ADDITIONAL INFO AT

THEONLYTIME.ORG

The Only Time Richard Got Angry at Me

New Discoveries in the Zodiac Killer Case

By James Bigtwin

Covering events and coincidences through October 9, 2024

Published December 31, 2024

ISBN# 979-8-9922712-4-9

Permission to quote from Repo Man is gratefully acknowledged. Many thanks to Alex Cox for this honor.

Contents

Opening Soliloquy...3

Preface...5

ACT I ==THE SET UP ======== 9

No way. No way. 9
What Do You Do When You Find Out a Friend
Might Have Been a Serial Killer?.................................11
    DNA or Other Possible Evidence 12
The Seeds of Coincidence.................................13
    The Face of It 14
The View from Left Field 17
Stanford University.................................20
The Stanford Chaparral.................................21
    A Brief History of the Chaparral and H & C 23
    The Stanford Chaparral's "Political Era".................................27
    1974 - The Resurrection 28
    Chaparral Pranks 29
    Who Shot R.R.?.................................31
Walk the Prank.................................32
    The Instantaneous Prank.................................33
    Damage ≈ Evidence.................................34
    Pranks are like Real Estate 34
    People are Really, Really Literal 35
My Prank Career at Stanford 36
    The Super Bowl.................................36
    Lambo 37
    File M for Meat 39
    The Horrible, Horrible Pie Incident.................................40
The Summer of 1986 41
Oskie Bear's Excellent Adventure 42
    The Proposition 42
    The Heist.................................43
    What Do You Do with a Hot Bear? Part 1 50
    Fresno.................................51
    Oskie's Broken Foot.................................52
    The Ransom Notes 53
    RF's Spectacular Oskie Idea.................................53
    What do you do with a Hot Bear? Part 2 55
The Smoke-Filled Rooms of Madison Avenue 57
    Hidden In Plain Sight 58
    Night Shift.................................60
    Technoromantics.................................60

San Francisco 1993 61
The Day I Met Richard 62
Politics. Art, Music. and Computers, but mostly Politics. ...62
The Only Time Richard Got Angry At Me 66
The Day Richard Gave Me a Tarot Reading 68
My Second Tarot Reading with Richard 70
Another Day at Richards 71
2002 - Back to Indiana 72
Visit to San Francisco 2006 73
So What Would You Do? 74
I Needed to Organize This Stuff Anyway… 75

ACT II = THE FACTS AND THE ACCUSATIONS = 77

Richard Gaikowski Bio 77
Richard at Good Times 79
Richard the Filmmaker 81
Richard and Computers 82
The Zodiac Crimes ---------- 84
Blue Rock Springs 84
The 408-code 85
Murders in San Jose 86
August 4, 1969, Enter The Zodiac 86
408-code Solved - Mostly 86
The Concerned Citizen Letter 87
Lake Berryessa 88
Paul Stine Murder 89
Paul Stine Letter 89
San Francisco Examiner's Message to the Zodiac 90
October 22, Oakland to Dunbar to Daly City 90
November 8, 1969 - The "Dripping Pen" and 340 Code 91
November 9, 1969 Letter 91
December 19, 1969 – Call to San Jose CHP 92
December 20, 1969 – Letter to Melvin Belli 92
April 20, 1970 92
April 29, 1970 93
June 26, 1970 – Mt. Diablo 93
Enter The Mikado 93
July 24, 1970 93
July 26, 1970 94
October 27, 1970, Happy Halloween! 96
A pause in Zodiac activity? 96
Los Angeles Times letter 97
Sierra Club card 97
Kathy Bilek 98

The 148 Code 98
Albany Letter 1973...98
The Exorcist Letter – Mikado Revisited...........................98
Other Possible Zodiac Communications...........................99
The Accusations ----------- 99
My Observations on the Facts and the Accusations 101
Problem - Binary Thinking...101
Problem - Needing Singular, Monolithic Motives..............104
Problem - Taking Assumptions as Facts 104
Earth, Water, Ball, Fish..105
Problem - Taking Snippets of Info and Expanding Them...107
Problem - Any AH can say "Zodiac"................................108
Problem - Tribalism 108
The 2007 Movie, The Zodiac 108
Lake Herman Road... 110
Blue Rock Springs... 110
Michael Mageau...110
Men Wanting to Date Darlene Ferrin...............................111
Could Darlene and Richard have known each other? 112
Nancy Slover and the Voice of Zodiac.............................112
The 408-code...114
Good Times July 31, 1969..115
Paul Stine.. 116
Graduate Student...116
Paul Stine and the Haight-Asbury Switchboard.................117
Could Stine and Gaikowski have known each other?.........119
October 22, The Voice was Not Low Enough....................120
7 Seconds of Fame 120
Specifically, Regarding the Accusations about Richard......121
Blaine 122
Blaine Did Write for Good Times.....................................122
Blaine also wrote for Berkeley Tribe................................123
Berkeley Barb, Berkeley Tribe, and Good Times 123
Richard Gaikowski's Politics.. 124
What was it about Reagan and Astrology? 125
The Idea Zodiac Stopped Killing after 1969.................. 126
Zodiac's Handwriting and Quirks................................... 127
Deaf / Punk...127
My Pieces of the Puzzle... 129
Richard was a Computer Programmer...............................129
Richard wrote a Tarot Card program on his Amiga. 130
The Man going to Prison 130
Richard Getting Angry about Reagan and Astrology..........130
The End of the Road...132

The Plague 136
   Hammer & Coffin Zoom Banquet 1 136
   December 2020 – The 340 Code Cracked 137
   Hammer & Coffin Zoom Banquet 2 138
The Stanford Chaparral Magnum Opus 139
   Loose Lips Sink Ships 141
   How to Make a Zodiac Code 142
   A Long, Tough Slog 144
   That's Not My Issue 146
   Busted 149
   Researching the Hippie Era 150
Stanford Macabre 151
   The 1970s Stanford Murders, Solved 153
   Janet Taylor, March 25, 1974 154
   Arlis Perry, October 12, 1974 154
   David Levine, September 11, 1973 - COLD CASE 155
   Eric Abramson, Dec. 20, 1973 – COLD CASE 158
   There are Always Two 159
   Could Richard Gaikowski have known David Levine? 159
   A Tale of Two Murders 160
   The Zebra Killings 161
   No more Zodiac research, just Chaparral 161
   The Radical Libertarian Alliance 162
Fake Names in Good Times 163
   Ben Dover 164
   Goatkirk 165
   Clandes Stine 168
   revoman 168
   Bear 169
Fake Names in the Stanford Chaparral 169
   Chaparral Political Era Covers 170
   "Good luck with that, buddy" 170
   The Conventional Wisdom 173
   Where Could You Find Computer in 1969? 174
   I Asked a Computer 176
   Computers in the 60s & 70s - Info from One Who Knows. 177
The Missing Link 178
   One F of a Coincidence. 181
Who was Dick Geikie? 182
   Dick Geikie in the Stanford Daily 183
   Richard Geikie 186
   Where's Dick? 187
   The Flip was Total 188

My Dilemma.. 189
    If Dick Geikie really is Dick Gaik................................190
    Stanford Daily's Message to the Zodiac Killer..................192
    Coming On Campus..194
    No One By That Name...195
    Non-Students on Campus..196
    Open Campus..196
    The Midpeninsula Free University...................................198
    Chaparral Staff Photo...198
The 408-code Revisited.. 200
    408-Code Deep Dive..203
By Knife By Gun By Rope By Fire............................... 206
    By Fire..206
    Stanford's First Bomb Incident.......................................207
    1970 Arson at Stanford..209
    Summer Daily 1970?...209
The Summer of 1971... 210
    Dinkelspiel Protest...210
    The Riot..211
    The Sunshine Express, or Maybe Brigade.........................212
    President's Office Bomb...213
    Junipero Lounge Fire...213
    More Bombs...214
    Willy and the Poor Boys...214
    Hospital-Related Bomb?...214
    The Second Time Around...215
    SLAC Bomb...216
1972... 216
    Stanford Rehabilitation Movement..................................216
    Encina Fire..218
    Knife Attacks...218
    More Fire...219
Emma Sharon Brown.. 220
By Rope - Edward Alan McNeill...................................... 220
Same Day, Same Serial Killer, Different Paper.............. 221
    The Missing Pages..222
    A Friendlier, Heartfelt Message to the Zodiac...................223
    Now There are Two of Them..225
    Blaine's Post..226
    The DR-70 Astrology Computer......................................227
    Fake Names in the Ithaca High School Yearbook...............228
So Close, Yet So Far – April 2023.................................. 230
    People Living in the Chappie Office.................................231
    High Chaparral Films..233

Trip to San Francisco May 2023 233
    In the Chappie Office 234
    All Chaparral issues seen 237
    The Mystery of the Blank Pages 238
    2023 Trip Aftermath 238
    The Oil Bird 239
    Call with D 240
    Blank Pages, Wrong Date, Fake Issue, WTF? 243
There was only one way it could happen 243

ACT IV = YOU WANT MIKADO? YOU FIND IT == 251

    Stabford 251
The Greatest Cover Story of All Time 251
    The Cavalry Arrives 255
    The Year of Living Deathily 255
    Laughing to Death 256
    Doodles Weaver 257
Further examination of The Missing Link 258
    The Double Exposures 259
    Threes and Fives Again 259
    March 1971 261
Even Further Examination of the Missing Link 261
Lynda Kanes 263
What Really Happened to the Chaparral in '69 265
    A3Mania 265
    Dawn of a New Era 266
    The Secret Salaries 267
    The Empire Strikes Back 268
    I've Got a Little Listing 269
    The Journalism Years 271
    Defense of the Journalism Years 271
Where Do You Hide a Tree? 272
    Page 394 273
    Delay in the Chappie 125 Book 275
    20 Days in November 276
    Mea Culpa to the Mea Culpa 277
My Dilemma 278
    Where Do You Hide a Tree? Part 2 279
    Sending Off the Chappie 125 Book 279
The Halloween Stanford Daily - October 31, 1969 281
    The Sparkling Mikado Review 282
    The Layout of the Mikado Review 283
    The Electric Zodiac 284
    All of the Articles Aligned 286

White Spots on the Daily 288
    The Recurring 3-Spot Pattern 290
    The Main Spot on the Mikado Article 293
    The Unique Spots on the Nov. 17, 1969, Daily 294
    Slick Tracy 294
    Who's There? 295
2024 - CHAPPIE'S 125TH YEAR 297
    The Dawn of the Second Renaissance 299
    The Stanford Daily Archives 300
Return to Stanford - April 2024 302
    That's Heavy, Man...302
    The Chaparral Office 303
    The Stanford Daily Offices 304
    The Stanford Daily MICROFILM 305
    Stanford Daily Summer 1970 Volume 307
Watch Me Make These Spots… Disappear................... 308
    Spots on Paper 310
    Occam's Coincidences...311
    It's Around..313

ACT V =THE BURRITO at the END of the UNIVERSE 321

    What would you do?...321
    Coincidence? Or CoincidenSe? 322
Observations and Conjectures...................................... 323
    Conjecture: Zodiac worked in newspapers or printing 323
    Conjecture: The Dick Tracy Zodiac comic
    was a coincidental opportunity. 324
    Conjecture: Zodiac was NOT a resident of Vallejo.............324
    Conjecture: Zodiac was a resident of San Francisco. 325
    Conjecture: The Zodiac mostly told the truth. 325
    Conjecture: There are indeed more Zodiac murders. 325
    Conjecture: Zodiac killed by gun, by knife,
    by fire, and by rope..326
    Conjecture: Zodiac indeed used Fake Clews 326
    Conjecture: The 408 Code is indeed solved
    by the Concerned Citizen letter 328
    Conjecture: Zodiac Planned a Mikado-themed Murder......328
    Conjecture: The 340 Code was Computer Assisted 329
    Conjecture: Zodiac's interest in computers.........................329
    Conjecture: The call to Palo Alto Times was authentic. 330
    Conjecture: The Daily's Zodiac Message suggested...........330
Happy Halloween Eve! 330
    How work Gets Done at a Student Publication...................331
    Conjecture: Later that Day at the Printers 332

Conjecture: Zodiac Calls November 4, 1969 333
The Seven Symbols - Chaparral Dec. 4, 1969 334
Stanford Murders - What If Zodiac was at Stanford? 335
The Bloody Handprint...336
A Lot of Strange and Bizarre People 337
David Levine 337
Conjecture: The Zebras did not kill Levine nor Abramson.338
Conjecture: Who killed David Levine? 339
Conjecture: Who Killed Eric Abramson? 340
By Knife 340
By Fire 341
By Rope 342
By Gun 342
Good Times – Stanford Coincidences.................... 343
Chaparral Good Time Places 343
The Magus...343
William Hinton...344
Lanh Dao Caoboy...344
Kelsie 344
Oil Bird 344
A Warship Can Be Stopped 345
Who was Dick Geikie? 345
The Missing Link Issue of the Chaparral...................347
Lynda Kanes...347
Etc. 349
National Treasure... 351

ACT VI == THE END (FOR NOW) ===== 355

The Tower..355
Coinc'o'dences...356
Cover Story 358
THE END - As of October 9, 2024 358
31 Questions 361

EXTRA STUFF ===== 366

Acknowledgments 367
Bibliography 369
Websites 369
Video and Film...369
About the Author 370
My Credentials 370
Endnotes 372
Index.. 380

The Only Time Richard Got Angry at Me

"A lot of people don't realize what's really going on. They view life as a bunch of unconnected incidents and things. They don't realize that there's this, like, lattice of coincidence that lays on top of everything."

– Miller, Repo Man

Opening Soliloquy

What I'm about to recount to you is a riddle, wrapped in an enigma, encased in a clusterfuck. I wouldn't blame anyone if they didn't believe this tale, filled with coincidences so strange, so incredibly, I dare say, coincidental, that they HAD to be made up. But aye, there's the rub. They are indeed true.

Even so, if it weren't for this one conversation, this one out of character moment by an old friend some 30 years ago, that gave me the slightest pause, a saga that will likely change the entire conception of a decades old cold case would not be known; an entire, multi-year odyssey, all on account of a single moment of the mask being lowered, the true self revealed.

Even after looking into the macabre story I discounted it all, until amazing coincidence found me again.

And when the ultimate trails converged, and the evidence pointed to a conclusion so fantastical, so improbable, so coincidental that it strains credulity, I tell you I would doubt it as well, if not for the discovery of something that could only exist by being the work of the perpetrator.

It's almost enough to make one believe in a sort of Divine Shakespeare. Almost.

Such is how my story begins, written here in a way to not reveal any relevant facts as to what I am talking about, so you can learn them as the story unfolds.

THE ONLY TIME RICHARD GOT ANGRY AT ME

Preface

From the moment I decided to write this book, there has always been a question of whether it was titled "The Only Time Richard Got Angry at Me," or "One F of a Coincidence." Because while it started with that one moment with Richard, it is perhaps more a story of a crazy coincidence. Several actually, across my lifetime.

This book will indeed cite new information and may very well solve the case of The Zodiac Killer, the serial murderer who terrorized San Francisco and the Bay Area in the late 1960s and early 70s with taunting letters and codes accompanying grisly murders. The media-craving, or perhaps more correctly, the media-savvy psychotic killer, even knew to give himself a name to add to the hype. Now with literally millions of people following the case, and thousands trying to crack it, The Zodiac is arguably the most famous remaining cold case of the 20th century.

It seems prudent to write something here, in the beginning of this book, explaining that I will be writing about many things other than Zodiac—like the humor, hi-jinks and pranks at the *Stanford Chaparral* and their rival, the *Stanford Daily*, the smoke-filled offices of Madison Avenue, concepts in cognition and interspecies communication with pioneering scientist Dr. John C. Lilly, work with Japanese media company Digital Garage, underground psychedelic rave culture and more.

This is a story of coincidences, strange, decades-long coincidences.

So much of my life has involved alternative communications; jokes and pranks, national advertising billboards, television broadcasts using "virtual reality" (both in the traditional and non-traditional sense), computer coding, interspecies communication with dolphins, and also dogs, cats, sheep, pigs, ducks, crows and more... I don't think I would have been able to comprehend what I was looking at without my previous experiences, which all play a role in this tale.

I was born a farmer and have worked as a banker, performed at

Montreux Jazz Festival[1] and on Dr. Demento[2]. Puns and wordplay are my afflictation. I have experience pulling pranks; have attempted to create a language both humans and dolphins could speak; have experimented making codes and ciphers. I have hidden secret art in other art, and left Easter eggs in publications.

And even after all these years, I still call myself a Chappie. A "Chappie," in this context, is a member of the *Stanford Chaparral*, the humor magazine of Stanford University, sort of a west coast *Harvard Lampoon* just without a castle.[3] I called myself a Chappie in 1986, and in 1994, and in 1999. When The Onion asked me in 2002 for a name to accompany my photo in their article "Stoner Uncle All Kids' Favorite," I gave them the name of Chappie legend Mike Dornheim.[4] I still called myself a Chappie in 2006 when Dornheim saw me for the first time since the article and said "You die," and I still am a Chappie in 2024. I fully agree with the Chaparral motto, "'tis better to have lived and laughed, than never to have lived at all." The people I have known through working on the Chaparral are some best and most creative one can ever hope to meet.

That said, I am not the first person to observe that Chappies seem to have some strange, random, psychic power, or, just the ability to foolishly wander into events in bizarre and comical ways. It seems to be happening again.

So yes, I knew Richard Gaikowski, and that started me down this path, but it was only because of my life experiences that I could recognize what I was seeing. And only because I was a Chappie that I bumbled upon the key discoveries. Who would believe that through the *Chaparral* would be the path that might solve this mystery? And that the *Stanford Daily*, the student newspaper of Stanford University, was also central to this tale? It's quite a bizarre concept to get one's head around. The long running rivalry and sometimes contentious relationship between these two Stanford student publications would make this story comical, if not for the seriousness of the subject at hand.

I would like to suggest that Zodiacifiles regard this book like one might the John Lennon / Yoko Ono album Double Fantasy (that might be better called Love is Deaf). Other than writing a bad review for it, the best strategy for that album is just to listen to the tracks you like. For such readers I recommend Acts II and V of this book.

There is also a huge reason to write more rather than less: This is

THE ONLY TIME RICHARD GOT ANGRY AT ME

still a cold case. No one knows what is relevant or not. And while you can indeed hide a tree in a forest, even unintentionally, at least the tree is there. (In the book, *The Chappie – 125 Years of Issues*, you can find that tree on page 394.) On the other hand, it would be a tragedy if the tree inadvertently happened to end up on the cutting room floor. If the conclusion to this story is anything like the beginning and middle of it, then there is likely a big sequoia or banyan right in the middle that I haven't seen, that we all have missed. Someone out there knows more about the tale I'm about to tell, and even crazier, they may not even know that they know.

While some existing dots may be connected, this book starts a whole new page of dots previously unknown to the public. Synapses will re-fire. The shroud of the years will fall off. And whether your metaphors are trees or dots, it should be interesting. Quite.

My own wonderment at this particular vista is a feeling somewhat beyond description. Before last year I had not written any book, now I will have produced two. And while I would have believed that I might one day produce a coffee table book about my beloved *Stanford Chaparral*, I would have been hard pressed to believe I would write a book such as this one. I would have been even more incredulous at the idea that I find possible clues to a crime in actual *Chaparral* and *Daily* issues, and even completely unbelieving that I would reprint those key clues in that huge Chappie anniversary book.

But I did.

It happens every day. Right?

ACT I ==THE SET UP =========

No way. No way.

"No way. No way. Richard was the nicest guy. No way he was a murderer. No way he was a… serial murderer."

From the moment I read that Richard Gaikowski was accused of being the Zodiac Killer, I was in disbelief.

The year was 2016, surfing the internet from our farmhouse in rural Indiana. My wife Kate and I had finally gotten DSL after years of dial up, part of our gradual return to normal society after a decade plus of dropping out of pop culture--what we jokingly called going Techno-Amish. We didn't have cable or satellite TV, just rabbit ears for local TV. We had gotten rid of cable around the year 2000, even while I was still working in television—with my work airing on five shows at the time, ESPN, ABC, Discovery Channel and others. (We not only cut the cable, but gave up TV and participation in pop culture, largely for the next 15 years. Add in moving from New York City to rural Indiana, and for certain we were in a bit of an information bubble.

We were already aware Richard had died because we had attempted to see him on a visit to San Francisco in 2006, and found he was no longer at his home on Guerrero. Calling his phone produced the three-tone "this number has been disconnected" recording. When we got home I searched for him online and found his obit.[5] He had died in 2004 from lung cancer. There was nothing online about him being a Zodiac suspect at that time.

Now ten or so years later, on some random evening, I was enjoying our upgraded and fast internet by googling people I used to know. Some names would get a couple hits. Some a couple hundred. Some none. When I typed in the name "Richard Gaikowski," there were thousands and thousands hits. "What the ?..."

And there it was, Richard had become one of the leading suspects in the Zodiac Killer case. There were websites about him. There had been a TV show. I was incredulous.

I knew Richard Gaikowski from 1993 to 2002, first while living in San Francisco from September 1993 to May 1994, and then continuing to visit him on frequent trips to SF through 2002. For years my routine when visiting San Francisco was this: land at SFO, get a rental car, go to the Jack In The Box on Bayshore Boulevard, then go see my friend Richard. We'd have great discussions that could last for hours.

Richard and I shared many likes and interests in common, and we became fast friends. Richard also sold very high-quality grass.

I was a raver, artist, videographer, and computer programmer in my late twenties. Richard was an artist, filmmaker, and bohemian in his late fifties, with many stories of his "hippie days" that I loved to hear about. We both shared an interest in discussing and debating politics, pop culture, psychedelic culture, history, art, technology, and religion. We were also both Midwesterners, Richard from South Dakota and me from Indiana. Richard was one of the only people who I've ever met on either coast who knew the difference between the Farm Bureau and the Farmer's Union. Such a subject is obscure even for Midwesterners, but Richard and I shared this obscurity.

I would go to Richard's to pick up grass, and we would invariably spend an hour or more talking. He'd take some of his stash and grind it to a fine powder in an electric coffee grinder. I'd never seen anyone do anything like this, but it was genius. The finely ground marijuana allowed for an immaculate joint, making the burn smooth and even, the high better. He would roll a joint and we would talk in his kitchen, which was just a small room to the back and right of the main room of his home, a converted storefront on Guerrero Street in the Mission.

We became friends. We traded computer graphics. I gave him some webpage backgrounds I had created, and he used them on his site. We linked our pages. Richard pointed a link to my "Pulsators" software I had made in Macromind Director.

In September of 1993, I moved into a house in Bernal Heights, a neighborhood in San Francisco, and became bi-coastal as I also kept part of an apartment in west Greenwich Village, New York City. In San Francisco I lived with Rose-X, a husband-and-wife team of video artists specializing in psychedelic videos, most notably Alien Dreamtime featuring Terrence McKenna. We also shared the house with JG, an idealistic younger guy learning to play the didgeridoo. It was a short walk, and shorter bike ride, to Richard's place.

In New York, I had founded a group/party called Technoromantics in 1989, centered on computer art and artists, who were encouraged to bring their art or something for discussion to our gatherings. It blossomed into sort of a 'scene'--New York Magazine later called these parties "salons."[6] I was eager to start Technoromantic meetings in San Francisco.

When I described the idea to my roommates, they said more or less immediately, "We should invite Richard."

He indeed came to the party I hosted, and a few days later I went to visit Richard at his home on Guerrero Street. It was the first of many visits with him over the next nine years, 1993-2002.

What Do You Do When You Find Out a Friend Might Have Been a Serial Killer?

What do you do when you find out your old friend is a leading suspect for one of the greatest remaining cold-case serial murders of the 20th century?

Well, the short answer is you flip out. I mean, sorta. It's just not a run-of-the-mill thing to consider. I mean really, it's just not normal and it definitely affects your day. And then some.

You search through your mind for anything you remember. You see if you can recall anything that seems out of place.

Upon reflection, you wonder if you were in danger. And I really didn't think I was in danger; Richard couldn't be a serial murderer. The whole idea was ridiculous. Even so, you search through your memories to think if there was some moment you were alone with him. Of course, I was almost always alone with Richard, there were only a couple times when I was there with someone else.

You think awful things like, "well if he was a murderer, at least he's dead now." I mean, that's awful, but I'm just telling you the truth of what went through my mind.

The idea of Richard being a killer was very far-fetched to me. Richard was a friendly individual, interesting, smart, and he could carry on a great conversation. I remember him smiling, with a quick wit and a lot of laughing. Richard was obviously a very intelligent guy, with many interests. And Richard sold really good grass.

Now this was in the days before the super-weed hit the scene. There was a lot of "dirt weed", or just what people considered normal back then. A lot of grass just gave you a light buzz. Some grass wasn't very good. But not Richard's—his was always top quality. Some of the first stuff I would come to call super-weed. To me, Richard was an affable guy into films and computers who helped make ends meet by selling marijuana. If you had asked me in a vacuum, who in my 50+ years of life might have been a murderer, a serial murderer, I would have never come up with Richard.

The entire subject of murder has never really been of interest to me. I'm not a true crime fan, I don't like movies with sicko violence, I never paid attention to serial murder stories. About the closest I have ever come to being interested in murder was watching Sherlock Holmes movies or Colombo.

But this was something different, a whodunnit in real life, intriguing enough for me to spend an evening or two reading through a lot of Zodiac websites to see if I had anything to add, or if anything jogged my memory. I mean, who knows? Maybe I had a piece of the puzzle.

DNA or Other Possible Evidence

Eventually I got a clear thought: "DNA!" Did Richard ever mail me a postcard? It seemed like a reasonable possibility. I'm not totally a pack rat or hoarder, but I'm close. As an artist, I have kept many things to document my work and life. And I like things. I have boxes and rooms of old stuff.

I looked through my mementos. I've kept many old invites, rave fliers, and other ephemera, quite a few of them from San Francisco. I went looking for a stamp or envelope Richard might have licked, or something else that might have his DNA. Or just anything from that time. In 2016, my items from the 1990s were stuck in random places, including boxes, folders and attics in Indiana, along with an apartment in New York City.

It took several months to even get to everything.

After some time, we were finally able to get to New York City where I could look through many items from my art and rave life. The best and weirdest things had stayed in NYC when we moved to Indiana. Of course, many of these best, weirdest items were from San Francisco.

To my disappointment, I did not ever find a possible licked stamp from Richard, although I did find an invite to the Roxie, the theater Richard owned. It was for Alien Dreamtime, the video made by my roommates, Rose-X, which includes a lot of my video art. Alien Dreamtime, a film of psychedelic graphics mixed with Terrence McKenna speaking, has achieved somewhat of a cult status. But the postcard was unaddressed and hadn't even been mailed--I likely just got it from my roommates directly—so it was no help.

But I did find something of interest, my most important artifact from this era: the sign-in book for my various art show openings. In that book, from the March 16, 1994, opening reception of my art show at Artists' Television Access in San Francisco, was Richard Gaikowski's signature.

The Seeds of Coincidence

Artists' Television Access (ATA) is a gallery and art space that still exists today, on Valencia near 22nd Street. It's a great scene and shows great art. It was also very close to where both Richard and I had lived.

ATA was an important place in my life for many reasons. They gave me my first big gallery show in San Francisco and allowed me an installation in their storefront window. Most important to me, it was the first show of Dukey, a serene dog I built in Swivel 3D, wearing VR glasses and a pixelated peace sign, with his two dog friends in an analog gouache junkyard with UFOs in the sky. The original Dukey painting had appeared in MacWorld magazine,[7] and now I had a series of five for this show.

It was at ATA, while my Dukey paintings were on display in March and April 1994, that I met Mr. Big, the CEO of Digital Garage in Tokyo. He and his entourage were brought to the show by my Japanese friend. It was a very fortuitous day for me. Mr. Big bought one of the main paintings, as well as a smaller study, and he invited me to Japan. From this meeting, I became his friend and ended up working for Digital Garage for many years, doing early web and interactive projects including a VRML website, and then as webmaster for Dr. John C. Lilly.

Dr. Lilly is known for many things: the first person to map the brains of primates; the inventor of the isolation tank and the science of sensory deprivation; cetacean research and human-dolphin interspecies communication research; and a leading authority on the scientific study of LSD and ketamine. His life is the basis for two movies, Day of the Dolphin and Altered States.

Through the mid to late 1990s, I would travel to Japan, and to Hawaii, where Dr. Lilly lived, often stopping in San Francisco to and from, and on my way to Burning Man, which I attended annually from 1995 to 2000.

I ended up becoming quite close with John Lilly, travelling with him and assisting with his presentation at the International Dolphin and Whale Conference (ICERC) in Tokyo in 1998, and then co-presenting with him at the ICERC Conference in 1999 in Paris. I continued to visit him in Hawaii until his death in 2001, and still maintain his website today, johnclilly.com.

Dr. Lilly is a controversial figure, who pushed the limits of exploration of consciousness, both human and "animal." He also wrote extensively about coincidence, devoting large sections of his books to E.C.C.O., a quasi-mystical system of beings that arranged coincidences for human travelers.

Now I don't exactly describe it the same way John did, but it has been my observation that there are indeed Coincidences, things that happen that are almost beyond belief or explanation. Two or more things that are seemingly related, but are truly just random occurrences, at least in the way we understand reality.

Some coincidences will be described in this book, like the *Stanford Chaparral* debuting a "Who Shot R.R.?" parody on the same morning in 1981 that Ronald Reagan was indeed shot. That fateful event plays a part in this story too. Coincidence? I really don't know, but as you read my story, keep in mind that the secondary title for this book is "One F of a Coincidence." It is also the actual title of Act III of this book, because wherever the facts lead, what happened really is one F of a coincidence.

The Face of It

Murder. You probably couldn't pick a subject I was less interested in, let alone a serial killer. Clicking on the first few Zodiac sites and reading for the first time about the murders, shootings and knifings, was a very distasteful endeavor. The whole experience felt negative and creepy. And the idea that it could be my old friend was just beyond. Beyond my ability to process, at first.

Eventually I saw a link for the Zodiac police sketch. I wondered if it would look like Richard.

I clicked on the link, and for the first time since learning of Richard's alleged Zodiac involvement, I became spooked. The sketch looked a lot like Richard. The shape of the head, the mouth, but most of all, the eyes and his large glasses. I'm not saying it is an EXACT match, but it is strikingly similar.

I will describe a feeling often in this book. It is related to when the hair stands up on the back of your neck, or less dramatically, when you find something that gives you pause, or more dramatically, when you see something that blows your mind. When I get this feeling, I often hear the music from the movie Close Encounters of the Third Kind in my head, music from the scene where Richard Dreyfuss sees Devil's Tower on TV, and finally understands the image he has been seeing.

The moment of seeing the Zodiac police sketch was such a moment.

"What do you think?" asked Kate.

"This sketch," I replied, "is just a little bit too close for comfort."

Still, even with the similarities of the police sketch, the idea that Richard was the Zodiac Killer was hard for me to believe.

And really, how many people had thick-rimmed glasses in 1969? Like a bazillion? In 1969 we were landing on the moon, but optometry had decided that glasses had to have big black frames, an unmistakable marker, "Hey look, I'm wearing glasses!" Not that there's anything wrong with that, but jeez...

The same could be said for buzz cuts. There were literally millions of guys with buzz cuts and thick glasses in 1969.

That said, the sketch could not have looked like him. It could have had no glasses. It could have had long hair, a beard, a long, thin face, or some other feature that would make it obviously NOT Richard, but it didn't.

If the sketch did not look like Richard, it would go a long way towards discounting him as a subject. But it does indeed look like him, so he is not discounted, at least not by the sketch. And even though the set of 1969 men who look like the sketch is quite large, Richard is indeed in that set. As someone who knew him, my point is this: It absolutely does look like him.

For the record, Richard was never an official police suspect, although he was apparently looked at by the police for a while. Upon reading various websites, I learned the accusations against Richard have been mostly based on the accounts of a single individual. There are many people who believe this individual, and there are many others who don't. There is a large Zodiac subculture online. If you visit websites or read books about the zodiac killings, you will find there are many camps, or groups of people who have their favorite suspect, and they have become tribal, with endless arguments and comment boards that can become nasty and combative.

I discussed the accusations about Richard with Kate, who had also met Richard a couple times with me in the very late 90s and early 2000s. As I have already stated multiple times but will state again to simulate my state of mind at the time, I really couldn't believe he was being accused of being a serial murderer. For a couple of days I kept saying that Richard was always friendly, and I never remembered him ever getting angry.

But then I did remember.

I don't know how the mind or memory works, but this is what happened to me. All of a sudden, I remembered that Richard DID get angry one time, but what was it about? I remembered it was over something I thought was stupid, but what was it? I reflected some more, and then I remembered.

And then, again, I sort of freaked out. A little more than the first time.

It was a silly thing he got angry about. A trivial thing. And surprising because it was very out of character, and about something that seemed so small, so inconsequential, frankly ridiculous, it was quickly forgotten. There were certainly dozens of positive Richard memories to counterbalance this one bad one. But once I remembered, there was no forgetting.

Sorry, I'm not going to give it away this early. I'm not going to tell you now, you'll get the details about this later in the book. Let's just say the only time Richard got angry at me was a memory that made the hair on the back of my neck stand up and the spacey music played in my head. I couldn't NOT think about it. This went on for a couple days with no sign of abetting. It was consuming more and more of my consciousness and internal dialogue. I needed either to address it or forget it.

So, I decided that I would go for it; spend some time diving deeper into this memory and topic. This strange out of character moment by Richard spurred me to investigate the Zodiac murders, reading books, websites, comment boards, googling all kinds of murderous terms, looking for anything that might connect with my memory. Despite my resistance to the material, the whole macabre subject, I would explore it on the off chance I had a piece of the puzzle that could solve this mystery.

The only time Richard got angry with me is where this story begins But because of how this story ends, I need to fill in how I got there.

The View from Left Field

I was three years old when the five official Zodiac murders occurred, and I didn't meet Richard until 1993. I wasn't aware of his connection to the Zodiac murders until 2016, when I had my memory. But I didn't think I had anything relevant and had put it out of my mind by 2018, save for the occasional sarcastic comment or joke. But no amount of joking, sarcasm, and hunching about it was able to prepare me for what I discovered, quite by coincidence, in 2023. I think it's apt to note the longshot nature of this story.

I grew up on a farm in southern Indiana. The primary business of the farm was pigs, but we also had sheep, grew corn, soybeans, wheat and hay, and always had dogs and cats. I was the youngest child by a many-year gap, with three sisters 12, 11, and nine years older than me. When I say "left field," the field part is real. Literally.

Now we weren't totally isolated. My father listened to opera and would read the New York Times to us during dinner, often asking our opinions on the news of the day. My mother was artistic, a seamstress, from a well-educated family who sent all children, male and female, to college back into the 1800s. And we traveled, going on annual vacations, to Colorado, where my mother was from, New York City, or long road trips across multiple states, including California.

On one such trip in 1983, while looking for colleges for me, we went again to the West Coast. UC Santa Barbara had sent me some recruiting letters for basketball. Getting some financial aid via basketball was the general plan for my higher education. After our visit at UCSB, we decided to drive up to San Francisco, where we had so much fun on a trip a few years earlier. We were travelling north on I-280 when we saw a sign for Stanford University.

"That's a good school," said my father. "We should stop in there."

I wasn't that interested. Honestly, at that moment I had never heard of this school. And besides, I was trying for a basketball scholarship and was hoping to go to either Columbia or Cornell. Nevertheless, we drove to Stanford and went to the admissions office. We learned there would be an orientation group meeting in about an hour, so we stayed and looked around the campus, including White Plaza and Tresidder Union, then went to the meeting and got the application materials.

A half year later, sometime between Christmas and New Years, my father asked if I had completed the Stanford application. He was not happy that I hadn't, so I went to my room and filled it out--sarcastically. I don't remember it entirely, but I do remember a question along the lines of "What event changed your life the most?" which I answered recounting the time I impersonated Elvis with my best friend, the two of us performing at the high school talent show and calling ourselves the Elvi, like Belushi and Ackroyd from a Saturday Night Live skit.[8]

Now to be clear, by this time I was learning that Stanford was ranked as high as the Ivy League. And I had learned it was the school involved in "the Play," the crazy end to a football game where some team lateraled five times and crashed through the band of the opposing team to win the game. I had seen this on TV many times, but never bothered to learn who the teams were. "Oh, those guys," I said. As I discovered, Stanford was the losing team. Bummer.

I figured my chances of going to Stanford were zero. It was very expensive and there was no chance I could go to such a school without a basketball scholarship. I might make an Ivy League team reserve, but the Pac 10, Stanford's league, was certainly above my abilities.

That spring, I was accepted at Columbia and was going to play on their basketball team. I was pretty psyched about going to NYC for college. But then the acceptance letter came from Stanford. It included a financial package that equaled Columbia's, with no implied requirement to play basketball.

High school basketball in Indiana is something like being in the military. Any team sport at a high level requires much commitment, my Columbia experience would indeed be dominated by basketball, and practices would indeed be quasi-military. I was prepared for that. But when I got the Stanford letter I thought, "College at a top school AND I don't have to play basketball! Like, I could be in plays or something? Or just time to explore other things?" I had been psyched to go to NYC, but now California sounded pretty cool too.

"You can go to New York after you graduate," said my dad. "And it might be a good idea for you to go to California first before New York City."

So I did it. I picked Stanford. When I finally got to Stanford and sat around with my other incoming freshman classmates, I learned that for some people, their entire lives had been devoted to getting into this place. Some had torn themselves apart for getting even an A- in high school, or middle school, or elementary, and expressed sadness that some of their friends had to go to UCLA, USC, or even… Berkeley.

I was incredulous—at my own actions. Can you imagine what the admission people thought of my application?

Stanfordites, or perhaps Stanfordians, will remember Dean Fred Hargadon, the affable and universally loved Dean of Admissions from 1969 to 1984. Hargadon is credited with helping Stanford ascend to the pinnacle of American universities with his wise choices for incoming freshmen. But the Class of 1988, my year, was his last year. I might have been Dean Fred's very last admission. Maybe it was a sarcastic gag for him too?

Sitting around a dorm room with my fellow freshmen in our first nights at school, they were in disbelief, some of them sort of irritated, that I had never heard of Stanford until I was a junior in high school. When they heard I filled out the application as a joke, they were not happy. It was a funny introduction to Stanford.

I'm not saying I was totally naïve, just uniquely. Back in Indiana when a student in my high school sociology class read from an article about the punk band Dead Kennedys, reading the lyrics of "I Kill Children" aloud to abhorrent gasps from my classmates, my teacher Mrs. S asked the class "Do any of you have any of this band's records?" I was the only one to raise my hand, so on that level I was the only one in tune with what was going on in pop culture. That said, there is a giant "but" coming in this story.

In olden times, there was no internet. You could read about bands in magazines, you could hang out around record stores and you could listen to alternative radio. I was lucky to be near WOXY, broadcast out of Oxford Ohio. "The Future of Rock and Roll." I was thoroughly turned off by mainstream music and craved something different.

I had read that punk rock was the heaviest, hardest rock out there, that the Dead Kennedys were some of the heaviest. They also had the funniest name. I went down to Northgate Mall in Cincinnati, went to the record store and bought the Holiday in Cambodia/Police Truck 12-inch single album. I brought the album home, played it, and agreed it was the heaviest, most satanic-sounding music I had ever heard. I played it for my friend T, and he agreed with me.

The thing is, the album looked like a regular 33 rpm album, which is the speed we played it. And not even WOXY played the Dead Kennedys, so there was no way to know we were playing it slow. It sure sounded satanic. I never looked at the writing on the disk. Read?

A year later, at Stanford, I heard the Dead Kennedys for the first time at regular speed. Funny, at normal speed the Dead Kennedys and other punk to this day sound Mickey Mouse to me.

Such was my knowledge of pop culture, and grasp of reality, upon my arrival in the Bay Area in 1984.

Stanford University

My first months at Stanford during the Fall of 1984 were everything all at once, all the time. I was in Branner Hall, the largest freshman dorm, and I was immediately with 300+ other freshman from all over the country and world. In my first hours on campus I got drunk for the first time, and then the second and eleventh time in the next few days. The very first evening I returned to my dorm room from a registration event, I found it full of guys hitting a three-foot tall bong, guys who were clean cut and had all their teeth (I had only seen rag-tag hillbillies and rat people smoking grass in Indiana). I resisted their offer for pot for a couple weeks. Soon I got my first girlfriend, and finally had sex.

But the academic side of my Stanford experience was a deteriorating situation. For the first time in my life, I was getting bad grades, and was coming to terms that I had never studied in my life and had little chance to learn how now. The partying didn't help, although it was fun as hell. I sorta held it together, but by January I was getting depressed and thinking of leaving Stanford.

When my freshman dorm attempted and failed a prank during the Super Bowl, a prank where I was one of the ringleaders, I became particularly despondent.

Then a miracle happened. At a lunch in Branner Dining Hall, a classmate had a copy of the campus humor magazine, the *Stanford Chaparral* that was just out, titled Death, Decay, and Tribulation. I had never heard of the *Stanford Chaparral* before. I looked at the issue and was hooked. Finally, something that spoke to me. I looked up their office on the campus map and went there that afternoon.

The Stanford Chaparral

The *Chaparral*'s offices were on the second floor so-called "Penthouse" of the Storke Student Publications Building, which also housed the campus newspaper, *Stanford Daily*, the *Quad* yearbook, and the *Sequoia* poetry magazine. The utter squalor of couches, joke items, signs, old beer smell, and shelves and shelves of issues dating back to 1899 made an immediate positive impression on me. The door was open, and a guy was playing pinball, Editor MC. He welcomed me right off, and showed me the rest of the office, with paste-up room, office, photography darkroom, and a balcony where you could drink, and taunt and wave at Daily staffers and other students. He told me to come back on Wednesday at 8pm to their weekly meeting, which I did. At that meeting, I had more insults and jests thrown at me by more people than I had ever experienced. Insults piled upon witty banter and more jokes washed down with more than a few beers. I was home.

The *Chaparral* very much changed my experience at Stanford for the better, and it's reasonable to say if it weren't for the "Chappie," I might not have stayed there.

Just to clarify, The *Stanford Chaparral* is also referred to as "The Chappie." *Chaparral* staffers are also called "Chappies," and as you will see, the term *"Chaparral"* and "Chappie" get thrown around inter-changeably by those familiar with it. I certainly do it. About the only thing I would say I've never heard is "The Stanford Chappie." That is definitely wrong. Don't say it, or if you do, it will be really, really, uncool.

The Chappie was a place where anything and everything could be mocked, would be mocked. But you also had to produce. Your stand-ing in the group depended on how funny you were, how well you could draw, or just how you could hang. Straight up partiers with noth-ing else to offer lost face with those who actually made the magazine. That said, there was almost always a party going on at the *Chaparral*.

We absolutely spent more time on the magazine than on classes. We absolutely drank and smoked every day. Hoping not let my parents know what was really going on at Stanford, I wrote my first pieces for the *Chaparral* under a fake name, Moose Neumann.

At the beginning of Sophomore year, some of the upperclassmen took me aside and asked me if I wanted to become business manager of the *Chaparral*. Because I was still quite naïve, I believed what they told me about what the job entailed. AND, I thought to myself, "gee, Business Manager might be the fourth or fifth highest position." My old, smarmy, student over-achiever self was interested in that, and I took the job.

The things the upperclassmen had told me weren't exactly lies, but they definitely were exaggerations—rosy platitudes about how much money we had, how many issues we sold, how easy it would be to sell ads. While the truth was somewhat to the negative, there was much to the positive. As business manager, I controlled the money, mostly, and as I settled into the job, I found you could (sort of) become the sec-ond most powerful person, and sometimes the first. For example, we were in debt, but we were liquid. So, if someone wanted a case of silly string or an NO2 tank "for the purposes of making a giant whipped cream cannister," as business manager I might be able to find the funds for a worthy Chappie activity.

My first year as business manager I served three different "Old Boys," as the editor is known, even when they are female. The first was the larger than life character MC, the first person I had ever met at the *Chaparral*. He is McCartney-esque, both good at writing lyrics and looking reasonably like the Beatle. He was a great leader for the

THE ONLY TIME RICHARD GOT ANGRY AT ME

Chappie, but as such, this also made him a great politician. He was one of four Chappies who successfully ran for Council of Presidents in the Stanford student government, the unfortunately named ASSU.

This caused the editorship to be passed on to RH, a good artist who loves to joke about religion, and masks a dark sense of humor underneath a harmless face. He produced a memorable issue with a cover by PC, finding a humorous aspect of the Space Shuttle Challenger disaster. Then in spring quarter, comic writing legend JW became Old Boy. JW went on to write for The Simpsons and created the cult cartoon series Mission Hill.

I liked the *Chaparral*, and hoped that someday I might become Editor. I was also eager to add my own chapters to the prankster legends of the Chappie.

A Brief History of the Chaparral and H & C

The *Stanford Chaparral* was founded in 1899, by Bristow Adams and Larrey Bowman. The first issue was October 5, 1899, and by December they were in debt--and they say reality isn't fractal. Anyway, they righted the ship in Volume 2 and the Chappie was off to the races.

In 1903, in what is the first known strange coincidence of the *Chaparral*, one of its members wrote a play about a great San Francisco earthquake. In the story, the quake is set in 1906, includes the destruction of Stanford's Great Arch and Memorial Church, and results in two people dying on campus. The story proved to be a bit more prescient than planned.

The *Chaparral* was growing into its place at Stanford, popular with the students and advertisers, but increasingly running up against opposition, namely the administrators of the university and the Press Club, a society of individuals who had worked on student publications with no real power other than its presumption of wielding influence. The Press Club had successfully hijacked the Chaparral in its first year, producing the last 3 issues of Volume One with Bristow Adams and Larrey Bowman's name forced under an obnoxiously larger CHRIS MASON BRADLEY on the masthead.

The Press Club had been held off but by the 1905-06 school year, the Chappies were tired of being jerked around by these turkeys. The year had been marked by outrageous material in print, public controversy, a duel between the Chaparral editor Morrie Oppenheim and the editor of Berkeley's Daily Californian, and punishment from Stanford administrators. By the spring session, the *Chaparral* staff was fed up. Old Boy Oppenheim was particularly exasperated.

On the night of April 17, 1906, Oppenheim and other members of the *Chaparral* met at their usual watering hole, Charley Meyer's Pub in Menlo Park. That evening they formed the Hammer & Coffin Society, to publish the *Chaparral,* and be an organization for *Chaparral* alums. The name Hammer & Coffin refers to the slogan "We're going to sock 'em with a Hammer and lock them in a Coffin." That is what Chappies are supposed to do to the "stuffed shirts" and "pompous." Of course, this is all a metaphor. The society was formed near midnight on the evening of April 17, 1906. The drinking continued until the wee hours. The group "went to sleep plastered."

A few hours later they "woke up plastered," as the great San Francisco quake of 1906 hit. It is a popular joke in Chaparral lore that the quake was indeed caused by the cosmic Jester, who proclaimed the birth of the organization by striking the ground with their comic hammer.

As the story from three years earlier had predicted, the earthquake destroyed Stanford's Great Arch, nearly destroyed Memorial Church as its great spire was obliterated, and as predicted, resulted in the deaths of two people on the Stanford campus.

Coincidences seem to follow the *Chaparral*. For those inclined, one could say it has a strange psychic energy. Even the secular-oriented would have to admit the *Chaparral* has had several strange coincidences throughout history. The events described in this book may be yet another.

But I digress.

From its auspicious founding in 1906 to present day, the Hammer & Coffin Society, or H&C as it is called, has published the Stanford Chaparral. I was "initiated" into the society in April of my sophomore year at Stanford, an honor offered to individuals who have worked on the Chaparral a year or more. The editor of the Chaparral is the president of the Hammer & Coffin, so I held that esteemed position for a year, 1987-88. The current co-editors of the Stanford Chaparral are the current co-presidents of the Hammer & Coffin.

I was told by any number of members that the Hammer & Coffin was a "secret" society, and while there are aspects of that which are comically true, this most certainly and provably a joke. I always figured it was a joke. I mean, students often run for Stanford student government, the unfortunately named ASSU, as the "Hammer & Coffin Slate."

Through my research for the Chaparral 125th anniversary book I learned the Hammer & Coffin certainly was not at all a secret from its founding up through present day. There are countless newspaper articles mentioning the group, their actions and plans regarding the magazine, dealings with the university and the like, as well as many press mentions noting individuals' membership Hammer & Coffin, the same way one would mention being in the Rotary Club or Kiwanis. Wedding announcements, obituaries, articles about promotions and the like all include that so-and-so was a member of Hammer & Coffin or the Hammer & Coffin Auxiliary.

The H&C Auxiliary was created in the 1930s for female Chappies, as women were not allowed to be full members. Despite the fact that the very first page of the very first *Chaparral* issue is written by May Hurlburt, one of the nine founders of the *Chaparral*, the Hammer & Coffin Society was men only. This outrage remained until the late 1970s, when the Chappies, both female and male, revolted against the byzantine misogyny of the organization.

For 68 years, 1899 to 1967, the *Chaparral* was a humor magazine. It was a general interest/literary format for two more. Then in 1969 it transformed into a political and protest tabloid akin to the underground press of the time. It stayed in tabloid newsprint format for five years, until 1974, when it returned to a humor format, continuing to print today as a color slick magazine.

From the 1920s through the 1950s, the *Chaparral* was one of the most important groups on the Stanford campus. It was a coveted thing to be a Chappie, and there were annual tryouts to get on the staff each fall. The Old Boy was a campus celebrity, people vied to be the business manager as it paid very well. The staff was large, with every class initiating several members into the Hammer & Coffin.

The *Chaparral* grew in popularity and status at Stanford, with the late forties and entire decade of the fifties being a true Golden Era. Magazine popularity in the United States reached its zenith in 1955, before television took much of its place, and the *Chaparral* largely mirrored the industry, peaking in circulation the middle years of the 1950s.

In 1951, the *Chaparral* published the legendary Purple Ape issue. While no one article was cited, Stanford Dean of Students Don Winbigler suspended *Chaparral* editor Stan Norton under the official reason of "general tastelessness," making headlines all the way to San Francisco. The *Stanford Daily* ran a huge block headline akin to Men Land on the Moon, or NIXON RESIGNS. This was big news. Norton would go on to become Mayor of Palo Alto.

In 1961, *Chaparral* published Layboy, a parody of Playboy, and Dean Winbigler struck again, with the temporary suspension of editor Brad Efron. Like Giordano Bruno, Efron had been punished for making light of the Virgin Mary (although not as severely as Bruno). Efron went on to be a celebrated Professor of Statistics at Stanford, winning many awards in a distinguished career over the next 50 years.

The *Chaparral* survived these controversies. Then came social change and chaos of the 1960s.

Always a mirror of the times, the *Chaparral* issues of the early sixties pushed social limits, publishing ever more explicit material on sex and drugs. While the 1961 Layboy issue was relatively tame yet resulted in a suspension, the 1965's Layboy Revisited included a topless centerfold of San Francisco dancer Carol Doda but received no discipline.

The 1966-67 school year included a *Chaparral* "LSD" issue called Legalize Spiritual Discovery and Pornography, complete with psychedelic hippie lettering and a jester as a multi-armed bodhisattva. Contrary to legend, the issues were NOT dosed with acid, but it makes a great story, and the current students' eyes grow wide at the telling.

That year was rounded out with Groin, a parody of a men's magazine that basically bankrupted the *Chaparral*, followed by Crash Comics, which included a nude centerfold of Vicky Drake, who had famously run and almost won Stanford student council president with nude and topless fliers for her candidacy. Time Magazine reported that this was the first time in history a college publication had printed a totally nude model[9].

The Layboy parodies of 1961 and 1965 had been huge successes—some of the highest selling *Chaparral*s of all time, but not these latest entries. More issues had been printed in anticipation of greater sales, but only a scant few were sold. Boxes of Groin became like supplemental office furniture in the Chappie office. "Well finally there were enough places to sit," quipped one Chappie about the state of the *Chaparral*'s still new offices in the Storke Building. Even in my years at the *Chaparral* 1985-88, there were boxes of Groin sitting around, along with boxes of many other issues.

It is amazing to think how quickly public sentiment changed in just a few years.

By the 1967-68 school year, the old *Chaparral* was on life support, converting to a general-interest magazine to mostly poor reception. The *Chaparral* only printed one issue the '68-69 school year, an election issue in the fall. The entire winter and spring quarters of 1969, there was no *Chaparral*, and perhaps not even a staff. The magazine was also in considerable debt. It seemed that this was the end of the line for the Chappie.

Was the *Chaparral* dead? Or was it just having an out of body experience? Fortunately, the little bush did not die. As stated in *The Chappie – 125 Years of Issues*, "Ironically, the capitalist demand of 1969 was for socialist material and sensibilities."[10]

The Stanford Chaparral's "Political Era"

In the fall of 1969, Stanford student Michael Sweeney convinced the Hammer & Coffin to give him something over $19,000 to restart the *Chaparral* as a "literary magazine." I suppose one could argue that since it had printed words on paper it was indeed literary magazine, but that is about the extent of it. Approximately $16,000 of the sum was used retiring the *Chaparral*'s debt, with around $3,500 as an operating budget. For those keeping score, $19,000 in 1969 is about $164,000 in 2024.

The *Chaparral* was changed into a newsprint, underground press format, more akin to the *Berkeley Barb*, or perhaps *Good Times*, than the *Paris Review*. It was not just a publication. The *Chaparral* became a focal point of campus and mid-peninsula protests, and certainly the center of the OFF-ROTC protests of spring 1970. The *Chaparral* office became a headquarters for the protesters.

The old Hammer & Coffin guys were NOT amused. In fact, they were livid.

And after protests, broken windows, buildings burned, and the infamous *Chaparral* OFF-ROTC issue, the University wasn't amused either. Sweeney and others faced punishment from both Stanford and the law, and it was the end of his editorship of the Chaparral.

The *Chaparral* continued to print in 1971 to 1974 in the tabloid newsprint format, and gradually became somewhat less radical in its editorial content, and doing some solid journalism. In fact, the 1971-72 *Chaparral*, and the 72-73 edition were quite organized and productive. These two school years tie for the most Chappie issues printed in any one year, 17, printing an issue every two weeks during the term. But I didn't learn any of these facts until the 2020s.

Back in the late 1980s, the "political era" of the *Chaparral* was described to us youngsters as a dark time, when the magazine had been taken over by radicals, and most disparagingly, wasn't funny. This was the entirety of my knowledge of the *Chaparral* circa 1969-74 until present day. But I want to make clear now, in the 2020s, that the description of that time was unfair, and in a word, wrong. The *Chaparral* has always been a reflection of the times it existed in, interspersing eras when it is a cutting-edge antenna/lightning rod, with other eras when it is on life support. In these aspects, the *Chaparral* during the years 1969 to 1974 fits right in.

It's not clear to me what the exact situation was at the Chaparral in the last years of this era. It wasn't until present day, through reading a July 16, 1974, article in the *Stanford Daily*, that I learned the university discovered people living in the *Chaparral* offices and publishing non-Stanford publications while there.[11] The university kicked these people out people out of the offices. The article didn't name the individuals, group, or publications removed from the office, but did include that the locks to the Chappie office were changed. The *Chaparral* was yet again in debt, and publication was suspended by the ASSU Pub Board. The Chappie was dead. Again.

1974 - The Resurrection

The *Chaparral* was resurrected in fall of 1974 by Mike Dornheim, known to Chappies as "The Field Marshal." He was given that name for his leadership qualities and deft maneuvering to wrest control of the *Chaparral* from MB, an individual not associated with the *Chaparral*, but who had presented a management plan for it to the Publications Board.

Dornheim seized the day by printing an issue of the *Chaparral*, a 12-page mini-format issue, 100 percent a college humor magazine, entitled *Fiscal Responsibility*. When the issue appeared, MB withdrew his proposal, and the Pub Board recognized Dornheim as the head of the Chappie[12]. He returned the *Chaparral* to its original humor format that it maintains to this day.

The Chappie re-devoted itself to comedy, perhaps even more exclusively than its original issues, when an occasional prose or poem might appear. By the mid-eighties, a full decade of comic tradition had been rebuilt. The 1970s and 80s brought a new heyday for college humor, what some are calling the Animal House Era. At that point, the *Chaparral* absolutely resembled the Deltas in the movie Animal House. Meetings were raucous. There was likely something going on in the office every night. There were a lot of funny people, jokesters, pun masters, drinkers, partiers, and of course, pranksters.

It was in this *Chaparral*, I found a home at Stanford.

Chaparral Pranks

In addition to producing a magazine, the *Stanford Chaparral* has a long history of pranks, with a particularly legendary period of pranking from the mid 1970s through the early 1990s.

One of the favorite outfits to prank was our old rival, the *Stanford Daily*, the student newspaper that even when it is full production only comes out five days a week. Weekends notwithstanding, five days a week is a worthy accomplishment. From the earliest days of the *Chaparral*, the *Daily*, which was the *Palo Alto Daily* from 1892 to 1926, was a rival. It became *The Stanford Daily* officially with their September 30, 1926 issue, and has been so ever since. Printed barbs, parody issues, staff football games, and pranking are all a part of the long history of the two publications. In olden times, Chappies were known to drop bags of water from their second-floor office on to *Daily* staffers coming in and out of their office.

In the fall of 1974, new *Chaparral* editor Dornheim pranked the *Daily* and the entirety of both Stanford and UC Berkeley. Traditionally, a Big Game issue was printed by the *Stanford Daily* for the Stanford/ UC Berkeley football game, even when the game was in Berkeley. In the first months of Dornheim's leadership, he learned the Daily would not be printing this edition because of a lack of advertising.

Dornheim saw the opportunity of the prank presenting itself and got the staff to spring into action. There was a wild paste up night at the Chappie office, and a 4am ride into the belly of the beast, Berkeley, to place the fake Daily in newsstands around the UC campus. The prank issue, with its lead story that the Stanford Axe, the prized trophy awarded to the winner of the Big Game, was missing, created quite a stir.

Comically, the next year the *Daily* tried to copy Dornheim's prank issue by producing a fake *Daily Californian*. In the issue, they made several jokes about Cal's All-American running back Chuck Muncie. Well, the result was not good--like a famous scene in the movie Fast Times at Ridgemont High. In that movie, a really good, really big, and really angered-by-a-prank football player goes WILD on his opponent. In this case, all of Cal was pissed, and they absolutely destroyed Stanford, 45-14, with Muncie literally running roughshod over us. Thanks a lot, *Daily*.

The *Chaparral* has made fake issues of the *Stanford Daily, Sequoia, Campus Report,* the *San Francisco Chronicle* and others; has sent fake registration letters to clueless freshmen, spliced hardcore sex films into the ASSU movie night, and changed the sign of the *Stanford Daily* to say *Stanford Dairy*. The Chappies did such a good job with the change that it was not noticed for weeks. Chappies also put a Mickey Mouse on the new campus clocktower in the wee hours before its official unveiling, and the prank was revealed in front of the university president, the trustees, the donor, and other university officials.

In what is widely held to be the greatest *Chaparral* prank of all time, Chappies swapped out the feature photo and caption that was supposed to appear on the front page of the May 2, 1980, *Stanford Daily* with a photo of themselves pretending to be the Stanford Bowling Team along with text that they had just died in a plane crash en route to a tournament in Indiana. The headline, "Tragedy Strikes Bowling Team," was not enough of a joke for people to understand it was a fake. It will be forever debated if the words "None Spared" should have been added to make it more obvious. For brevity's sake, I will just say that this prank caused a large, multi-week shitstorm on campus, and punishment for the seven not-dead bowlers, the details of which remain sealed to this day.

The *Chaparral* loved a good prank. But sometimes, reality seemed to prank the Chappies.

THE ONLY TIME RICHARD GOT ANGRY AT ME

Who Shot R.R.?

On March 21, 1980, in the final, cliffhanger episode of the TV show Dallas, protagonist-villain J,R. Ewing is shot by an unknown assailant. Thus began "Who Shot J.R.?" mania, which swept the nation, and the world. People recant that upon arriving in Europe in the summer of 1980, Europeans questioned the Americans on if they knew who did it. Even Larry Hagman, the actor who played J.R. was questioned about who did it by the Queen Mother. He refused to divulge the secret, even to royalty.

On November 4, 1980, Ronald Reagan defeated President Jimmy Carter to become the 40th President of the United States.

On November 21, 1980, the largest television audience in history watched the Dallas episode Who Shot J.R.? The murderer was revealed to be Kristin Shephard, J.R.'s sister-in-law and mistress.

Sometime in January 1981, the words Datebook Parody were written on the *Chaparral* chalkboard, and its headline article, Who Shot R. R.? was proposed by JM during a Chappie "germ session." A germ session is a meeting where the Chaparral staff gets together to come up with ideas ("germs") for the upcoming issue. The editor writes the ideas on a chalkboard, and the issue begins to take shape. These meetings were particularly raucous.

JM wrote the article in February, and it was edited and laid out into March. Final art boards were sent to the printer around St. Patrick's Day, and the printed issues were returned to Chappie staffers about ten days later. Weekend plans and other fun stuff caused the staff to delay selling the issue until the following Monday when they were likely to catch the largest number of students, actually going to class.

And so it was on the morning of March 30, 1981, the *Stanford Chaparral* debuted their new issue, Art, Music and Generics, containing its centerpiece printed-on-pink-for-authentic-Datebook-parody cover story, Who Shot R. R.? Datebook was a recurring section of the *San Francisco Chronicle*, with entertainment features, TV listings, games and puzzles. Some of the Datebook parodies were even printed separately for added comic use. The cover included a picture of Ronald Reagan, with the suspects Jimmy Carter, Nancy Reagan, and a horse. As with the debut of any Chappie issue, the staff was quite excited to see the fruits of many months of work. A sales table was set up on Stanford's White Plaza around 10 am, Pacific time.

Ninety minutes later, 3,000 miles away, on the other side of the nation, President Ronald Reagan was shot. For real.

Now if you were to tell someone that on a particular day a comedic article about an assassination would be printed from the home state of a particular politician, and on that same particular day, that politician is indeed a victim of an assassination attempt, one might say that it was impossible it could be a coincidence--there MUST be some connection. Government agents indeed thought that too and sent investigators to Stanford and the *Chaparral* offices. But after a full investigation, they came to their conclusion:

It was indeed, just a coincidence.

Keep this in mind as you read the rest of this book. I'm trying to keep it in mind as I write it.

Also remember an additional strange comic quirk that has no significance to this tale other than its comic value: Because of this assassination attempt, Nancy Reagan placed a call to "a lady in San Francisco," as Donald Regan called astrologer Joan Quigley in his 1987 tell-all book, *For The Record*, where he exposed the Reagan's use of astrology to plan all White House functions.[13]

Nancy Reagan had been in communication Quigley previously, asking her advice during the 1980 Presidential campaign. But now, Joan Quigley became the central person scheduling all things for the President and the White House based upon her astrological readings[14].

That's right, an astrologer in San Francisco planned the schedule, arranged the timing, and okayed all actions done in the Reagan White House after the assassination attempt. Who knew?

Walk the Prank

As I have said, the *Chaparral* is a humor magazine, but is equally proud of its pranks. If you wanted to become someone in the *Chaparral*, or the Hammer & Coffin Society, your college career would have to include pulling some pranks. I was excited to join the *Chaparral*, and eager to add to the long history of Chappie pranks.

As young as ten, I was engaged in Halloween pranking, mostly with a jovial man who lived across the road. Stringing toilet paper, spreading shaving cream, misplaced for sale signs, and toilets springing up in front yards were all part of the hi-jinks.

My first big prank came during high school graduation, when I got some of my father's herbicide and under the cover of night went up on the side of the Brookville Lake Dam with my friend and Non Musicians bandmate, BG. We burned an 84 into the grass of the dam, although we didn't do it very well. We should have brought ropes, it was hard to see, and it was quite steep. Nevertheless, you could see the 84 well into the next year. It was such a hit that it led to the Army Corp of Engineers mowing the year of the graduating class into the grass on the dam annually, a tradition that continues to this day. The '84 "crime" went unsolved until 2008, when I confessed to it at a community meeting in front of local Army Corp of Engineers staff.

At Stanford, I came into my own as an accomplished campus pranker, both individually, and after joining the *Chaparral*.

To me, the essentials of a good prank are:
1. Don't get caught;
2. No one gets hurt, including property, and;
3. It is funny.

By far the most important one of these things is to not get caught. Ok, ok, of course you don't want anyone to get hurt either, but not getting caught means no one knows you did it. It means you don't face consequences. It means you don't have to plan what to do because of those consequences. It's really the way to go.

Actually, I was TERRIFIED of getting caught, at least for some pranks, and would think through plans and scenarios so as to successfully NOT get caught. If I had gotten suspended or put on probation by Stanford, my father would have had a heart attack. Perhaps my mother too.

So, given the importance of not getting caught, it behooves you to spend some time thinking it out. Here are some of the things to consider when pulling a prank where you don't get caught.

The Instantaneous Prank

A key factor in pranking is operating quickly. An instantaneous prank, if such existed, would be an uncatchable prank. It's just simple mathematics. But since an instantaneous prank is not possible, you should instead strive for a prank that takes the shortest time to commit. That minimizes the chances of you being seen, of campus police happening by, of any number of things. Speed is of the essence in a successful prank.

Damage = Evidence

As previously stated, another key to a great prank is that no one gets hurt (except maybe their feelings). That includes property. If you can get into a building, an office, without breaking anything, that is very preferable to the alternative. The key point is that if you don't damage any property, you cut your chances of leaving any clues, which is of tantamount importance. Damage Equals Evidence is the equivalent of No Damage Equals No Evidence.

If you perform your prank quickly, and there are no clues, you get people thinking up various alternative theories of how it happened. Most of those theories are certain to be wrong, but they often gain traction, and as they do, your chances of being caught grow lower. Once wrong theories become conventional wisdom, also known as "CW", you are off scot free.

Pranks are like Real Estate

I have always been amazed at how pranks are like real estate. What do I mean by that? Well, I mean you can't always get the ideal situation you might dream up, so you have to take the situation as is. In real estate, you have to choose from what is available. You must make your plans work within the aspects of that property. Oftentimes a prank opportunity, like a real estate opportunity, just happens. You weren't planning to buy that certain property, but it became available and it makes a lot of sense. Same in pranking. You weren't planning to prank, but hey, the key was in the lock. It was almost like reality was daring one to seize the opportunity.

So many pranks work this way, stemming from a situation that already exists; an opportunity that presents itself. A happenchance occurrence where you realize you could pull a prank. Like Dornheim realizing the annual *Daily* Big Game issue was not going to print that year.

When a group of Chappies in 1983 wanted to do a spring prank, they looked in the paper and saw that the clocktower was soon to be dedicated, and so the Mickey Mouse on the clocktower prank was hatched. In 1986, the heist of the Berkeley Bear was born upon the discovery that the glass case in the Union was unlocked. The entire caper would not have happened if not for this fact. And yes, another famous

Chappie prank began when they discovered a key in the padlock of one of the large map cases at the entrances to campus. And yes, the key worked on every case at every entrance. That led to the placement of a large dot in each case that said "You Are Here." Without the discovery of the key in the padlock, that prank would never have happened.

Pranksters look for such opportunities. The prankster is as much reactive as they are proactive. They see an opportunity, and then do the prank. They work with what is given to them and then take it from there.

It is my observation that Zodiac was a prankster. A psychopathic, evil prankster, but a prankster nonetheless. Certain things were planned, but other things just happened, truly just by random chance, and they acted on that random chance. Later in the book I will discuss that the entire name of The Zodiac, and moreover, the black hood used in the Lake Berryessa attack are possibly such a random occurrence that aligned with the comic strip Dick Tracy--all of which the killer took advantage of.

People are Really, Really Literal

Another thing to consider when pranking is that most people are really literal. I'm not certain I understood this while I was a college student, but after my time on Madison Avenue and decades of work in communication and cognition I can say without a doubt: People are Really, Really Literal.

Moreover, people are very much oriented to their *initial take* on things. If you can give someone a context to an event and they think they absolutely know what that context is, that will shape most, if not all, of their comprehension of it over time. Once you have a bunch of people with a false initial take, and they exchange their false opinions on the matter, you are probably safe and have gotten away with your prank. This is similar to the "CW" observation I made earlier, but emphasizes that peoples' first impressions are the primary driver of what becomes "CW."

People tend to like their first take, tend to hold to it. When information comes that disputes it, they often think it is the exception. When data comes that affirms the take, they embrace it. This is just another way to say that people have confirmation bias.

This phenomenon and variations of it has been used to frame ideas for billions of people over thousands of years, in many categories like religion, politics, advertising, grifting, the selling of cheap products and the like. It is also a key element in successful pranking.

My Prank Career at Stanford

Freshman year I stole a few signs; building signs, directional signs, stupid stuff. But what about something cooler? Along with my friend, C, we cooked up an idea for a bigger prank, one that if successful would gain national attention. When I say pranks are like real estate, the metaphor here was Monopoly, and we had just happened upon Park Place and Boardwalk, right there at Stanford. The Super Bowl was coming to campus! We decided to prank the it - we just needed an idea.

The Super Bowl

Super Bowl XIX was scheduled for January 20, 1985, at Stanford Stadium. I lived in the school's largest freshman dorm. How often does the Super Bowl come to your campus your freshman year? Well, like only one time. It almost seemed too good to be true, and it seemed that we were SUPPOSED to do a prank, or at least attempt one.

It's not so much the game that was exciting, it was the buildup, the preparation. Tents, RVs, and people all started showing up on campus two weeks prior. Parties were springing up all over campus and the local area. Of course, we were in 49er territory, so there were lots of fans. I was and am a Bengals fan, so I wasn't too thrilled about the Niners, but even so, it was a fun extra to freshman year. A couple of us in the dorm wanted to pull a prank but didn't have a good idea. Then about a week before the game, the Goodyear Blimp showed up. It was pretty surreal, this large balloon orbiting the skies of campus. I realized I had only seen the blimp on TV before. It's quite impressive in person and captured our imagination.

And so the idea of the Branner Football Balloon was born, a giant football balloon twenty feet in length and ten feet in diameter, made from brown garbage bags cut and taped together, with the word BRANNER written across it. The idea was to fill it with helium balloons as well as regular air balloons to make it zero gravity. We would attach lift balloons raise it over the stadium, released by pulling a fishing line. We figured it would hang over the Super Bowl for some extended amount of time, possibly, hopefully, floating down onto the field.

We marshaled the dorm, we assembled our materials through the week, then worked through the night and created the enormous football balloon.

What we did not calculate was the helium loss of 1,000+ balloons across even just a couple hours, so even though we had a great balloon in the dorm, by the time we got it outside the stadium it didn't have good lift. We also had waited until the start of the second half, which was less chaos outside the stadium, but just meant we lost even more helium. Outside the stadium we frantically did what we could to make it lighter, but it was just barely floating. It did eventually get up over the edge of the stands. Some of our classmates said they saw it from inside the stadium, but it got caught on the trees outside the stadium and fell back to the ground. All in all, the prank was a failure.

Lambo

Ten months later, at Big Game November 23, 1985, the three main builders of the Super Bowl Football vowed to do it again, and this time succeed.

Now Big Game is not the Super Bowl, but to Stanford and Cal-Berkeley, it is close. The rivalry is one of the oldest and most contested in all of college sports and includes a long history of pranks by each school against the other. Stealing The Axe, the trophy awarded to the winner of the game, is the stuff of legend. Other pranks throughout the week preceding the game have always been part of the rivalry.

This time we had experience, and better engineering, than during our Super Bowl attempt. Most notably, we used painter drop cloth instead of garbage bags, meaning less seams and much less duct tape, which made the balloon simpler to make and lighter overall. Plus, we went bigger, fifteen feet in diameter and thirty feet long.

Since the drop cloth was clear, we needed brown balloons to make it look like a football. Very late in the process we discovered that no vendor could get us the 3,000 or so brown balloons we needed. In fact, the only color they had in those quantities was white.

And so the idea of a balloon that was a sheep, which we named Peggy, was born, and it wasn't thirty feet long, it turned out to be thirty-five or more feet in length because we added a head. It was constructed in the main lounge of my residence, Terra House, starting Friday afternoon and working through the night for the Saturday afternoon game.

The developing project in the Terra lounge was met with varying reactions, from disbelief to enthusiastic support, to outright scoffing. We needed 1,500 regular-air balloons blown up to go with our 1,500 helium balloons, no small task. A lot of people stopped by and blew up five or ten balloons for us. We rearranged the furniture in the lounge, using couches and the corner of the room to make a balloon bin where we could stash the 1,500 regular air balloons.

We had to calculate how fast we could blow up 1,500 helium balloons, so we could wait as late as possible to start that process. We set the start of the helium inflation for 6 am.

Helium balloons were blown up using a tank, with an assembly line process of one person feeding balloons to another, who was running the tank, with the inflated balloon handed off to another person to tie them and then put the balloons directly into the plastic skin of the sheep. Slowly we had enough balloons to hold up the plastic, and the shape of the sheep began to form. Now the Terra lounge is pretty large, and it has series of double doors opening to the outside, but by late morning we had to move Peggy outside to fill it to its full capacity. We set up shop in Terra's front courtyard. Luckily it was not windy. Before heading to the stadium we spray painted RAM EWE CAL on one side, and LAMBO on the other, as well as a Hammer & Coffin logo.

The rest, as they say, is history. We got it over the stadium. We pulled the fishing lines to release the two lift balloons. One of them was released as planned, but the second one stuck, so it didn't float down to the field, just stayed high over the stadium. We were ecstatic. We ran in the stadium and celebrated while it hung over the field for many minutes. People started chanting, "RAM EWE CAL!"

Instead of floating down to the field it just floated right over and past the stadium. Old Stanford Stadium officially held over 80,000 people, but many more on a Big Game Day. People were sitting in the aisles. Student sections were packed with cheering, partying, students. When the sheep floated over the stadium and beyond, we tried to get out quickly but it was impossible. We were stuck in the stadium.

Then a miracle happened. While trying to make my way to an exit I heard the crowd swell and turned around to see the sheep being blown back over into the stadium. It must have caught a stronger wind, as it was spinning and moving faster than planned. It went high up into the air and back over the stadium again, before coming down into the stands on the other side of the field. For a moment it was being pushed down towards the field by the crowd, but then it ripped open, releasing the 1,500 helium balloons and 1,500 regular air balloons. It was quite a sight.

At the time, I had joined the *Chaparral*, but did not know what the Hammer & Coffin Society was. I just figured it was some Chappie symbol. I had painted an H&C logo on the sheep, making some of the upperclassmen upset. But Editor MC embraced it and printed a photo of it in the next *Chaparral* issue. The sheep made it into the newspapers[15], and I'm told it was on TV and radio, fully described by the play-by-play announcers. Back at Terra House, some, but not all, of the naysayers apologized for doubting us.

File M for Meat

In Spring of 1986 we produced the Let's Eat issue of the *Chaparral*. The cover was a girl in a bikini, chef's hat and apron holding a grilling fork stuck into a big porterhouse steak. The photo shoot for the cover was on a Thursday night, and when we were done, we had this steak leftover. We had been handling it and it had not been refrigerated, so we didn't want to eat it. It was just going to be thrown away. Or....

Chappies had been sneaking into the *Stanford Daily* offices for years. We went in and out many times with no forced break-in, and with no keys. How? Well, you could pull out the nails on the vent of their office door, pop out the vent, and then reach up and turn the handle. Once in, we would return the vent to its original position and replace the nails. Then after some mischief, we relock the door handle and pull it shut, in and out with no evidence of how. We would do mild pranks, rearrange things, leave things in their office, but we never left any evidence of how we got in there. Conventional wisdom would lead one to think that someone who had the key, likely a *Daily* staff member, was doing the pranks.

That night, at 3 or 4 am, we went into the Editor's office of the *Daily* and put the steak in the file cabinet, filed under the letter M, for meat. We replaced the vent, relocked the door and faded off into the night. Then we waited.

Nothing Friday. Nothing Saturday. Nothing Sunday. Then in the Monday May 19, 1986, edition of the *Daily* we saw an ad for Daily staffers. There would be a grilling question for the new editor candidates, with hard-hitting questions including "Why does the *Daily* office smell like a dead rat?"[16]

The next day we were in the *Chaparral* office when we heard water squirting from a hose. We went to the balcony to see the file cabinet with all the drawers pulled out, getting hosed down.

A couple days later, the *Chaparral* Let's Eat issue debuted, with the steak on the cover. But no one ever put it together. At least, no one called us out on it.

The Horrible, Horrible Pie Incident

On Tuesday, May 27, 1986, members of the *Stanford Chaparral*, including me, entered the Associated Students of Stanford University Senate, the unfortunately named ASSU, meeting wearing masks and other disguises, and threw whipped cream pies into the faces of some the senators. Six of us went in, but only three came out. I went back to help get the three captured guys out. The Daily reported our four names, but when the punishments were handed down, only the three who were caught faced discipline. The Senior of the punished, RH, had his diploma withheld at graduation. Others faced consequences that lasted into their post-Stanford careers. Do you need more proof that when you pull a prank it is CRITICAL that you don't get caught?

The Summer of 1986

By the end of sophomore year, it was becoming ever more clear that Stanford was EXPENSIVE and draining my parents' finances. Two more years of this would be pretty painful. I did everything to save money, and many things to earn it, like being a research subject at the Stanford Medical Center. I got a fun and unique summer job with a company that inspected fire sprinkler systems in buildings, which took me to the very top of the Transamerica Pyramid (not the top floor, but the top point). And for housing I found the thriftiest accommodation in the Mid-Peninsula, the Chappie office.

I was at the office all the time anyway, and by then I had been the *Chaparral* Business Manager for a full year, so I was sort of "in charge" of the space already. Old Boy JW was back East and everyone else was gone for the summer. The office had a sink, and a fridge, and the Storke Building had bathrooms downstairs. Roble Gym was a block away and open each day, with showers and an occasional hoops game. I crashed on a couch in the office for a couple nights, before moseying up to Roble dorm after dark, going in a side door, up some steps, and grabbing a mattress from a random vacant room of a higher floor. Never missed. Maybe never even noticed. Down the steps, behind some pine trees, eucalyptus and other vegetation on a mostly deserted campus after dark, I slipped the mattress up the back steps and into the Chappie office without much trouble.

I worked Monday to Friday, sometimes extra on Saturday, and ate sandwiches and Jack In The Box. For partying, I calculated that the cheapest buzz was the biggest plastic bottle of cheap vodka, with the biggest bottle of chaser, both swigged from the bottle. I'd drink as much vodka as I could without vomiting, then do the chaser, some kind of lemon-lime-grapefruit mix. I'd sit up on the balcony and watch the people go by, and in and out of the *Daily* office, where they were still putting out a paper two days a week.

A couple of times I would yell down at them or make some clever comment. A couple times, *Daily* people might come up late night while working on their issue.

A few weeks in, I got a call from B. He was back East and BORED and wanted to know what was going on at Stanford. I told him nothing, other than drinking straight out of the vodka bottle, and there was plenty of room in the Chappie office. So B. flew out and became my roommate at the Chappie. The night he got there, we moseyed up to Roble dorm after dark, in the side door, up some steps, and into a random vacant room of a higher floor many doors past the room I had visited before and grabbed another mattress. Never missed. Even easier the second time. Through the pines and eucalyptus. Up the back steps and into the office.

And that's where we lived, summer of 1986. I created a nice little apartment in the corner room with the balcony. B took the paste-up room, which still left the main room for general partying. At least until the night of August 3, but that story begins in late July.

Oskie Bear's Excellent Adventure

The Proposition

I was in the *Chaparral* office when B and N came in.

"We've got an idea, and we want to know if you want in on it," they said. "We've been in Berkeley, in their Union, and the glass case for their big stuffed bear is unlocked."

"Unlocked?" I exclaimed.

B and N explained it was a freestanding glass case, with a trophy case lock on it, and it was unlocked, in the lobby of their Union. The lock was there, but it wasn't engaged. If we can get into the building, we could get the bear without breaking a lock or any glass.

Remember what I said about no clues, and no property damage? This piece of prank real estate sounded like an incredible opportunity. I mean, the greatest legends at Stanford, or Berkeley, were the stealers of The Axe, but Stanford already had The Axe, it would be stupid to steal it from ourselves. But Oskie, Cal's Golden Bear mascot in the glass case in the UC Union would be almost as cool, maybe even cooler.

We decided that we all three of us should return to Berkeley, to case the location, see how we might get into the building, and plan the prank. Luckily it was Olden Times, when there were not many, if any, security cams. We went to Berkeley the next weekend, and it was as B and N had described. The case was unlocked, and the door somewhat ajar. We pushed the door back in a bit, to make it look more normal and less obvious it was unlocked.

We walked around the Union on that day and looked at our options. There were many rooms in the building, seemingly many not in too much use. Large parts of the building were mostly uninhabited. And so the plan was hatched.

One of us would hide in the building, and just stay there after hours. Then at some pre-arranged time, he would let us into the building, and we would liberate the bear. There was a parking garage beneath the Union, and there was an elevator close to the bear case that opened right into the parking garage below. We would move the bear into the elevator, down to the basement parking garage, into the car and away.

Since it was his idea, and since it was a bit INSANE, we let N be the one to stay in the building.

We went back to the *Chaparral* office to plan some more. We figured we would encounter the least number of people around the union early on a Sunday morning. So late that the last partier had gone to sleep. So early there wouldn't be a jogger or preacher awake yet. On this crazy drunken Saturday night in the *Chaparral* office, we set Zero Hour slightly more than seven days into the future, 4:30 am, Sunday, August 3, 1986.

The Heist

Saturday afternoon, we drove N's Jeep Waggoneer over to Berkeley, picking up Jack In The Box on the way. We dropped N off outside the Union and watched him go in. B and I proceeded to kill time in Berkeley for the next 10 hours or so. We went to one movie, and then another, ate, ultimately watching the midnight showing of *Rocky Horror Picture Show* at the U.C. Theater in Berkeley.

We brought a battery-operated alarm clock set to 4:15 in case we happened to doze off. And while I had indeed fallen asleep in the movie theater, as we got closer to Zero Hour, the adrenaline was more than enough to keep us wide awake.

At 4:30, we drove under the Union, to the basement parking garage, right up to the doors by the elevator.

But N was not there. We waited for what seemed like an eternity but was probably just a minute. From across the parking garage, a figure approached us. It looked amazingly like a Deep Throat scene out of All the President's Men. We hid behind the Waggoneer, but the guy was walking right towards us.

"B!" "J!" "It's N!"

B and I let out a collective exhale.

"The elevator's disabled. Locked."

"Oh fuck."

"We're still good," explained N. "I blocked the doors on the main floor, we can get back in. Let's go."

We had to exit the parking garage out onto a plaza next to the Union. We quickly crossed the plaza to the propped open door, went in and closed the door.

We approached the case. Would it still be unlocked? We grabbed the trophy lock and tugged. The door opened.

We had naively hoped the bear would just lift off his base, perhaps slide off of stakes. But it didn't budge when we tried that. We grabbed the base and slid it out onto the floor. We then attempted to rock it back and forth to loosen it, but it wasn't working.

Now this glass case was in the main lobby of the UC Berkeley Union, with A LOT of windows all around. We were taking too long and doing it with the great potential of being seen, even at 4:30 am, plus however many minutes we had taken so far. Each passing minute raised the likelihood of a passerby. We had to think fast.

The elevator was right there, the intended path of our escape, now blocked to us. But would the doors still open? Someone pressed the button and lo and behold, the elevator doors opened.

We quickly moved the bear and its base into the elevator and let the doors close. Now in the elevator, which luckily was quite large, we flipped up the base to reveal the bear was attached to the base with two large threaded screws with perhaps one-inch nuts on them securing the bear.

While I can brag about our preparation, I still must admit that we did not bring a wrench big enough for that size nut, a completely idiotic lack of planning on our part. I was sure we were screwed. Our only chance was that the nuts would spin with only hand power.

I put my hand on the first nut, and it spun!

Far from a rusty farm or basement nut and bolt, this was a pristine, shiny university nut and bolt. Both nuts spun off with no trouble, and we detached Oskie from his base. He wasn't very heavy, I don't think more than twenty-five pounds. The problem was that he was a bit unruly to carry. We thought about two people carrying, but that required coordination and made it harder to be quiet, and invisible.

Oskie, including his extended arms, was about seven feet long. I am 6' 8" and experienced with baling straw and hay. I suggested that I could carry the bear alone.

We decided on our next move.

When the elevator doors opened, N would head out first, clearing the way, opening doors and making sure the plaza was clear of people. I would carry the bear, as quickly yet as normally as one could carry a large stuffed bear. B would shut the case, leaving our calling card and joke, an 80s-fad "Animal in Car" window sign (a sarcastic second-wave response to the "Baby On Board" signs that had been the rage) attached to the glass, grab any tools or anything we might have inadvertently left, close the doors, and get out of there.

We listened to see if we could hear anything, but it was still silent, so we opened the elevator doors and hightailed it out of there--out the door that had been propped open, across the plaza, down into the parking garage and into the back of the Waggoneer. We pulled out of the parking garage nice and smooth—no screeching tires or anything to call attention. We drove south, away from Berkeley into Oakland, presumably a different police jurisdiction, and then made our way onto the freeway, back to Palo Alto. I remember looking at my watch while riding away. It said 4:51.

It was still darkish when we got back to Stanford, coming down I-280 to Sand Hill Road, taking "the back way" onto campus, the easiest access to the Chappie offices, and more importantly, closest to the HVAC room above the *Stanford Daily*'s bathrooms in the Storke Building. We backed into a spot as close as you could get to the Storke Building, then got out to see if anyone was around.

During this part of such a prank, the key is to not call attention to yourself. Just act naturally. No one is looking to see if you have Berkeley's bear in your car. If no one knows a crime has been committed, no one is paying any attention at all. On the other hand, if the crime has been discovered, maybe they ARE looking to see if you have Berkeley's bear in your car. It was still way before 6 am, and it was a Sunday. We correctly thought we had several hours before the crime would be discovered.

Stanford was still deserted at this time. We went to the Wagoneer, got the bear, now wrapped in a blanket, and calmly walked it into the doors of the *Stanford Daily*, turned all the way to the left where the bathrooms were, and into the men's room. In that bathroom there was a ladder and access to the HVAC room above. One of us went up, and the others lifted Oskie through the service entrance. The HVAC room was quite large, even with the equipment, so there was plenty of space. We could prop him up so he stood on his feet—or rather the big screws that came out of the bottom of his feet, while leaning on a vent. Dry. Secure. Very secret.

We closed the door to the ceiling, putting it back just as it had been. It looked perfectly normal. And other than the off chance that someone went up there to service the equipment, very well hidden. And, most importantly, not hidden in the Chappie office. We likely took leaks in that bathroom and tried to maintain composure walking out. "Just usin' the john…"

But no one was there even upon exiting the Daily. No one was watching us. The realization that we had done it was setting in. The rush of energy that came from successfully lifting our rival's mascot out of their own Union and hiding it in the ceiling of the *Stanford Daily* was a fantastic feeling. Certainly, we would become legends, added to the list of Stanfordites who had successfully pranked Berkeley. We headed straight to Safeway where we bought six bottles of Cook's Champagne, two for each of us. We went back to the Chappie office and got really, really drunk.

And so it was that in August 1986, three members of Stanford's Class of '88, B, N, and I, used the *Chaparral* office as a base of operations on a mission that helped UC Berkeley's Oskie (as we jokingly misspelled his name throughout the prank) expand his horizons. We let him out of his glass cage in the UC Union in Berkeley, to a couple week stay in the HVAC room over the Daily, then on to a Redwood City storage locker for a few months, and then a year or so at N's house in Fresno.

There were no signs of break in, and no clues other than that Animal in Car thingy that we left in Oskie's case. The lack of any sign of forced entry, either on the building or on the case, led people to initially think it was an inside job.

We planned well, and executed well, and had everything covered except for one key item, what to do with Oskie after we succeed - the one item we hadn't considered. So, over the next fifteen months we had to keep cover, and a straight face, while both campuses were abuzz with Oskie speculation, while even our close friends and employers talked about it, while we sent letters to the Bay Area press creating a small media event, unknowingly and ironically mimicking the actions of someone it would be years before I even heard of, the Zodiac Killer.

News reports stated that this was being treated as a felony,[17] as I'm sure it was. A quasi-realistic stuffed bear, beloved by thousands of Weenies, as Stanford students derogatively refer to Berkeley students, is certainly worth more than $500, the value threshold for felony theft. One press account mentioned the bear had "acquired the status of a deity or icon to the campus community."[18]

The prank was big news around the Bay Area, showing up in newspapers, TV and radio. I was riding across the San Mateo Bridge with my boss when the news came across the radio. He turned up the volume and was said, "Hey! Did you hear about this?" I feigned excitement, or at least feigned not knowing anything about it. I had pulled pranks before, but I wasn't really prepared for all this. KGO radio offered a $500 reward, no questions asked[19]. Phil Frank drew Farley cartoons in the *San Francisco Chronicle* about the heist on successive days, imploring us, the bear stealers, to communicate, a letter, a ransom note, anything[20]. It was in the news, and on people's lips—all in all it was quite surreal. We hadn't thought this part through at all.

I knew the *Chaparral* would be a prime suspect in the heist, as would the Stanford Band, and any of Stanford's fraternities. I figured it was inevitable that someone would contact us, and so I imagined what a Chappie like myself, known for pranks and other campus hi-jinks, would think of the theft of the bear being done by someone else. As expected, a call came to the office. Luckily the call didn't come from the police, but from the *Stanford Daily*.

"Hi, I'm so and so and I'm calling to see If you know anything of the whereabouts of the Berkeley bear?" they asked.

"I heard! It's fucking awesome!" I said. "Totally incredible! What do you know about it?" The Daily reporter then proceeded to tell me how the bear was estimated to be 800 to 1000 pounds[21], standing eight feet tall, and that it was last seen in a vehicle heading north out of Berkeley. It was all I could do to keep from laughing, because all of those "facts" were completely wrong! To be fair to the Daily reporter, those were the "facts" in the initial reports in the press.

The truth was that the Bear weighed perhaps 25-30 pounds, it might have been longer than seven feet, INCLUDING its outstretched arms, and it left Berkeley to the south. Rather than an enormous and heavy Ursidae Maximus, think of something more like a furry piñata.

And the best part, while I was quoted in the August 8, 1986 *Stanford Daily* as knowing only what I had read in the papers[22], Oskie was at that moment residing IN the *Stanford Daily* offices, in the HVAC room above their bathrooms in the Storke Building! For me, this particular aspect of this particular prank is the pinnacle. To be in the rival *Stanford Daily*, talking about my prank, with the crux of the prank actually IN the offices of the Daily is a coup of incredible pranksterness. It is hard to describe how satisfying this was.

The thing is, lack of evidence can become "evidence" in itself. Since there was no sign of a break-in at the Berkeley Union, and no broken case, it led to people thinking it was an inside job. The longer that idea was around, the more people who ascribed to it. It soon became conventional wisdom that it was an inside job.

"We didn't do it," said the *Stanford Daily*, in an editorial in the August 12, 1986, *Stanford Daily*, which includes a quote from Stanford Police Chief Marvin Harrington to the Berkeley Nation regarding the missing Oskie: "Look closer to home."[23]

Having both the Stanford Police and the *Stanford Daily* inadvertently helping us cover our tracks was extremely satisfying. It is worth taking note of how this worked, and works, on matters such as this. And there's more.

That issue of the Daily was yet another coup. In addition to the Daily editorial staff unknowingly running cover for us, the front page contained a story about the horrible, horrible Pie Incident, including interviews with my three *Chaparral* compatriots who said their pun-

THE ONLY TIME RICHARD GOT ANGRY AT ME

ishment for such a harmless and fun prank was too high[24].

Because I had been one of the *Chaparral* Pie Throwers, but didn't get caught, I faced no consequences. But right above that article, in the top right of the page, was a photo of the empty glass case in the Berkeley Union, where Oskie once stood. Two stories about two pranks on the same front page of the Daily! Neither story mentioned me, but I had a hand in both. All while the Daily staff was writing editorials that Stanford didn't do it. It was an amazing time in my prank career.

I kept waiting for the police to call or arrive at the *Chaparral* office, but it never happened, except for the night of the theft.

I know I should have told you this before now, but it just didn't seem to fit anywhere. Ironically, the police DID visit the offices of the *Chaparral*—the very night of the bear heist, or rather, the next morning. At 7am, joggers reported that three guys in their underwear were having an unusually raucous party at the Chappie. The police visited us and confiscated our illegal items including our booze and a makeshift bong. They also asked us if people were living in the *Chaparral* office, because they saw the two mattresses, the toothbrushes and food there.

I was sure that this would lead to us being caught. Certainly, upon hearing of the bear's theft, any police detective would ask for a run down on any abnormal or strange events that occurred on either campus that night, especially the Stanford campus. That's what Columbo, or Sherlock Holmes would do. That's what I would have done if I were a police detective. We had screwed up by celebrating. Soon we would be questioned and almost certainly be caught.

But the questioning never came. Apparently, a drunken party at the *Chaparral* offices was deemed as a normal event.

As for living there, we tidied up and went to our friend's house in Los Altos for a while, then came back to the office when the heat was off. Nevertheless, fall term was starting soon; students, professors, campus life would be returning. Some quiet evening, behind the pines and hedges, in the side door, up the steps, back to the random rooms, back on the still empty bedframe and springs, we returned the mattresses to Roble dorm. Had anyone noticed? It didn't look like it, and now that the mattresses were back and everything restored, and we were out the side door and into the night, no one would. At least for the mattresses.

As for the bear, I always wondered if the Stanford Police didn't try too hard to catch us. Telling Berkeley to look for an inside job could have stemmed from Stanford pride. Yes, there were no signs of break in, neither on the Union's door, nor the glass case. But ask yourself, who would steal the mascot of UC Berkeley? Come on, is this an idiot test? The perpetrators are most certainly from Stanford.

What Do You Do with a Hot Bear? Part 1

Did I mention we planned well, except for the part where we succeeded, and then had to decide what to do with the Bear?

As we approached Big Game 1986, we bounced around many ideas, all more implausible than the next. All involving risk. Various ways of getting the bear onto the field, which would be hard as the game was AT Berkeley. We thought about leaving it at the home of Stanford coach Jack Elway. Or getting it into the locker rooms of the team. Eventually we realized we didn't have to do anything with the bear, THIS year. In fact, perhaps we could hold it until after we graduated.

When we realized we didn't need to do anything until Big Game 1987, that easily became the most popular idea. Doing nothing was very appealing at the time. Even so, the secrecy and stress of this was a constant theme for all of us.

As the days counted down to Big Game, there was a fair amount of Oskie speculation in the press. Cal accusing the Stanford Axe Committee, police questioning them and the Stanford Band. But we stayed silent. Apparently, annoyance with the situation was building up inside the Cal boosters and football team. Because...

On that Big Game, Cal avoided having their all-time worst record by completing one of the greatest upsets in Big Game history, November 22, 1986, beating heavily favored Stanford 17-11. I have always wondered if we, the Bear Stealers, were in part responsible for inspiring Cal to kick Stanford's ass so handily that game.

The Hammer & Coffin Vault

For a while, JW had talked about the Hammer & Coffin vault. I didn't know if he was joking, or if he had really heard something about it. Either way, we had wondered what might be in such a vault. I mean, an 80-year-old "secret" organization of Stanford grads might reasonably have items they wanted to hide, I mean to keep safe.

We would go to San Francisco for occasional Hammer & Coffin meetings to discuss what was going on with the *Chaparral*, or make plans for the annual banquet. The board of the Hammer & Coffin were mostly graduates of the 1950s, but might have individuals who graduated from the 30s to the 70s. Even then, it was unclear (at least to me) who the H & C board were, but at that time it seemed to be run by T, editor of the *Chaparral* in 1955. We met in the board room of T's business, in a skyscraper in downtown San Francisco. As one of these meetings was ending, I approached T.

"Does the H &C have a vault?" I asked, "I have something I may want to put in it."

"Vault? We don't have a vault," said T. "What on earth are you talking about?"

"Well…." I paused. "I thought it might be a good place for the Berkeley Bear."

A look of panic came across T's face. He put his hands over his ears, turned, and walked hurriedly down a hallway to his office. I followed.

"No really," I said, "You don't need to know…"

"Please, stop talking," said T. "Look over there." And he gestured to the office directly across the hall from him.

I looked into the other office. There were blue and gold Cal items on every square foot of wall space, on the desk, on the shelves, logos, pom-poms, bears, pennants, blankets, hats, plaques, mugs, stress balls and doilies.

"This is what I have to deal with," said T. "Every day. I don't want to know anything about the Bear. I can't know anything," he said. "And what is this nonsense you are asking about a Hammer & Coffin Vault? There is no such thing."

Fresno

After paying for a storage locker in Redwood City for a few months, and with the 1986 Big Game come and gone, we decided it would be cheaper and safer if we took Oskie to the home of N. The three of us, plus B's roommate K, drove Oskie out to N's home in Fresno where he could be safely hidden and stored for free.

Of course, this was the perfect time to take pictures of Oskie, to prove we had him and to show how much fun he was having, so we took photos of Oskie barbequing in a Stanford T-shirt and hat, lounging by the pool, and drinking a beer with us.

And then we just cooled out for a year.

The funny thing about Fresno was that the following fall the Stanford Band performed a halftime show titled, "Where's Oski?" (they spelled it the Cal way) and it's worth noting a funny coincidence about the show.

As it would be, I was the only bear stealer in the stadium for this show. I watched the band do their routine, consisting of several songs, where they suggested various places Oskie might be, like Hawaii, Vegas, and other famous locations. But then, for the finale number, they revealed where Oskie REALLY was: Fresno.

How did they know? Only a few people knew, and it wasn't anyone in the Band. Their suggestion Oskie was in Fresno turned out to be a joke, the same way Johnny Carson would joke about Fresno. But in fact, the real cosmic joke was that at that exact moment, the Oskie the Bear was indeed in Fresno.

"Who is writing this shit?" I asked?

Oskie's Broken Foot

We also were deep in discussion about what to do about Oskie's broken foot. It seems during the theft of the bear, Oskie's right foot fell off, but we did not discover this until some weeks after the heist. We were despondent, as we had never intended to damage him, and thought we had been careful. We wondered about Stanford-friendly taxidermists, or even distant taxidermists. For many months our favorite plan was to drive Oskie to Colorado where my family has a cabin, and find a taxidermist there, hoping they had no idea about the Berkeley Bear.

Then a miracle happened. Comically, and thankfully, at one point when we were moving the bear, we noticed a strange tab of leather on the broken foot, with fur attached to it. It looked like torn fur, but I touched it and felt a claw. It was a flap of fur that had flipped up, and attached to it was…Oskie's missing foot! Oh my god we were so happy.

The Ransom Notes

The next year, Senior year, we knew we had to do something with the bear. We still had all of the options from before, all still as impractical and risky as the previous year. But it was also getting lame that we weren't doing anything with our prank. We had done it, we had stolen the bear out of Berkley's Union, but now those days were long past. We needed an idea now. And so, we decided to take Phil Frank up on his suggestion, and send a ransom note.

We made some ridiculous demands, mainly around the police or Cal or Stanford agreeing not to prosecute us. We wanted a letter "on really nice paper" pledging no prosecution, signed by the President of UC Berkeley, Stanford's President Donald Kennedy, California Governor Deukmejian, Sammy Davis Jr., the President of Round Table Pizza, and a few thousand UC Berkeley students.

The letter was roundly disparaged, and no wonder—our demands were sort of stupid.

Did investigators still think this was an inside job? If so, one would have had to believe the perpetrators were trying to frame someone from Stanford. It's likely Berkeley investigators would have given up on the inside job theory by this time. As for Stanford, police must have had their doubts too. Or was it convenient for the Stanford community to still maintain they had nothing to do with it? Was it tribal loyalty to Stanford to not try so hard to catch us? Or, did they really believe it was someone from Berkeley, given no forced entry and no broken locks? One way or another, we were never questioned. This point really illuminates the value of leaving no damage, and thus few clues, when pulling a prank.

After the ransom notes hit the press in early October 1987, Oskie fever was back on. Even though our demands were completely ignored, Oskie was again on the lips of the Bay Area.

RF's Spectacular Oskie Idea.

RF was a recent alum, a well-respected prior Editor of the *Chaparral*, with a prank history of his own, the mastermind of the Mickey Mouse on the clocktower. In other words, he had prank credentials. And as an older "Old Boy," he held rank over me, and I rightly held much deference to him.

He had an idea for the staff that sounded hilarious. But as he told us his idea with obvious excitement in his eyes, I experienced something like a "Hitchcock effect", un-zooming the camera while trucking in, producing a strange film-noir thriller effect.

"What you need to do is make a fake bear," he said, "and then put it in the back of a pickup and drive around. Drive around Stanford. Drive around Berkeley. You're sure to eventually be stopped by the cops, but when they do, the bear is fake!"

At the time of this story, there were only seven people who knew about the bear, and R was not one of them. He just thought it was a funny idea.

"That's a great idea!" said one of the Chappies. Then they turned to me, "What do you think, Jim?"

Can you imagine? Spending a lot of your time trying to devise a payoff to the Oskie prank while not getting kicked out of school, and here comes this idea presented to you, one you SHOULD be very excited about and eager to take up. This is a great idea… for everyone who is NOT an actual stealer of the bear. All in all, this moment was surreal. I remember, my brain repeating, "Oh my god! Oh my god!" (OMG had yet to be invented).

"Oh, yeah, that's a cool idea…. But isn't that just cashing in on some else's prank?" I said.

"Yeah! That's the beauty of it. You didn't steal the bear, it's just a fake! You're not doing anything illegal. You don't have anything to worry about because you didn't steal it."

Now I had practiced for the police or the press asking me about the bear, but I had not envisioned this.

"Umm, umm… I dunno." I said. "It's funny, but it will take a lot of time…"

"It's just papier Mache. It's an art project. It's one fun evening with beer."

"Well, we'd want it to look realistic, otherwise this will be lame. The paper said it's eight feet tall," I said.

This was one of the many times I conveniently used the incorrect reports in the press of the great size and weight of the bear to throw people off. Estimates in the paper put the bear at seven to eight feet, and weighing hundreds of pounds.

RF was clearly disappointed that I wasn't so enthusiastic with his idea. I really did try to see a way, but in every scenario it would cause people to notice us. If I wasn't on the police's radar screen, why do anything, even a joke, to put myself on one? If I were the cops, the *Chaparral* would already be on a short list of suspects. So, we did not make a fake bear and go driving around Stanford and Berkeley. I declined to do RF's prank idea, much to his disappointment.

What do you do with a Hot Bear? Part 2

While we didn't do his idea, the concept of using a fake bear to hide the real bear was incorporated into our thinking and seriously considered in various ways right up to the conclusion of this prank. For example, we likely couldn't carry the real bear on to the football field, but we could bring a fake one, especially, as had been pointed out, if it were big and clunky and obviously a home-made substitute. We considered it for quite a while, but even though revealing the real Oskie inside of the fake one in front of a Big Game crowd would have been legendary, we still couldn't figure out how to do it without being arrested, and worse, expelled.

We discussed what to do with Oskie extensively, over many months. We revisited the idea of leaving it in the yard of Coach El-way's house or in the locker room of the Stanford Football Team; skydive the bear on to the field, all kinds of ideas were considered. But any possible scenario we came up with seemed to lead to our getting caught and punished.

With no traction from the first ransom note, we sent a second with reduced demands and even less of a response. The head of the Stanford Axe Committee remarked in the press that it looked like we were getting desperate. We were.

So with another Big Game approaching and no good idea, we did the most logical thing--which still could theoretically get the bear on to the field during the game--but more importantly would be getting the bear off of our hands. The only people with a reasonable shot at getting the bear onto the football field was the group many people thought had taken it all along, the amazing, incomparable, irreverent Leland Stanford Junior Marching Band.

Of course, as one of the organizations most likely to have stolen Oskie, it would be hard for them to say that it just "showed up" in the Band Shak. So that's where we put it.

We knew that the band was playing at the Thursday night Big Game bonfire rally on the other side of campus. During the rally, two of us would put the bear in the shack. The other two would watch the area and make sure no band members or random people wandered near the Shak, and if any did, our guys would attempt to delay them.

We took the bear, wrapped it in garbage bags, and slipped into the Band Shak while the pep rally was going on. The place was deserted. Quick in, nice and quiet, leave the package leaning up against the wall, and right back out into the night. The one and only time I was ever in the Band Shak, I left the Berkeley Bear for them.

We got back to the Chappie office and called the Band Shak, getting their answering machine. In my best disguised voice, I told them that Oskie was there.

As we would learn months later, the leaders of the Band got back to the Shak before the rest of the Band. When they found Oskie there, they FREAKED, and quickly got him out of there.

When those guys returned to the Band Shak, they said they found the band members, "dismantling" the Shak looking for the bear. The mass of Band members had returned from the rally and played the answering machine message. I think they may have been drinking too.

The Bear was out of our hands, Big Game 1987 came and went without anything about it.

The following year we learned that Oskie had made his way back to Berkeley, by way of a fountain in San Francisco. The Stanford Axe Committee had left it there, sometime after the Band had gotten it to them.[25]

All three of us, and our accomplices, graduated from Stanford in June of 1988. I got out by the skin of my teeth, with the minimum number of credits and minimum grade point average allowed. I was outta there, and off to New York City.

The Smoke-Filled Rooms of Madison Avenue

Now where does someone go to work who has experience creating comic magazines, good computer skills, and the demeanor and knowledge of how to pull off a prank? Well, Madison Avenue of course.

Upon graduation in 1988, I was able to get immediate work in New York as a desktop publisher. I was also able to live at the loft of my friend Don Dickson, on the third floor of the notorious 55 Grand Street in Soho. Don was jazz guitarist Stanley Jordan's manager.

Back at Terra House at Stanford, Don had given me the nickname Bigtwin, which I now embraced as my "art name." Before leaving Stanford, Don and Stanley had also sent me to see this weird guy in East Palo Alto, Jaron Lanier. There he showed me the software Swivel. He even gave me an early version of it, saying it wasn't even "beta" software. We made a joke that it was "gamma," and so for many years all my Swivel files were named "gamma," including all of the Dukey, UFO, and flower 3d models used in my art. Access to this software helped me get an edge in 3D modeling on a Macintosh, and propelled me into a career in computer graphics and virtual reality over the next decade.

The 55 Grand loft was the location for many late-night parties, where people would come after their gigs. Also living in the loft was Brazilian percussionist, Valtinho Anastacio. Between the three of us and the many visitors, the pad was almost always partying, particularly from 4 to 8 am. During these days, I would try to go to sleep at 9 or 10 pm, so that I could wake up at 4 am, when the crew would show up after their gigs. Kenny "DocTone" Kirkland and Jeff "Tain" Watts would arrive, with an extended crew including Joaquin, Fernando and others. Joaquin had been the drummer for Jimmy Cliff. I often went to work still "under the effects" of the evening's festivities. Good thing I worked in an ad agency.

My *Chaparral* experience, and a quick understanding of computer graphics helped me to rise in the field of desktop publishing and 3D modelling in the late 80s and early 90s. I appeared in many magazines including *MacWorld, Publish, Adweek.* In Fall of 1988 I was selected to be the artist for an *Adweek* Magazine experiment, to create the first, or one of the first, Postscript ad in a major magazine. I used both Aldus Freehand and Adobe Illustrator to create the full-page trade ad for *Playboy.*

Hidden In Plain Sight

A year into my time in NYC, I was hired by Young and Rubicam and began working on the Joe Camel account, using the computer to produce hundreds of variations on layouts, ingratiating me to the boss. I started to draw my own designs and after a year I switched from being Production, the people who took orders, to Creative, the people who thought up the ideas and gave orders to the production staff. The computer upended the entire workflow of an ad agency. Art directors got the power to create on their computers, and the strict separation of production and creative departments dissolved. Half of my initial job at Y&R was to train art directors how to use the computer. We got them Macs with color screens, Photoshop, Illustrator, and Macromind Director.

My boss at Camel, advertising mastermind MZ, demanded many versions of an ad. You did not just make one layout. If you did, you'd be fired. You made many layouts and needed to be prepared to make variations of them. Prior to the computer, presentation boards were used with many overlays, flaps, and type silkscreened on transparent film, so that variations of the same idea could be shown. The department used incredible amounts of photostating as art directors would order various sizes of the same art that they could use to compose into these boards. Dedicated typographers designed headlines and taglines working in conjunction with the art directors. Expert layout and paste up artists also assisted the art director to physically compose a complex board.

The computer blew all of that away. We made thousands and thousands of Joe Camel ads on the computer. Some individual ads could have several hundred layout variations alone. By 1992 or so, I was a top designer of Camel national ads: billboards, print ads, phone booth posters and the like.

Sorry for the long set up, but my point is about public perception, conventional wisdom, urban legend, and pop folklore. I can see the Joe Camel drawing the same as anyone else. It's fairly obvious that his nose looks like a penis. This is public knowledge. Even though these ads were outlawed decades ago, people still know that Joe Camel's face was a penis.

Now layered on top of this, or behind, is the urban legend that the Camel pack had subliminal drawings on it, like a naked man, or the word "quality." It is my observation that the owners of Camel, the RJ Reynolds Corporation, didn't mind at all about these urban legends. The mysteries of the Camel pack was a common topic of conversation and made it into the marketing.

We worked crazy hours at Camel. Many nights until after midnight, 2 am, 4 am, even the not-so occasional all-nighter. One such late night, we finally saw it, the true face of Joe Camel.

Joe Camel's nose is indeed a penis, but his mouth is a vagina.

Yes, I said that.

A vagina with a cigarette sticking out of it. Once you see it it's impossible to unsee. Now, no one told us this, it was our own observation, the observation of the creative team paid to make Joe Camel ads. We laughed so hard our stomachs hurt, and still laugh about it to this day.

Occasionally, even now in the 2020s, the subject of Joe Camel comes up, and the general public pretty much still knows, and you can still hear outrage, that his nose is a penis. No one talks about, or even knows that his mouth is a vagina. Hidden in plain sight for decades. Hilarious!

Now for those who think all big advertising has subliminal messages in it, I think I have to disappoint you. There are almost no top-down, management-level plans or conspiracies to put subliminal messages into ads. I'm not saying it never happened, but it's rare. Consider the reality of the advertising business—chaotic! Most ads are produced under tight schedules. Yes, you had months to develop an ad campaign, but 48 hours before the deadline, the client wanted something else. It was hard just to keep a coherent liminal brand narrative, forget trying subliminal.

But at the illustrator and layout artist level, the late-night crew level, stuff like this does occasionally happen. We did put some jokes into Camel layouts. In one drawing I made a clock at the time 3:33, a 666 joke. Another time we had the Camel drummer trying to start a fire by rubbing his drum sticks together, drawn in such a way that the sticks made an inverted cross. Both of these had limited public runs, if at all and then I think mostly on match books, and were printed so small the jokes weren't even really viewable. The point is--yes, sometimes people work jokes, or subliminal material into ads or publications, or whatever—not as some grand conspiracy, but as the late-night joke of the hands-on workers.

Night Shift

Camel provided access to really good computers and printers, and in off hours we made our own art. I was also able to buy very good computers for my home. With the help from the guys at the Apple store, I was able to get what they said was the fastest Macintosh in the city, making both print graphics and video. A new era of psychedelic art, rave art, cyber art was dawning, and I was right in the middle of it.

Technoromantics

As stated earlier, in 1989 I started a group/party called Technoromantics, centered on computer art and artists, who were encouraged to bring their art or something for discussion to the group. It was not a "user group," which is what most computer art groups were at the time. Technical user groups did nothing to address what artists were THINKING about when they made art. How they felt emotionally, or even spiritually, making computer and other tech-based art. That is how Technoromantics was different. What were people trying to say, what did they feel? What was their artistic theory? We also explored the mystical and spiritual in regards to technology. Technoromantic meetings were some really great parties. What had started as just a gathering of a few friends had grown into an event with more than 100 attending. I guess you could have called it a "scene."

By 1993, I was feeling wanderlust. I had naively pronounced I would be in New York for five years, and now, five years had passed. And the rave scene, as well as the "cyber" scene was centered in San Francisco.

So I decided to become bi-coastal. I let go of my great space in Queens and got a share of an apartment in Greenwich Village, while I put out feelers for a place in San Francisco. I planned to live in both cities, but primarily in San Francisco. This broke some amount of momentum that the Technoromantics had in NYC, but I was very psyched to move to west.

San Francisco 1993

I always had wanted to live IN San Francisco, even though I went straight to NYC after graduation. Five years later, I was ready to try. I mean, San Francisco. Cyber city. Rave city. Cloud City. When the fog comes in over the hills and sifts in between the Victorian houses, immersed in flowers or other sub-tropical ecology, chilling on a Tuesday, or any day, afternoon.

Despite the famous quote falsely attributed to Mark Twain that the "coldest winter he ever spent was a summer in San Francisco," someone else might describe the weather as perfect. It's never THAT cold, but you always need a jacket, which is cool because it means you have pockets, perhaps many pockets you can use to carry stuff: floppy disks, flashlights, food, twine, business cards, a pipe, markers and pens.

And in the 1990s, San Francisco was cheaper than New York. Really, it was! So on my New York money I could live pretty well in San Francisco.

My friend DC had lived in San Francisco in the 1980s, and knew some people there who needed a roommate in their house in Bernal Heights. They were video/computer artists too, so it could be a good fit. I moved in with Rose-X, and our other roommate, JG, who was learning to play the didgeridoo.

In San Francisco, I got my first email account, at The WELL, the Whole Earth 'Lectronic Link. I have kept this email all these years and it has come in very handy.

I also joined the SFnet, a hip scene of people posting on bulletin boards from various coin-operated terminals in bars, clubs, and coffee shops around San Francisco. While creating my first account on SFnet, the prompt asked me: User Name? I typed in "Bigtwin," and almost hit enter, but I stopped. I hit the delete key, and instead typed in "Sheep in an Anthrax T-Shirt." That name, and various other "sheep" names, became my handle. SFnet exchanges were some of the greatest improvised comedy, sarcastic discussions I have ever participated in.

San Francisco is a very fun city. Great restaurants, beautiful scenery, and an amazing club and rave scene. Soon after I got there, I attended a Wicked Full Moon Rave at Bonny Doon, a sandy beach in a cove along the Pacific where guys would take a generator, turntables and speakers and throw an all-night party, incredible!

Such was my life and headspace in the Fall of 1993. Here we come back full circle to the day my roommates suggested inviting Richard to my Technoromantics party.

The Day I Met Richard

I met Richard in the living room of my house in Bernal Heights, when he came to the first west coast Technoromantics meeting.

The first Technoromantics in San Francisco was held in the living room of our house. About a dozen people attended, including Richard. I introduced myself to the group and talked about what had been going on in New York, then showed a video and some of my artwork, 3d-modeled images printed out, cut out, and collaged into gouache paintings. The paintings included computerized dogs—the Dukey series—as well as flowers, and UFOs on Impressionist-ish painted backgrounds. I was very cautious around the group of mostly total strangers, as it was not only an "art" party, but I might be meeting future business contacts.

After perhaps a half an hour, a woman asked if she could smoke pot. I said sure, and then every single person in the room broke out grass. It was hilarious. I was in San Francisco now, with a bohemian lifestyle even a bit beyond New York's.

As the party progressed and became less formal, I got to speak with Richard. I remember him being very personable, interesting, a great addition to a party/discussion about computers and art, technology, consciousness, etc. We got along well right off the bat. I learned he had been living in San Francisco since the sixties—artist, bohemian, film-maker and distributor, theater owner, an old hippie, a real cool guy. He was interested in computers and the internet too. He also let me know that he could take care of anything I might need to buy, as in cannabis. Things were getting off to a great start in San Francisco.

"You should come and visit me some time," said Richard, and he gave me his address and phone.

Politics and Art and Music and Computers,
But Mostly Politics.

I visited Richard many times, discussing anything and everything, politics, art, computers, music, drugs.

Richard made films, and psychedelic video mixes on his Amiga. And he had Vietnam-era stories, protest stories, hippie stories, art stories. I had often wondered what it would have been like to have been 20 in the sixties, and to some degree wish I had been born earlier. We compared the current rave scene to 60s music festivals and communes; the Video Toaster and Macintosh of the 90s compared to oil projections of the 60s. He could talk about technoromantic ideas like spirit and emotion in the context of technology, theories of consciousness and if computers would affect such, and on and on.

Richard was also into computers. He and I were both beginning to experiment with websites. And while I was the "computer guru," at least in my young, myopic mind, Richard was sometimes more advanced technologically than I. Richard was the first person to tell me about mp3s, for example. He did have a lot of old technology and electronic things around his house. I really didn't know what I was looking at.

I also remember discussing music with Richard. I was surprised that he didn't bring up the bands from of the sixties and seventies very often. Richard was interested in punk rock. He explained that he had hung around the punk scene and had even made a film about it. I had some interest in punk rock, but I had never heard of any of the bands Richard spoke of. I remember being a bit embarrassed and bemused that this "old guy" knew more about this sort of thing than I did. The only band he mentioned that I had any knowledge of at all was The Dicks.

I had seen The Dicks at a party in a frat house at Stanford, and I went to a Dead Kennedys show at the Keystone in Palo Alto. I told Richard my story about playing Holiday In Cambodia too slow to his laughter. But I was not a punk rocker, not at all. I was someone a true punk rocker would hate, a college student, from an expensive private university no less. That said, Circle Jerks, Black Flag, and the Repo Man soundtrack had joined the Dead Kennedys in my record collection. But I'd conjecture that a true punk would note I only had "sellout" bands and view me with even greater contempt.

I remember talking about Church of the SubGenius, the Furry Freak Brothers, and The Residents, who we both had a connection to. Richard knew those guys, and some of the early Residents videos were made by Macintosh 3d modelling pioneer artist JL, an acquaintance of mine and a good friend to one of my best friends. I do remember him saying he had lived in New York, but not New York City, saying that he had been in the Army.

Of all the discussions I remember with Richard, the topic I remember talking about most often with him was politics, American national politics and the underlying economics and sociology driving it. We talked about the evolution of the Republican party, from its roots with Lincoln to Roosevelt, Taft, Harding, Coolidge and Hoover, to Ike and Nixon to Reagan. Then we would break down the Democrats. These were the Clinton years. Clinton was a Dem from a rural state, but had he sold out to corporate interests? Was he a country populist or just Bush with a saxophone?

I told Richard of my parents, who, while they identified as Republican, were true swing voters, voting for Kennedy, then Goldwater, then Nixon, then McGovern, Carter then Reagan then Mondale. My father hated Reagan, saying, with examples, how he had screwed the farmers. He was suspicious of the Bushes, voting for Ross Perot in 1992. Richard would talk about how it was in South Dakota, which is quite far from Indiana geographically, but quite close culturally, grouped together by the sensibilities of farming people and rural life, and definitely with a different point of view than the coasts.

We talked about the Midwest and farming. My father had been active in the Farmers' Union in Indiana. Richard had worked for them in South Dakota. We shared a few laughs over their acronym "FU."

Richard was obviously very intelligent, very well read, and it was always an interesting conversation. And when you couple these conversations with some of the best marijuana you could find, it was a great experience. Unlike today, super-power weed wasn't common. There was a lot of varying quality, some pretty mediocre stuff. Not Richard's. The stuff Richard had was of a different level, much more powerful than the average street weed of the early 1990s.

Richard also attended some of my art shows in San Francisco. I was making mixed media paintings, gouache and computer printout gelled together. I had shows in 1993 and 94 at the Falling Dog Café, Brainwash, and Artists Television Access on Valencia, where Richard signed my book.

In the entirety of the time I knew Richard, September 1993 to January 2002, I do not remember any mention of the Zodiac, nor any subject even remotely like it. Crime stories, murders, dark tales were not my cup of tea. I definitely remember talking with him about the protests of the 60s and 70s, and the violence associated with that.

Richard almost exclusively used the term "pigs" to describe the cops, but so do a lot of people. I'm sure I have occasionally used that term, when joking or in certain crowds, but Richard always used it, like a lot of old hippies, but perhaps more than anyone I have known personally. I always got a kick out of a person with a normal and or short haircut doing or saying counterculture things out loud. The clean-cut Richard always calling cops pigs was funny.

My bi-coastal experiment of living in both San Francisco and New York ended by May 1994. It was VERY difficult to keep one's life together with two apartments in two cities if you are not rich enough to pay for a personal assistant. As a freelancer, I did my own accounting. I found myself packing financial and other documents as I traveled between NYC and SF and back again. It was also hard to keep straight where certain possessions were. I would go to the closet looking for something, and then remember that the item I was looking for was indeed in the closet, just in the other city.

Most importantly, I learned that I really did prefer living in New York City. I actually liked the changing of the seasons, the fast pace and glib honesty of New Yorkers, and New York was the place to be for national advertising and television. So, I packed up my Oldsmobile and headed back east. My "San Francisco Sojourn" ended, at least as far as living there.

Work and travel still brought me to San Francisco multiple times every year from 1994 to 2002. I still would see Richard often, returning to SF for work, or on my way to Hawaii or Japan or Burning Man. I am a lover of habit and routine, and my routine upon arriving in San Francisco became sort of a personal joke—land at SFO, get a rental car, go to the Jack In The Box on Bayshore, and then go to Richard's. A visit to Richard's was always a highlight of the trip.

He never even got angry.

I recounted all of this to Kate.

I spent a couple days incredulous about Richard being a murder suspect. It was a weird experience, thinking that this man I had known might have been a serial killer. How could someone say that? Why Richard? I thought about the many other people I had known in life.

There were many other people I would have guessed to be a murderer before Richard. I mean, Richard was always pleasant.

Of course, your mind thinks of all kinds of things. You wonder, what if it was true? Was I in danger all those times? It goes on and on. Your mind goes round and round.

Reading the websites about the Zodiac was unpleasant for me. It seemed that most of the case against Richard stemmed from a single person accusing him, and apparently the police had dismissed his story. The various websites offered a few possible suspects, and the various camps of people who believed one or another were engaged in quite a bit of vitriol against each other. It was hard to know what to believe.

I tried to put it out of my mind, but honestly, it was hard NOT to think about it.

Richard was a great guy. He was warm and engaging, intelligent, funny. We spoke on all kinds of subjects; politics, art, computers, pop culture. I couldn't even remember him getting angry.

And then I remembered...

...there was this one time Richard did get angry at me.

A creepy feeling came over me, a mixture of goosebumps, and apprehension, while the Close Encounters music played in my mind.

"You know, I DO remember Richard getting angry once. Very angry."

The Only Time Richard Got Angry At Me

We were sitting at Richard's kitchen table, like so many other times, and we were sharing a joint that Richard had rolled, some of his very good marijuana, finely pulverized in his coffee grinder, for a very evenly-burning experience. As I remember it, we had been talking for some time.

During a critique of political personalities, the subject of Ronald Reagan came up. I remarked that Reagan was perfect to be a president, superficially, because he looked the part. A Hollywood leading male, who looked good on a screen, on TV, and who could deliver the lines that were written for him impeccably.

"Well, you know that Reagan's success was directly tied to him having the best astrologers," said Richard.

Now this was the mid 90s, and Reagan and astrology was a well-known story for many years, from the *National Enquirer* to *Time Magazine* to TV. It was a joke, akin to Bigfoot. I have no doubt that I made a face showing how ridiculous I thought the idea was.

"Oh, come on, that's just tabloid B.S. Reagan was such a success because he was an actor and played his role, very well. He could read the words written for him and deliver a speech like no other."

Richard became agitated. "He did everything by astrology, as governor and as president. He was sworn in as governor at 2am…" I had heard that already, and said something to the tune of people were superstitious, and that it had been confirmed he used, or his wife used, astrology, but I didn't buy that using astrology accounted for his success.

I am not going to tell you I remember every detail of this moment, but Richard was truly angry, and he stood up from the table. "It was astrology" he demanded. He was looking right at me. His lip quivered.

The thing is, it wasn't that important to me. Reagan hadn't been president for years, so who cared? Who cared, even if he was the current president? Who cared at all? It seemed to me to be a weird thing to be hung up on.

Now I don't poo-poo astrology, nor tarot, nor non-organized religion for that matter. But I also don't demand that they work, either. I would never use them as the basis of my political opinions.

Personally, I am science-oriented about things like medicine, farming, and public policy. But I'm not a scientist nor socially tied to a set viewpoint--I don't care about losing face with atheists or other scientists or reductionists for entertaining the idea that some so-called "pseudo-sciences" have some amount of merit. I've seen too many weird things to discount the spiritual side of things, whatever that means. We do seem to be "connected" in ways that science has not yet discovered.

But I would never get angry because someone had a disagreement about such a speculative and unprovable topic as astrology. To demand that Reagan's political success was because of astrology, to me, was nuts. To get angry at someone for not agreeing to that seems weird.

Strangely weird. It was an awkward moment, but it was clear Richard was really upset about this, and he demanded that I agree with him.

So I said some placating statement, agreeing that ASTROLOGY was why Reagan succeeded.

This conversation did not end our friendship. I just passed it off as an old hippie being very particular about their hippie ways and opinions. Sorry to generalize, but I found hippies were often very particular about things others might find trivial. You might be able to eschew the wearing of clothes, you could paint your car with flowers, you could stop using clocks or commercial toothpaste and that would all be accepted. But you also might do something like wearing your seat belt in a car or pass the pipe the wrong direction ("it MUST be in the direction of the sun…") and someone might get very upset. It has been my experience that it is hard to predict what is taboo to those in the counterculture, hippie, raver, or otherwise, but hippies had more such things than other groups. Richard getting angry about Reagan's use of astrology was just one of those quirky hippie things.

But anyway, I totally forgot about it for 20 years. I only remembered it after reflecting on my memories of Richard for a few days. It remains the only moment I saw Richard angry.

Other than this conversation about Reagan, I do not remember talking to Richard at all about astrology. I also do not remember any conversation about making ciphers, or serial killers, or any other subject that might be related to Zodiac.

Reflecting on the memory, it still seems like such a strange thing to get upset about, and more so for a guy who didn't normally get mad. Of course, this is not evidence, but nevertheless it happened. I was faced with the nagging idea that Richard Gaikowski COULD be the Zodiac.

The Day Richard Gave Me a Tarot Reading on His Computer

In April 1999, I attended the Hammer & Coffin banquet. It was a bigger event than normal as it was the centennial year of the *Chaparral*, which was founded in 1899. I flew to San Francisco, got a rental car, went to Jack In The Box on Bayshore, and then went over to Richard's.

"I want to give you a tarot card reading with my new software I've coded," said Richard.

"Wow! Sure." I said. "Coding your own tarot program? That's cool."

Richard and I were already linking to each other from our webpages, and I knew about his filmmaking. I hadn't realized Richard was actively coding. And when I saw the software, I was surprised and impressed that he was such an experienced coder. He was a pretty advanced programmer. Richard wrote the tarot card program on his Amiga.

He asked me if I would like a reading, and frankly, I was very excited to say yes. I previously had very profound moments with tarot card readings. I eagerly agreed was intrigued how it would be done by computer.

Richard began the reading.

"What is a big question you have, a big life question?" asked Richard. "Or something important to you that you've been wondering about. Don't tell me what it is, just think of something, some question, and fix it in your mind."

It was a ridiculously simple question for me at that time, because for years I had stewed over the idea of returning to Indiana to help my parents, who were still farming into their (very) old age. I knew that would happen one day, and as the years passed, that day was certainly getting closer. It weighed heavily on my mind.

"Okey dokey, I got one," I said.

Richard pressed a key.

Boom. First card. The Fool.

I was blown away. The *Chaparral* mythology and more was not lost on me. I had identified with The Fool card for many years at that point as it was akin to the "Jester" of the *Chaparral*.

Richard baritone voice began from the computer. "The Fool, The Wanderer, folly, mania, extravagance, intoxication, delirium…"

It was really nice software. With each card drawn on the computer it would speak the meaning, a recording of Richard's baritone radio voice, very dramatic. Richard had a very distinctive voice. Then the card animated into its place on the screen and the next card was drawn. The cards were placed in a pattern I recognized, an arrangement of six cards in a cross pattern and then a column of four cards to the right of the cross.

I don't remember every card drawn, but I do remember laughing so hard my stomach hurt. I remember the first card, The Fool, and I remember the last card, Death, with Satan and the Wheel of Fortune somewhere in between. It was an entertaining reading that basically said my foolish endeavor would be one of learning, fulfillment, and ultimately death, which sort of happened in the coming years.

I really liked the reading. Actually, I was blown away by it and told Richard so. But then he said something that really surprised me, that the reading was no good, that it was useless.

"I haven't yet programmed in that cards can be upside down, which is very important. It completely changes the meanings of the cards." said Richard. "I'm glad you enjoyed it, but as an actual reading it was useless."

So in his opinion, the reading was useless because the programming for an upside down card was not yet in place. I remember thinking he was quite particular about all of this. I had gotten previous tarot readings from people who said that whether a card was upside down or not was not important, but it sure was to Richard. It was yet another instance of Richard being very precise and serious about an occult subject.

Now a tarot reading is not an astrology reading, but it is indeed related. I looked through the information presented online about Richard and did not find that he did tarot readings, nor that he was a computer programmer. For what it's worth, programmers refer to themselves as "coders."

My Second Tarot Reading with Richard

Richard gave me another tarot reading sometime during one of my last visits to his home, with Kate accompanying me. I had described the first reading to her, and I asked Richard to give me another one. Richard did as before, asking me for a question to keep in my mind, but to not tell him. In my mind I asked about the dolphin communication research we were helping with. Also, during the reading, Richard required that Kate leave the room. She went to Richard's kitchen.

This reading was not so memorable. It didn't really click with me, and it seemed there was no clear message. It was also strange that Kate was asked to leave the room. All in all, it was clear that Richard was very particular about his occult practices.

Another Day at Richards

Another day I flew to San Francisco. I landed, got a rental car, drove to the Jack in the Box on Bayshore, and then visited Richard. I had not called ahead like I often did.

When I got there, Richard was there with two other people. A guy named B, and another heavy-set Latino or Hispanic man.

"I'll get your stuff," said Richard, "But I can't visit today." Richard wrapped up an eighth in a sandwich bag.

Richard explained that B had brought the other man there to spend the night with him. That man would be entering prison soon, and he needed to know what went on inside of a prison before going in. I assumed at the time that Richard was referring to homosexual sex and similar things one might encounter in prison because it was mentioned that the Latino man "had never been with another man."

I have to admit, it was not the average situation I had encountered, but on the other hand, in a bohemian culture one hears all kinds of things. And while prepping for prison was not a concept I had ever considered, it did seem like an immensely practical thing.

I thanked Richard for the purchase and was on my way.

2002 - Back to Indiana

As I have described, the 1990s and into the 2000s were an era of cyber-psychedelic counterculture globetrotting; California, Japan, Hawaii, and six consecutive Burning Mans, from 1995-2000. I came to San Francisco often for business, conferences, and worked for various periods in the Bay Area.

On September 11, 2001, everyone's life changed. And while we were fortunate not to lose anyone on that day, it spelled the end of my work situation in downtown New York City, vastly lowering my income. After September 11, there were no new clients for the video studio I worked with.

On September 30, 2001, John Lilly died, further removing the reason for our trips to the Pacific.

By early 2002, things were getting financially strained for me, to say the least. I was becoming unable to afford my rent. Luckily, Kate and I had found each other, and were planning a life together.

In the summer of 2002, I vacated my apartment and moved in with her. The year had already seen my father turn 80 years old, while still running the farm full steam. The economy of lower Manhattan, certainly regarding advertising, TV and computer graphics, had not recovered from 9/11. Prospects were slim.

I did find a little work with Voice of America in Washington DC. Even so, it was barely enough to live on, and I had to commute there from New York. That didn't make much sense. I had always thought I would one day return to Indiana to help my parents with the farm. If not now, when?

So, in November 2002, we packed up a Penske truck and moved to the farm in southern Indiana. My life as a globe-travelling cyber-artist was suspended, my identity as Bigtwin was put on ice, and I re-assumed my original identity as Jim Suhre, a Midwesterner.

Life changed very much. I cut my hair and shaved. We looked for "straight" work while helping my parents farm. Freelance advertising out of a farmhouse wasn't really feasible in that time and place, so I eventually took a job in the local bank. Kate and I re-founded the town's canoe race festival and got involved in local politics. In 2006, we witnessed Mike Pence tell a group of 3rd graders that "…they might be looking at a future Vice President…." One wonders, who

THE ONLY TIME RICHARD GOT ANGRY AT ME

tells a group of children they might be looking at a future VICE president? That's strange. But I digress...

I didn't promote, or even bring up, my previous life to the people in Indiana, other than the points that I worked on Madison Avenue and in TV. We lost contact with a lot of people. I continued to exchange occasional emails with Richard into 2003, but then the correspondence ended.

So, you can tell from what I am describing, I was friends with Richard, but not so much that I knew when he died. And because of our situation, we lost contact with a lot of people. Richard Gaikowski was one of dozens of people I would have had no contact with for many years, starting in 2002. I didn't think to contact him, I didn't try. I still considered him a friend, but the counterculture aspect of my life was over and there little reason to even attempt to blend them together.

Visit to San Francisco 2006

In April 2006, Kate and I travelled to San Francisco, so I could attend Hammer & Coffin's 100th reunion and banquet festivities at Stanford. It had been over four years since going to the Bay Area, a lifetime compared to the previous years. As normal, after landing at SFO, we got a rental car and we went to the Jack in the Box on Bayshore. I tried Richard's number from there and got the three-tone, "this number has been disconnected" message.

"I'm worried," I said to Kate. "Richard's number is out of order, with the "no further information" line. I hope he's ok."

When we got to his place on Guerrero, it was obvious he didn't live there anymore--the windows were all different, it didn't look like anyone was living there, and when combined with the phone out of order, it was clear he wasn't there. We proceeded on to Haight Street, where we had a room at the Red Vic.

I searched for Richard online and found his obituary. He had died two years earlier in 2004. He had a long and glowing obituary and obviously had a positive effect on many people. That was the last I thought of Richard for ten years.

Yes, at long last, this story is back to 2016, when I discovered the accusations against him, while surfing the internet from an Indiana farmhouse.

So What Would You Do?

So what would you do? What actions would a reasonable person take in lieu of this situation? As I said before, I was not interested in crime stories. Becoming a true-crime internet sleuth was not an activity I would have ever predicted for myself.

But here was a real-life story, this actually happened to me. And as I reflected more on my San Francisco memories, and my very unique friend Richard, who knew? Maybe I did know something relevant to the investigation. Honestly, at first it just seemed ridiculous. As remote as I thought that possibility, days passed, and I was still wondering about it. It seemed I HAD to investigate it, at least a little, just so I could stop thinking about it.

I mean really, why would someone who seemed so together and who wasn't known to get angry, indeed, get so angry about something as trivial as laughing at the idea of Reagan and astrology? That topic really triggered him. The only thing I ever remember triggering him. Truly, "The Only Time Richard Got Angry at Me."

It all gave me pause.

So, against my initial predilection, and with full hesitancy of thinking this all might be a kooky black hole of time and effort, I came to the conclusion to go for it.

I decided to find out all I could about Zodiac, and Richard, to see if there were any pieces of the puzzle I might be able identify. Was there a Reagan connection? A tarot card connection? A computer coding connection? Was there anything in the Zodiac crimes that might be something I remember Richard talking about? Anything to substantiate a memory of an interaction from twenty-plus years ago, when we were undoubtedly really stoned?

I considered the concept of the serial killer in earnest for the first time, and the particular oddity of The Zodiac. What type of person could commit such horrific crimes while providing much more evidence with their letters, codes and taunts? Each action a potential to screw up, yet still they avoided capture. What sort of person would write those codes? What would the day-to-day actions of someone hiding such a secret be?

I Needed to Organize This Stuff Anyway...

I started to go through my extensive possessions, justifying spending time on this project under the premise that I would be going through piles of stuff organizing and throwing away unneeded junk. I am somewhat of a pack rat, but moreover kept anything to do with my art or career. Any magazine with my art, or an ad I designed, many fliers, party invites, art invites. I have hundreds of old computer disks: floppy, SCSI, Zip, CDs, DVDs. By 2016 this situation was borderline out of hand. This could be a good opportunity to go through a lot of old stuff, and maybe throw out (eyeroll) stuff that was out of date.

Was it possible that I had something from Richard? Did he mail me an invite, in which there may be DNA? Did he lick stamps on a postcard I might have? Did he ever give me a button?

And so I began in earnest. Sometime around 2016, I started my research into Zodiac. I wrote down everything I could remember about Richard, and reviewed as much Zodiac material as I could find. I started a spreadsheet about Richard and my San Francisco memories.

For what it's worth, I did not read the Graysmith Zodiac books, as I was an unknowing pioneer of the phrase and behavior, TLDR. But we did watch the 2007 Zodiac movie...

THE ONLY TIME RICHARD GOT ANGRY AT ME

ACT II === THE FACTS AND THE ACCUSATIONS ======

And so I studied the Zodiac, and I also researched the man I had known who was being accused.

Here I provide just the basic facts, the most agreed upon points to this matter, and present them, much as I understood them from 2016 to 2018.

Richard Gaikowski Bio

The first thing I searched for was an obituary for Richard. As I said, we had found and read Richard's obituary in 2006. The *San Francisco Chronicle* ran a glowing and loving article about his life, describing him as a bohemian and a "bon vivant."[26]

A search of newspaper archives yielded many stories by Richard, and about Richard, from his high school days through his work in South Dakota, New York, and California from the 1950s to the 1980s.

Richard was born in Watertown, South Dakota on March 14, 1936. As a high school student, he was a state finalist in an American Legion oratory contest. One of 13 competitors, his presentation was titled,

"The Constitution—Temple of Liberty."[27]

Upon graduation from high school, he served in the Army as a medic from 1955 to 1957. After the Army he then went to Northern State College, earning an economics degree and was the editor of the student newspaper his senior year.[28]

In 1960 Richard is the Regional Director of the Young Democrats[29], and on the campaign staff for South Dakota Governor Ralph Herseth.[30] By December 1960, he is employed as the State-News Editor at the *Aberdeen American-News*[31].

The February 1, 1962, *Huron Daily Plainsman* reports that Richard has taken the job of Public Relations Director of the South Dakota Farmers Union with the unintentionally comic headline, "Webster Native Joins State F.U. Staff Here."[32] The job description includes editing a bi-weekly Farmers Union newspaper, as well as production of educational materials for television and radio.

In 1963, the *Daily Plainsman* reported that CBS Television contacted Richard in his position at Farmers Union to arrange their filming of the Wheat Appreciation Rally in Aberdeen.[33]

On July 31, 1963, the *Rapid City Journal* reported that Richard has resigned from the South Dakota Farmers Union.[34] The article continued that Richard intended to attend graduate school at the University of California.

I was unable to confirm if Richard did attend the University of California, but later in 1963 he was employed by the *Daily Commercial News* in San Francisco.

The December 8, 1964, *Martinez News-Gazette* reported that Richard had been named managing editor of the *Morning News-Gazette*[35] The article mentioned his degree from Northern State College but did not mention the University of California.

From various press reports, it appears that Richard assumed a management role as well as one of community outreach for the Martinez paper. For example, there are help wanted ads in the *San Francisco Examiner* looking for a sportswriter for the *Martinez Morning News Gazette* with Richard listed as a contact[36]. In May 1965, Richard was a guest speaker at a dinner recognizing student journalists at Martinez's Alhambra High School.[37] That October he returned to that school for a journalism workshop that included students from other high schools

THE ONLY TIME RICHARD GOT ANGRY AT ME

including Richmond, Albany, Brentwood, and Vallejo.[38]

In October 1965, Richard got himself purposely arrested and jailed, under what he describes as a "secret plan" with his employers to write an article about the conditions inside a jail.[39] Initially having difficulty getting arrested, Richard drove around committing traffic violations in plain sight of police, but found they only gave him warnings. He ultimately drank alcohol in his car in front of a law enforcement officer, but then only succeeded in getting arrested when he refused to sign his citation. He then spent 38 hours in the Contra Costa County Jail. His experiences were chronicled in a 4-part series of articles running in the Martinez and Vallejo newspapers.

On December 31, 1965, the *News Gazette* reported that he resigned from that paper to take a position with the Albany, New York *Knickerbocker News[40]*.

Richard works in at the *Knickerbocker News* approximately two years and then returned to the Bay Area sometime around the fall of 1968 or spring of 1969.

Also in fall 1968 or winter 1969, Richard apparently traveled to Europe. He authored an article about The Troubles in Northern Ireland reporting from Belfast, printed in the *Knickerbocker News*. The date of that article is January 31, 1969.

In 2004, just months before his death, Richard wrote an essay called "My Albany Sojourn," which chronicled this era of his life. In it, he said he left New York for Europe in the fall 1968. This self-authored article is a keystone to those who have discounted him as a suspect.

Regardless of the timeline of his trip to Europe, we know Richard relocates back to the Bay Area in 1969 and was living at the *Good Times* Commune in San Francisco by the spring or summer.

Richard at Good Times

In April of 1969, the *San Francisco Express Times* becomes *San Francisco Good Times*, a tabloid underground press newspaper produced by the residents, members, family, comrades, (I'm honestly not sure how they regarded themselves) of the Good Times Commune. It was is a weekly paper from April 1969 to May 1971, when it went bi-weekly, which it continued as until its demise in July 1972.

I have seen speculation that Richard started working at *Good Times* as early as April 1969, but his first byline isn't until July 17, 1969, under the name Dick Gaikowski[41]. After that, he always appeared as "D. Gaik" or "d. gaik" or "Dick Gaik." He used one of these bylines in 48 out of 135 total *Good Times* issues. It is also stated online that Richard was the editor of *Good Times*, but I have never found an instance in a *Good Times* issue of him being referred to as editor. There is never an issue where anyone is referred to as editor, nor are their staff boxes or other types of credits. Whether he was "the editor" or "an editor" or "sometimes an editor" is inconclusive based on the actual printed *Good Times* issues.

Speaking of Richard's bylines in *Good Times*, they are very inconsistent in terms of their frequency. Any way you describe it, they appear haphazardly. After his first article, Richard wrote again in the next issue about a group in Berkeley doing Astrology[42]. But then he does not have a byline for the next six issues. Then he appeared in three consecutive issues, September 11, 18, and 25, 1969, then not in the next four 4 consecutive issues, before appearing in the October 30, 1969. After that, he is not in 10 consecutive *Good Times* issues, not appearing until January 22, 1970. At least his byline does not appear. There are many obvious fake names in *Good Times*, so it is entirely possible he is one of them and still worked there.

The very sporadic nature of Richard's bylines in *Good Times* continued through 1972.

Including that January 22 issue, he wrote in 16 out of 18 issues up to June 29, 1970. He then did NOT appear in 10 straight issues. Then, starting with the August 21 issue, he appeared in the next seven out of nine issues, but then in only four of the last nine issues of 1970. After the December 18, 1970, issue, he missed 16 consecutive issues, with no byline until April 30, 1971. The whereabouts of Richard in the early parts of 1971 is the source of much speculation.

On May 14, 1971, *Good Times* announced they would go bi-weekly[43], with their next issue on May 28. Richard has a byline in that issue, then misses the next two (a period that is now four weeks). He is also in the July 9 issue.

Starting with the August 6, 1971, *Good Times*, Richard had a byline in 12 out of the next 13 issues. In the one issue he missed, there is a byline for a "Guy Du Lac."[44] This is the only byline anywhere for such a person in any search engine for any publication in the time period. It is quite likely this is a fake name and also quite possible it is Richard. The end of this string is Richard's last byline, January 28, 1972. He does not appear in the final 13 issues. *Good Times* comes to an end, printing its last issue on July 21, 1972.

The very real possibility exists that Richard did write under fake names, in which case he would be a part of many more *Good Times* issues than the 48 he appears under "D. Gaik" and its variations. In that scenario, we might find his sporadic activity was less whether he wrote for a *Good Times* issue, and more what name he wanted to appear as.

Richard the Filmmaker

Richard started making films while he was still at *Good Times,* with his directorial debut, This Is My Black Movie, a 6-minute film short made in 1970. The film is described as dream-like scenes of a woman seducing a man intercut with images of spiders, faces and skulls.

In 1972, Richard's name appears in the San Francisco telephone directory. By 1973 Richard is operating The Storefront Cinema at 14th and Guerrero Streets[45]. The 1980 *SF Free and Easy* guide described it as a "clandestine scene" that ran 18 months before the cops shut it down.

In 1973 Richard made Drummer, a film that interspersed sequences of an artist making a clay drummer with footage of drummers on the streets of San Francisco and in Golden Gate Park.[46]

In 1976, he and two partners purchased the Roxie Theater in the Mission.[47] The venue had been a porno theater, and was in very bad repair, allowing for a reasonable purchase price and new management. Richard and his partners rehabbed the building and revitalized the scene, turning it into an independent repertory theater where pretty much anything could and would be shown. The *San Francisco Examiner* reported that Richard's favorite filmmakers were Bunuel, early Fellini or Pasolini, and that he hoped to show lesser-known films from Poland.[48] In its heyday, The Roxie was regarded to be one of the premier independent movie theaters in the country.

At some point in the 1970s, Richard began his film distribution business, One Way Films, with a catalog of counterculture and underground films and videos.[49] The catalog included many films documenting the punk and new wave music scenes.

In 1978, Richard made "Festival of Bards" documenting a poetry festival at the Greek Theater in Berkeley. The film includes many poets including Alan Ginsberg and Robert Bly.[50]

In 1979 Richard made the film DEAF/PUNK, a six-minute short documenting a night at the San Francisco Deaf Club and a performance of the punk band The Offs.[51]

In 1980 Richard made another 6-minute short "Moody Teenager,"[52] a film whose style has been compared to that of Kenneth Anger.

In 1983 Richard wrote a review for the movie "Taking Tiger Mountain" in the *San Francisco Sunday Examiner and Chronicle*.[53] The post-apocalyptic film starred Bill Paxton in one of his earliest roles. The review noted that the film would be premiering at the UC Theater in Berkeley before playing at the Roxie. While Richard wrote several movie reviews in *Good Times*, this is the only movie review by him that I found in other newspapers.

Richard and Computers

In the mid-1980s, Richard started one of the very first computer bulletin boards, NewsBase, an information clearing house and early digital community for progressive news.[54]

For the nine years I knew Richard, 1993 to 2002, he lived in a storefront apartment on Guerrero, and presumably supported himself via his film distribution service and other retail sales. That said, I only can conjecture about Richards financial livelihood. I do remember him remarking that Amiga computers were much cheaper than Macintosh, and gave you just as many features, if not more. The Mac had nothing like Amiga's Video Toaster, the workhorse hardware board and software for countless video artists, video mixers, and those who wanted to make psychedelic rave video from the early 1990s to the 2010s. It was also a very good tool to make "straight" videos as well, with a good character generator and video switcher.

I also owned a Video Toaster, but otherwise I was all-Macintosh in those days, so that likely inhibited our computer discussions.

I remember Richard showing me a film (technically a video) he made about the Cannabis Club of San Francisco. It includes interviews with founder and San Francisco counterculture legend Dennis Peron and others. I found the video on YouTube and watched it again here in the 2020s. Occasionally there is a voice coming from off camera, but it does NOT at all sound like Richard to me. As I have stated, Richard's voice was baritone. The voice on this video is much higher. I am not aware of the exact date of this video, although it must have been in the 1990s.

Richard died on April 30, 2004, from lung cancer. From his obits and comments by others, he obviously had a great effect on many people, very much to the positive. I have to agree—he had a positive effect on me.

Such is the public record of Richard's life that I know, as confirmed by newspapers and other contemporaneous publications.

The Zodiac Crimes ----------

Lake Herman Road

The first official Zodiac murders were on December 20, 1968, at a lover's lane pull-off on Lake Herman Road in Solano County, California. A gunman attacked two teenagers, David Faraday and Bettilou Jensen, sometime after 11 pm on a Saturday night. Faraday and Jensen were on a date, presumably attending a function at Vallejo High School, where they were both students.

Each victim made it out of the car, but was unable to escape, Faraday dying from a bullet to the head, and Jensen dying from five bullet shots in her back. Police did not name a suspect.

I say these are the first official murders, because there is significant speculation that there is at least one, if not more, murders by the individual who was Zodiac that occurred in southern California earlier in the 60s. Specifically, the murder of Cheri Jo Bates by stabbing on October 30, 1966 in Riverside is conjectured to be Zodiac. After the murder, letters were sent to the police and to the local newspaper, and a note was written on the underside of a desk months later, all similar to Zodiac.

Assigning this murder to the Zodiac remains speculative, and even though later Zodiac letters reference his "Riverside activity," that may be a boast or leaving "fake clews," as it is spelled in one of his letters. So, while there is much speculation, officially the Lake Herman Road killings are the first Zodiac crimes.

Blue Rock Springs

Slightly over six months later, just after midnight on July 5, 1969, another couple was attacked on at another lover's lane at Blue Rock Springs Park parking lot, just 3.5 miles from the Lake Herman attack. Darlene Ferrin, aged 22, was murdered from multiple bullet wounds. Her date, 19-year-old Mike Mageau was shot several times. He miraculously survived the attack.

From Mageau's account, while they were parked in the lot, a car drove up behind them. Darlene seemed concerned it was someone who had been stalking her and was relieved when the car drove off. A few minutes later the car returned and parked behind them, leaving the headlights on. The driver of the car got out and approached Ferrin and Mageau's car, and immediately began to shoot. It is believed the shooter fired five rounds, some hitting both individuals, and then fired two more, before speeding off.

Approximately 40 minutes later, a call was placed to the Vallejo Police Department. The call was taken by police dispatcher Nancy Slover. As recorded in Slover's police report, the caller said,

"I want to report a double murder. If you will go one mile east on Columbus Parkway to the public park, you will find the kids in a brown car. They were shot with a 9 mm Luger. I also killed those kids last year.... Good-bye."[55]

The 408-code

Up until this point, the two attacks were a story in Vallejo and Sonoma County. But this case was about to become a big story, not just in the Bay Area, but the entire United States.

On July 31, 1969, three letters were mailed, one each to the *Vallejo Times-Herald*, the *San Francisco Examiner*, and the *San Francisco Chronicle*, each containing facts about the Lake Herman and Blue Rock Springs murders that only the perpetrator could know, and each containing one part of a code. This code has come to be known as the "408-code" because that is how many characters are in it. The author of the letters demanded that the codes be printed on the front pages of each of the three papers the coming Friday, or he would, in his own words, "go on a kill rampage."

The killer detailed the brand of the ammo used, the number of shots, the positions of the bodies and some of the clothing for both the Lake Herman and Blue Rock Springs murders, which confirmed the author of the letter was the killer.

Each letter is signed not with a name, but a symbol, a circle with a cross through it; like a gun sight, or a printer's registration mark, or the astrological symbol for earth, or something else. Over time, the circle with the cross hairs became the logo, so to speak, of the killer.

The three letters are hand-written, and are identical, word-for-word, with one exception, the letter to the *San Francisco Chronicle* has the added sentence "In this cipher is my identity."

All three papers did reprint the code in their papers, but not on the schedule desired by the killer. The *Solano-Napa News Chronicle*, sister publication of the *Vallejo News Herald*, did run it on the front page of the August 1st issue[56], but the *San Francisco Examiner* only printed an article about the codes but not the code itself[57], and the *San Francisco Chronicle* ran their portion of the code on page four of their Saturday, August 2 edition[58]. The *Examiner* then printed all three codes together in their Sunday, August 3, 1969, edition[59].

Murders in San Jose

Also on August 3, two teenage girls were brutally murdered by knife in the hills near an upscale San Jose neighborhood.[60] Debrah Furlong, age 14, and Kathie Snoozy, age 15, were killed by multiple stab wounds, each perhaps hundreds of times. There was a lot of overlap of these crime stories in the press. For example, the *Vallejo News-Chronicle* article about these murders shares the same page with Zodiac's 408 code.[61] Whether Zodiac specifically claimed these murders, or he implied it, or it was conjectured by others, is unclear to me, but in 1971, Karl Francis Werner confessed to these crimes as well as another covered later this section.

August 4, 1969, Enter The Zodiac

In the articles accompanying the codes, investigators issued public calls for the murderer to provide more details about the crimes, to confirm it was him. On August 4, the killer obliged. And for the first time he used the name he is known as to this day, The Zodiac[62].

In a presumably hand-delivered letter to the *San Francisco Examiner*, the letter begins:

Dear Editor, This is the Zodiac speaking. In answer to your asking for more details about the Good Times I have had in Vallejo, I shall be very happy to supply even more material. By the way, are the police having a good time with the code? If not, tell them to cheer up; when they do crack it, they will have me…

The letter goes on quite a bit longer and "The Zodiac" indeed provides more details about his crimes.

408-code Solved - Mostly

On August 8, 1969, the 408-code was solved, except for the final 18 characters of the *Chronicle*'s portion of the code, by Don and Bettye Harden of Salinas, California[63]. The hobbyist puzzle solvers used a simple letter-substitution method to solve the code, although it wasn't quite so simple. There were multiple symbols used for many characters.

The solution reads, divided in its three parts:

I LIKE KILLING PEOPLE BECAUSE IT IS SO MUCH FUN IT IS MORE FUN THAN KILLING WILD GAME IN THE FORREST BECAUSE MAN IS THE MOST DANGEROUS ANAMAL OF ALL TO KILL SOMETHING GI

VES ME THE MOST THRILLING EXPERENCE IT IS EVEN BETTER THAN GETTING YOUR ROCKS OFF WITH A GIRL THE BEST PART OF IT IS THAE WHEN I DIE I WILL BE REBORN IN PARADICE AND ALL TH

E I HAVE KILLED WILL BECOME MY SLAVES I WILL NOT GIVE YOU MY NAME BECAUSE YOU WILL TRY TO SLOI DOWN OR ATOP MY COLLECTIOG OF SLAVES FOR MY AFTERLIFE. EBEORIETEMETHHPITI

Without any obvious name in the cipher, it is theorized that either the killer lied, and his identity is not in the *Chronicle*'s code, or the identity is in the final 18 unsolved characters at the end. That is what the Harden's assumed, writing "signature" over the remaining characters. The Harden's solution, confirmed by investigators, ran in many newspapers on August 9.

It is certainly an assumption that the 18 unsolved characters are where the Zodiac's identity lies, but it is not without merit. These characters of the *Chronicle*'s code, the part of the code the killer says contains his identity, remain a mystery to this day, and are the basis for much speculation and debate about the case.

The Concerned Citizen Letter

On August 10, 1969, an anonymous letter with the correct solution to the 408-code was mailed to the Vallejo Police Department Sergeant John Lynch. On a typewritten 3 x 5-inch notecard, the letter reads:

Dear Sergeant Lynch, I hope the enclosed "key" will prove to be beneficial to you in connection with the cipher letter writer. Working puzzles criptograms and word puzzles is one of my pleasures. Please forgive the absence of my signature or name as I do not wish to have my name in the papers and it could be mentioned by a slip of the tongue. With best wishes.

The key was written on a separate white sheet of paper and was indeed a correct solution of the cipher. It would appear there are three possibilities for this letter: 1. The letter writer is a separate individual who solved the code independently; 2. someone who read about the code being solved in the paper two days earlier and who then sent this as a hoax; or 3. the letter was written by perpetrator.

Lake Berryessa

At approximately 6:30 pm on Saturday, September 27, 1969, a couple was attacked on the shores of Lake Berryessa, approximately 40 miles north of Vallejo in Napa County. Cecelia Ann Shepard and Bryan Calvin Hartnell, both students at Pacific Union College in Angwin, were on Twin Oak Ridge, a piece of land that extends into the water on the west side of the lake[64].

A man approached them wearing a black hood. The circle and cross symbol the Zodiac signed his letters with was painted or sewn on the hood in white. Originally demanding Hartnell's wallet and keys, it seemed like a robbery. The perpetrator mentioned he was an escaped convict from Montana. Then the hooded man produced white clothesline out of his jacket and demanded at gunpoint that Shepard tie up Hartnell, which she did. Hartnell asked if the gun was loaded, and the man showed him a fully loaded clip. Then the man tied up Shepard.

The hooded man proceeded to knife Shepard and Hartnell in the back with an estimated nine to twelve-inch knife, which was one inch wide and possibly sharpened on both sides.

Ultimately Shepard was knifed ten times, and Hartnell six times. Both feigned death and the perpetrator left the scene. Hartnell was able to get up and stagger to the road above and flag down help. Both victims were able to describe the assailant and the black hood. Footprints of the assailant were found, military-issue Wing Walker boots.

Sometime around 7:45 a call was placed from a pay phone in Napa to the Vallejo Police Department, claiming the murder.

Later that evening, writing was discovered on the side of Hartnell's car. It started with the familiar circle and cross hairs logo, and then:

"12-20-68   7-4-69   Sept 27-69 – 6:30 By Knife"

Two days later, Celia Shepard succumbed to her wounds and died in the hospital. Bryan Hartnell survived[65].

To my observation, this incident is the strangest of all, with many unanswered questions. Why the hood? Did he want to get caught? Not want to get caught? Was he fooled the two were dead, or did he purposely leave the two alive? Why put the symbol on the hood?

The following day, September 28, 1969, the *San Francisco Examiner-Chronicle* Sunday Edition and other newspapers around the country ran a Dick Tracy comic strip where "The Zodiac Gang" wore black hoods with white astrological symbols on them[66].

Paul Stine Murder

On Saturday, October 11, 1969, someone hailed a cab somewhere in downtown San Francisco and gave the cabbie the address of Washington and Maple as the destination. The cabbie recorded the intersection in the cab's logbook. One block farther west, at Washington and Cherry, the cab's driver was shot in the head at point blank range with a 9mm pistol at approximately 9:55 pm[67].

At some point, three teenagers who lived at the intersection witnessed the stopped cab with two men in the front seat, one slumped over the other, apparently dead. They had not heard a gunshot. The other man appeared to be emptying the pockets of the dead man. The kids watched for several minutes as the perpetrator wiped down the dashboard of the car, and then the outside doors, both passenger side and then driver's side.

The perpetrator fled on Cherry Street heading towards the Presidio a block to the north. Initially, police mistakenly searched for a black man. Seven dog teams were brought in, but there was no arrest.

From the accounts of the teenagers, the Zodiac police sketch was created.

Paul Stine Letter

On Monday, October 13, a letter was received by the *San Francisco Chronicle* that contained a piece of Paul Stine's bloody shirt, with text that read:

> *This is the Zodiac speaking. I am the murderer of the taxi driver over by Washington St & Maple St last night, to prove this here is a blood*

stained piece of his shirt. I am the same man who did in the people in the north bay area. The S.F. Police could have caught me last night if they had searched the park properly instead of holding road races with their motorcicles seeing who could make the most noise. The car drivers should have just parked their cars and sat there quietly waiting for me to come out of cover. School children make nice targets, I think I shall wipe out a school bus some morning. Just shoot out the front tire & then pick off the kiddies as they come bouncing out.

On Wednesday, October 15, news of the letter, and that the Zodiac was in the city, threatening to kill school children, gripped the public in fear. "Zodiac Mania" was officially on.

San Francisco Examiner's Message to the Zodiac

If there were any doubts about Zodiac Mania, the top is blown off that Sunday, October 19, 1969, when the *San Francisco Examiner* takes the extreme action of running a front-page editorial above the masthead titled, "Message to the Zodiac Killer." The editorial asks the Zodiac to give himself up, says they offer him no sympathy, but they offer to get him medical help, to guarantee his full legal rights, and to tell his story, and included their phone number for him to call[68].

Can you imagine, an editorial at the top of the front page, above the masthead of the paper itself? The unprecedented action was seen by almost everyone in the Bay Area.

October 22, Oakland to Dunbar to Daly City

Around 2 am, someone claiming to be Zodiac called the Oakland police twice and asked to speak to Melvin Belli or F. Lee Bailey later that day on the Jim Dunbar TV Show. The police confirmed that this call was is the Zodiac, as they relayed information only the killer would know[69].

Melvin Belli agreed to appear on the live TV show, and around 7 am someone who called themselves 'Sam" did indeed call the show and speak to Belli. They arranged a meeting for 10:30 am that day in Daly City. Sam never showed, but there was a bit of a circus at the Daly City location, as police and news teams flocked to the spot later that morning. ABC News did a particularly great report from the scene.

THE ONLY TIME RICHARD GOT ANGRY AT ME

The audio from the TV show was played to three people who had heard the Zodiac speak, the Oakland patrolman who took the calls earlier that day, Vallejo Police Dispatcher Nancy Slover, and Brian Hartnell, and they all thought it was not the voice they had heard before; the Zodiac's voice was lower than the caller to the show[70].

Sam continued to call Melvin Belli at his home, through December and into the next year.

November 8, 1969 - The "Dripping Pen" and the 340 Code

The "Dripping Pen" card was sent to the *San Francisco Chronicle*, along with another piece of Paul Stine's shirt, and a cipher that would come to be called the "340 Code," because it contained 340 characters. The commercially printed card has the title, "Sorry, I haven't written, but I just washed my pen." The card refers to "bad news" that the public won't get for a while, and asks for the cipher to be printed on the front page of the paper. At the time I learned this, in 2016, this code had not been cracked, and many people conjectured that it was just a gibberish code, since no code breaker had made any headway on it. This code was finally solved in 2020.

This communication includes what appears to be a victim count. At the end of his writing, underneath his signature crosshairs logo, he writes:

Des July Aug Sept Oct = 7

Investigators conjectured how he got to a count of seven, and noted that "Aug" was included. What murders could they be? It was posited that he might be including the Furlong and Snoozy murders in San Jose[71].

November 9, 1969 Letter

The next day a multi-page Zodiac letter was delivered to the *SF Chronicle*[72].

The letter begins:

> *"This is the Zodiac speaking up to the end of Oct I have killed 7 people. I have grown rather angry with the police for their telling lies about me. So I shall change the way the collecting of slaves. I shall no longer announce to anyone. When I committ my murders, they shall look like routine robberies, killings of anger, + a few fake accidents, etc."*

This is very important—Zodiac said he Would change the way he killed. He wouldn't announce his murders anymore, but instead make them look like explainable crimes. And while Zodiac letters continued to be sent, the only specific confessions to murders contained in these future letters are those believed to be committed by someone else.

The letter also taunted the police for not catching him the night of the Paul Stine murder and described at length that he used airplane glue on his fingertips so he wouldn't leave prints. He also said that he wiped down Paul Stine's cab after the murder in order to leave, as he spelled it, "fake clews."

Zodiac again claimed seven murders, as he had in his communication the day before.

But these important points are only part of this letter. It has become known as the "Bus Bomb Letter," or the "Death Machine Letter," because of its extensive description of a bomb/device that he claimed would be used to blow up a school bus of children. He included an ingredient list and a diagram of the bomb he described as a "death machine". Mention of the bombs, the "death machine," and the threats against children were withheld from the public, only revealed several months later, on May 1, 1970[73]. This information was withheld from the public out of the opinion that the "death machine" claims were so outrageous they were likely a hoax, and over concerns of creating public panic from the threats.

December 19, 1969 – Call to San Jose CHP

Someone claiming to be Zodiac called the California Highway Patrol in San Jose, and threatened to kill five police officers as well as a family of five[74].

December 20, 1969 – Letter to Melvin Belli

In the midst of Sam's hoax calls to Melvin Belli, the real Zodiac mailed a letter to him[75]. The letter is certainly authentic as it includes another piece of Paul Stine's shirt, the third piece he sent. In this letter, with strangely immaculate penmanship, the killer asked for help, and referred to "this thing in me," explaining how it won't let him seek help and that it is hard to keep under control. Zodiac implied he has killed eight, and he said he might take his ninth and tenth victims soon.

April 20, 1970

Zodiac sent a letter to the *San Francisco Chronicle* claiming ten victims and included what has become known as the "13-Character cipher." This code remains uncracked today and is particularly taunting to the public and law enforcement, because the letter literally says, "My name is-" before the single line of coded letters[76].

The letter continues, with the killer saying he did not plant the bomb that recently killed cops, almost certainly referring to a pipe-bomb on February 16, 1970, at San Francisco's Park Police Station that killed one policeman, blinded and severely maimed another, and injured eight more.

April 29, 1970

Zodiac sent a get-well card featuring a cartoon of someone riding a dragon to the *San Francisco Chronicle*. Writing in the card referred a couple times to a "blast," and said the way to avoid the "blast" would be for Zodiac to see people wearing Zodiac buttons around town[77].

June 26, 1970 – Mt. Diablo

Zodiac sent a letter to the *San Francisco Chronicle* that included a 32-symbol cipher. He complained that the citizens of San Francisco were not wearing Zodiac buttons, and he included a description of a bomb, along with a Bay Area map to find that bomb. The map has a Zodiac logo drawn over Mount Diablo, a high peak in the East Bay. The letter also said that he had shot a man in a parked car and now claimed twelve victims[78].

Enter The Mikado

July 24, 1970

Zodiac sent a letter to the *San Francisco Chronicle* where he again stated he was unhappy that people were not wearing nice buttons, and so now he has a "little list." This letter is first referenced in print in Paul Avery's November 16, 1970 article in the *San Francisco Chronicle.*[79]

This letter has become known as the "Kathleen Johns" letter, as he references driving a woman and her baby around a few months earlier, likely referring to the ordeal of Kathleen Johns and her baby in March of 1970, near Tracy, California. On that evening, a pregnant Johns and her 10-month-old baby were motioned off a road by an apparent good Samaritan, presumably to fix her tire. But instead of fixing it, the individual loosened the tire, making the car undrivable. Johns and her baby were forced to ride with the man for 90 minutes, until they could escape. While at the police department later that evening, Johns saw the police sketch of Zodiac on the wall and identified her abductor as the same man.

The Mikado is a Gilbert and Sullivan comic opera first performed on March 14, 1885 in London. At one time, The Mikado was one of the most produced stage shows of any kind, although its production is much rarer today, given the reaction against Asian stereotypes in the show. In 1967, there was a feature motion picture produced of The Mikado[80].

I note this letter as the first known Mikado reference in a Zodiac letter. I have not seen anyone else make this connection, but it is clear Zodiac is referencing a little list. In his next letter, Zodiac removes any doubt that this is a Mikado reference.

July 26, 1970

Two days later, Zodiac sent what has become known as the Little List letter, because it contains the entire lyrics of the song As Some Day It May Happen (I've Got a Little List) from The Mikado. The letter begins with two pages of ranting about people wearing buttons and threatens to torture all 13 of his victims. And a large zodiac logo with SFPD – 0, and – 13 next to the crosshairs. He then proceeds with two-and-a-half pages of lyrics. In the song, the character Ko-Ko, whose title is the Lord High Executioner, sings about the people on his "little list" he has slated to kill, included here with Zodiac's spelling and punctuation.

As some day it may happen that a victom must be found,

I've got a little list. I've got a little list,

Of society offenders who might well be underground

who would never be missed would never be missed!

There is the pest-ulential nucences who write for autographs,

All people who have flabby hands and irritating laughs.

All children who are up in dates, and implore you with implatt.

All people who in shakeing hands shake hands with you like that –

And all third persons who with unspoiling take those insist.

They'd none of 'em be missed. They'd none of 'em be missed.

There's the banjo seranader, and the others of his race

And the piano-organist I've got him on the list.

All the people who eat pepermint and phomphit in your face,

they would never be missed they would never be missed!

Then the idiout who phraises with in-thusastic tone

of centuries but thi, and every country but his own.

And the lady from the provences, who dress like a guy

who doesn't cry

And that singular abnomily, the girl who never kissed

I don't think she'd be missed I'm sure she wouldn't be missed.

And that nice impriest that is rather rife

the judic-ial hummerist I've got him on the list

All funny fellows, com-ic men, and clowns of private life

They'd none of them be missed. They'd none of them be missed.

And uncompromiseing kind

Such as wachamacallit, thingmabob, and like wise,

well- never-mind,

And tut tut tut tut, and whatshisname, and you know who,

but the task of filling up the blanks I rather leave up to you.

But it really does-n't matter whom you place upon the list,

for none of them be missed, none of them be missed.

Can you imagine the investigators reading this? I mean, the case was already bizarre. Literally psycho. Then they receive this letter.

Zodiac's quoting of Mikado lyrics was not released to the public in hopes that some other Mikado reference would be made, either helping to confirm the veracity of a future communication, or better yet, creating a slip-up that could help identify the killer.

When neither of these materialized, investigators changed tactics. The Zodiac-Mikado connection is publicly released on October 12, 1970, in a Paul Avery article in the *San Francisco Chronicle*[81].

That article also made public what is known as the 13-hole Postcard, that had been sent to the *Chronicle* on October 5, presumably still claiming 13 victims as he did in July of 1970.

October 27, 1970, Happy Halloween!

A Halloween card was sent to *San Francisco Chronicle* reporter Paul Avery, addressed as "Paul Averly" on the envelope. It featured a skeleton on the front, wearing a pumpkin around its waist, and giving an okay symbol with its hand and a 14 written in the hand. The card says "From your secret pal" on the top, and, "I feel it in my bones, you ache to know my name, And so I'll clue you …"[82]

Inside, there is another skeleton, obscuring the line, "But then why spoil the game?" and "Happy Halloween!" The type, "4-TEEN" appear over the skeleton, and "BOO!" next to it. The card is signed with some undecipherable markings, the letter Z, and the usual circle and cross hairs Zodiac logo.

The back of the card has the word PARADiCE printed vertically with SLAVES printed horizontally, with the words sharing the A, making a cross. Then "By FiRE" "By GUN" "By KNiFE" "By ROPE" is printed in the four quadrants around the cross. The letter I is always lowercase in an otherwise all caps section, and the N of "KNiFE" is printed backwards.

It's worth noting that the 2007 David Fincher movie Zodiac incorrectly shows this Halloween card being delivered to Avery with a piece of Paul Stine's shirt included. That did not happen, the movie is conflating separate events. The *Chronicle* did indeed receive a piece of Paul Stine's shirt on Oct. 13, 1969. The Halloween card to Paul Avery was received on Oct. 27, 1970, but did not contain a piece of shirt.

A pause in Zodiac activity?

The frequency of Zodiac letters trails off in 1970. Is it a pause? Is it sputtering out? Are subsequent letters authentic or are they hoaxes? By late 1970, Zodiac had been in the news so much that it appears people were indeed making fake letters. Imagine that.

To another extent, this was all becoming exhausting and old news to the public. However one looks at it, the communications become more sporadic, less frequent, and harder to categorize and authenticate. In 1971 there are few authenticated Zodiac communications, interspersed between speculation about various murders in California.

Los Angeles Times letter

On March 13, 1971, Zodiac sent a letter to the *Los Angeles Times*, that said they wouldn't bury him on the back pages like some of the others[83]. The letter is postmarked from Pleasanton, California, about 50 miles southeast of San Francisco. This was the first authenticated Zodiac communication in six months, and it was sent to Los Angeles, not San Francisco.

Sierra Club card

Nine days later, on March 22, someone sent a post card to Paul Avery, again addressed to "Paul Averly." This "Sierra Club card" is believed to be authentic as handwriting experts deemed it consistent with other Zodiac communications[84] It is the subject of much speculation, but it was thought from the beginning to be tied to the September 1970 cold-case murder of Donna Lass in South Lake Tahoe[85]. The card hints that this is his 12th victim, but has a total count of 17 or more.

For many years the incident was classified as a missing person as no body had been found. Then in 1986 a skull was discovered that many believed to be Lass, but even then, the skull's identity was still unknown. It was finally confirmed to indeed be her by DNA analysis in December 2023[86].

Press references to the Zodiac Killer in San Francisco newspapers basically stop after this card, save for speculation about the similarities of the murder of Trudy Hiler, a Chico State student murdered in the Lake Tahoe area in July 1971.[87]

It is unclear if this is from a lack of Zodiac activity, or a new strategy to not report his actions in the press. Regardless, there are no significant articles about this case after the Sierra Club card for the rest of 1971, all of 1972 and into 1973. By May of 1973, there is speculation in the press that Zodiac may be dead.[88]

Kathy Bilek

High school senior Kathy Bilek was murdered on April 11, 1971, near Saratoga.[89] There was speculation early on that it could be Zodiac, but by April 13 investigators cast doubt on that theory and said the crime had much more in common with the murders of Kathie Snoozy and Deborah Furlong.[90] A few days later, investigators became certain the crimes were committed by the same person.[91]

On April 29. San Jose college student Karl Francis Werner was arrested for the murders of Furlong, Snoozy, and Bilek.[92] On September 1, he pleaded guilty to the crimes.[93]

The 148 Code

Sometime in May 1971, a letter and code were sent to the *San Francisco Chronicle* from Fairfield, California. The authenticity of this letter has not been confirmed. It included a cipher containing 148 symbols. Now to this untrained eye it looks like different handwriting. The 408 and 340 codes were hand drawn, but very straight and aligned in both rows and in columns. This code is just written out, more like handwriting, with slanted symbols that have only a slight similarity to the previous codes. Perhaps at this point neat penmanship on the codes was passé? In this letter, the author claims to have killed 21 times.

Albany Letter 1973

In August of 1973, a letter postmarked in Albany, New York, arrived at the *New York Knickerbocker News*, saying they "will kill again." In the letter, threats are made against the Albany Medical Center. The letter contained a short code that remains unsolved.

It is unclear to me whether this letter is deemed by the police as authentic. It is also unclear to me if there are other letters sent around the country as Zodiac, authentic or hoax. But there is no crime in Albany, New York, nor anywhere, tied to this letter.

This letter is of great significance to those who think Richard is Zodiac, as he lived in Albany from 1966 to 1968.

The Exorcist Letter – Mikado Revisited

On January 29, 1974, Zodiac sent a letter to the *San Francisco Chronicle*, that said they had seen The Exorcist, and thought it was "the best satirical comedy they had ever seen."[94] Then the letter proceeds to quote Ko-ko from The Mikado again:

"Then he plunged himself into the billowy wave, And an echo arose from the suicide's grave. 'Titwillow, titwillow, titwillow!'"

It's worth noting that the actual lyrics are 'Oh, willow, titwillow, titwillow!' It would seem Zodiac quoted the lyrics from memory, rather than copying them from a lyrics sheet. Whoever Zodiac was, they liked The Mikado and knew much of it by heart.

The letter includes "Me/37 – SFPD/0," a possible claim of 37 victims. It is my understanding that investigators view the "Exorcist Letter" as authentic.

Other Possible Zodiac Communications

There seems to be quite a few more letters of unknown authenticity sprinkled throughout the seventies and into the early eighties besides the ones previously noted. This includes a February 1974 letter talking about the Symbionese Liberation Army (SLA), the terrorist group that most famously kidnapped Patty Hearst,[95] and a couple other letters sent in July 1974.[96] There are dozens of possible Zodiac letters. I had to stop reading about them as they seemed to drift farther and farther from the clear facts of the case.

I had vowed not to get sucked into the black hole of Zodiac research, and I had indeed gotten sucked into the black hole of Zodiac research. I decided I had read enough. Anyway, that's the basic rundown of the Zodiac case, and how I understood it in 2016. I'm sure many people will say, with some merit, that I've left stuff out. I'm sure I have.

Of course there is A LOT of speculation online about other murders, and of course, Zodiac himself alludes to many other murders. There are plenty of cold-case murders to choose from. I have stuck here to a summary of what has been confirmed to be Zodiac, and other items that may be relevant to Richard Gaikowski, like the Albany letter.

The Accusations ----------

At some point in the 1980s, an individual known as Blaine, and sometimes Blaine Blaine, began to suspect Richard was Zodiac, and began to record his conversations with him. He had known Richard for many years, but only then began to suspect him. In August 1986, Blaine sent a letter to law enforcement with his accusations against Richard. Richard was then put under surveillance for a short time.

This was more or less not in the public awareness until into the 21st Century. I certainly didn't know anything about it when I knew Richard 1994-2002.

Public awareness does begin with the 2009 History Channel documentary series MysteryQuest and the episode, titled San Francisco Slaughter[97]. This is how I learned about it as well, along with many various websites devoted to the Zodiac killer case, most notably Tom Voigt's zodiackiller.com. A Google search of Richard Gaikowski currently yields 277,000 results, the vast majority of results regarding Zodiac.

In the MysteryQuest episode, Blaine, under the pseudonym 'Goldcatcher" makes his accusations against Richard public: That he was indeed the Zodiac, that he continued killing into the 1980s, that Richard had threatened him to keep quiet. Blaine had secretly recorded Richard talking about the Zodiac and about codes, including gibberish codes.

Since the airing of that episode, Richard's name is often included among top Zodiac "suspects." I put that term in quotes because he was never an official police suspect. Only one person has ever been named by law enforcement as a suspect, Arthur Leigh Allen. Allen is the preferred suspect by the famous Zodiac author Robert Graysmith, but DNA evidence has led investigators to the conclusion that Allen is not the killer.[98]

The online debate about Richard is about as lively as any in the Zodiac world. There are many people who feel very strongly about this, on both sides. On one side is primarily Zodiac researcher Tom Voigt, who was contacted by Blaine now years ago, who names Richard as his top pick, and who has a large following who agree with him. On the other side are a great many people. There is a lot more information and material about both sides of this debate online.

So there you have my summary of the Zodiac crimes and timeline, a summary of Richard's life as assembled from contemporaneous newspaper articles, my memories of Richard, and the state of affairs as I perceived them around 2016.

My Observations on the Facts and the Accusations

While the previous material has been presented chronological-ly, it is impossible to correctly portray the piecemeal nature of how I learned it. Writing in 2024, with the benefit of hindsight, it can all seem so obvious, with one thing leading to another. But I did not learn these facts in chronological order. From 2016 to 2018 I learned the facts of the Zodiac case, or rather what is reported as facts, as I found them--meaning out of order, with some points I now know to be im-portant not discovered until closer inspection years later.

As noted in this book's long and meandering Act I, people are VERY oriented to their first take on things, and that includes me. And compounding this problem, I learned all of this in the internet era, which means it all came with the online commentary of the public-at-large.

So I know that my opinions are distorted. Furthermore, I have not studied criminology, nor any other murder cases. I am not a psychol-ogist, sociologist, nor any other "ist." I'm just another amateur "inter-net-sleuth."

That said, my observations are honest ones that I can back up with examples. In my opinion, much of what I was reading online was riddled with logical mistakes and faulty reasoning. Before you even get to the actual facts, one must wade through so many inane takes it is hard to verify what is fact, what is opinion, what is urban legend. In my opinion, the public perception of the Zodiac case has been greatly harmed by poor reasoning. I want to address this before discussing the specifics of the case.

Problem - Binary Thinking

So much online material about Zodiac is inundated with binary thinking. And what I mean by binary thinking is absolutist statements pronouncing something has to be one way or the other, when they are likely partialities. Binary is a computer term that means either/or. In a computer, at its basic level, things are either zero or one. No nuance. In regards to this case, I call binary thinking the demanding or absolute consistency across crimes, motives, and victims. Binary, all one way, no gray area. Never an exception.

There are indeed binary things. For example, if it is indeed the case that you were in San Francisco at 11 pm on October 11, 1969, then it is a certainty you were not in New York at that same time. Those sorts of things are binary.

But most things are not binary. Someone telling a lie, or just honestly misremembering something ONE time does not mean they are doing it EVERY time. Witnesses are not ALL credible, nor ALL non-credible. Witnesses are mostly credible, or mostly not credible.

When assessing someone's credibility, it shouldn't be viewed as a binary question, one should try to discern which things the person says are likely true, and which are likely false.

All of us do a lot better when we insert "possibly" or "might" in and around our statements. The level of discourse would improve, not only from a civility standpoint, but from a logical one.

Another aspect of binary thinking is demanding that motives and situations must be consistent, exactly consistent, each time, every time. With Zodiac, Lake Herman, Blue Rock Springs, and Lake Berryessa are clearly lover's lane sites. But what then of Paul Stine? The statement "Zodiac only attacked lover's lane type places" is false. The statement, "Most of Zodiac's attacks were at lover's lane type places" is true.

We must also recognize also that motives don't have to be absolute. It could be the case that a killer has a primary motive for a crime, and also a secondary one. Random events can also come into play. Motives need not be simple. To demand that each crime have a simple, consistent motive is just not tenable.

Binary thinking negatively affects discussions about method and motive. Were all attacks spontaneous? Or were they all planned? It doesn't have to be all one or the other.

Did Zodiac know his victims, or were they all random? In all these cases, the answer can very well be both, and neither, depending on the particular case. Actually, multiple and varying motives and methods would be quite likely, especially if some of the additional claimed murders are indeed true.

But, like seemingly everything today, online discussion about these matters becomes a pissing match between absolutist camps on any one of these points. Some DEMAND that ALL Zodiac attacks were random attacks. Others DEMAND that Zodiac knew his victims. Mathematically, especially the higher the victim count, the most likely is that Zodiac knew some of his victims and others were random strangers. I keep an open mind on this point and try to avoid making absolutist statements about things which can likely only be conjecture.

The question of whether Zodiac was honest in his letters is also harmed by binary thinking.

It seems that many people take Zodiac's claims of the first five attacks as truthful, but then regard the subsequent years of letters and claims of victims as lies or boasts. While there are indeed things in Zodiac letters that have been shown to be untruthful, that in no way means it all is untruthful. It is not good logic to regard all the letters beginning November 1969, and through the 1970s as lies. Keep in mind that the prior communications about Lake Herman, Blue Rock Springs, and Paul Stine were indeed truthful, verified by evidence.

It is believed, reasonably, that Zodiac's claims of the South Bay murders of Debra Furlong, Kathie Snoozy, and Kathy Bilek to be a lie, especially after Karl Francis Werner confessed to them. This point has been one of the cornerstones of those looking to discount much or all that Zodiac communicated from approximately November 1969 into the future. It's worth noting that for 51 years, the other cornerstone of this opinion was the unsolved 340 code, held by many to be gibberish and further evidence of a lying Zodiac. The code's solving in 2020 has obliterated that point.

But it is not just my opinion, I believe mathematics would back me up--the most reasonable position is that some of the Zodiac material from November 1969 into the 1970s is indeed truthful, and some of it is false. Which means it's very likely there are indeed additional Zodiac victims, who and how many is the only questions.

And there are other things in Zodiac letters that are certainly or likely lies. Beyond the claimed murders that were ultimately charged to other people who confessed to them, I believe I can show where Zodiac is clearly lying, not as a boast, but to throw people off the trail.

Problem - Needing Singular, Monolithic Motives

As a very wise child once said, "It's simple, but it's complicated."

Isn't that how pretty much everything is in life? And isn't everything combinations of things, rather than singular entities. Consider something like fried chicken, assuming you like it. Do you like it for the crispy batter, or the tender meat? Do you like the eleven herbs and spices advertised by the national chain, or the seven ingredients espoused by journeymen fryers of southern Indiana?

My point is that it is certainly a combination of factors that determine things we like.

Now, let's talk about things we don't like. In fact, let's talk about people who piss us off. Does one single thing they do aggravate you, or is it a combination. Did your dislike of a person accumulate over time, or was it one, monolithic reason? Of course it is a combination and a cumulation.

Treating Zodiac's motivations as monolithic and methods as always consistent is just not sound reasoning.

Problem - Taking Assumptions as Facts

I saw this paraphrased statement on a message board: Zodiac wasn't a gay man because gay men don't kill women. I'm not aware of the statistics on this, but I am sure in the entire history of the earth, there has been at least one gay man kill at least one woman. I hope the sarcasm of this statement is obvious. It is certain that across all of history, there have been many gay men who have murdered women. Misogyny is not limited to heterosexuals.

Now if that comment had read, "I think it's unlikely that Zodiac was a gay man because statistically they murder women at a lower-than-average rate," I would have less problems with the statement, even though I would question such a statistic, and here's why:

First off, are we talking only about out gay men, or closeted ones as well? There are many, many, closeted gay men, so any such statistics on this subject are suspect. But that's just the tip of the iceberg.

Sexual angst is strong among human beings, and sexual guilt is a key-component of society, a foundational concept of our religions. It was an even bigger thing in the late 1960s than today. The shaming of homosexuals, the entire psychodrama that some in society, the Church and more, put on homosexuals, is despicable. It is too much for many people to endure, especially young people. Especially in homes where such was shamed.

Then there is just sexual angst in general. The depression that can come from lack of success in dating, the jealousy that can stem from seeing the object of one's desires dating others, the pain of loneliness.

I believe the number of men who have killed women over sexual issues is immeasurable, accounting for the majority of all murders from the beginning of time until now. Heterosexual, homosexual, bisexual, asexual. Jealousy and angst go hand in hand with humans and can be especially ugly in the human male. It wouldn't surprise me if killing about sex outranks people killing for money or food or survival.

So, we don't know anything about the sexuality of the killer, only that their first three attacks are all on lover's lane couples. The fourth attack was not. What that means is unclear.

Earth, Water, Ball, Fish

This story bears telling here.

In November 1999, I traveled to Europe with John C. Lilly to attend the International Cetacean Education Research Centre (ICERC) Conference at Versailles outside Paris. At this conference, I assisted John with his presentation. I showed the programming work I had been assisting with for cetacean scientist Dr. Ken Marten at Sea Life Park in Hawaii.

One experimental piece of software was a little app I made called the Type-O-Tonalator, that applied one note to each letter of the alphabet, starting on the low part of the keyboard for A, and going up one note until Z. As you typed, the software played the notes. You could also save certain words and associate a graphic with each. Some of the words just sounded awful, but some were quite melodic. I created a demo using four words, four that not only sounded quite nice, but were also relevant to dolphin communication research, EARTH, WATER, BALL, FISH.

EARTH makes a nice riff, the E and A are both low, the R and T are similar high notes, and back down for the H. Remember, A is the lowest note and Z is the highest. WATER is also nice, and almost sounds like cascading water, starting with the high W, then very low A, then not as high T, then not as low E, then not as high again R. BALL is perhaps the easiest one to learn, as it is two adjacent low notes, B, A, then two identical relatively higher notes L, L. Finally, FISH, three notes each higher, FIS, then a lower note to end. To me, FISH sorta sounded like a fish in water, similar to the way the animals have songs in the symphonic tale for children, Peter and the Wolf.

I demonstrated this software to about 300 conference attendees. I told them that this was just an attempt to make a tonal language that perhaps both humans and dolphins could understand and speak. Then I assured all of them that they could indeed learn this language and played the four words for them on my computer. I played the tones for each word twice.

Then I turned off the screen and said it was now time for their test to see how well they had learned the new language. I played WATER, and most of the crowd said WATER. I played EARTH, and the entire crowd said EARTH. I played BALL, the easiest of the four, with two low notes and then two identical high notes. Everyone got that.

Then, I was about to play FISH when I had an inspiration. Instead of playing FISH, I played BALL again. Upon hearing the notes, half of the people said BALL, and half of the people said FISH.

There is a lot going on here.

First, people were able to learn a tonal language, and in just a few minutes. They were able to recognize the patterns of the tones and know they were coded data meant to stand in for English words.

Second, people were able to perform simple logic and anticipate the fourth word. I had indeed said I was going to play all four words, but ended up not doing that, so people were trusting of me, and they were able to remember that the fourth word, the word not played yet, was FISH.

But most importantly, and the point of this story, is that half of the people weren't really listening by the fourth word. You had to be actually paying attention.

Equally important, and why I can say I taught some people a tonal language that day, is that half of the crowd indeed recognized I played BALL twice. They indeed understood the tonal language.

For those who said FISH, I can only point out that tricksters, propagandists, and other kinds of linguistic hucksters frequently use the fact that half of the people are no longer paying attention to ply their schemes. People latch on to their first take. People stop paying attention after they think they've gotten it. People jump to conclusions based on partial data. Some people jump to iron-clad, if-you-don't-agree-you-are-an-idiot conclusions as their standard operating procedure, when all they have is their first, assumption-riddled take.

I think Zodiac operated knowing this flaw in human behavior, and I say that with respect and in the hopes of truly solving this crime. It is of tantamount importance to listen and perceive what is actually being said and seen, not what we have assumed we will hear and see.

In France, I was asked, why were we trying to teach dolphins English?

I replied, "It is because dolphins really have no chance pronouncing the French R."

Problem - Taking Snippets of Info and Expanding on Them

Problems in comprehension like the one previously illustrated are in all parts of human experience, and certainly with people interested in this case. I see conventional wisdom taking over discussions about the Zodiac, and certain facts are seemingly accepted by everyone, but they are assumptions and are misleading. Then, those assumptions are built upon, growing as a subject and getting enshrined in everyone's mind as fact.

Any number of aspects of this case, verified or not, have been expanded into multi-decades-long discussions. Certainly, some have merit, and just as certainly some are a total waste of time and brain power. Things like where Zodiac lived, what was his ethnicity, and what were his politics all have been expanded into a sort of dogma. Later I will discuss how a snippet of information about Paul Stine has been expanded into rigid opinions about his murder.

Of course, any theory of the case that uses conjecture to any degree will be guilty of what I am describing. What I find detrimental is not the speculation per se, but the rigid and argumentative defense of such speculation. A tempered and reserved tone is a much better path to follow.

Problem - Any AH can say "Zodiac"

Upon hearing of a crime, a cold case in the 1970s, one can say "I think it was Zodiac" without anything to back it up other than your lips flapping. "Unabomber!" "Son of Sam!" "The Manson Family!" They can all be spoken or typed, and because they are known entities in this macabre subject, people feel it is ok to posit them for any and all cold cases, regardless of the plausibility, even if it is totally and utterly ridiculous. This phenomenon is a huge problem in the current public discussion of the case.

Problem - Tribalism

I can understand rooting for your sports team, or your country. These are perhaps the only places where tribalism makes any sense.

I can somewhat understand tribalism in partisan politics, although being for your side, regardless of what they say or do, is a recipe for our leaders to become corrupt. I would hope that Americans still hold the leaders of their own political party to account with the same standards we hold the other party's leaders to. Once in a great while, we still do.

But I do not understand tribalism as a function of cracking the Zodiac case. In fact, going tribal in your attempt to crack the Zodiac case is a certain way to distort your interpretation of things and a likely path to confirmation bias.

It appears that so much time is wasted, so much brainpower is wasted, on just trashing other people. Once someone has stated that they don't believe someone else is credible, there is little need to add needling statements in more or less every sentence uttered about them. And there is no need to write two thirds of your articles about how wrong someone else is.

The 2007 Movie, The Zodiac

I'm going to be honest, this is a GREAT movie. Director David Fincher weaves a compelling story and you really feel like you are in 1969 San Francisco. That said, I have learned that certain facts were handled loosely, and creative license was used. I'm not going to go into detail, but I found the website zodiackillerfacts.com, maintained by crime researcher Michael Butterfield, to be very helpful on this subject. He correctly notes several things that are factually wrong with the movie.

I was disappointed to learn this, and I was also disappointed to learn that DNA evidence had already cleared Arthur Leigh Allen in 2002, five years before the movie was made. Now I can understand some things from a filmmaking point of view—I don't think the film is outright disingenuous, but I don't think the film gains anything by not following the events exactly as they happened. My point is this, as with everything: one should verify, or at least try to verify, any claim you see independently. Anyone reading this book should absolutely verify for themselves what I present and conjecture.

So, the movie is great. Very entertaining, but not a tool for research.

Let's Remember We are Talking About a Psychopath Here

I conclude with this, because this is a big one. I must tell myself this all the time: We are talking about a psychopath here. No one knows what they would do.

No one can say, well so-and-so would certainly do this… or it wouldn't be rational for someone to do x…, without realizing that all such statements come with not just grains of salt, but bags of it. Truck-loads of it. We're talking about a psycho killer. Who knows what he thinks is rational? So, there's no reason, actually less than no reason, for any high-browing about what the perpetrator would do. It is all conjecture and speculation, and those who do not acknowledge that are way off on a limb.

Such are my observations about the problems in the investigation, and moreover in the online discussions of Zodiac. Now I will discuss each event.

Lake Herman Road

I don't have too much to add here, other than an observation. It is true that the Zodiac claimed the murders, and he provided police with details of the crime not known by the public. It is usually described that the Zodiac letters contained facts that only the killer would know. My observation is that such facts could possibly be known by a friend of the killer too. It is a tenet of the Zodiac investigation that the killer operated alone, but that is just an assumption.

Blue Rock Springs

Michael Mageau

I am surprised that the testimony of victim Michael Mageau is not given more weight. In the 2007 film, This is the Zodiac Speaking, he said that Darlene Ferrin told him she had a stalker, and mentioned that he thought she said his name was Richard.

Now there are people who very much discredit his account. They say he is totally unreliable as a witness. Mostly I have heard people dismiss him, citing that he has given different accounts at different times.

This is some of that binary thinking I was talking about. I don't understand the inability of some to grasp why the victim of such a horrible event might have inconsistent memories. It's not like the event happens and then they just move on like nothing happened. The emotional and mental damage such an event would cause is possibly more damaging than the physical. Beyond that, the body and mind have defense mechanisms.

One must be able to grasp the difference between a judgement opinion, from a factual opinion, and doing so about a moment when you were bleeding from multiple gunshot wounds including through your neck. A good investigator would look for other emotional or physical cues as to whether Mageau at any one time was lucid, or at another may very well be experiencing a state that most of us cannot even imagine. I present that certainly would be able to relay MANY factual things and be absolutely reliable for much testimony.

For example, did Michael Mageau still know his own name? Did he know what day it was? What model of car they were in? Where were they parked? What was the name of his date? I imagine he was able to state all those facts correctly. So that means that some of his testimony IS reliable. So why wouldn't he be able to recount correctly something Darlene said to him? Why wouldn't he be able to remember the name of the stalker? Why wouldn't we weight his opinion, someone who was on the scene, much higher than someone just ranting online?

Of course, trauma causes unpredictable actions and distorts memories. Such would account for inconsistencies in his account. In any case, you cannot just dismiss his accounts out of hand.

In reality, there is little-to-no basis to discount his statement that the stalker was named Richard. There are many, many names. Why that one and not another?

As for Mageau supposedly saying he laid their for 8 hours before help came, it seems to take forever when you are in pain. Now imagine how slow the clock goes when you've been shot multiple times. Certain things you might perceive differently. The body's shock systems would certainly have taken over. I think we should cut him some slack about how long he laid their bleeding.

But even with a whole lot of this, a Zodiac victim, someone infinitely closer to this crime than any of us, said Darlene had a stalker named Richard. Why shouldn't we believe him? It is amazing this fact isn't heavily valued in this case.

Men Wanting to Date Darlene Ferrin

It is not a value judgment, just a statement of fact, that it is possible the Zodiac Killer either dated Darlene Ferrin, or wanted to date her.

It is also not a value judgment, just a statement of fact, that a young woman dating many men and boys, even while she is married, twice by age 22, who is out at a lover's lane at midnight with a man that is not her husband, is at risk of male aggression. Some would say she was playing with fire.

It is a simple and awful fact of life, that a sexually active woman makes many men angry. So while it is possible that her murder at a lover's lane with a man who was not her husband was random, it is extremely possible it was NOT random. The perpetrator could have easily known she was there, and jealousy could easily be the motive. The police reports state that Blue Rock Springs park was a known place Darlene went with dates.

There is dispute and speculation whether Darlene held a painting party at her house months earlier. Some demand that it never happened, others are certain it did. I'm not here to demand either way, but it is entirely plausible, if not likely, as she had recently moved into a new home.

Those who believe it happened posit that Darlene asked many of her male friends to come to her painting party to paint a room in her house. A painting party is a way to get other people to work for you. Did any of the men who came to the party think that working for her would increase their chances with her romantically? Of course some did. From a statistics standpoint, the probability that not one man at Darlene's painting party thought it would increase their chances with her romantically are very rare, almost impossible.

The Zodiac online discussions are often clouded by moralizing on this point, as if the public sentiment of the 2020's has any bearing on a crime in 1969. And even if they did, it has nothing to do with solving this crime. It's just moral grandstanding.

Could Darlene Ferrin and Richard Gaikowski have known each other?

The short answer is of course they could have. She was a waitress at various establishments around Vallejo. She is described as attractive, always with many boys around. There is absolutely no way to know the extent of the people she knew, from good friends to boyfriends to casual acquaintances to customers.

According to Tom Voigt on his website, zodiackiller.com, Napa County Sheriff Detective Ken Narlow said Richard Gaikowski was at Darlene's painting party. Voigt also makes the case that Richard moved to Albany the same time Darlene did and moved back to California the around the same time as well. It is easily confirmed that Richard did live in the Albany, New York area from 1966 to 1968. I have nothing to add to these points, other than observing that it would be entirely possible that Richard did indeed know Darlene.

Nancy Slover and the Voice of Zodiac

I can say from having many conversations with him, Richard Gaikowski had a very unique voice. I work in advertising and have many times handled the production of audio for television and radio commercials, voice overs and jingles. Richard had what you would call a classic radio voice. Baritone, no heavy accent, perhaps one could hear a tinge of his Great Plains roots, but moreover a good voice to be an announcer or sportscaster. Good enunciation and pronunciation. A sort-of, American Shakespeare. I would not describe it as a common voice, I would describe it as distinctive.

In the tarot card software that Richard wrote, his recorded voice described each card when it was turned on the screen. His recorded voice said which card had been pulled and described it with force and dramatic pauses.

"The Fool. New beginnings, Innocence, Leaps of faith. Originality. Spontaneity. Jocularity."

On Tom Voigt's website, zodiackiller.com, he has recordings Blaine made of Richard speaking. For what it's worth, I can confirm that the recorded voice is indeed Richard. I think it is reasonable to say it would be relatively easier to identify Richard's voice than many other voices because his voice was indeed exceptional.

Nancy Slover was the police dispatcher for the Vallejo Police Department and took the call from Zodiac in the early hours of July 5, 1969. At various times, Nancy Slover has identified different voices as the Zodiac. A few of those times she has identified Richard as the voice.

So obviously this cannot be counted as airtight evidence. But just as solidly it cannot be dismissed. When questioned about herself identifying different people's voices as the Zodiac, she confirmed that Richards's voice did indeed match.

Now I have seen some people online completely dismiss Nancy Slover's voice identifications. Please, that is just not rational. There is no way one can dismiss them.

What I can say is this: if at any time Nancy Slover identified Richard's voice as the voice she heard, then she was confirming the Zodiac's was a distinctive baritone voice. What we can state with near certainty is that any voice that she heard but misidentified, must have also had the baritone timber as well. We can conclude that Zodiac spoke with a deep voice.

Nancy Slover passed away in 2012.

The 408-code

As we know, the 408-code was sent in three parts to three Bay Area newspapers. It is obvious that Zodiac took great care in preparing this cipher. It was sent more than three weeks after the Blue Rock Springs attack. By sending it to the three newspapers, with two of them in San Francisco, it was guaranteed to be a Bay Area wide media event. The "prank" was sure to get a lot of press, requiring newspapers and law enforcement of multiple jurisdictions to get involved and coordinate with each other. The buzz that the 408-code generated was off the charts. I don't think this was all done on a whim, it was planned and deliberate. That it was planned and deliberate is something I think important to keep in mind when thinking about it.

There are three handwritten notes, one each accompanying each code. They are word for word the same, EXCEPT in one place: In the letter to the *Chronicle* accompanying part three of the code, there is one extra sentence: "In this cipher is my iden(t)ity."

Then, in the code solution of that part three, he specifically says he will not give us his name. Reading that part of the solution made me laugh out loud. This guy is really jerking us around. In addition, the final 18 characters of this part three remarks were not solved—and remain unsolved to this day. Either those characters do not use the same cipher key, or they are gibberish. It seems quite plausible that the killer's identity is in these 18 characters, or perhaps it is more evidence that we are being jerked around. I imagine how he must have laughed about the conundrum he was causing investigators and the public.

I think the importance of this section of code cannot be understated.

In the fourth line of this part of the code, the letter sequence GYKE occurs. Those four letters solve to AUSE, the last letters of the word "because." Those who believe Richard to be Zodiac make much of this. At minimum, it is strange coincidence that GYKE and AUSE make up two-thirds of "Gaikowski". It is certainly a possibility that it is there on purpose. Online debate on this point is some of the most heated one can find.

Despite the coincidence, many people just dismiss this as ridiculous. They cite that Richard never spelled his name "Gyke." I would just like to point out that he also didn't spell "ows" as "ause" either. If it is his name, it is his name PHONETICALLY, not literally. If this is just a coincidence, it is one F of a coincidence.

THE ONLY TIME RICHARD GOT ANGRY AT ME

The detractors also state that there are all kinds of letter sequences in the 408-code, that possibly make all kinds of names. Of course there are. But do these letter sequences solve to other parts of a relevant name? I have yet to see where someone was able to find Arthur Leigh Allen, Lawrence Kane, or any other name, suspect of otherwise, in part three of the code.

Some also point out that in the solution to this code the killer states they will not give us his name—and they seemingly take that as truth. To me, this passage makes it even more likely that his name, or rather his identity, is indeed in this section of code. The perpetrator is an evil jokester. He is taunting the police, and the public. He has taken the time to make up this elaborate scheme, and he enjoys that no one can figure out his prank. I think what he enjoys is actually putting his identity in the code, but in such a way that no one can figure it out.

That said, with 18 characters still unsolved, perhaps we should just focus on deciphering that section. Either way, no one can definitively say what is going on with this code, and people should always couch their opinions in that light.

Good Times July 31, 1969

Those who believe Richard is Zodiac make much of the *Good Times* issue of July 31, 1969. Indeed, that is the same day that the three-part 408 cipher was sent to the three Bay Area newspapers. The cover of that *Good Times* issue is indeed split into three equal parts, the only such cover in the entire history of *Good Times*. The three sections are photos of Bobby Seale, Peter Fonda, and Swami Dananda. The issue contains interviews with each of the three. The Fonda interview and the Swami Dananda interview are conducted anonymously, or at least uncredited with a byline.

D. Gaik, or any obvious modification of that name, is not printed in this issue, no byline or other reference. But it is still possible that Richard conducted one or more of the interviews. For example, in the December 18, 1970, issue of *Good Times*, Dick Gaik conducts and interview with William Hinton, the author of the book Fanshen.

One of the things I noticed about this *Good Times* issue, is that in the interview of Swami he says, "Man is a thinking animal."

The 408-code contains the text "…man is the most dangerous animal of all." It seemingly has been assumed this is a reference to the story and movie The Most Dangerous Game. This has become conventional wisdom, but the possibility exists it might be a reference to this article.

Other than that, it doesn't seem like much more than a coincidence this issue's cover is divided into thirds, and there is a rational explanation WHY it would be divided into thirds: There are three interviews which are the main articles of the issue. If the three articles were seen as of equal editorial value, one might handle the cover this way. If the three articles were by three different staff members, all of equal standing in the group, one might have such a cover.

If it turns out that Richard was the Zodiac, it could very well be something intentional--if he had control of the cover layout. Otherwise, this point about the issue in thirds doesn't seem to be that compelling to me.

Paul Stine

Washington Street

Those who believe Richard is the Zodiac make a big deal that Richard Gaikowski's cousin lived on Washington Street, the same street Paul Stine was murdered. On the surface, that sounds like an interesting coincidence.

But when you map the locations, you see that the cousin lived 20 blocks away from the site of the Stine murder, a distance of 1.9 miles, not exactly walking distance. I don't think this even counts as relevant at all. It is purely circumstantial evidence and should NOT be used in a case theory of Richard.

Graduate Student

One thing that may be mostly overlooked about Paul Stine, is that he was a grad student. It is quite common, for Stine to be described exclusively as a "San Francisco cab driver," and of course that is true, but it frames one's opinion.

Early on, reading the first accounts of the Zodiac killings, I had a vague idea along the lines of: Perhaps the cabbie said something about Zodiac? People often talk to their cab driver, especially back in the day before the plexiglass walls had been installed in cabs. Perhaps Paul Stine said something about Reagan, or poo-pooed the idea that he was governor because of astrology. Perhaps he said that this Zodiac guy was a psycho or punk. "Cab Driver Paul Stine" sounds like a stereotype of a person. No offense to cab drivers, but they tell it like it is, they are street-savvy. Cabbie is a working-class job, and they indeed work hard for a living. It's not hard for someone to have a stereotype of a cabbie in their minds.

I was floored to learn that Paul Stine was a graduate student, a PhD candidate in Philosophy, and had also worked in journalism, and maybe still was working in newspapers. He was just driving a cab to put himself through school. And not just an undergrad degree, a doctorate. He only drove cabs to earn side money while he was a grad student. "PhD candidate and soon to be Dr. Paul Stine" certainly sounds a lot different, right? But seemingly everywhere Paul Stine is described as a cab driver. That's it. As if his entire life was all about driving a car around San Francisco for money.

So there still is the chance my and many others' original take is true, that Paul Stine just got the wrong passenger, completely at random. Maybe he did say something that set Zodiac off. Maybe Zodiac wanted to do a murder in the city of San Francisco but couldn't find a lover's lane remote enough to pull it off? So instead, he decided to send a cabbie to a location where he thought the streets would be deserted. Or perhaps he picked the location for an escape route into the Presidio?

On the other hand, if your theory is that Zodiac wanted to get time on a computer and realized that befriending a graduate student at a local university would be a likely way to do it, the "cabbie" Stine starts to look more like a student, more like some of the other victims. Oh wait, I'm getting ahead of myself.

Paul Stine and the Haight-Asbury Switchboard

There is a fair amount of disagreement on the relevance of Paul Stine living two doors down from the Haight-Asbury Switchboard. Tom Voigt makes the case that this switchboard worked very closely with *Good Times*. Some people may have referred to the Haight-Asbury Switchboard as the "Good Times Switchboard." Others dispute this, and say it was never named "Good Times Switchboard," and there is no good connection between the *Good Times* paper/commune, and the Haight-Asbury Switchboard, thus it is irrelevant that Paul Stine lived near it.

Upon review of all *Good Times* issues, it is clear there was indeed a close working relationship between *Good Times* and the Haight-Asbury Switchboard during 1969, trailing off in the first part of 1970. By mid-1970 through the end of Good Times in summer 1972, the actual mentions of the switchboard in *Good Times* issues shows the close relationship does not exist anymore.

But from April 1969 through early 1970, I believe many people likely DID call the Haight-Asbury Switchboard the "*Good Times* Switchboard," and that Good Times people would have been hanging around the Switchboard location on a regular basis. Let me explain:

The precursor to *Good Times*, the *SF Express Times*, started printing telephone numbers for a few switchboards around the Bay Area in their final issues in March of 1969. The initial issue of *Good Times*, dated April 1, 1969, did the same.

Beginning with their second issue in April 1969, *Good Times* ALSO printed a list of names of people who had messages waiting at the Switchboard. This was a unique and important added feature to the Switchboard AND to *Good Times*, as you could get a *Good Times* to see if you need to go to the Switchboard, but also the Switchboard could tell people to look in *Good Times* to see if there was a message waiting for them. The general public learned that they could check *Good Times* to see if they had a message. The listing of people in *Good Times* who had Switchboard messages was beneficial to both entities, and the public. And it would require coordination and regular contact to be effective.

In these issues with the printed names, *Good Times* often just refers to the Haight-Asbury Switchboard as "The Switchboard." It does not do so for other Bay Area switchboards. *Good Times* would often publish the names, addresses and phone numbers of other switchboards, but always identified them with a descriptor, such as Mission Switchboard, or East Bay Musicians Switchboard. Also, *Good Times* never printed the names of people with messages waiting for any switchboard other than the one located at 1830 Fell Street, the Haight-Asbury Switchboard.

During these years, *Good Times* used the names Haight-Asbury Switchboard, the San Francisco Switchboard, The Switchboard, or just Switchboard to refer to the switchboard at 1830 Fell Street.

In issues where the names of people with messages waiting were printed, *Good Times* often ran a paragraph explaining that The Switchboard was located at 1830 Fell St., sometimes not. In the classified ads and messages in *Good Times* in 1969, there are many instances that say to contact so-and-so at *Good Times* or the Switchboard, underline mine. Clearly to the people placing the ads, AND to the people receiving the calls, calling one or the other is of similar effect.

Good Times ran the names of people with messages at the Switchboard in every issue from April 16 until the November 27, 1969, when they missed doing it. Then the names were printed for two more issues before missing another, December 18, 1969. The practice began again in January 1970, but it sputtered out by March. People with messages waiting are printed in the March 19, 1970, issue but not again until three months later in the June 5 issue. The listing mentions that the Haight-Asbury Switchboard was under new management in June 1970, so perhaps *Good Times* was helping them get started, because otherwise the practice of *Good Times* running Haight-Asbury message names was over.

So, while there is no instance that I could find where this switchboard is named in print as the "*Good Times* Switchboard," it is obvious that in 1969 the two entities worked closely together and had a large overlap of people in from April 1969 to March of 1970. It is also reasonable to think that some people would specifically get a copy of *Good Times* in order to see if they had a message at The Switchboard, and could have colloquially called that particular switchboard the "*Good Times* Switchboard."

In addition to these names being printed, *Good Times* issues were sold at the Switchboard. The evidence of overlap and a working relationship between *Good Times* and the Switchboard is confirmed in print, and in full swing during the summer and fall of 1969, when Blue Rock Springs, Lake Berryessa, and Paul Stine murders occurred.

Could Paul Stine and Richard Gaikowski Have Known Each Other?

The short answer is, it's possible.

Those who allege that Richard was the Zodiac conjecture that Richard knew Paul Stine. Some say Richard attended Paul Stine's funeral. I have no information either way about these ideas.

But I have confirmed that Paul Stine did indeed live just two doors away from the Switchboard, on the same side of the street, no more than 30 feet away. It is entirely possible Richard Gaikowski could have met Paul Stine via the Switchboard, and outright dismissals of this possibility are ill-founded.

And there's more.

In the entire time *Good Times* published the names of people with messages waiting at The Switchboard between April 16, 1969, and the spring of 1970, a message for "Paul," with no last name, occurred three times: August 28, September 11, and September 18, 1969. These are all approximately one month before the murder of Paul Stine on October 11, 1969. Of course this is not proof of anything. There certainly would be more than a few Pauls in San Francisco at the time. Mathematically, it is likely someone else. But the possibility exists that it's Paul Stine.

October 22 - The Voice was Not Low Enough

As noted, while the calls to the Oakland police were verified to be authentic, the calls to Melvin Belli on the Jim Dunbar TV Show were hoaxes, identified by three people not to be the correct voice, and ultimately traced in February 1970 to a man calling from an asylum and not Zodiac.

Also note that the three people all said the man on the phone's voice was not low enough. I can confirm that Richard had a low, baritone voice.

7 Seconds of Fame

While the October 22, 1969, calls to the Jim Dunbar show turned out to be a hoax, the media coverage was quite real, with local and national news covering the event, including ABC News, which filmed at the Daly City location later in the day. During that broadcast, in a clip you can find on YouTube if you search for "Zodiac Killer, Real Voice, Police Say Calls Never Traced," a man wanders into frame at 3:20 and for seven seconds walks right at the camera.

I am here to tell you now, it looks very much like Richard Gaikowski, the shape of his head, his hands in his windbreaker, his glasses. It is reasonably close to his height and build as I remember him.

This is yet another funny coincidence. Because most likely, this is NOT Richard. It's just so funny that it looks so much like him. And it really does look like him.

And even funnier, consider the alternative, rational explanation for this: You have to imagine an individual who is crossing the street, presumably unaware there is a news crew filming. This person then sees the ABC News crew, with cameras, lights, and likely a van with large letters saying ABC NEWS on the side. In 1969, the TV lights would be very bright. Despite all this, they still have randomly wandered into frame, then discovering they have done so, THEY THEN decide to walk DIRECTLY towards the reporter and camera for many steps. That's quite a clueless individual.

Or not.

It's funny that all the descriptions one could use for this man, white, average height, 30-40 years old, with horned rimmed glasses could all be applied to Richard, as well as thousands of other people who could have been crossing the street that day, walking straight at the reporter. It is totally explainable that it looks exactly like him. It's also very funny.

Specifically, Regarding the Accusations about Richard

As noted earlier, the source for all accusations against Richard come from an individual known as Blaine, who originally made the claims in 1986, but was only known to the public via the airing of the History Channel's MysteryQuest episode on the matter in 2009.

I have read the vociferous pushback against the accusations. It comes in two forms—from those who knew Richard, and those who didn't.

I completely understand people who knew Richard pushing back against accusations that he is the Zodiac. As one who knew Richard, I get the feelings and disbelief. It is entirely plausible to me how someone could think the accusations are completely untrue and to be angry about it. If not for my memory of Richard's strange anger about Reagan and astrology, I would probably be 100 percent in that camp too. Even so, that memory is not enough to sway me that Blaine is right. I have so many other memories of Richard always being friendly, helpful, a good guy, and could imagine thinking there is no way he was a serial killer.

Richard obviously had a positive effect on a great number of people. Even to today, 20 years after his death, people mark his birthday in social media posts. Many regard the accusations as completely unfounded and impugn the reputation and motives of Blaine and those who believe him. Personally, I cannot fault Richard's friends for coming to his defense.

But some of the other pushback one sees doesn't come from people who knew him, but rather from people who just decided that he is not the perpetrator and have taken to attacking those who think he is. Some of this is over the top and not of sound reasoning. Many have strong opinions based on conjecture or incorrect data. Some have even insinuated that the accusations are entirely made up. Some have tried to claim Blaine wasn't even around *Good Times*, or that *Good Times* and the Switchboard did not work closely together. Again, I believe that people have become tribal about this subject, and that is never a good idea.

Blaine

At the time of this writing, I have never met, nor corresponded with Blaine, nor Tom Voigt, nor anyone else who is a Zodiac researcher. I have had no way to assess Blaine's credibility other than by finding corroborating evidence that either supports or contradicts what he has said. So that's what I endeavored to do.

Blaine Did Write for Good Times

Searches for Blaine in the archives of the underground press, indeed yield bylines for Blaine in *Good Times*, as well as a few in the *Berkeley Tribe*.

Blaine wrote at least 24 articles for *Good Times* over a period from July to December 1969, writing an instalment called CopWatch. His first byline in *Good Times* is July 3, and then his work is in twenty straight issues through October 30. He missed the November 6 issue, before being in the next four, through December 4, 1969. That is the end of Blaine's bylines in *Good Times*.

In six *Good Times* issues, both Blaine and Dick Gaik have bylines. In the July 24, 1969 issue, articles by Blaine and Gaik share the bottom of page 6. Blaine's article is his CopWatch article. Next to it is

Capricorn Reports by D. Gaik, an article about an astrologers' group in Berkeley. Gaik's article mentions that some members are starting to use computers to practice astrology.

It is possible there are more *Good Times* issues that they both worked on, given the frequent use of fake and/or joke names, but these are the only ones confirmed by their established bylines.

There are also some conjecture that Richard was the editor of *Good Times*, and worked on every, or almost every issue, even when he had no byline. I was unable to verify this either way, and it never says as much in the scattered mastheads *Good Times* would occasionally print. Nevertheless, the *Good Times* articles prove Blaine and Richard knew each other, and that they knew each other in 1969.

There are detractors of Blaine, who say they don't remember him at all at *Good Times*.

One of the people who casts doubt Blaine's assertions about Richard uses the defense that they worked for *Good Times* and don't remember Blaine ever working there. But Blaine wrote for *Good Times* from July to December 1969, and this person did not start working at *Good Times* until August 1970, nine months after Blaine left. They can say truthfully say they don't remember Blaine, when in fact, he had been there a year earlier. Someone who only started at *Good Times* in August 1970 would indeed never have met Blaine, and would have little to no relevance on debunking him.

That individual also cast doubt on the description of the Switchboard and Good Times, which we already showed had a regular working relationship in 1969 when Blaine was there, but, by August 1970, there was NOT a close working relationship. So, the individual who arrived in August 1970 would indeed not remember that, but they would not be credibly debunking Blaine.

Blaine also wrote for Berkeley Tribe

A search for Blaine's byline in the *Berkeley Tribe* revealed six results. In 1969, he appears in the September 19, October 3 and 17, and November 19 issues, and in 1970 the January 30, and May 8 issues.

Berkeley Barb, Berkeley Tribe, and Good Times

In the April 1, 1969 issue of *Good Times*, the inaugural issue, the

Berkeley Barb is called "the sister publication" of *Good Times*. But by the summer, the *Barb* split into two, with a group calling itself the Red Tribe breaking off. On July 11, 1969, this group published an issue called "Barb On Strike." A week later they produced Issue 2 under their new name, *The Berkeley Tribe*.

The *Tribe* prints 137 issues from July 1969 until May 1972, and in my opinion seems to be more of the "sister publication" to *Good Times* than the Barb, based on reading the issues of the era. In any case, its relevance here is any overlap between the *Barb* or the *Tribe* with *Good Times*. Blaine is one of a few people who contribute to that overlap.

In October 1971, *Berkeley Tribe* reran a *Good Times* story about Richard getting arrested by draft police. From the printed material of both papers, it is reasonable to say that there was overlap between the *Berkeley Tribe* and *Good Times*.

There are audio recordings online that Blaine claims are of conversations between himself and Richard. I can confirm that the voice on the recordings sounds exactly as I remember Richard's.

The bottom line is this: There are cases when I have confirmed things that Blaine has said, and in no case have I been able to prove something Blaine said is incorrect. But I have NOT confirmed anything Blaine has accused Richard of, not by a longshot.

Richard Gaikowski's Politics

I see in many places Richard described as a radical leftist.

That may be so, but my own opinion is a bit different. Certainly, Richard was left of center, and on many subjects I'm sure people would view him as wildly left wing. But my impression of him was that his politics were much more complex and nuanced. Keep in mind he was a business owner and property owner--the Roxie Theater. Richard also had his film distribution business One Way Films, and as mentioned, his cannabis business.

Richard had also been the Communications Director for The Farmer's Union, FU, in South Dakota. Now the FU is not exactly a left-wing organization, but it is absolutely to the left of Farm Bureau, the largest political organization of farmers. Of course, that's not saying much, as Farm Bureau is very right-wing. My father told how the big split between Farmer's Union and Farm Bureau came over Social Security—which was not available for farmers when it was first initiated. Farmer's Union lobbied hard for farmers to be able to join Social Security, while Farm Bureau opposed it. Farmer's Union eventually won the battle, and farmers joined the Social Security program in 1955.

Despite this left-of-center effort, family farms are the epitome of small business, and such farmers are very independent, holding some firm libertarian ideas mixed in with collective policies like Social Security. And while what I have described might seem to those on the outside as contradictory, it is indicative of the complexities that it is to be a farmer in a technologically advanced country. Farmer's Union was an organization that exemplified these complexities.

Richard was FU's public relations manager back in South Dakota. Not that one adopts the politics of your employer, but that employer did indeed have a leftish slant, all the while holding some beliefs quite right wing, and very right wing compared to hippie sensibilities.

I don't remember Richard spouting radical leftist politics at all. Socially left, absolutely. Interested in art and counterculture, for sure. But also, a business owner. An independent thinker. More of a libertarian than anything.

What I remember more than left wing politics was his ability to sarcastically speak of the extremes of both sides. I remember him talking about the completely impractical aspects of a commune. For example, there is absolutely no way that a commune does not reward the laziest, least-contributing member, and penalize the most-contributing member. It's a mathematical fact. Richard had lived in a commune, now he lived alone. And while he could say this, he hated Nixon, Reagan, and the other stars of the right wing. I remember Richard dishing out sarcastic comments across the political spectrum.

Now Richard did absolutely despise the police. I don't think I ever heard him refer to police as anything other than "pigs" or "the pigs."

What was it about Reagan and Astrology?

Reagan using astrologers was well known when I met Richard in 1993. It was well known WHILE Reagan was President in the 1980s.

By 1993, Bill Clinton was President. Reagan had been out of office for more than five years. The world had known about Reagan, and especially his wife Nancy's use of astrology since Donald Regan's tell-all book in 1987. From there it was in all the news, from legitimate sources to the tabloids.

There is just no rational explanation for one to get angry at another for not believing that astrology was the reason for Reagan's political success. It was bizarre how angry he got. Especially strange because it was so out of character for him. It truly was the only time Richard got angry at me. Something about this specific point set Richard off. Was it mostly about Reagan, or mostly about astrology? Honestly, I think it was more about astrology. What on earth could be the reason?

The Idea Zodiac Stopped Killing after 1969

As we have seen before, in the November 9, 1969, letter Zodiac stated:

"This is the Zodiac speaking up to the end of Oct I have killed 7 people. I have grown rather angry with the police for their telling lies about me. So I shall change the way the collecting of slaves. I shall no longer announce to anyone. When I committ my murders, they shall look like routine robberies, killings of anger, + a few fake accidents, etc."

Up to that point, Zodiac had been completely "truthful" in his communications. I put truthful in quotes because he shouldn't get any credit for being truthful about abhorrent acts, and he is clearly maintaining this entire alternate persona, which is dishonest. But stripped away from moral judgements, we have someone telling us about true events, events that check out with the facts.

So the most reasonable take on this communication is that it is also indeed true. Zodiac is going to keep on killing, but there will be no announcement, and many of the killings will look like other things.

As for what these things look like, Zodiac tells us of some: routine robberies, killings of anger, fake accidents, etc. The "etc" is most interesting, because it opens the door to even more methods. I believe it entirely possible Zodiac disguised some actions by making them look like political protest. Perhaps some were disguised to look like ritual murder. I think it's quite possible Zodiac framed people, perhaps even influenced people to murder. Could "etc" be extended to making a murder look like a suicide?

Zodiac had been, to that point, truthful in his diabolical writings.

Even the 340 code that was held by many to be just gobbledygook has turned out to be a real cipher. So, if we accept that Zodiac is still being truthful, we must realize that there are murders he committed that we are perhaps even unaware of, others that are still unsolved, or some murders that were incorrectly solved.

Zodiac's Handwriting and Quirks

While investigation of Zodiac's handwriting is central to the case, I have rarely seen it noted that he has, at least to these amateur eyes, two distinct penmanship styles.

The most prevalent is a very slanted style, that appears to be written quickly, perhaps at a breakneck speed. The individual letters are not just slanted from the upper right to lower left, sentences tend to slant too. This style appears in many Zodiac communications.

But then there is another style, much more precise, very neat—almost like that of an elementary school student doing their writing lessons. One sees this style in his December 20, 1969, letter to Melvin Belli, and the penmanship on the Halloween card sent to Paul Avery.

Of course, I am not a handwriting expert, and everyone has good and bad days, even the Zodiac. I would like to point out that in the Melvin Belli letter Zodiac refers to "the thing that's in me," implying he has an identity, and the murderer is a separate identity or "thing" inside him. I only speculate that a "thing" might have a different handwriting.

Further support for this kind of idea might be found in the 1974 Exorcist letter. The movie deals with the demonic possession of a child, yet Zodiac refers to it as the greatest satirical comedy of all time. I almost feel this is an admission that he feels he is possessed, by a demon, by something. It would be another instance of Zodiac referring to another entity in his body and person.

These points are just my observation and are only put forward because I haven't seen them discussed much in materials about Zodiac.

I did find one piece of Richard's handwriting that game me pause.

Deaf / Punk

In 1979, Richard made a film called Deaf / Punk, capturing an evening at the San Francisco Deaf Club with a performance by The Offs.

The ending credits are titles written in white chalk or paint or perhaps even Wite-Out on black paper. The credits say "FiLM by RiCHARD GAiKOWSKi." The sequence of upper case and lower-case letters is reproduced as written in the credits.

Now I don't know who wrote the credits, but the most likely person truly is Richard. Assuming he did indeed write out the credits, we must note the similarities to his writing to aspects of Zodiac communications.

Now I'm not a handwriting expert, but two things just jump out at you: the use of the small i in otherwise ALL CAPS words, and the "by," where the tail of the letter sharply hooks to the left under the "b".

Zodiac uses the small y in more or less all of his communications. Even capital Ys in Zodiac letters and codes are just large lower case y characters. He often hooks the tail of that letter to the left. I'm sure this is subjective, but some of Zodiac's y characters look quite a bit like the y used in these movie credits.

But regardless, the most interesting similarity of the DEAF/PUNK movie credits is the ALL CAPS writing with the exception of the letter I, which is written in lower case with its dot. Such a method, all caps, but with the i always in lower case is a prominent feature of the Zodiac's Halloween Card sent to Paul Avery in 1970. On that card, Zodiac writes PARADiCE, By FiRE, and By KИiFE.

The Halloween card also has the y characters with the aforementioned hook, drawn larger than the other letters. Also of note on the Halloween card, the N in KИiFE is backwards. The significance of the backwards И, the lowercase I characters and the other Zodiac penmanship quirks is unknown.

The film credits have three more screens, written here as they appear in the credits: "CAMERA JOEGH BULLOCK", "SOUND/ CAMERA DOUG KiPPiNG ASSIStANCE: CLAUDIA OBAtA", and "DEAF/PUNK".

In the second of these, it is worth noting that the small "i" motif is used twice, but then there are two more instances when it is not. But, on this screen, the t characters are lowercase, and look like crosses. Again, the significance of this is unknown, if any, but it is interesting.

My Pieces of the Puzzle

By now, my review of the Zodiac case had gone on for many months, a year going on two. Not all the time, thankfully, but the review took up enough of my time that it was becoming an annoyance. I decided I had spent enough time going down the rabbit hole.

I had read too many websites, watched too many videos. I had gone through my old scrapbooks and piles of art. I had found Richard's signature in my artist's guest book, but so what?

I had an invite for Alien Dreamtime showing at the Roxie, but this was created by my roommates, not Richard. No licked stamp. No hand-addressed postcard. I had lots and lots of rave invites. Fliers for my art shows, invites from people on SFnet. But nothing from Richard.

I did have the WayBackMachine, that showed that Richard's website and my website linked to one another starting in 1999. I also found some email correspondence between the two of us from the late 1990s that-extended into early 2003. Those are both proof we knew each other, but not evidence of anything other than that. My original idea that I might have something that could be a clue turned up empty.

And while it was true that I saw nothing in the Zodiac case that connected to anything I had, or remembered about Richard, it was clear I did indeed know some things about Richard that were not stated in any website or documentary I could find. These were:

Richard was a Computer Programmer

Richard was a computer programmer, known in the business as a "coder." Now that's just a coincidence, but a strange one indeed. And it shows a certain amount of skill that could be very helpful in the creation of codes. Computer coding is ultimately taking information, data and commands, and "coding" it, turning the initial information into different information. Computer coding would be invaluable in creating the cyphers, and especially the cyphers where there was an additional coincidence in the code: Reserving certain areas for certain symbols, while the computer kept track, able to show options, etc. Honestly, the creation of the cyphers, most notably the complex 340 cipher with its offset letters, would be extremely difficult to create without computers. I found nothing in the Zodiac information on Richard that said he was a computer coder, but can say with complete certainty that he was.

Richard wrote a Tarot Card program on his Amiga.

His computer programming skills were such that he could write a very nice piece of software, and that he used those skills to create software for mystical or perhaps occult purposes. The two tarot card readings also illustrated that Richard was very particular about these esoteric things; I had to keep my question secret, the lack of the software having upside down cards made the reading in Richard's words "useless;" and no other person could be in the same room while he did the reading.

The Man going to Prison

Richard's assistance to someone entering prison was empathetic and teaching a presumably heterosexual man what he might encounter once incarcerated there did seem like a practical thing to do. That said, this item is not your everyday sort of occurrence. How did that man know to find Richard? It was implied that Richard's friend B had brought the man to him. What was the larger story here?

Richard Getting Angry about Reagan and Astrology

And lastly, my strange encounter with Richard, when he got angry about Reagan and astrology, the strange out of character moment that gave me pause and started me on the path of investigation.

The four things I knew are really not that much—just anecdotes, just sort of interesting and odd facts about Richard. It's not like I had a document that proved anything, or any missing link to this story.

Nothing I had been on the lookout had turned up. There was nothing in the story of the Zodiac that spoke of an obsession with Reagan. No time Zodiac talks about Reagan having the best astrologers. No mention of Reagan at all in Zodiac evidence. At least nothing I had found.

There was nothing in the Zodiac information about The Tarot either. I had speculated that tarot references might be something that someone who called themselves The Zodiac would find interesting. Now I know tarot and astrology are separate occult topics, but even so, I thought it would be reasonable to find some references--but there were none. No Death Card, no Fool Card, no Ten of Swords.

There was nothing in Zodiac materials that seemed strangely like the Farmers Union, or Midwest politics. No information, nor anything that jogged a memory, or led to any type of realization.

There was nothing in Zodiac about marijuana or pulverizing it in a coffee grinder.

There was nothing about Zodiac being a computer programmer, and the idea was entirely my speculation.

I do find the GYKE letter sequence in the 408-code is interesting, but if it turned out to be a coincidence I could believe that too. Funny coincidences DO happen.

As for Blaine's accusations against Richard, while I never found an instance where it could be shown Blaine was inaccurate, I also could not corroborate any accusation. I confirmed Blaine did know Richard and did write for *Good Times* in 1969. His audio tapes are indeed of Richard.

All in all, I would totally believe it if it turned out that Blaine had many things wrong, including his main point—that Richard was Zodiac. I can also see why some people would question Blaine's story, the way he presents it is not exactly standard. It would just be too weird for many people.

I do find the vitriol of those dismissing it out of hand, trashing Blaine and those who believe him, really not necessary. The derisive comments from some people towards Blaine and those who have taken his accusations seriously don't do anything other than make the deriders look petty, and ironically it also makes them less credible.

I do understand the anger towards Blaine by those who were friends of Richard. If Richard had never gotten angry at me, over what I believed to be a trivial piece of pop culture history, I would likely be in total agreement with them.

In all of this, I have tried to keep an open mind, and especially regarding Blaine. People who have chosen an alternative lifestyle, people who have taken psychedelic drugs, people who don't fit into the mainstream are no less credible, or more credible, than anyone else. There are honest people and dishonest people in all walks of life, including the counterculture. And of course, no one is totally one or the other. Life is complex, people are complex. The entire story of Zodiac is complex and strange.

Those who voice strong, absolutist opinions on the Zodiac case while perhaps not knowing anything other than what they have read online are really out on a limb. If I knew Blaine, I might be able to have a more definite opinion, but I don't. Blaine and I do share one thing, we both knew Richard. As an individual who knew Richard, who knew him in 1969 and for many years after, Blaine's accounts would have value, some value—and certainly more value than countless modern-day critics.

But here is the bottom line: I came to the same conclusion that apparently the law enforcement community has come to as well, that Blaine's accusations have not met the standard to have Richard be named as a suspect. I can say that without deriding those who disagree and think he is the perpetrator.

The End of the Road

As for my memories about Richard, while it may be interesting background information, that is all it is.

The thing about the only time Richard got angry at me, is that the incident can easily be explained without meaning anything else. I can guess that the number of people in California who are very into astrology and who lived either under the governorship of Reagan in California or the presidency of Reagan in the United States is quite large. There would be hundreds of people, if not thousands, in the Bay Area alone who believed Reagan's success was explained by astrology.

My memory of an old hippie getting angry and demanding that Reagan's success was because he had the best astrologers is really not that big of a deal. It is of passing relevance due to the other accusations, but that's it. My contribution to this mystery would be somewhere between minuscule and zero.

Nevertheless, my information was, at minimum, not in the public. Who knew if the police had it? Who knew if there was something that the police did think was interesting? The possibility did exist that something I knew might provide a clue that they were looking for.

Reflecting upon this matter, one comes to the realization that the victims deserve all efforts to solve the crimes against them. It often feels that this point gets lost in all of this. The truth was that I did have information about an individual being accused, and I had no way of knowing what the police might find relevant.

So, in that spirit, I sent an anonymous letter to the San Francisco Police with the things I knew about Richard. In July 2018, I mailed the letter from a non-descript mailbox in suburban Kansas City while on a cross-country road trip, so it would be even more anonymous and more untraceable.

And so ended my Zodiac research.

"You are responsible for your short-term coincidences, to eat, to not get hit by a bus, or avoid certain people. The Universe is in charge of your long-term coincidences, who you meet, where you go, what you are shown."

– John C. Lilly, 1996

ACT III ===
ONE F OF A COINCIDENCE ======

I met Dr. John Lilly for the first time in 1996, in the midst of a decade of traveling, both physically and mentally, that often brought me to San Francisco. I was selected to make his website, and to do so I would go and live in his home on Maui. The previous quote is something he told me one of the first times we hung out. John relayed his ideas about "Earth Coincidence Control Office" to me, and also explained how the entirety of Western Science was still encumbered by religious dogma, and said the so-called "Scientific Observer" was just a secular version of the Judeo-Christian "soul," and as such was a spurious, untested assumption.

Honestly, what John was saying was a bit more metaphysical than I was at the time, I was more interested in his scientific discoveries and interspecies communication with dolphins and whales. I was more of an atheist/reductionist then.

But now as an older, wiser individual, I've come to have a similar set of opinions. Western science is still encumbered by religious dogma, the Scientific Observer is indeed a problematic concept, and more to the point for this book, coincidences DO exist. And they are so multi-layered, intertwined, often incredibly and outrageously funny, it does seem like "the Universe" or "the Fates" or some kind of Earth Coincidence Control Office has set them up.

Such is the next part of this tale.

The Plague

By 2020, Kate and I had left Indiana and were now living on the East Coast. After my parents passed away, it became clear that I was no farmer, and that rural Indiana was sub-optimal, so we moved back east, where you could live rural, but have things like trash pickup and solar panels. We would also be just a short drive to NYC. We had an idea to restart our art and counterculture lives. Something like that.

That plan was coming along nicely, looking up New York and Japan and California contacts. I started to do art under the name Bigtwin again, only this time as James Bigtwin. We reconnected with many old friends.

Our long period in the wilderness was seemingly ending when the fateful year of 2020 came along. Covid hit in early March and so the lockdowns began. Like many people, we had some time on our hands. We decided to turn the days of plague into something productive.

One thing I had been lax about over the years was documentation of my art, 30 years of materials and projects—a lot of that stuff from Act I-- including working with John Lilly and dolphins, paintings, virtual reality work with Jaron Lanier and the Montreux Jazz Festival, and then with broadcast television, ABC and ESPN, designing Joe Camel billboards and ads, and being the basis of a cartoon character on the cult series Mission Hill. Then there was the TechnoRomantics, parties and raves, mandala programming, virtual set sketch comedy, Burning Man, Disorient, Japan, Dr. Demento…paintings, programming, parties, 3D modelling, video and music… a lot to document, files to organize. I also looked up my beloved *Stanford Chaparral*.

Hammer & Coffin Zoom Banquet 1

One morning in April 2020, I woke up to an email, the annual Hammer & Coffin banquet was cancelled due to covid. I was on a large group email known as the Old Farts, Hammer & Coffin members who have graduated, but I don't think I ever responded to one, perhaps not even looking at them. I had not been to a Hammer & Coffin Banquet since 2006, and basically had not participated in anything since then.

But I had just begun to Zoom, perhaps that week, and wondered why we weren't doing anything like that. I sent an email to the group. As I would grow to learn over this saga, the usual response to an email of the Old Farts list is crickets. A couple days went by and there was

THE ONLY TIME RICHARD GOT ANGRY AT ME

no response, so I just did it. I got a Zoom professional account and I set up a call on my own. I sent out email invites, prepared some funny green screen backgrounds for myself, and on a Saturday night in late April 2020, held the first Hammer & Coffin Zoom Banquet. The event was a hit.

The zoom was attended by perhaps 30 people, with many regrets sent by those who could not make it, so much so that I held a second one a week later. The second one was smaller, but still well attended, and with many new people who were not in the first one. Reconnecting with so many people from the past, with lots of funny stories, memories, and the incredibly funny digs and insults that Chappies exchange, was the spark that led to my reconsideration of the *Chaparral*, and its alumni association, the Hammer & Coffin Society.

I started looking myself up in the *Stanford Daily* archives, for evidence of my past pranks and hi-jinks. One year I was also a columnist for the Daily. It was a good exercise in discovering that I'm a mediocre writer at best, but I did pen Anarchism Fosters Intellectualism,[99] an idea that too much control stifles creative thinking—an idea society is in even a more dire need of than it was in the 1980s. There were stories of when I was part of a group of Chappies who ran for student body president. Don't laugh, *Chaparral* slates had won twice before, including the group directly preceding ours.

To my disappointment, the *Chaparral* itself didn't have much in the way of archives. There were websites, but they had not been updated in many years; there were some *Chaparral* covers uploaded, but at very low resolution, and many of them were mislabeled. Not that I had a right to complain, I certainly had not done anything nor helped anyone else. I had been incommunicado with the Chaparral and Hammer & Coffin since 2006.

And with the anemic action on the Old Farts email list, it seemed there was not much interest in getting *Chaparral* stuff organized online. I spent the most of 2020 lockdown focusing on my own archives, my art and career.

December 2020 – The 340 Code Cracked

In December 2020, I saw in the news that the Zodiac's 340 code had been cracked. Of course I was interested and read a few articles about it. The team of David Oranchak, Sam Blake, and Jarl Van Eycke had done it, more than 50 years after the code was created in 1969[100]. It had been cracked using computers running over 600,000 simulations, ultimately discovering that the letters were not just substituted, but then run in a pattern that offset the letters across the entire code. The offset was that of two over and one down, the knight's move in chess. The chess move was used on two blocks of nine lines each, comprising the first 18 lines of the code. The final two lines of the code also used the knight's move, but alternated down then up, producing a braided effect. You can find more information about how they did it as well as color-coded diagrams of their solution method online.[101]

The hopes that cracking this code would reveal the killer's identity, or provide a big clue, were dashed when the ciphered solution just yielded more of Zodiac's boilerplate language. A message similar to his other letters, nothing unique or of interest. It did seem that the Zodiac was just regurgitating old material. That said, the formation of the code itself did interest me.

"Man, that coding looks computer generated," I thought. "Machine precision." My conjecture that Zodiac could have been into computers was enhanced. I also noted, as did many, the chess move in the methodology.

I wondered if Richard played chess. Some months later I indeed found a picture of Richard playing chess--against members of the Black Panthers!

But despite reading these articles, I wasn't returning to Zodiac research, I was entering the sarcastic phase of my Zodiac journey. A joke here, an oblique reference there. It was like joking about being hit by lightning or winning the lottery. It's never going to happen, so a joke is especially in order. A deadpan line about a serial murder, farcical lines about writing things in code, or even a bloody handprint, just became part of my often-dark sense of humor.

Hammer & Coffin Zoom Banquet 2

By April 2021, Covid was still raging, and it appeared that once again there would be no Hammer & Coffin Banquet. I waited to see if "The Management" was going to hold a Zoom call, but no invitation came. So eventually I just went ahead, sent out invites, and held the second Hammer & Coffin Zoom Banquet.

By this time, the advertising/branding guy in me had figured out that 2024 would be the 125th Anniversary of the *Chaparral*, which had been founded in 1899. Classic (re)branding of an old idea is what we had done at Camel—what so many olde-time companies need to do, and an anniversary is the perfect time to do it. I had experience with planning anniversaries, including the 200th birthday of my hometown in Indiana, which went so well that I was recruited by the neighboring town for their 200th. I had also handled the 60th, 100th, 120th and 160th anniversaries of various advertising clients—banks, hospitals, restaurant chains. Anniversaries are not just great ways to revitalize a brand, they are great excuses for having a party. And for organizations and non-profits, it is like shooting fish in a barrel for doing a fundraiser.

So, at that April 2021 Hammer & Coffin Banquet Zoom, I announced I would be holding monthly zoom calls, the first Wednesday of every month. I invited everyone to come, but especially the next one, May 2021, where I would lay out my ideas for what became to be known to me as the 125 Project, and the creation of a large, heavy, *Stanford Chaparral* history book.

The Stanford Chaparral Magnum Opus

During the May 2021 Zoom call, I outlined plans for a 125th anniversary of the *Chaparral*, with an event in October 2024, the creation of a digital archive of all *Chaparral* issues and other ephemera including photos, articles, fliers and news articles, and the creation of a big, coffee table book, a huge, super-tome of biblical weight, hundreds of pages, with an embossed cover, gold ink, and a satiny ribbon for a bookmark. I envisioned alums from each era writing up stories about their time at the *Chaparral*, supplementing the vast amount of raw material he had from Chappie issues.

The idea was received enthusiastically by some, and quite a few people said they would contribute. There was also a fair amount of skepticism, anywhere from "It will never happen," to "print is dead, no one will want a big tree-killing book." I ignored the naysayers and proceeded on the idea. Of course, many people remarked, "2024? That's so far in the future…." But I knew better. I gave the group one year, until June of 2022, to submit articles and ideas for the 125 Book.

I began the process of finding *Chaparral* issues. I possessed about twenty that I had kept in boxes since leaving school in 1988, and a smattering of issues I had from going to banquets after graduation. I started scanning issue covers and started to receive covers scanned by other Old Farts. Between all our efforts, searching old boxes and attics, and more *Chaparrals* I found online, we soon had a couple hundred issue covers.

I had plenty of space in my Dropbox directory, so I made a new folder and started to upload anything and all *Chaparral* and Hammer & Coffin. The issues, art, news stories, ads, funny anecdotes, bios of famous Chappies, and accounts of the many pranks.

I searched online for issues being sold through eBay, Etsy, Amazon, bookstores and collectible sites.

Eventually I had to make a spreadsheet to keep track of the issues, as it appeared there would be 500 or more. Also, with a spreadsheet, it would be easier to track missing issues and finally get an accurate estimate of how many *Chaparral* issues existed. At the request of a current *Chaparral* staff member, the Stanford Library scanned the covers of many of the early issues. We also got help from the State of California libraries, and the Library of Congress in DC. We searched the internet for all manner of *Chaparral* tie-ins and discovered people who worked for the *Chaparral* that we didn't even know about.

The process was consuming more and more of my time, but it was fascinating. So much good art.

It became clear there were many more issues than we thought, perhaps seven or eight hundred. Out of necessity we just focused on scanning the covers because scanning the entirety of each issue would be a MONUMENTAL task. Besides, getting the cover allowed for the issue, or "Number," as it was called in Olden Times to be documented and put into the spreadsheet.

Of course, I set up spaces on the spreadsheet for issues from 1899 to the present, but had vast areas of unknown sections, including the era 1969 to 1974, known to us as the "political era," when the *Chaparral* was a newspaper printed in tabloid format. Some of the old guys were still upset about this era of the *Chaparral* and were still grinding an axe about it in the 2020s. I didn't really know much about it, and with hundreds of issues to find, I placed 1969-1974 issues as a low priority.

Monthly zoom calls continued through the summer and fall and into 2022. As time went on, our discussions veered away from our book project and more into memories of our time working on the magazine.

Loose Lips Sink Ships

By 2021, *Chaparral* alums and the not-so-secret Hammer & Coffin society, or at least our "non-representative alums" were having monthly zoom meetings that I hosted. All manner of topics were brought up. Keeping the focus on the task at hand was often difficult. One night I blabbed about the Bear prank.

After graduating Stanford, I had never divulged the Berkeley Bear prank to anyone, except my wife. I never told my friends or parents or the rest of my family. By 2020, I had reconnected with DL, who by chance, knew of the heist the night it happened. He knew of it because we had thought that we needed a fourth person on the caper, someone to stay with the car all the time, so we called X, who refused to join us. DL was with X during the call, so there were five people who knew about the prank as it happened.

I asked DL if I should remain quiet, or if I should tell people about the Bear heist.

"It's been over 30 years, you should tell people," said DL.

So, one evening on a Zoom call in late 2021, I revealed the story of the Berkeley Bear prank to the group of Chappies attending. People were fairly amazed, almost overjoyed at the story. One very respected alum was very excited about the story and advised me to contact *Stanford Magazine* or the newspapers. They were very insistent, but I had to tell them I was not interested in that.

At the next month's Zoom call, this same alum brought up the suggestion again. I again said I was not interested. Then they said words to the effect "Well someone should do it," which set off a red light in my head. The implication that "someone" WAS going to do it and seemed a passive admission that they were thinking of doing it. I was fairly certain that they intended to do it.

I had to think fast. Had I blown it by speaking about this prank? They say loose lips sink ships, and I tend to believe that saying. Were the others not going to honor my wishes after I had let them in on it?

It seemed like this was where it was going, so I made up something, quick and on the spot.

"Look," I said. "You can't tell *Stanford Magazine* because… the Bear prank is actually not completed. There is still one key part of it yet to be played. We need total secrecy."

"Really? Oh wow. What are you going to do?" they replied.

"Sorry, I can't tell you. But rest assured we are planning something that will be a big joke on Cal, while we reveal the Chappie's role in doing it."

Luckily, this was accepted by the person, and the threat of their writing to *Stanford Magazine* with this scoop about the bear was averted.

But one should take care at what one jokes about, because jokes often have a way of coming true. Especially if you help them.

Through the course of planning a *Chaparral* history book, the idea of an encyclopedia became less and less attractive. A comic book or story book would be much better. We should be less documenting what went on in the past, and more telling a story making new and living thing in the present. Pranks were a big part of the *Chaparral* history.

Upon reflection of my quick excuse, the idea that the bear prank wasn't finished yet became more and more real in my mind. Maybe the bear prank indeed WASN'T over.

I pondered what steps I could take to add to the 35-year-old Bear prank. Finally, an idea came to me that in retrospect was really a bad idea. Keep in mind that in 2021 I had no idea what the future would hold. I was just trying to make a joke. And now I am forced to confess what I did, so I can tell the entirety of this story truthfully. So here it is.

How to Make a Zodiac Code

It is so important that I must say it again: In retrospect, what I decided to do to continue the bear prank sounds like a really bad idea, but who would believe the path this story would take? It was January 2022, I had no reason to think I would actually find Zodiac-Stanford coincidences. It was just a gag.

This gag is the beginning of what I call "My Dilemma," a concept I will expand on later.

To complete the bear prank, I decided to make a code, like the famous 408-code in three parts. In it I would confess to the bear prank, maybe even make some Richard references too, but it would be primarily to confess to the bear. I would create the codes, and prepare envelopes—three copies sent to the *San Francisco Chronicle*, the *San Francisco Examiner*, and maybe the president of Berkeley? That sounds about right.

I did not intend to send them for several more years, thinking I might leave the codes as instructions in my will--because this idea was too crazy to do while I was alive. At minimum I would have to be much older before mailing these. Or I could get a set to DL, and if something happened to me the codes would be mailed, and the mystery of who liberated Oskie from the Berkeley Union in 1986 would be answered, via a parody Zodiac code.

It seemed funny at the time.

I started out in earnest. I downloaded a copy of the 408-code. As we know, part three of this code is where the sequence "GYKE" is found.

I decided that the first two parts of the code would be confession of the bear prank, and the last third, the "GYKE" part, would be where I told what I knew about Richard.

In the "GYKE" position, my code would say OSKI or BEAR. Or maybe OSKI could cipher to BEAR. (I decided to use Cal's spelling "OSKI" instead of our spelling "OSKIE" since it was four letters.)

I formatted the downloaded code on some 11 x 17 paper, lightening it so I could write on the paper, and printed out a couple of copies of it. Remember, I'm a graphic designer, I have a large format printer and lots of graphics software and hardware. I also made some letter charts, A-Z with boxes to write my symbols in.

Not too far into the process, I realized that making a message cipher, with other coincidences you wanted to have happen, like making "OSKI" appear in the right place, was difficult, more difficult than I assumed. Just the presumably simple task of writing a message that was the correct length took a few tries. I was getting nowhere fast.

I decided to stop what I was doing with paper and pencil and got on the computer instead. I started to code a little app written in the programming language PHP that could do what I needed.

Through the use of my custom-written Zodiac code maker, I was able to not only land the word BEAR at the same location as GYKE in part three, I was also able to put OSKI in the same location in part two of the code, and HAND in part one. You may not understand the significance of HAND, but the next letter, in the fifth position, I made a C, making HANDC, as in Hammer & Coffin.

With the code completed, I wondered if I could take the code even further. I thought about how Zodiac had some letters backwards, some symbols other than letters, things like that. I decided to make some of the symbols in my cipher outlined, white letters with a black outline. I counted up and I found I had enough letters to spell "STANFORD-CHAPARRAL". Not in order of course, just the letters that would anagram to it.

The Zodiac Code I made was a clever piece of work. It would have been a great prank and a funny way to confess to the Berkeley bear caper, sometime in the future, near or after my death. But this book and the other things I have discovered superseded it.

The prank got as far as me making the code, printing out the copies, preparing the envelopes and addresses, to the *Chronicle*, the *Examiner* and the President of UC Berkeley, and a set for DL with the solution. Given what I was to discover in the two years that followed, I am VERY happy those letters were never sent out. I only confess to this now because of the need for a complete, and I do mean complete, Mea Culpa about "My Dilemma," the creation of fake *Chaparral* issues, fake Zodiac-style codes, and any and all joking I did about Zodiac during the months leading up to February 2023.

But in 2021, Zodiac had indeed become a joke to me, a piece of pop culture. Meanwhile, the rest of this story unfolded.

A Long, Tough Slog

Isn't that how Donald Rumsfeld described Iraq? What a fucking disaster. Well anyway, it could be a description of the *Chaparral* 125 Project. Not the disaster part, the slog.

As I said earlier, the *Chaparral* had a small online presence in 2020. Whereas I could search vast archives of our rival, the *Stanford Daily*, we only had a couple dozen issue covers, very low resolution, often mislabeled, and only some recent issues online. The vast history of the *Chaparral*, covering more than a century and hundreds of issues, was nowhere to be found.

I had never done anything towards making an archive, so I had no right to complain. But I was now going to help fix this as best I could. Had anyone ever looked into the entire history of the magazine? Perhaps an illustrious Chappie from the class of 1955 had done so in the fifties. It was high time to do so again, scan, research, write a history, and to make a large online archive available to the public.

This Chappie begrudgingly admits the *Stanford Daily* archives are really great. Its search capabilities are very good, and one can find any number of things filtered by time and keywords. Of course, a lot of items relevant to the entire university were found. Reading the old issues in our possession was even more interesting when compared to the press stories of the day. From around WWI to the sixties, there was almost certainly a *Daily* article about each *Chaparral* issue, and stories about new editors or other relevant news. *Chaparral* meetings were announced in the Once Around the Quad calendar section. And of course, stories of the scandals of the day, editors being suspended, administrators and community members offended.

From these *Daily* articles about the *Chaparral*, one could piece together many eras where there were had missing issues, often learning the title of the issue and its date.

The spreadsheet was getting filled in, and with much real data and a few estimated years, it looked like there would be around 800 total *Chaparral* issues.

As a practical matter, I had focused on the humor years of the *Chaparral*, 1899 to 1969, and 1974 to the present, and not covered the political era of 1969 -1971.

During my time as a student in the late eighties, the *Chaparral*'s political era was treated like it didn't exist. We had issue covers on the walls of the Chappie Office, but only the comedy years. The 1960s issue covers progress from somewhat normal to Layboy2, the first college publication in history to feature a topless centerfold, followed by the first with a nude centerfold and a full on psychedelic LSD rock and roll poster style cover with the Jester as a buddha, then a year as staid literary magazine, and then… NOTHING.

The covers on the walls in the square inner-office of the *Chaparral* stop. They trail off about half-way across and the rest of the wall is blank. The vast unknown. The wall, like the years it represents, were a mystery.

Then in the far-left corner of the next wall is an issue from 1974-75 school year, and the issues begin again. By the late 1980s, we had mostly completed that wall and the next, reaching the floor-to ceiling windows on the fourth wall. The years of 1969-1974 were unknown by us, and even yearbooks were no help. The *Chaparral* kept copies of the Stanford Quad yearbooks, but one wasn't produced in 1972 or 73. The 1971 yearbook was a hoot though. Lots of pictures of hippies, and...

JW showed me something he had found in the 1971 yearbook. In the senior photos was a picture of a guy in an embrace with a girl. His name was Paul Sigourney, and his hometown was "Havoc," and the girl was a dead ringer for Sigourney Weaver![102] "She went here," said JW. "She's the niece of Doodles Weaver." Now I hadn't heard of Doodles Weaver at that time, but it turned out he was one of the most famous Chappies of all time. Stanford class of 1937, the right-hand maniac of Spike Jones. He briefly had his own show in the early days of television. Sigourney Weaver would have indeed been on campus, so it could really be her in the picture. I've never found out for sure.

The months ticked on, and 2021 became 2022. By summer, all but 30 out of an estimated 850 comic *Chaparral* issues had been added to the directory. As for the political era, I only had one, the infamous ROTC issue.

Searching for the *Chaparral*, year by year, in the *Daily's* archives, I finally arrived at 1969. Boy what a difference a few years makes.

That's Not My Issue

I had started work on the *Chaparral* archive and 125th book on my own. No one asked me to do anything. I started having monthly Chappie zoom calls because I became enamored with the idea of video conferencing, virtual conferencing, and how it could revitalize the H & C. I started assembling *Chaparral* covers and issues online of my own volition, so, I had no right to be upset at anyone for not helping, helping not very much, or just ignoring the entire effort.

As the hundreds covers were assembled, and the task changed to the much more difficult process of scanning entire issues, and as the responses to the posting of said issues became less and less, I began to wonder if anyone was enjoying the issues we had put online, or had even read the issues.

"I bet I could make a fake issue, and no one would even notice," I thought to myself.

"But that would be unethical," I replied.

So, I soldiered on. And besides, there WERE some people helping. My God, PC was a researching, article-writing animal.

Even so, the paltry participation from so many was depressing. How many years would it take me to scan every issue? The answer? Many. Plus, some issues were really faded, while others looked brand new. Some were on glossy paper, and some issues weren't printed very well in the first place. I bought a new, oversize format scanner and played with the settings for a few days, trying to find the magic bullet, a setting I could just brainlessly, QUICKLY, use, which it turned out did not exist. Each issue, and often each page, needed its own separate adjustment. So, I decided to just scan, and not color correct; it was the only way we could get 100 issues scanned, let alone 800.

Then one day I uploaded some issues, and someone did respond. I was happy to see that X responded to my email. But then I read it. He was complaining about the quality of the scans.

And so the Duck Number was born.

The Duck number was constructed from a cartoon of Mutherfucker Goose, flipping us all off, and while it had been drawn for the Chappie in 1986, looked amazingly old school. When combined with some fading and scratches, it reasonably passed for a 1920s cover. I added and old-timey *Chaparral* logo, and the title Duck Number on the artwork, and uploaded it.

No one responded.

And so I modified the Duck Number and replaced the issue name with "Hey Al X!" and re-uploaded it into the directory.

I made other fake covers, a jester in a classic Black Death plague mask, one with pointy nose that complimented the Jester's tri-point hat very well for the Plague Number. I made a 1912-looking Gaseous Discharge Number, in honor of our long history, as noted by the Harvard Lampoon, of making fart jokes. I changed the famous Harry Truman photo of him holding a newspaper saying "Dewey Beats Truman" into a one saying "Winbigler Suspends Chaparral" for a 1951 fake issue. I made a 1970 Nude Hippies issue in the newsprint format of that era, and I used a photo of Oskie from our bear heist and put it into a 1940s style issue titled "Smarter than the Average Bear." (I go into all of this in much greater detail in the Mea Culpa section later in this book.)

I realized that you could really tell people almost anything, even things about themselves, and they would likely buy it. People were not readily able to recognize these fakes, even from their own years.

This is not to say that real work on the project stopped. Far from it. Fake issues were just my hobby, my little prank to my classmates. The collection of covers was growing, I now estimated the total number of *Chaparral* issues would be in the 800s.

In April of 2022, Kate and I went to the Library of Congress in Washington, to find and photograph a large number of missing issues.

The missing comic issues tended to cluster in a few years, one gap in the 1990s, and a couple of gaps in the 21st century. You'd think that we would be missing issues a century old, but it was this relatively recent history that was wrong, or misnumbered, causing the gaps.

Previously I had tried encouragement, sweet talking, funny pictures, funny videos, limericks, and any and many other methods to try to get people to find and scan the issues of their time at school. Group emails, individual emails, direct calls, whatever. But half of love is 'tough love,' and now it was time for that.

I sent out an email, praising the effort to get some 800+ issue covers, and noted that there were only a few "eras of lameness" that still had not gotten their issues into the database.

That finally got some action.

Within a few days, some of the missing issues were sent. It turned out that some of those issues were actually not missing, they were just misnumbered and in the wrong place in the directory. I don't mean the files were misnumbered when archiving, the issues themselves had the wrong dates on them. This is not a dis on any particular era of lameness, there are misnumbered issues throughout the history of the *Chaparral*.

In addition to receiving some truly missing issues, the 1990s Chappies also sent some obviously fake issue covers. One of them was even a cartoon of me. Finally! The organization had a pulse!

I considered my options.

In the *Chaparral* digital directory we were building, there was a folder for Chappie office photos. The majority of photos were of the office in the Storke Building, where the *Chaparral* lived 1965 to 2009. In the center office room, we would put up the covers of issues, making quite a historical record. In the main room of the office, there were shelves of issues, hundreds of them, in stacks or in bound volumes. I took the fake covers sent to me and Photoshopped them into the office photos. I uploaded the doctored office photos into the directory and told no one.

At a subsequent zoom meeting, a particularly innocent Chappie brought up that he believed the 90s guys had sent fake issues.

"I know, I thought that too. I mean, look how crappy they are." I replied, "but I was looking at some old office photos, and look: THERE THEY ARE ON THE WALL." I showed the doctored office photos and they were completely accepted as real. We spent some time theorizing that in the early 90s, computer graphics were still pretty rudimentary, and that is likely why the covers looked so shitty. Luckily, none of the 1990s guys responsible for the fake issues were on the zoom call, and the meeting went on normally.

Busted

As Halloween 2022 approached, no one had yet publicly pointed out my fake issues in the directory. It was unclear to me how many people were even paying attention. It was sort of pissing me off.

So I decided to try my most brazen forgery yet. My most sarcastic. And in retrospect, my most ill-advised fake *Chaparral* cover. I took the infamous Zodiac Halloween card sent to Paul Avery and worked it up into a fake 1918 *Chaparral* cover, which I attached digitally to the interior pages of another old issue. I uploaded this fake issue, along with some real ones, sent out the email and waited.

After a few days, I was finally contacted by a former editor, BH, who pointed out that I had posted a fake cover.

"Finally, someone with some brains in this organization. H&C has a pulse," I replied.

"I don't know about that," wrote BH in reply. "I just know about Zodiac. My whole family are aficionados of the case. I'm the only one in my family that has NOT visited Lake Berryessa."

I replied with a joke, "I'm using my *Chaparral* research to mask my Zodiac research."

I'm not sure how they interpreted what I said, but I understand the strangeness of such a statement. At the time, it truly was a joke. But as I was about to find out, the joke was on me.

Researching the Hippie Era

I was born in 1965. Not what is derogatorily called today a Boomer, I'm a Gen-Xer. Not that I care, but I always looked upon the hippies as separate. I remember making hippie jokes as a kid.

One time I rewrote the story of Jesus and the disciples to be a Ken Kesey-esque story on the back of a Methodist church bulletin. I'm sure I didn't even know who Ken Kesey was, but I knew about hippies, and hippie busses, going on the road. Jesus and the apostles had long hair and sandals too, and they were traveling around. It was perfect to make a parody hippie story, with Mark from Detroit, Luke from Oregon, another wild guy Slack Dog, and Jesus providing free food at Woodstock. Most Sundays I made paper airplanes out of them, but this one was a funny story. I was proud of it. My mother saw what I had done, reached out, and crumpled it with a single hand, never to be seen again.

Right up through college, when I decided to sorta "drop out" myself, in a much lamer, 1980s sorta way, I always wondered what it would have been like to be born a decade or two earlier, a hippie, a radical. Being 22 in 1968 would have been a lot different than my experience in 1988.

The funny thing about researching the hippie era is there are indeed a ton of underground newspapers in addition to straight newspapers, to use the lingo of the day. But woe to you if you are looking in the underground papers for a masthead, a staff box containing the names of everyone working on the paper. You are very often SOL.

Even the usually reliable school yearbooks, which had faithfully documented campus life for 70 plus years, now became a place for experimental acid art, or just ceased to exist at all. The *Stanford Quad*, which had provided key, well-organized information for the *Chaparral* history project, now spun into uncharted territory, producing one final book in 1971, the issue JW had shown me with Sigourney Weaver, with tantalizing storylines and clues as well as off beat pop culture, before succumbing to the times, and no funds, ceasing publication during a critical era in our historical endeavor. There was no Stanford *Quad* in 1972 and 73.

As I described before, we hadn't focused on the *Chaparral* years 1969-1974, but now it was time. In the late summer of 2022, we asked the Stanford Library to help us out again and scan the covers of that era. As usual they were very helpful. We asked how many 69-74 issues they had, and they reported that they had a complete set, every single issue without gap, 44 issues in total.

I had no idea there were so many issues from these years. It turned out that during the political era, students had printed a lot of issues, seven in 1969-70, three in 70-71, seventeen in both 71-72, and 72-73, and four in 73-74. This pushed the total number of *Chaparral* issues printed to over 900! The library said they would need a few weeks to scan them all, and then would send PDF files. I became excited to commence research on this unique era in *Chaparral* history.

Stanford Macabre

In olden times, it seemed like so many movies, horror, sci-fi, comedy used the plotline of something being on an 'Indian burial ground.' By 2022, I was beginning to wonder if it was true for Stanford, realizing the probability that at least one Native American buried somewhere on the property was quite high. I had spent hours researching, collecting articles about *Chaparral*, and of course reading much about the news of the day on a wide range of topics, coincidentally including murder.

I learned for example, that a *Chaparral* editor in the 1920s, David Lamson, was accused in the 1930s of murdering his wife Arlene, up in the "faculty ghetto," which are actually really nice homes up in the hills where many Stanford professors live[103]. It was a huge scandal resulting in multiple trials; an initial conviction overturned on appeal, then multiple hung juries[104]. I had never heard of this incident before.

I also learned of the theory that Jane Stanford herself was murdered in 1905 in Hawaii[105]. Frankly, it was a pretty bizarre thing to learn in the context of all this.

"Who's writing this stuff," I said to myself jokingly.

I wasn't considering either of these stories for the *Chaparral* anniversary book. In fact, given my past doing Zodiac research, I was not interested at all in such subjects for the 125th anniversary book. There were plenty of quirky factoids and stories to tell without getting anywhere near murder, despite the *Chaparral*'s love of making death jokes. And now here I was, with all this Zodiac sarcasm, working on the anniversary project. I told PC I did not want to cover the Lamson murder in the Chappie 125 book, perhaps sarcastic references to it, but no article.

But, even though I didn't want to put murder in the book, as it would be, murder came up as a subject all on its own.

One evening during one of the monthly Hammer & Coffin zoom calls, someone brought up the murders on the Stanford campus in the early 1970s. Somehow I had never heard of these; not when I went to school there in the 1980s, nor in the time since. I had even somehow missed seeing any mention of them while doing my recent research. I know that's hard to believe, but it is indicative of my sensibilities prior to this story, I was not a true crime fan. And as I've said, the era of the Chappie's history I had paid almost no attention to was 1969 to 1974. So perhaps it made sense I had not heard of these murders. Regardless, I heard about them during this zoom call. It was all a strange and creepy surprise. Four murders in the early 1970s at Stanford? Wow.

They all occurred quite close to each other, both in location and timeline, between February 1973 and October 1974. Two bodies were found up in the foothills, Leslie Perlov and Janet Taylor; there was the "ritual murder" of Arlis Perry in Memorial Church, and there was a physics student murdered near Meyer Library, David Levine.

I listened to the discussion of the people on the zoom call.

"I don't believe this." I thought to myself.

The good news, according to the people on the Zoom call, was that all the murders had been solved in recent years. Modern DNA techniques had produced the evidence to find the killers. While listening to the gory details, I was relieved that they were all solved and none of them needed to enter my head regarding anything Zodiac.

It was too good to be true.

As it would happen, before the end of the call, someone must have been googling, we found out that all the murders had NOT been solved; only three out of four were. The fourth was still a cold case, the knife attack on the physics student David Levine near Meyer Library. A knife attack with a blade of eight to ten inches.

"Wow! Who knew?" I joked that this sounded a lot like Zodiac.

Then it was my turn to get on google. While the Zoom call was still going on, I brought up Google, But I didn't search for David Levine, I typed in "Lake Berryessa," because I wasn't sure, but that sounded a lot like the weapon used in that attack. And there it was. The weapon used in Zodiac's Lake Berryessa attack was indeed approximately a 10-inch knife.

I got the same eerie feeling I got the first time I remembered the Reagan astrology argument with Richard. Wisps of the eerie Close Encounters music played in the background. My mind started to wonder. Could politics or protesting have brought Richard to Stanford? Is there any possible way he might have crossed paths with David Levine?

The 1970s Stanford Murders, Solved

When people talk about the Stanford Murders they mean the four that occurred in 1973-74: Leslie Perlov, David Levine, Janet Taylor, and Arlis Perry.

Investigators have declared three of these murders solved. Cold cases for over 40 years, the murders of Leslie Perlov and Arlis Perry were solved in 2018, and that of Janet Taylor in 2019.

Leslie Perlov, February 13, 1973

Leslie Perlov was found on February 16, 1973, in the foothills, at the entrance of a quarry off Old Page Mill Road, sexually assaulted and strangled with a scarf.[106]

She had gone missing on Tuesday February 13, and a search for her began on Wednesday February 14, in and around the quarry where she was believed to be. The next day, February 15, they found the body of Mark Rosvald, age 25, of Barron Park, a neighborhood in Palo Alto. He died from a gunshot wound to the chest, with the shotgun held by one hand. The death of Mark Rosvald was ruled a suicide.

The first press accounts of Perlov's murder state that investigators suspected she had also been sexually assaulted, but by February 21 the Peninsula Times Tribune reported that there had been no sexual attack. Across the subsequent 40+ years after the murder, press accounts vary as to whether there was a sexual component to the attack, with both sexual and non-sexual being cited.

In 2018, John Getreu was arrested, as his DNA matched with semen found on Perlov's body. It was again an instance of advanced DNA technology cracking a cold case.[107]

Janet Taylor, March 25, 1974

If it hadn't been devastated already, the Stanford community was horrified by the murder of Janet Taylor, daughter of former Stanford Football Coach and Athletic Director Chuck Taylor.

On March 25, 1974, Janet had been on the Stanford campus visiting a friend. Around 7 pm she decided to hitchhike back to her home in La Honda. Her body was found the next morning, off Sand Hill Road near Searsville Lake. She had been sexually assaulted and strangled with a piece of her own clothing.[108]

Coincidentally, Janet Taylor was the Menlo-Atherton High School classmate of Barbara Rocky, a Brigham Young University student slain two weeks earlier near Salt Lake City, Utah.[109] It is unclear whether investigators think these crimes are connected.

In 2019, DNA analysis also linked her murder to John Getreu, already in jail for the murder of Leslie Perlov.[110] In 2021 Getreu was convicted for the murder of Janet Taylor and received a life sentence.[111] Facing trial for the murder of Leslie Perlov, he confessed to the crime in 2023[112]. Later that year, Getreu died in prison[113].

Arlis Perry, October 12, 1974

Arlis Perry, the wife of Stanford student Bruce Perry, was murdered in the evening of October 12, in Stanford's Memorial Church. Conjectured to be a ritual murder, she had been killed with an ice pick and had been sexually molested.[114]

Arlis Perry's murder remained a cold case until 2018, when advanced DNA analysis definitively linked security guard Stephen Crawford to the murder. On June 28, 2018, police arrived at Crawford's apartment with a search warrant. Crawford locked the door and committed suicide with a pistol[115].

And so, as it stands in 2024, three of the 1973-74 Stanford murders are regarded as solved. The remaining cold case is the second of the four, David Levine.

David Levine, September 11, 1973 - COLD CASE

In the early hours of September 11, 1973, undergraduate David Levine was murdered, stabbed approximately 15 times near Meyer Undergraduate Library on the campus of Stanford[116].

David Levine was a physics major from Ithaca, New York, the son of a Cornell professor. He was a standout student, and by all accounts, a brilliant, energetic and empathetic person. He was the star undergraduate of the Stanford Physics Department and was described by friends as someone who loved to discuss and debate politics for hours on end in the dorm lounge. He was on track to graduate in just three years and was doing work normally reserved for graduate students. He was working on a device that would be an alternative to an electrocardiograph. And because computers were scarce at the time, he was building his own computer.

An incoming freshman in the fall of 1971, he ran and was elected a student senator in fall of 1972. But his main focus was academics. He decided to stay on campus and attended summer session in 1973. Summer Quarter at Stanford ends in early August, yet he still stayed on campus to work on his project. Early September is one of the most deserted times on campus, save for workers and others preparing for the fall term that begins near the end of the month.

Levine left his lab and was presumably heading back to Mirrielees House where he lived. Levine's wallet was empty, but intact, so the motive for his attack was not robbery. Police said they believed it was a surprise attack because there was no sign of struggle.

The site of the murder is one I am very familiar with, having lived on that side of the campus all four years of my time at Stanford, and spending MANY hours in Meyer Library. I also lived at Mirrielees in 1987-88 when I was a senior

In those days, and mine, most classrooms and labs were generally to the west of the site of the murder, with mostly dorms and housing to the east. Like many Stanford students who lived on that side of campus, I have passed by Meyer Library, the site of the murder, perhaps thousands of times, at all hours of the day and night. I did so between the *Chaparral* office and my housing a decade later.

I must remark that my doubts about the investigation into David Levine began the first time I read newspaper accounts about it. My impression from the articles is that the investigators were not very savvy about campus life. For example, in the September 11 edition of the *Palo Alto Times*, the day of the murder, a detective stated, "We have no idea why Levine was out on campus at such an early morning hour."[117]

Really? Students working late on their research, or partying, at all hours is viewed as strange? Those cops obviously never spent time on a college campus. This statement shows a general lack of understanding towards the situation they encountered, and I can only wonder what other details they may have been oblivious to.

David Levine had decided to stay on campus during the summer to work on his projects. I would posit that David Levine often left the lab, or wherever he was working after midnight. Many nights. Perhaps most nights. To not understand why he would have been outside the library after midnight is to not understand what normal life to a college student like David Levine was.

By the next day, investigators were positing that it was a surprise attack because there was no struggle.[118] This view very much dominates any discussion about David Levine's murder to this day.

Now I understand that the investigators interviewed people over many days, trying to ascertain a suspect, and were not able to find a single one, at least not one ever reported in the news. But this idea of a surprise attack has been stated from the very beginning of this case, before those interviews or any investigation had occurred. Was the fact that they didn't find a suspect a self-fulfilling prophecy? Did it become conventional wisdom and/or part of groupthink? There are a lot of victims who are murdered by people they know. A lot of people who kill people they know; settling a grudge, jealousy, revenge, unrequited advances.

It is an unfortunate fact that some in society take it as impugning the victim's character to even conjecture that someone wanted revenge on them. This is not the case at all. Such is a necessary discussion in the effort to solve the crime. I think it's quite possible that the investigation did not fully explore possible suspects in this case out of respect to the victim and the family.

From my first reading of the account, I thought the idea of a surprise attack did not make sense. That would require that someone got to Levine without being seen, or heard, and was able to level a lethal blow the first time. Campus is well lit at night. There are few completely dark places. I wondered how someone got close enough to Levine to strike a blow without him noticing, able to move away or defend at all.

I think it's possible that he was murdered by someone he knew and trusted. In that case, one could get very close, which could make that first strike easier. "Wow, look at that, David? What do you think of that?" Or even, "look how well you can see Cygnus tonight," of course referring to the constellation that is prominent in September in the Northern Hemisphere. Such a scenario would make access for a clean shot more likely than a surprise attack out of the bushes.

I think the idea of an assailant hiding in this high-traffic area is less than likely. You could set up your surprise attack in a dark corner of campus, and hope no one would see when you revealed yourself, but the location of the murder was absolutely NOT some dark corner, quite the contrary. And they had to be hidden well, yet still be able to see well enough to pick their victim? If the attacker can't see, they might jump out and find the intended victim is larger and stronger than they are. The assailant's quick first stab must incapacitate the victim, otherwise they could retaliate.

As noted earlier, conjecture about what is rational is difficult because we are theorizing about a murderer, so anything, truly, is possible. On the other hand, that killer has avoided capture for over 50 years. To me, the surprise attack just doesn't sound probable.

The murder occurred sometime between 1 and 3 am, so there's obviously much less traffic than at other times. But it is still a major juncture for everyone living on the east side of campus, up to half of the student population. Residents of Mirrielees, Branner, Wilbur, Stern, the Trailers, Escondido, and the houses beyond Campus Drive could all come by this spot on their way from the academic buildings to their homes. Even with school out of term, there would have been someone coming by every few minutes or so. Other parts of campus would be much more deserted.

So, the police believed that the murderer hid at this juncture, and just waited for someone to come by when no one else was there. Waited unseen, till a suitable victim happened by, then was able to sneak up on and kill that person without being noticed, delivering a perfectly fatal blow on the first attempt. I mean, it's possible. But is it likely?

It is also no small detail that the murder weapon is almost exactly the described weapon of Zodiac's Lake Berryessa attack and murder, an approximately 10-inch blade knife. It's also no small detail that such an attack occurred not just on David Levine; but on two college students.

Eric Abramson, UC Berkeley, Dec. 20, 1973 – COLD CASE

Just three months after David Levine's murder at Stanford, a Berkeley grad student was murdered with details eerily similar. On December 20, 1973, Eric Benjamin Abramson, a 23-year-old majoring in physical chemistry from Ardmore, Pennsylvania was murdered at UC Berkeley, at night, on campus.[119] He was returning from the lab around 10:30 pm, while school was out of term. He was killed by multiple knife wounds to his chest from an approximately 8 to 10-inch knife.

In some ways it feels an understatement to say that these events were just similar. They are almost identical except for one fact: Abramson fought back.

Abramson was found in a garage area near the UC Women's Faculty Club. As with the Levine murder, robbery was not the motive. Police did search for a suspect. A woman stated she heard a scream and saw a tall black man in a grey sweatsuit running. It is unclear this individual was running from the scene, as other reports describe him as a jogger. It's possible he was just wanted as a witness.

A trail of blood stains approximately 200 feet long led police to Abramson's body. Police searched the area and found a leather knife sheath to hold a knife 8 to 10 inches long. They also found a bloody pencil and a pair of glasses near the murder scene.

Two science students, both murdered with a similar knife, both when school was out, one at Stanford and one at Berkeley just seemed too coincidental to me. On the other hand, there were MANY murders in this time period, so it's by no means certain they are related. Even so, it seemed weird. I mean, where would you go to hide after a murder at Stanford?

Berkeley?

There are Always Two

I know that's a hokey movie line from the movie Star Wars. But for a latent Taoist, it's sort of true too. I'm going to say it again: Two science students murdered, one at Stanford, one at Berkeley, both at night, by knife, and when school was out of term, just three months apart.

And now it seemed like I didn't just have two research projects, the *Chaparral* and the Zodiac, now there were two murders to investigate. Stanford and Berkeley, the ancient rivals, two schools in a dyadic relationship whether they liked it or not.

Regarding long-term, coincidences I was at this vista point: While I had been researching the *Chaparral* for nearly two years, I had focused on the humor years, 1899 to 1969 and 1974 to the present. Now at the precise time that I was beginning research the 1969-1974 *Stanford Chaparral*, all-this new information about murders at Stanford came to me.

I don't know how I had never heard of these things before, but I hadn't. It was a big surprise now. A spooky surprise. Seemingly, the stars had aligned for me to restart Zodiac research for a possible connection at Stanford, during the years 1969-1974. One couldn't write such a coincidental story, yet here it was happening, in reality. For those who like synchronicity and unity of purpose, this was one of those half-chocolate, half-vanilla ice cream cones.

For those who like coincidence, it was a hot fudge sundae.

Literally, the job in front of me for the *Chaparral* 125th anniversary project was to do a deep dive of Stanford 1969-74. Could there be a more synchronistic and efficient way to see if Richard Gaikowski and or the Zodiac, whoever he was, could overlap with the murder of David Levine? If there was, I sure couldn't think of one.

Could Richard Gaikowski have known David Levine?

If it could be shown that Richard Gaikowski and David Levine were at the same event, same protest, or members of the same group, that would increase the likelihood that they knew each other. Just showing that they could have known each other, or even that they traveled in the same circles, would be significant.

Really, it seemed like such a longshot. But if it were so, what sort of things would have occurred to make it happen? What possible ways could there have been?

Well, political protest could have brought Richard to Stanford, either actively participating, or covering for the press. If I could discover such, perhaps there would be additional details that might lead to finding an overlap. Which group was protesting? What issue? Protests could have theoretically brought Levine to San Francisco as well, but I didn't think that was as important because the crime happened at Stanford. What would bring someone to campus?

Richard might have also been trying to get time on a computer, and Stanford would be a good place to try. David Levine was building his own computer, and into politics. If they had somehow met, they might have had a similar type of friendship that Richard and I had.

Finding other common interests would be a way they might have met, I know Richard was into films, making films, having a film distribution business and running a theater. Was David Levine also into films?

All of these things seemed astronomically unlikely, nevertheless they crossed my mind.

A Tale of Two Murders

I'll say it a third time: David Levine and Eric Abramson were both murdered on their respective campuses at night while school was out of term, and both with an 8 to 10-inch knife.

David Levine was a top physics undergraduate student at Stanford, building a computer for the department. Eric Abramson was a graduate chemistry student at Berkeley, with plentiful access to computers. In both cases, police ruled that robbery was not the motive. In both cases, there were no suspects. In both cases a reward was offered for information, but with no success in either case. Months later, both cases still not only had no suspects, they both had no leads.

For a short while in the months after the murders, the theory that they were connected was referred to in the press. By spring of 1974, both cases were at dead ends. Then it seemed there was a break, in both cases.

The Zebra Killings

In May of 1974, eight months after Levine and five months after Abramson, both murders were indeed grouped together, with great fanfare, along with dozens of other murders attributed to the Zebra Killers, by San Francisco Mayor Joseph Alioto[120].

According to Alioto, the Zebra Killings were perpetuated against whites, by a "black terrorist group," who was responsible for over 50 unsolved murders around California. The Zebra list is morbid, shootings, knifings, dismemberments - a long list of murders in California from the late 60s to 1974.

It is unclear what information Mayor Alioto used to include the Levine and Abramson murders in the Zebra Killings data, and why he was commenting on murders outside of the City of San Francisco. Nevertheless, the theory that Levine and Abrahamson had been murdered by the Zebras entered the public consciousness.

I read the accounts of more than 50 of these murders. It was a bit too much.

No more Zodiac research, just Chaparral

One morning Richard Dreyfuss wakes up in the movie Close Encounters and tells his wife Teri Garr all the pictures he has drawn of some strange mountain are coming down. His character had become obsessed with this vision of a rock formation, drawing it, building out of mashed potatoes--it was putting a strain on their marriage. At some point the Dreyfuss character gets the feeling this is all a big waste of time. The fever has broken, there is nothing more to this. I felt the same way.

Researching the Zebras really wore me out. And I realized I was spending almost all my time going down various rabbit holes of dark subjects, which not only had slowed gathering data for the *Chaparral* and the planned anniversary book, but also wasn't even about Zodiac so much anymore, I was reading about 50+ murders of various types all over California. WTF?

As I stated previously, any loudmouth, joker, idiot or asshole, can spout, "Maybe it was Zodiac?" with nothing more than the bullshit words coming out of your mouth. To even spend any time at all on such a subject makes one at least part idiot internet conspiracy expert.

And maybe more so for me, given I knew a Zodiac suspect, and had attended Stanford. This tale just sounds like I'm just blending all my personal history into a far-fetched theory. And even if it's only partially far-fetched, how would one even hope to prove any of this? It seemed like more than a longshot, and certainly a black hole of time.

I resolved to just stick to researching the *Chaparral*. Zodiac was a unique sidebar, but that's it, and it was a hell of a time-waster.

"So just put it out of your mind," I told myself. "Stop researching Richard. Don't even think about David Levine. No. More. Zodiac."

The Radical Libertarian Alliance

I set out with this new directive, literally and dutifully working for the *Chaparral* 125 Project, not Zodiac. But like Dreyfuss' character in Close Encounters, that didn't last long. A couple days tops.

While searching for the *Chaparral* in the *Stanford Daily* archives, I took note that there was a 1971 Once Around the Quad calendar listing for a group called the Radical Libertarian Alliance, and they were holding their meeting IN the *Chaparral* office[121]. In fact, the listing said "regular closed meeting," so this wasn't a fluke or one-time thing.

"That's weird," I said to myself. "Libertarians? I thought the Chappie was left-wing."

I was born in 1965, and I barely paid attention to politics as a kid, but my impression by high school age in the 1980s was that Libertarians were right wing, more so than even Republicans. I was also under the impression that the *Chaparral* of the early 1970s was very left wing. Radical Libertarians didn't sound very left-wing to me. What were they doing holding meetings in the *Chaparral* office in 1971?

I googled the Radical Libertarian Alliance, and found that it was a short-lived but nationwide group that attempted to unite the left and right wing under a libertarian banner. People noted then that it was a unique alliance, united largely around anti-draft sentiments. The *Daily* described the group as an individualist anarchist organization "However, it sees little difficulty in working with communitarian anarchists like David Harris, former ASSU President. Communitarian anarchists

THE ONLY TIME RICHARD GOT ANGRY AT ME

believe that individuality can really be expressed only in freely-formed communes. The RLA sees itself both as part of the national libertarian movement and as part of the New Left."[122]

I was surprised to learn there were left-wing libertarians, and a group that had both left and right. They were described as *'buzz-cut guys who called cops pigs.'*

I had another one of those moments. "Wow, that sounds like Richard," I thought.

Now it was just a hunch, but it really reminded me of my political discussions with Richard. I remembered that we had spoken about the politics of the Midwest, of farmers. People don't realize, but old school farmers were much more centrist than they are today. And the Farmer's Union, which Richard had worked for, was truly hybrid, advocating for farmers to get to join Social Security and other programs some view as socialist, balancing that with the fact that family farms were all small businesses, and very much FOR capitalism. Could you call them "libertarians?" I thought the term was apt.

Richard didn't have a buzz-cut when I knew him, but I was well aware of his previous hair styles. He did indeed have a buzz cut in the 50s and 60s. As for Richard's politics, this concept of right and left-wing libertarianism together just seemed to me to be very much how I remembered Richard.

There was one other definite thing: Richard only called cops pigs. I don't ever remember him not using the term pigs when talking about the police.

I googled "Radical Libertarian Alliance" and "Gaikowski" and came up empty.

I googled "Radical Libertarian Alliance" and "*Good Times*" and there was a hit! A 1971 *WIN Magazine* from New York City covering Libertarianism contained a classified ad selling the book of the Radical Libertarian Alliance as well as a letter talking about an article from *Good Times*[123]. The letter was signed by Ben Dover.

Fake Names in Good Times

It was time for another deep dive on *Good Times*. To clarify, it was not to find out if someone out there really was named Benjamin Dover, it was time to diagram all the names, real or fake, in the totality of

Good Times' print run.

The *Good Times* bylines have many obvious fake names: Rip Van Winkle, Jando Noone, Ben Dover, Goatkirk, Bear, revoman, and the like. There are many more that might be fake. The hippies seemed to love to make up fake names. There were so many new search terms to try.

Ben Dover

So what about "Ben Dover"? One wonders how long ago that joke was first made, perhaps centuries, right? I remember hearing or making Ben Dover jokes in grade school in rural Indiana. Surely the joke is universal, at least among English-speaking people with a certain sense of humor.

Ben Dover writes in *Good Times* often, with seven bylines in 1969. In the October 16, 1969, issue, Ben Dover authors Fuck You, Sir, an article about how having an obscene tattoo can get you discharged from serving in the military[124].

The article gives four suggestions, the first two involve tattooing FUCK YOU or EAT SHIT on the karate-edge of your hand, and thus visible when saluting. The article suggests you could also do FUCK YOU, SIR or EAT SHIT, SIR. The third suggestion is to tattoo your back with two large breasts and nipples on your shoulder blades and a belly button on the small of your back. The fourth tattoo suggestion is to have a wolf and rabbit with the rabbit on one buttock about to jump into your asshole. The article continues that the military will not draft homosexuals, but you need proof, with the suggestion to hire a hustler at the bus stop and photograph him blowing you in the photomatic machine.

Of course I'm paraphrasing.

As noted earlier, Ben Dover also wrote a letter to *WIN Magazine*, a New York City underground press tabloid.[125] Their March 1, 1971, issue was titled Libertarianism and the paper covered that topic. The issue spends a great deal of content on a new idea: right-wing libertarians, with both pro and con takes on the movement.

Also as I noted earlier, this was a surprise to me, as I had only known Libertarianism as a right wing movement. To my post-Reagan knowledge, people who were Libertarians were more to the right than Republicans, although I did hear libertarians summed up once as "Republicans who smoke pot." But here in this 1971 publication was evidence that libertarians had been viewed up to that time as left-wing. This was a fascinating discovery for me.

Well anyway, Ben Dover described his "tatoo" article (he misspells 'tattoo' all five times he uses the word), and said he learned this information in Seattle, and then mailed off his article to *Good Times* and they printed it. Nevertheless, by the time of this letter, Ben's address is printed as San Francisco.

This same issue of *WIN* includes a classified ad selling the book of the Radical Libertarian Alliance[126]. This issue is the one and only time this ad ran in *WIN* and is the only search engine hit for the group in that publication. Given the issue was devoted to Libertarianism, those selling the Radical Libertarian Alliance book must have known ahead of the issue's subject, and viewed it a reasonable publication to place an ad in. The fact that the same issue mentions *Good Times* (in the Ben Dover letter) is just another funny coincidence in all this. Add in that the Radical Libertarian Alliance held "regular meetings," as the calendar listing noted, in the Chaparral offices, well, such a coincidence might be called hilarious.

For what it's worth, in the September 8, 1970, issue of the *East Village Other* (NYC), a cartoon called Pair of Dice Lost includes a character named Ben Dover[127]. I am not saying this is significant, I only note the additional comic coincidence that in his letters and codes, Zodiac consistently misspells the word paradise as paradice.

Goatkirk

In the September 4, 1969, *Good Times*, there is an introduction to Tarot article written by "Geo Ati Kirk."[128] The article explains this is the first of a series of articles on Tarot, and then expands on the full subject. A large part of the article deals with The Fool card, explaining a certain amount of confusion in its numbering. Some maintain The Fool is tarot card number Zero, but this article says it is the only unnumbered tarot card. The article concludes with the author asking the public to send in their interpretations of The Fool, in preparation for the next article in the series which will be devoted to that card. Later in that same issue is a classified ad. It says, "Send in your interpretations of The Fool to Goatkirk, c/o *Good Times*. Those used may get a free tarot deck."[129]

The next issue, September 11, 1969, *Good Times* runs a Goat-kirk article, and prints some of the responses to Goatkirk. One of the responses is especially glowing in praise of Goatkirk's tarot introductory article, and asks if he has written more on the subject and/or is he teaching anywhere. Goatkirk's response includes his confessing that he has written under that name "Verne," "jando," and miscellaneous other people.[130] As for the tarot article in this issue, Goatkirk gives a short, sort of apologetic article for not writing about The Fool, referencing The Juggler, The Magician, and The Tower cards causing his house to fall apart. He says he hopes to write The Fool article the next week. The classified ad looking for Fool interpretations is rerun in this issue[131].

One week later, September 18, 1969, Goatkirk skips the article on The Fool, and writes an article on the next card, The Magus, aka The Magician, card number One in the tarot deck. The same classified ad is rerun again in this issue.

In the next issue, September 26, 1969, Goatkirk writes a general tarot article because he says that people have requested more general information rather than articles on individual cards. Included alongside the article are some more of the responses about The Fool card. The classified ad runs again.

There is no Goatkirk article in the October 2, 1969, issue, but the classified ad runs again[132].

Goatkirk's tarot article of October 9, 1969, answers a question from a reader, and includes more responses to the request for Fool interpretations as well as the classified ad[133].

The October 16, 1969, *Good Times* has no Goatkirk article. There is also a classified ad, but for the first time the text of the ad is different:

FREE TAROT study(?) for all you followers of Goatkirk. Drop me a line at Good Times or call here or 567-0880 so we can get together. Next column next week[134].

The next week, October 23, 1969, Goatkirk again writes a Tarot article that includes responses about the Fool from the public.[135] A particularly interesting response talks about the tarot deck of Aleister Crowley, famous British occultist and philosopher. The new classified ad from the previous week is rerun[136].

There is no tarot article in the October 30, 1969 *Good Times*, but the new classified ad is rerun again[137].

There is again no tarot article in the November 6, 1969 issue, but there is the classified ad[138]. There is also a Switchboard message in this issue for "Kirk," with no last name[139].

There is no Goatkirk, article or classified ad in the November 13, 1969, issue.

There is no article on November 20, 1969, but there is a new classified:

GOATKIRK is looking for a cool pad that is quiet to get his head together…can pay up to $50 mo. Has small dog and is hassling welfare. Any help would be appreciated. Write Goodtimes and 14 Isis St Apt 7 SF [140]

The next week, November 27, 1969, Goatkirk writes a non-tarot article, the first time that his subject has ever changed[141]. The article is a review of a Flying Dutchman album, referencing *Ramparts* magazine editor Robert Scheer's experience at Santa Rita after being busted at the People's Park hassles. This article is on the right side of page 12, directly next to page 13. The main article on that page is the same height of the album review, and would almost be viewed as the same article, if not for a black line separating them. It is titled "Astrological and Tarot Forecast November 23- December 22. At the end of the article is the debut byline for Swami Sivananda (more about him later). The article flows around a large box of graphic text that reads:

"zodiac strikes again" in stylish, but hand-drawn, typography[142].

The classified ad looking for housing is rerun in this issue, but that is the end of Goatkirk's articles in *Good Times*. His classified ad runs once more in the December 4, 1969 issue[143], the last time the name Goatkirk is printed in *Good Times*.

Is Goatkirk Richard? If so, the door is open that Richard used many other aliases.

The eight letters of GOATKIRK are seven out of ten letters of R. Gaikowski. If you switch the T and I, you get that all eight letters of Goatkirk are in R. Gaikowski.

The name Goatkirk also has the name Gaik in sequence: G o A t k I r K.

I searched the Goatkirk phone number in all *Good Times* issues, and found that in the February 13, 1970, issue, the same phone number is used in a classified ad "ROOM WANTED by *Good Times* reporter..." The ad concludes "Ask for Dick."[144]

During these years, Richard's name does not appear in SF White Pages nor City Directory.

In the 1971 San Francisco city telephone directory, there is a listing for H. Goat. That is the one and only year I could find a listing for H Goat.

The identity of Goatkirk is a central question in my mind. It is of course of particular interest to me as I have knowledge of Richard's tarot card computer software and his attention to detail about the orientation of the cards. If Goatkirk is Richard, we can not only know that tarot was an interest of his back to 1969, but also realize that he used many fake names and nom de plumes.

Clandes Stine

There is an article In the February 27, 1970, issue of *Good Times* titled Taking Liberty, with the byline Clandes Stine[145]. The article is about the Presidio 27, individuals charged with mutiny at the Presidio military base in 1968. This is the only byline for Clandes Stine that any search engine reveals for *Good Times* or any publication of the era.

Some note that the Paul Stine murder occurred just one block from the Presidio, and on the one-year anniversary of the protest. The relative importance of the Presidio protest in the narrative and editorial priorities of *Good Times* is just one more quirky coincidence. In addition, Paul Stine's wife was named Claudia.

revoman

Another byline used just once is revoman. It was used for the April 16, 1971 *Good Times* article about protests at the Stanford Hospital[146]. I conjecture it means something like "Revolution Man." This is not just the only time this byline appears in *Good Times*, it is the only time it appears at all anywhere. As with "Clandes Stine," I could not find another "revoman" byline in any other publication, any time or anywhere.

Guy du Lac and just Guy

Starting with the August 6, 1971 issue, there are Dick Gaik bylines in twelve of the next thirteen *Good Times* issues. The only issue he misses, the September 17 issue, is the only time the name Guy Du Lac appears in the entirety of *Good Times'* existence[147]. Again, this is just circumstantial, it is not for certain Richard, but I ask you to consider the opposite, that it is just a coincidence. That means that Richard just coincidentally wrote in twelve of thirteen issues, and the only one he doesn't write for just happens to get a submission from someone else named Guy Du Lac. The one and only time Guy, the "Man from the Lake" writes for *Good Times*. Sure, that is totally possible.

Now punsters and others can easily recognize the phonetic similarity to Gaik. In some ways Guy-du-Lac is kind of like GoAtkIrK. If you could prove Richard Gaikowski was Guy Du Lac, or that he was Goatkirk, it would be fascinating, proof he used many names. And the tantalizing question would be, are there more we have not yet identified?

In 1972, there are two consecutive issues with the byline Guy, on May 19 and June 2. In the second of these issues, Venceremos wrote a letter to *Good Times*[148].

Bear

In street slang, a "Bear" is a husky, hairy, homosexual man. If one were to look at the *Good Times* group photo published on January 1, 1972, the most likely person to pick out as a Bear would be the guy in the upper right, Richard Gaikowski.

The byline Honeybear also appears a few times.

There are many more fake names than the ones I've just mentioned.

Way more. Black Shadow, Grass Prophet, Wind Catcher, Evil Sugar, Gitchy Goomy and more. Those are just the obvious ones. *Good Times* is full of them. The crazy part is that prior to people having online handles, hippies were the masters of such names, groundbreaking pioneers. It only makes sense the killer, whoever he was, picked up on this cultural phenomenon and gave himself a handle, a fake name under which to commit their crimes. It couldn't be more 1969.

Fake Names in the Stanford Chaparral

At the *Chaparral*, we used to make up fake names all the time. My first pieces for the magazine were under the name Moose Neumann as a quasi-official nom de plum for me, but it was also commonplace to make a name right up to press time: Ferd E. Lizer for a farm advice column, Hammond Cheese for something else. Rich Smartass, Warren G. Wonka, and Anita Amanda Lay. It's what an irreverent zine like the *Chaparral* does.

Chaparral Political Era Covers

As the days went by, I was getting excited to receive scans of the political era from the library.

I was honestly at least as curious if they might contain the name of David Levine or Richard Gaikowski, as I was about their place in the *Chaparral*'s history. In many ways, it was a funny situation, but it provided the perfect cover. I didn't have to ask the library, and the dutiful younger Chappie alumnus who was my contact there, "Hey, I need scans of all this stuff, I'm trying to solve the Zodiac murders." I could instead ask about the *Chaparral*, and it was totally normal and legitimate.

And it WAS normal and legitimate, because I was the point person assembling the Chappie digital archive with the goal of making this big book. It was not my fault that it was simultaneously assisting my conjecture about a serial killer.

Do coincidences follow the *Chaparral*? Well that question is perhaps unanswerable, but in any case, it sure seemed like it was happening again. Amazing coincidence. One F of a Coincidence.

The Old One, the Jester, the Fool, was giving me a comical ride, with me being both a dithering idiot, happenchance sleuth, and willing participant in a story that was about to get surreal.

"Good luck with that, buddy"

One evening, S, who was a mid-70s Chappie, attended our alumni zoom call. During the call, people were talking about where they lived, Branner, Roble, Stern and Wilbur, when S mentioned that in the Fall of '73 he did not get campus housing, but then he did, because there was a student murdered at the beginning of the term. It's also how S came to the *Chaparral*, because his roommate was JH, the eventual co-editor of the *Chaparral* with Mike Dornheim in 1974-75.

I couldn't believe what I was hearing. There was that creepy feeling again, the eerie music in my head, this time somewhat stronger.

"So let me clarify," I asked. "you're saying that the murdered guy, David Levine, was the roommate of JH?"

"Yes, then I became his roommate. It was from JH that I learned about the *Chaparral* and joined."

At that time, I still had not confirmed that David Levine ever visited the Chappie office, it was just my conjecture that an interest in politics might have brought him there. David Levine had sponsored some left-of-center motions in the student senate, but he did not fit the profile of the leftists of his day. I wondered if the hybrid of right and left that was hanging out in the *Chaparral* might be appealing to him?

But now with the account of S, the probability that David Levine had visited the *Chaparral* office skyrocketed. At minimum, I had David Levine one step away. The *Chaparral* office was a place of frequent parties, and people would go there, even if they didn't work for the magazine. One might easily accompany their roommate there.

Furthermore, after freshman year, people very often picked their roommates, rather than have them randomly assigned. JH and David Levine were going to be juniors, so they almost certainly knew each other and were possibly friends because they possibly picked each other to room with. If that were indeed the case, it would be a fascinating piece of information.

While I tried to process what I had just learned, the group proceeded to discuss the four 1970s Stanford murders, and how three of the four had recently been solved, yet David Levine was still a cold case. As I said earlier, I had just learned of these murders a few months prior. As a 1988 graduate, I stayed silent while the older alums discussed these 1970s campus murders. Now, I just listened, and then started to jot down notes.

Some said they remembered the murders when they happened, how it was creepy for a while, especially as more murders happened.

Then DL said, "We were sure our housemate did the Memorial Church murder. He was a real weirdo. He'd walk around campus in a black hooded robe, and joke about Satanism. We lived on campus that summer, in the trailers…"

The trailers were the Manzanita Trailers, temporary housing near Branner and Mirrielees, on the east side of campus. It was reasonably close to Hoover Tower, which allowed for certain humor as to the quality of the accommodations.

"One summer I painted "Welcome to Hooverville" on the first trailer coming in from Campus Drive, with a great view of Hoover Tower in the background," said L. Hoover Tower is of course The Hoover Institution on War, Revolution, and Peace, which is not only the Herbert Hoover Presidential Library, but a prominent conservative think tank. As econ majors, both L and I found the reference to Depression-era encampments especially funny in the shadow of Herbert's tower. Manzanita Trailers as Hooverville is a joke for the ages.

Eventually the conversation came back to David Levine.

"The David Levine murder was a surprise attack," said S. "There was no struggle," said S.

"Yes," agreed another. "Wasn't it part of a terrorist group killings, the Zebra murders?"

"No, the cops are sure it was a stranger. Just a random, senseless murder."

I was completely blown away, and in retrospect, I think I wish I hadn't said anything, but I did.

When the conversation came to a lull, I said, "I know this sounds crazy, but I think there may be a way to connect a leading Zodiac suspect to David Levine, perhaps even meeting each other at the *Chaparral* office."

This sort of stopped the conversation cold, and I could tell that this information was not warmly received. As I said, I wondered if I should speak up. On the other hand, we might have been on the precipice of connecting them.

There was an awkward pause.

"Good luck with that, buddy," said S.

I decided to just drop it. You know, I had never been anywhere near such a thing before, a murder, and I hadn't really thought it through. For these alums, this was not a just piece of macabre history, this was a big and horrible event in their lives—while I had just learned about it in recent months, they had known about it for 50 years.

At the end of the call, I was stunned. I sat there for some time, thinking of the ramifications. This brought David Levine one full step closer to the *Chaparral*, where people who were like-minded to *Good Times* people might be hanging out. They were still many steps away, but little by little, they grew closer…

The Conventional Wisdom

I suppose there is a certain simplicity and a certain appeal to the idea that a complete stranger committed the horrible attack. In that case, the murderer is an outsider, not someone we know. There is no killer among our friends and acquaintances, it's someone else. Furthermore, the death was random, like a car wreck or freak accident.

That David Levine was killed by a surprise attack from a stranger has been the prevailing theory for nearly 50 years. Then, on a zoom call, an idea is presented that is quite outlandish, a wild and improbable claim, and if you add in the idea that our own organization might have something to do with this, well, it's not hard to figure out why it wasn't well received. Upon reflection I realize that perhaps it was just a bit too much to say out loud.

From 1973 until 2018, all four of the Stanford Murders were cold cases, theoretically they all could have been committed by random strangers. It was still possible to maintain that there was no one in the Stanford community who could have been the perpetrator, not a student, nor professor, nor employee of the university. Obviously that all changed when three of the four murders were solved.

But David Levine's murder is different from the other three, not just because it is still a cold case, but because the other three all involved sexual assault of young women. David Levine's murder stands out. There was no apparent motive, there was no robbery. Just a senseless murder in the middle of the night.

And with few clues, the idea that it was a random stranger took hold. I posit the theory was also accepted because no one wanted to think there was a killer among the Stanford student body or community? I'm just saying they had no leads, and as the months went by and they still had no leads, the stranger theory took hold.

However it came about, the idea that a complete stranger killed David Levine started with the original news reports the day of the murder and seems to remain to this day.

Based on the information learned in the zoom call, David Levine was not just a Stanford student who used computers and liked to talk politics, one who may never have even heard of the *Chaparral*, let alone visit their offices. Now he was the roommate and likely friend of a future *Chaparral* editor. Just on roommate status alone, it was possible he visited the *Chaparral* office at least at some point. Did he attend political meetings in the *Chaparral* office? Did he go to a party there, or just hang out? If he did, the chances he could have met Richard Gaikowski rose.

Keep in mind, "radical libertarianism" a union of left and right-wing concepts had only REMINDED me of Richard's politics. I had nothing other than this hunch that something like this would have interested him. It was just conjecture. It was also a conjecture that David Levine might have visited the *Chaparral* office or been interested in this group as well. But as unlikely as this conjecture seemed initially, everything I found seemed to increase that possibility. To be clear, the things I had found were in 1971, prior to Levine attending Stanford. My point would be that the "scene," those hanging out in and around the office could have existed through 1974, and if so would definitely overlap with Levine attending Stanford. I now had a possible path for Levine and Gaikowski to meet, and strangely enough, to meet in the *Chaparral* office.

So, despite my best efforts and continued intention to cease Zodiac research, I had been recaptured by my research into my own college organization, known for its irreverence and pranks. I was now investigating Zodiac as much as *Chaparral*.

"No one is going to believe this," I thought.

I freely admit that this story is hard to believe.

Where Could You Find Computer in 1969?

I was operating on the conjecture that politics was a way Richard might have come to Stanford. Another way I explored was through computers.

In a 1969 *Good Times* issue, D. Gaik wrote an article describing his visit to the Astrology Research Center in Berkeley.[149] The article stated that "some astrologers are now using computers." So I wondered, who had computers in 1969? Or moreover, who had computers you could do astrology on in 1969?

Well, I imagine you could have rented time on them, but if you were poor, you'd look for low-cost and specifically FREE access to a computer. You'd need a friend, perhaps one that worked on a computer at their job. Of course, it almost certainly would have to be on the down low. A business would likely have some kind of audit system in place for their equipment. Then there would be the question of why people were there at night, or the weekend.

A university is a much more plausible place for a person to be able to get on a computer in 1969. Even in non-protest times, students could be on the computer terminals at all times of night, and likely had a higher incidence of "shenanigans" on the computers. Beyond that, schools go out of term. Campuses are ghost towns at certain times of the year.

By the nature of this story, one would be looking for secrecy, not to access computers as part of a supervised effort or class. You'd try to make friends with someone. Someone with access to a terminal, but with a fair amount of autonomy. You are almost certainly looking for a grad student. And you'd want access at night, or better yet, at times when school was not in session. The most likely was that you would have a friend who would give you access.

So after thinking it all through, the conclusion that someone who wanted to use a computer for the non-scientific endeavor of astrology, let alone cipher-making, would be: 1. Looking to make friends at a college; 2. Want those students to have access to computers. Grad students or computer standouts, who would have a lot of unsupervised time on the computers; 3. Very interested in times when school was out of session; and 4. In all cases, prefer using the computers at night, when there would be less people and it would be easier to hide.

In 1969, there were few dedicated computer departments in the universities, but science departments had computers. Stanford also Stanford had SAIL, Stanford Artificial Intelligence Lab, run by Dr. John McCarthy, and a Computer Music Department. One time around 1985, I remember going up into the hills with my friend Don Dickson to Stanford's Music Department, sometime around 2 or 3 am where Stanley Jordan was doing some kind of experimentation with computers and music. It was very peaceful and remote up there, especially at night.

I Asked a Computer

It occurred to me: who better to ask about the origins of computers than a computer. In 2023, AI became all the rage. I asked an AI engine: Who had computers in 1969?

It replied that universities and research institutes, businesses, government agencies and the military had computers.

I asked if people used computers at Stanford and Berkeley to do astrology in 1969. It replied that while it was possible, there was no evidence for this claim.

I pointed out to the AI that astrology was not real science, and that Stanford and Berkeley might not like their computers used for such. The computer agreed, noting that both Stanford and Berkeley are top institutions, and would not want pseudo-science performed on their computers.

I asked if someone wanted to do astrology on a computer at Stanford or Berkeley, would they one have to sneak around? It replied that it sounded reasonable that you would have to sneak around, but it said to keep in mind that there was a large range of beliefs at both schools, and it's possible that some would be receptive to astrology.

I asked: When would be a good time to do astrology on a computer at Stanford or Berkeley? It recommended that I do not use a computer at Stanford or Berkeley as it would not be a sanctioned event.

I asked when it would be best to use the computers, if one found a sympathetic professor or student? It replied that the best times would be late at night, or early in the morning, when there would be less chance of being caught by someone not supportive of astrology.

I asked what times of the year would one try to do astrology on a university computer? It replied that it would be best when school was out of session, summer or winter breaks.

Now, a year later, it is widely known that AI can produce really bad answers, and often seemingly outright lies, so this discussion was just for fun. Nevertheless, the simple logical abilities of the AI pointed that late night times when school was out of session would be the optimal times for non-students to attempt to use a computer for astrology or other non-sanctioned uses.

For those of you keeping track, remember that David Levine was killed sometime between 1 and 3 am, on September 11, 1973. Stanford's summer term ends around August 10, and its fall term doesn't begin until the end of September. At Stanford, September 11 is a day when school is very much out of session. As for Berkeley, their fall semester ends in early December, and school is out of session until the first week of January. Eric Abramson was murdered on December 20, around 10:30 pm.

Computers in the 60s & 70s – Info from One Who Knows

In the 1960s and 70s, Stanford was a leader in making computers available to the public. Many people there in key positions advocated for the democratization of computers, getting them to the people. While a Bay Area resident of 1969 might look to any college as a likely place to get computer time, they might REALLY look to Stanford. A lot of people did indeed take advantage of this visionary opportunity.

In the 1970s, many were desperate, or at least eager, to get computer time. This led to computer users being up all hours of the day and night, every day of the week, both when school was in session and when it was out, literally 24-7-365.

Specifically, regarding the case of David Levine, he was building his own (his department's) computer. Until that computer worked itself, and even after, he certainly was jockeying for mainframe time along with many others. His computer time could quite possibly have been at night, possibly often after midnight.

Sessions on the mainframe were not haphazard; they were diligently scheduled. Computer time was precious, and people logged on exactly at the time their session began and the prior user's session ended. The schedule was known days ahead. The schedule of David Levine's computer use would have been seen by people who had access to the schedule. Someone with access to the schedule could have easily known that David Levine's computer time ended at a certain hour, and he would then be heading for home.

In their earliest reports, the fact the police say they had no idea why David Levine might have been out that late at night shows that the police really had no idea what the situation was. Without such an understanding, they certainly had little basis to know what to look for or what might be out of place, other than standard murder investigation questions.

The Missing Link

Sometime in fall of 2022, I got the PDFs of scanned *Chaparral* covers from the Stanford library. PT had been our ambassador to the library, and made the requests for scans. We really didn't need an ambassador, but he was willing to make the requests, and it was a way to expand participation in the project. Apparently, the issue covers had been posted for some weeks, but I hadn't seen the email.

Adding the covers from this era to our directory brought the total number of issues to over 910, and also brought us within single digits of getting them all. As comical as it sounds, we had one missing issue from 1914, and about seven missing from the 21st century, in the last 10 years of the magazine's history. Such is the truth about an organization like the *Stanford Chaparral*.

I had looked the PDFs over when I downloaded them, but really just breezed over them. I mean, I didn't expect to see a Chappie cover page with David Levine or Richard Gaikowski on it. I would have to wait until we got to see the interior of these issues.

An additional funny thing about Political Era *Chaparral*s is that often they had two things that could be construed a cover, the front page with the masthead, but also half of the back page, which on some editions was folded over with a large graphic on one half, making a cover. This made me have to decide which cover, the front page or the back page graphic, to use in the *Chaparral* online directory. In some cases it was easy, but in others there was both a great front page story, perhaps of historical significance, and the back page graphic, which also might be good.

The March 5, 1971, issue presented a unique problem in that it had two sections, each with its own cover. Other than that, it seemed to be an average issue, a Stanford-ized version of the underground and alternative press that was flourishing of the time. The front of the first section included two large pictures with the headline Justice at Stanford? The front of the other section was more like a newspaper with just one small picture. I decided to just post the front of the first section into the directory. I didn't look at section two much at all, and moreover, the directory was set up for one cover per issue. I uploaded the cover from the front section and moved on to the next.

I was looking for staff boxes, or coverage of the ASSU Senate, election endorsements and the like but not finding any. Of course, these were just the front pages. Anything like would likely be on interior pages. It didn't matter, with each cover uploaded we were getting ever closer to completing the task of getting a scan of every one. The directory project was going well. The book, not so much.

As 2022 ended, we did not have enough stories for the book, not even close. Or rather, we had stories, in our minds, but no one had WRITTEN anything. Someone suggested that the transcripts from the Zoom calls could be the basis of articles. In addition, you could share the screen of old issues and have the people who worked on that issue talk about it.

"OMG, genius!"

And so it was in that light that the January 2023 Zoom was set to be specifically for 1980s Chappies.

The idea worked well; we had a larger than normal crowd at the zoom call, and got some really funny commentary, some of which did indeed make it into the book. But we didn't get anywhere near completing the decade of the 80s, so the February meeting was announced to be Part 2 of the 1980s.

At some point in all of this I got a message from an older alum. "You're going to do one of these (Zoom calls) for the 70s, aren't you?"

"Of course," I answered.

March 1, 2023, was set up for the 1970s Chappie alumni Zoom call. In preparation, I extracted some more covers out of the Stanford Library's PDF. There were still 20 or more Political Era covers to upload into our directory. Even though the call was mostly for Chappies 1974 to 1979, the years when the magazine returned to its humor format, I thought it was a good idea to use the meeting to get all 70s covers up into the directory. Anyway, we wanted to heal the schism between the different 70s eras. The *Chaparrals* from 1969 to 1974 were just as much Chappies as any era.

And so it was that in preparation of the all-1970s Chappie Zoom call, that I looked at each of these covers more closely. I went through each cover, which is all we had, reading the articles, becoming familiar with the material looking for anything relevant, both for the *Chaparral*'s history, and the Zodiac--anything about politics, protests, San Francisco or other things that might overlap with *Good Times*. I also kept an eye out for computer-oriented articles, astrology articles, the Radical Libertarian Alliance, the Free University.

It was only then that I paid any attention at all to the second section of the March 5, 1971, *Chaparral* issue. And there, right on the front page was an article on computer music! Wow, an article on computers, something I was looking for. I was thrilled and proceeded to read the article. Computerized Music Challenges Old Pros was the headline, with the byline, By Dick Geikie.

I re-read it: By Dick Geikie.

To say that I heard that weird music again, to say that the hair on the back of my neck stood up, to say that I could not believe my eyes, would be an understatement. I wigged out. I mean, I seriously wigged out.

I sat in disbelief for many moments.

"Kate, you're not going to believe this…"

Yes, the weird, creepy feeling started again, but this time the discovery changed the entirety of my research and work on this matter. The article was written by Dick Geikie.

"Dick Geikie? Holy shit! Fuck, fuck fuck fuck fuck. Dick Geikie! Dick Geikie?

I had looked specifically to see if this article about computers might have anything that led to Richard Gaikowski, known for writing under the pen name Dick Gaik, and I see the byline is by Dick Geikie. Dick Geikie.

I tried to remain calm. I tried to get my head around what I was seeing. I knew that this may not be anything other than another funny coincidence. I also knew that proving Dick Geikie was NOT Dick Gaik, theoretically, would be quite easy.

A simple people-search finding a Dick Geikie would mean it was not Dick Gaik. Finding that a Dick Geikie went to Stanford during those years would mean it was not Dick Gaik. All that would have to happen was a single shred of data showing that Dick Geikie actually existed would prove it was not Dick Gaik. An obituary, a property record, a phone book listing, and any other type of hit a search engine could find could dispel that Dick Geikie was actually Richard Gaikowski.

However things went from this point, this was going to be a pretty funny coincidence. I thought my story was weird before, but now the long tale that started with an argument about Reagan and astrology had now come full circle with Dick Gaik under another version of his name now writing for the *Stanford Chaparral*? That's borderline unbelievable. Or is it the biggest coincidence of all time?

One F of a Coincidence.

As the Jester would have it, right above the byline for Dick Geikie there is a caption under a photo of a bike stand, The bike had been stolen, ripped off, and a tire chained to the bike stand was all that was left. The photo is captioned, The Missing Link.

It had just been a hunch that politics or protests might have brought Richard to Stanford, or to get computer time. It was additional conjecture that got him into the *Chaparral* office. I had never dreamed I might see his byline, for an article about computers, IN a *Chaparral*...

To be sure, it was not his exact byline, or a known byline. He wrote for *Good Times* as Dick Gaik, not Dick Geikie. But I realized that if these were indeed the same person, not only would that place Richard at Stanford, it would also show he was there using yet another variation of his name.

And if there were more variations of Gaik, like Geikie, then why not Gyke?

What Do You Do When You Find Out a Serial Killer Suspect May Have Written for Your College Magazine?

What can you say? I wigged out.

Things got pretty surreal in the hours after this discovery. It was a longshot conjecture—I certainly didn't really think I would be able to show that Richard had come to Stanford, and out of all the possible ways that might happen, who would believe this is how it was done? He WROTE for the *Chaparral*? It was almost unbelievable --someone named Dick Geikie writing about computers in a 1971 *Chaparral* issue.

If Dick Geikie was indeed Richard, this would be a discovery of almost unparalleled significance. The discussion about his potential as a Zodiac would be changed forever. Of course, writing for a college magazine is not a crime, but just the fact that he was doing so, under an assumed name, would open up a huge number of new things to investigate, and the speculation about this online would be extensive.

I realized I had A LOT of new work to do. I had to try to confirm that Dick Geikie was Dick Gaik, and to try even harder to confirm that he wasn't.

Who was Dick Geikie?

I took to Google. I searched "Dick Geikie" and "Stanford," nothing. "Dick Geikie" and "California," nothing. "Richard Geikie" and "Stanford." Nothing. Just "Dick Geikie," just "Richard Geikie," all nothing. Finally I just tried "Geikie" and I got a couple hits.

Eventually I got search results for a Richard Geikie.

"Shit, there's a guy who went to MIT, that could easily be the same person."

By this time, I had looked at enough Stanford alum bios to know you will often see an MIT, or Ivy League school in their resume.

I clicked on the link. Hmmm, no Stanford, just New England universities. How old? Well honestly, he could be a very likely age as his earned his undergrad degree in Massachusetts in 1968. It's entirely possible he could have hung out at Stanford during the spring of 1971. But if he did, there was no record of it. Even so, the only records of this individual were for things in New England. I would have to explore this individual much more later.

I tried various searches on a few different platforms, and found two more Richard Geikies in the USA, but neither were the right age. There were no Geikie even living in California. I went to Whitepages. com. "Dick Geikie" "Richard Geikie," just "Geikie." Again, no search yielded anyone who would be the likely age for a student, even allowing for a wide range of age in grad students. No Geikie had any tie to California.

I took to the Stanford Alumni website, and their Find an Alum search engine. I searched again for "Dick Geikie," "Richard Geikie," and just "Geikie." NOTHING. No one by that name was in their records. I went to the Stanford Yearbook archives. "Dick Geikie," "Richard Geikie," just "Geikie." NOTHING.

I realized that unless Dick Geikie was the Richard Geikie from New England, who earned his undergraduate and graduate degrees in New England, and who would have had come to Stanford without enrolling and had written an article for the *Chaparral* while there; unless ALL of that was true, I had NO plausible explanation for who Dick Geikie was. The chances that Dick Geikie was Richard Gaikowski were rising. But how on earth did he come to write for the *Chaparral*?

I went to the *Stanford Daily* newspaper archives and typed in "Dick Geikie" and low and behold, I got several hits…

Dick Geikie in the Stanford Daily

Dick Geikie has bylines on six *Stanford Daily* articles from June to August 1971, as well as one photo credit, and is also listed in the staff box twice. The following is a summary of Dick Geikie in the *Stanford Daily*.

June 25, 1971

The *Stanford Daily* printed an article by Dick Geikie on page seven titled Work-Study Program Initiated, about a program for Stanford Hospital workers.[150]

July 9, 1971

The *Stanford Daily* reprinted the March 5 *Stanford Chaparral* article by Dick Geikie about Computer Music. The article appears on page eight of the issue.[151]

Now I thought that was strange, I had never known that the *Chaparral* and *Daily* to share articles, but it made sense to me after I thought about it. Both publications were in newsprint format in those days, and I imagined the *Daily* needed content during the summer session. Dick Geikie likely suggested to the *Daily* to rerun it. I added a new column to the spreadsheets I was making: Chappie – *Daily* Overlap.

In the staff box of that *Daily* issue, Dick Geikie is listed under the heading Staff[152].

July 13, 1971

Dick Geikie finally made the front page of the *Stanford Daily* with an article, Campus Hosts Sixty Summer Workshops, about programs-at Stanford that were available to the general public[153]. For those looking for rational ways non-students could be on campus and not be out of place, here is some evidence. Presumed non-student Dick Geikie himself writes an article about it.

And if that sort of mild coincidence weren't enough, this issue's Once Around the Quad campus calendar has a listing for a meeting of the Radical Libertarian Alliance that very night, July 13, to be held in the *Chaparral* office[154].

"Who's writing this shit?" I bemused.

I had thought that politics might have brought Richard to Stanford. I had thought that something like "radical libertarianism" might be right up his alley. "Buzz cut guys who called cops pigs" just sounded so much like Richard. A mix of right and left politics reminded me very much of my long conversations with Richard in the 1990s. Now here they were in the same issue, in a meeting at the Chappie office. Who would believe it? I could hardly believe it.

July 27, 1971

Dick Geikie co-wrote an article about the demise of the *Midpeninsula Free* University.[155] That article contains an interview with Tim Coburn, a long-time *Chaparral* member and future editor. Tim Coburn was also a *Chaparral* evangelist. While working on the *Chaparral* book, I learned of at least five people who said they joined the *Chaparral* staff in the 1970s on the advice of Tim Coburn.

July 30, 1971

The *Daily* printed an article by Dick Geikie titled Med Clinic set up in San Jose[156]. There is a photo along with the article, also credited to Dick Geikie. The *Daily* staff box of this issue lists Night Lackeys "…who wished to remain anonymous."[157]

August 3, 1971

Page seven of this *Daily* issue lists Dick Geikie in the staff box under the heading Other Lackeys[158]. The staff box shares the page with a Once Around the *Quad* listing for a Radical Libertarian Alliance meeting in the *Chaparral* office that night, with Dr. Eugene Bleck giving a talk on educational vouchers at the regular closed meeting[159].

THE ONLY TIME RICHARD GOT ANGRY AT ME

August 6, 1971

The bottom of the front page of this issue contains the article, Sci-Fi Medium for Speculation, by Dick Geikie[160]. He is also listed in the staff box under the heading Night Staff, which also includes "and the masses."[161]

August 10, 1971

The *Daily* printed a smaller than normal four-page issue for its final issue of the summer. This was planned, as along with most of the student body, the publication always takes six weeks off at the end of summer. When summer term ends, the university becomes really deserted as it prepares for the new school year. Lots of maintenance, cleaning and repairs are taken care of in preparation for the students return near the end of September. There are no bylines or references to Dick Geikie in that final summer issue, but there is a farewell article that listed many events coming to the area in the next six weeks. The article concludes, "Whatever you do, have a good time. Until September 28th, Good Bye."[162]

I had all these new names to search for, in Google, Whitepages, and the Stanford Alumni Directory. I was eventually able to find some of the people in these *Daily* issues.

"What you have to understand, it was the summer," said U, "there were all kinds of people on campus, non-students, even high schoolers. And we were very short-staffed. We'd take help wherever we could get it."

I had experience in such matters: I had stayed on campus the summer of 1986, and understood implicitly about summer term. Sort of a wild, off-beat kind of time, with random people and hi-jinks on a sparsely populated, and at times, completely deserted campus.

So, I had someone named Dick Geikie who wrote an article for the *Stanford Chaparral* in March 1971, and who wrote for the *Stanford Daily* in June, July, and August 1971. And with initial attempts to identify this individual coming up empty, my head was somewhat spinning.

If Dick Geikie was Dick Gaik, then the entire story of Richard would have to be reconsidered.

Richard Geikie

It wasn't easy to find an answer about who Dick Geikie was at Stanford. No Dick Geikie in the Bay Area nor all of California. Two Dick Geikies in the Midwest, but neither anywhere near the age they would need to be, and neither any connections to California.

It was time to examine more closely a Richard Geikie from New England, as the only possible person who could be Dick Geikie. If so, this individual would have had to come to Stanford for the spring and summer of 1971, in between earning undergraduate and graduate degrees at New England universities.

I stewed on this possibility for two months, and finally broke down and contacted Richard Geikie's brother. Richard had passed way some years prior, and I found his brother's name via the online obituary. I found his phone number via another search engine.

I dialed the number, and… he picked up.

I told him I was working on the 125th anniversary of the *Stanford Chaparral*, which was true, hunting for bylines I had found in the *Chaparral* and *Stanford Daily*, which was also true. I told him I had the byline of Dick Geikie in a 1971 *Chaparral* and couldn't track down who that was, all of which is true. I did not tell him I was trying to rule out key exculpatory evidence in a murder case.

I asked him if his brother ever spent time at Stanford.

'Yes," he replied, "he went there often."

To be honest, I was quite disappointed to hear that, as my conjecture was now easily explained away. Dick Geikie was this individual.

"I just want to confirm," I asked, that your brother went often to Stanford University in California."

"California? Why no. I thought you said Stamford, in Connecticut. He often went to Stamford. My brother never went to California, as far as I know."

My dejection faded.

Richard Geikie's brother confirmed that not only did his brother not live in California at any time, did not study at Stanford, but by his memory his brother would have been in Austria in the summer of

1971. He didn't think there was any chance that the Dick Geikie in the Chaparral issue was his brother..

I thanked the gentleman and pondered the meaning.

Where's Dick?

Finding Dick Geikie was as elusive as ever, and the best possibility found so far, the only possibility other than it being Richard Gaikowski, had just been disproven. Dick Geikie was eluding all explanation via internet searches; Google, Whitepages, Spokeo, Radaris, newspapers.com, newspaperarchive.com, jstor.org, archive.org and more all came up empty for any Dick Geikie. None of the right age, none who ever lived in California. Stanford's Alumni Directory also had no Dick or Richard Geikie.

A distinct possibility was increasing in likelihood, that Dick Geikie didn't exist at all; that Dick Geikie was a fake name, a modification of Dick Gaik, Richard Gaikowski.

The situation led to a joke, "OMG, he didn't go to a mental hospital in 1971, he went to Stanford!" There is plenty of speculation online, that Richard was committed to a mental hospital sometime in spring of 1971. I have never been able to confirm nor disprove any of that, but if he needed mental healthcare, it made a perfect joke that he would be hanging around Stanford.

A funny coincidence is that if he did go to Napa State Hospital, he might have been examined by EB, editor of the *Stanford Chaparral* in 1952, who worked many years at Napa State Hospital eventually becoming its director. But I digress.

As for Stanford, political protest could have interested Richard. Part-time work could have been an attraction, or summer workshops. Or the lure of something rare and unique that Stanford offered: computer access to the general public.

When Richard started computer programming is an open question, as is where he might have had access to a computer as early as 1969. I previously conjectured that computers might also bring the Zodiac to a college campus, looking for time to code, likely during off-hours. What started as a hunch was now manifesting itself in the archived pages of the *Stanford Chaparral* and *Daily*.

The *Daily's* offices were part of the same Storke Publications Building as the *Chaparral*. The publications shared the same bathrooms—the bathrooms over which we hid the bear. The *Chaparral*'s balcony overlooked the doors of the *Daily*. Dick Geikie was writing for both the *Chaparral* and the *Daily* in 1971. There were political meetings in the *Chaparral* office during the same days, and nights, that Dick Geikie was there.

There was that creepy feeling again.

As for the effort to confirm Richard Gaikowski was NOT Dick Geikie, that had come up empty. The search continues to this day for some evidence, some record somewhere, or even plausible circumstance, that some other person than Richard Gaikowski, Dick Gaik, is the Dick Geikie at Stanford in 1971. None has been found.

The Flip was Total

So much for my Zodiac research ending. And so much for me joking about it. The flip had now become total. Yeah, I was making a *Chaparral* anniversary book. But now I had to reckon with the stark reality that I had indeed made an amazing discovery. And even if it turned out to be someone else, it's at least as funny coincidence as Who Shot R.R.? But if it were indeed true, this would be the greatest Chappie story of all time.

And I now had a very important question, the answer of which holds the key to everything:

"Who is Dick Geikie?"

It became a challenge to keep working on just *Chaparral* history, Zodiac research was taking over.

While I had started out primarily researching over a century of humor years of the *Chaparral*, with only casual interest in the five political years, now I changed 180 degrees to focus on the political years, 1969-1974. While collecting data for the Chaparral book, I looked for any and all information about Dick Geikie. What was the full extent of his activity at Stanford? Did it extend as far as September 1973? Could Dick Geikie and David Levine have known each other?

The flip was also fractal. I had been researching the *Chaparral*, with the Zodiac as a quirky sidebar. I had even joked to some *Chaparral* alums that I was doing *Chaparral* research as "cover" for my Zodiac research, but at the time it was truly a joke.

Now that "joke" had become the truth, and in many ways, the perfect cover to look into a VERY unsavory subject. Those five political years of the *Chaparral* that had always been such a mystery to Chappie friends and I were now the exact focus of this crazy story. The hippie years of the *Stanford Chaparral* became The Keystone.

My Dilemma

I also realized my loose lips and dark humor now became somewhat of a problem. No, they were an actual problem. A big problem. I had blabbed about Zodiac in a Zoom call. I had made fake Zodiac codes, and fake *Chaparral* issues, not to mention the fake Zodiac *Chaparral* issue. For that matter, I had made many fake *Chaparral* issues. I had fake *Chaparral* issues that other Chappies were accepting as real issues. This was all intended to be a funny prank that I had played on my fellow alums. But now because of the Dick Geikie discovery, this was going to absolutely be discussed in the context of the Zodiac Killer. And let's be realistic, the discovery of Zodiac AT Stanford University would be an amazing claims. When this news went public, there was only one thing to be certain of: It was going to be a shitstorm.

All my joking and fake issues not only had to stop, but I had to figure out how I would handle this problem of my own making. I began referring to this problem as My Dilemma.

The first thing I did was stop talking about Zodiac. I ceased all talk of murders, even the old time Chappie-adjacent murders. I hid the fake issue I had made and hid the joke code I had made about the Berkeley Bear theft. I went through my computer and removed all files, drafts, and other items related to the forgeries or the Zodiac from all of the Chappie directories. The entire topic was ghosted.

I wasn't sure what the ultimate solution to My Dilemma would be, but at least I had taken initial steps to address it.

And with that, I began an even deeper dive into the history of Stanford 1969-74, the *Daily* and the *Chaparral*, mapping it against the known history of Zodiac and other Mid Peninsula crimes of that era, looking for more evidence of Dick Geikie.

The Comical Problem of What Folder to Use?

By now I was downloading all kinds of articles, with the humorous dilemma of not knowing sometimes if I had a *Chaparral* item, or a Zodiac item, or both. It was often hard to decide what folder to put some items in. Does a layered photoshop document of all the 1970-71 *Chaparral* issues go in the *Chaparral* folder, or the Zodiac? The question was legitimate, and at the same time, ridiculous. There were so many questions like this.

The question was worse with certain files—some that needed to be in both folders. It sounds like a small thing, but as the number of files grew, over months that turned into years, it became an occasional comical event. And I had to make sure I didn't share my screen at the wrong time. One zoom call I caught myself at the last moment, about to share some *Chaparral* material while my desktop was otherwise full of Zodiac. That would have been a major mistake, that I thankfully avoided.

If Dick Geikie really is Dick Gaik

If Dick Geikie really is Richard Gaikowski, then a few other profound things are true:

Richard is on a college campus and is writing under an assumed name.

Richard is using yet another variation of "Gaik."

If Richard is Dick Geikie, then there is a much greater chance there are even more variations of Gaik. Most importantly, the chances increase that "Gyke" from Zodiac's 408-code is indeed another version of Gaik.

We know Richard liked to play with his bylines, mostly settling on Dick Gaik for his *Good Times* articles, but not exclusively. He might have also written under other names, joke names. We truly do not know the extent of the names Richard used. But if Dick Geikie is truly Richard, then it is another confirmed version of wordplay in his bylines. And with each confirmed alternate version, the likelihood becomes greater that he actually used many more.

I wondered if he used Dick Geikie for all of his Stanford activities? Did he perhaps take the computer music course or one of the 60 summer workshops he wrote about? If he did register for those classes as Dick Geikie, it is not just confirmation that Richard wrote under a fake name, but was conducting his life with a fake name. If so, that would be a profound revelation.

On the other hand, some might point out that Dick Geikie is so close to Dick Gaik that it doesn't matter. But if so, why bother changing it to Dick Geikie at all? What was the intent?

Then there were all those fake names in *Good Times*. He could be operating under a lot of names, and they don't have to have anything related to Gaik.

Richard is spending time at Stanford during a time of heightened bombing and arson.

This is just a simple fact. The dates of his bylines on the *Stanford Chaparral* and *Stanford Daily* coincide very much with the time of frequent bombings. Now this would be the case for anyone writing in the spring and summer of 1971, so it is by no means unexplainable. There is no judgement here, I only note that the opportunity existed.

Richard was hanging around the Storke Publications Building at Stanford

With bylines in both the *Stanford Daily* and *Stanford Chaparral*, Richard was clearly spending at least a moderate amount of time in the Storke Building. The Storke included the office of these publications, as well as the Stanford *Quad* yearbook and *Sequoia* poetry magazine offices. The building served as housing to many off-grid denizens, and included a dark room, great for photo developing and the go-to spot for romantic interludes in the facility.

To say Richard hung out around the Storke building is different than saying he hung out around the Tresidder Student Union, or any campus building, save perhaps the Band Shak. There was always activity there, official and non-official.

Richard never mentioned he was at Stanford, let alone worked for the *Chaparral*

To me, this is quite an important point, because the *Chaparral* was and is pretty much the entirety of my Stanford experience. I didn't exactly like the rest of the school; I spent most of my days at the Chappie office. My career is based on my *Chaparral* work, not my degree. When I talk about Stanford, I talk about the *Chaparral*. I'm positive I would have mentioned to Richard I was a Stanford graduate, it's how I started visiting San Francisco.

I am also certain Richard never mentioned that he worked for the *Chaparral*, because if he had I would have talked at length with him about it. I would want to see what he had written, asked him about the office, the parties, the scene, if he knew about the Hammer & Coffin. But he never told me. We talked about a lot of stuff, but this never came up.

I can take this one step further. I was helping Richard with his website as the 1990s approached its end. By 1999, we each had links to each other's website on our own websites. I also supplied Richard with the background for his site. Richard linked to my site from his, with a link named Eye Candy directing people to my Pulsators app[163]. On my site I had a Links page, with an offbeat listing of various things from John C. Lilly to Jaron Lanier to many other 1990s cyberculture miscellany. Richard Gaikowski listed right above The *Stanford Chaparral*[164]. There is no way I did not show him this page. There is no way we did not look at it together on one of my visits. What's more, you can verify this yourself, through the assistance of Archive.org and their Way-Back Machine, where the pages in question are preserved, both on my site and on his.

The point being: If Richard Gaikowski was indeed Dick Geikie, then he purposely did NOT tell me he hung out at Stanford, that he wrote for the *Chaparral* and *Daily*. So, while writing under the fake name Dick Geikie is not illegal, it is apparently not something Richard wanted to bring up, if indeed it was him.

The whole thing was either getting more bizarre or more comical, depending on how you looked at it.

Then I got an idea that in hindsight one would have thought was obvious: I went to the *Stanford Daily* archives and for the first time typed in a search term that I had never thought to try before on that particular publication. I put it in quotes just to make sure: "Zodiac Killer"

Stanford Daily's Message to the Zodiac Killer

I could hardly believe my eyes. There, in the October 24, 1969, *Stanford Daily*, at the top of page two, was an editorial titled, Message to the Zodiac Killer[165].

I blinked a few times. It was even too weird to hear the eerie music.

THE ONLY TIME RICHARD GOT ANGRY AT ME

I'll say it again: At the top of the *Daily's* opinion page on October 24, 1969, is an editorial titled Message to the Zodiac. I stared in disbelief. Then I started to read. The editorial asks Zodiac to give himself up, to the Daily, and invites him to a staff meeting the following Monday.

"Wow, that's ill-advised," I thought, or words to that effect. A college newspaper running an editorial inviting a serial killer on their campus HAD to be a bad joke, because it was certainly a bad idea. I mean, I've made jokes about Zodiac, but 50 years later, and I've never invited him to a meeting at my offices just twelve days after his most recent murder. That's a very bad idea.

Keep in mind, as a Chappie, I am well versed in bad ideas, ill-advised attempts at humor, at a university, in print. I'm sure the idea of printing this editorial sounded funny at the time, to someone. But even so, when I first saw the editorial, I had the same take. "Holy wow, that's a very bad attempt at humor," or words to that effect.

Even though I was vaguely coming to the conjecture that Zodiac could indeed have come to Stanford, I still didn't immediately think this editorial was relevant. Even an ill-advised-humor expert like me thought it was just a bad attempt at being funny.

In fact, it was indeed a parody, which is a form of humor.

I discovered that this editorial closely followed the pattern of the *San Francisco Examiner* editorial from the previous Sunday, also titled Message to the Zodiac Killer.[166] It was laid out in a similar way, with a black line around it, and it ran at the top of the page, although the *Daily* version is on page two rather than on the front page like the *Examiner's*. Stanford's version asked Zodiac to give himself up - to the *Daily* and invited him to a staff meeting the following Monday. It was either brave or foolish to invite a serial killer to your meeting. No, actually, just foolish.

"I wonder if this caused a shitstorm?" I thought.

Sure enough, the search results revealed that there were Letters to the Editor the following Friday.

When I clicked on that link, taking me to the October 31, 1969 issue, I was surprised to find only one short letter, titled Poor Taste. It was direct and to the point that the Message to the Zodiac editorial was inappropriate, callous, and that Stanford students should be smarter than this.[167]

And that was it. No shitstorm. The editorial and the following letter to the editor were the only two Zodiac Killer search results in the time period of the killings. It's so hard to predict what will cause a big blow up at Stanford. It often seems quite arbitrary. It seemed this one could have, or should have, but it didn't.

The next search result for "Zodiac Killer" was in 1974, and then again in 1978. Each were AP wire articles and not related to anything at Stanford.

Interestingly, there were eight more hits for Zodiac Killer from 1979 through 1985, where the Daily apparently reran the same article about San Francisco night clubs year after year. Yes, eight different times, for both summer guides and New Years specials, they ran an article that included the line: "San Francisco's nightclubs, even more than Herb Caen or the Zodiac Killer, distinguish this city."[168] Who knew?

I must somewhat disagree with this article. Everyone knew Herb Caen. A mention by him in his column brought instant notoriety and publicity across the Bay Area.

I also must somewhat agree. One reason I moved to San Francisco in 1993 was its rave and club scene, but I never heard of the Zodiac until well into the 21st Century.

Coming On Campus

By changing my search term in the *Stanford Daily* archives from "Zodiac Killer" to "Zodiac," I got significantly more hits, but almost all of them weren't relevant; ads for getting your chart done, astrology-themed products, and a record review for an album called *The Electric Zodiac*.

But I did find something interesting. Very interesting. In the November 5, 1969, *Stanford Daily* was a front-page story with the headline Zodiac Calls. It reported that the previous evening, November 4, Palo Alto police received a call from someone who claimed to be Zodiac and said they were coming on the Stanford campus in the next ten minutes. Police went on alert, but nothing happened[169].

Now you might think the eerie music would play, but my first take was that this was a prank call, likely related to the joke editorial. It appears that this is the collective take on the call as well. Just more stupid and tasteless college antics.

I ran a search in the newspaper archives including Palo Alto with Zodiac for fall of 1969, and I found it, or so I thought. But it was actually press reports of a different call, one to the *Palo Alto Times* on October 20, 1969, where the caller says they were leaving the city because they were "too hot." The caller also threatened to shoot children as they exit a school bus, a threat that had been widely reported by that time[170].

So, there were TWO calls to Palo Alto by someone threatening to be Zodiac, along with this joke *Daily* Zodiac editorial! I had missed these items when I read about Zodiac years ago. Of course, I wasn't looking for a Stanford tie-in back then. This was getting weird.

But even so, I still viewed all this as pranks. They were done at the height of Zodiac hysteria, October and November 1969. It was all over the news and on everyone's mind. My take was that someone around Stanford thought this was funny. Some drunk frat guys make the call, some *Daily* staffers think up the article, maybe the second call is from someone who happened upon the *Daily* article one night while really drunk or stoned, and picked up the phone. Even though I thought I might have Dick Gaik on campus in 1971, certainly Zodiac hysteria and bad college humor explained these events in 1969.

No One By That Name

Do you remember I was still working on the history of the *Stanford Chaparral*?

While researching for the 125th Anniversary of the *Chaparral*, I was able to ask the Alumni Association for help with names I could not find. I had several bylines from across the 125 years of people I could not find, so I submitted a list of them, with one of the names being Dick Geikie.

They confirmed to me that no Dick Geikie, nor Richard Geikie, ever went to Stanford.

Now, for the first time, an official body was confirming what I had suspected, that Dick Geikie was not a student, he was a visitor to Stanford. The odds that Dick Geikie was Dick Gaik continued to rise.

As noted earlier, there are a lot of non-students at Stanford during summer quarter, so this is not a smoking gun by any means. That said, if Stanford had been able to confirm Dick Geikie was a student, then this story would have been over. But they didn't.

Non-Students on Campus

As was described to me by another student of the era, "Stanford had all kinds of people from off-campus in those days. Earlier it was cheaper to live off campus, but that changed, and it became very expensive, so a bunch of people who had been living off campus came back on. There were also a bunch of non-students who started living on campus. People were sleeping anywhere and everywhere. Off campus people were common."

Crashing in the lounges, the common rooms, or nooks and crannies was also common in some of the houses at Stanford, and not just the communes. While a classic Stanford commune like Columbae might have had a permanent non-student component of residents, in this era there were non-students residing for periods of time in all sorts of campus housing.

Another individual described what it was like during the summer, with all kinds of non-students hanging out on campus. Some were high school students coming to campus the summer before their senior year of high school to see how they liked it. Some were students and professors visiting from other schools. Even Dick Geikie's computer music article, yes, that one, on the page with the Missing Link contains the passage "Most of the people taking the course," noted Dr. (Leland) Smith, "are from other universities. They are learning the techniques of generating computer music to return and set up similar departments at their own schools."

So, large numbers of non-students on the Stanford campus in the early 1970s is confirmed.

Open Campus

I found even more confirmation of this. In 1970, there was an Open Campus movement, with two weekends in May of that year devoted to it.

When I discovered that the summer 1970 *Stanford Daily* issues were not available, I started examining the spring issues more closely. The arson and Molotov cocktail attacks that occurred at that time were of interest, particularly those on computer facilities on campus. I knew from references in other news articles that there had been an attempted arson at the computer center in Polya Hall, but I did not know the date or details.

I eventually found an article on the front page of the May 18, 1970, *Stanford Daily*. As I filled in my spreadsheet, the sub-spreadsheet with just arsons and bombs on it, I looked at the rest of the page to see what it might yield. The top right-hand story of this *Stanford Daily* was an article about the Open Campus that had occurred the previous Friday, May 15.[171]

"I wonder who went to that?" I sort of joked to myself.

The article, First Open Campus Draws 400, describes a successful event, much larger than the organizers anticipated. They were also thrilled with the participation and level of discourse between the students and the outside people described as "businessmen, housewives, retired people, veterans of foreign wars, Birchers, Communists and anarchists."

Organizers stated they were issuing open invitations to the general public for the next few Fridays and Saturdays via open invitations in the local press. As directly reported in the article:

"One San Francisco newsman characterized the day's events as an attempt by students to reunite America and to dispel the notion that college students are engaged in a conspiracy against the broader society."

Now I understand that there were thousands, or at least hundreds, or even just dozens of "San Francisco newsmen" in May of 1970, but I hope you can understand my reaction to reading this in an article, when I was specifically wondering about who might be in attendance. Yet another One F of a Coincidence.

On May 25, 1970, the *Stanford Daily* reported on the second of such weekends, and printed an article titled, Open Campus A Success. Almost 800 people from outside the campus attended, double that of the previous weekend[172].

The Midpeninsula Free University

As I discovered, non-students on campus pre-dates 1970 by a lot. In fact, my ignorance of the situation was almost comical. The Midpeninsula Free University played an enormous role in ringing non-students on campus beginning in 1966 and right through to 1971.

The Free University movement was nationwide, in several locations across the country. One of the most vibrant locations of this movement was at Stanford with the Midpeninsula Free University.

Anyone could teach a course, or take a course, from art, to music to photography to gardening, to pottery, math and science, yoga and massage, from politics from computer programming to astrology, or hundreds of other courses from the practical to the esoteric. There were lots of classes for body and sexual awakening, and the catalog of classes might just show a young couple completely naked. This was the sixties. Classes were held both off campus and on, during the day and night, and there was a constant dialogue about which location for the classes was best. It brought hundreds, if not thousands, of people onto the Stanford campus.

The FreeU continued to thrive until 1971, when annual elections brought new management to the organization. Within six months, the Midpeninsula Free University basically ceased to exist.

Chaparral Staff Photo

In the online archives of Stanford's Green Library, there are some *Chaparral* and Hammer & Coffin materials. This archive was very helpful while working on the *Chaparral* anniversary. It was not really helpful at all in Zodiac research, with one exception.

There was a black and white photo of a group of 12 people in the *Chaparral* office, presumably the Chappie staff, and certainly from the political era, as one individual is holding a newsprint issue up for the camera, and the clothing and hairstyles in the photo are certainly of that era. The photo had no other identification, no year, no names, no caption.

But for what it's worth, I thought some of the people in the photo looked much older than college age. A man in the lower right and another in the upper left stood out to me. After learning about the Free University and the Open Campus movements, the conjecture that the two men could be non-students was not that far-fetched. What's more, the man in the upper left looked sort of like Richard to me.

I had seen online pictures of Richard at various times in his life.

The photos included one from 1964, where he has a buzz cut and classic 1960s thick-rimmed glasses, one from the January 1, 1972 *Good Times* cover where he was quite hairy with a full beard and wire-rimmed glasses, and another from around 1978 where he had a much shorter beard and a clean cut hairstyle also with wire-rimmed glasses. It's really amazing how different the same person can look over just 12 years, let alone a lifetime.

In the back row of people in the *Chaparral* staff photo there was a man who could easily be Richard. He was clean shaven, with wire-rimmed glasses and hair starting to get hippy but not yet—over the ears and almost to the base of the neck. I wasn't sure, but he looked close enough to Richard that I endeavored to identify everyone in the picture. Can you imagine if I actually had found a picture of him at Stanford in the Chappie office?

I downloaded the picture. It was of reasonable quality, but quite grainy when trying to look at details, like what issue the person was holding up, or identifying the papers strewn about on the table that the staffers were sitting around. Using graphics software, I blew up the photo and sharpened it the best I could.

I was finally able to identify the papers on the table, They said "A Warship Can Be Stopped." From there, I was able to learn that it was a tabloid printed for a protest on November 5, 1971, in support of the sailors of the USS Coral Sea. This was quite exciting. Not only did I have a date to work with, but this protest was also covered by *Good Times*.

I was also able to identify that one person was wearing a shirt that said "Blood Rock." Through more googling, I learned about the band and their one big hit, D.O.A, released in 1971. By any measure, the song is macabre, fairly creepy, telling a first-person account of a couple in a motorcycle wreck, bleeding to death, arriving at the hospital dead on arrival.

Let me tell you, that song was an apt soundtrack for my research, and I played it over and over during this period.

I wasn't completely without ideas of who was in the picture, I had some names of Chappies from the general era. I also had access to Stanford yearbooks, at least the 1969, 1970, and 1971 editions. There was no *Stanford Quad* yearbook in 1972 and 1973, a point that made a lot of this research much more difficult than it would have been otherwise. There were also a few Stanford Froshbooks online, books with photos of all incoming freshmen, but also with a few years missing. If the protest era did anything, it was to break the faithful chronicling of the school year by the yearbook, first being replaced by stream of consciousness layouts, followed by years of just not printing a yearbook at all. So while my task of identifying people in an old photo would have been difficult enough, it was even more difficult because of the particulars of era.

I spent quite a bit of time on this, and little by little, started to identify people in the photo. Eventually I had four identified, and I even found their emails through the alumni association. Through correspondence with them, I got a few more identified, but none of the people remembered the individual who I thought might be Richard. It was a tantalizing line of research, with the potential of absolutely confirming that Richard was at Stanford. This photo was a central part of my investigation for several months.

The 408-code Revisited

With Dick Geikie actually writing for the *Stanford Daily*, and with the possibility I had a photo of him in the Chappie office, I decided to dig in deeper on some Zodiac items I had been wondering about. One of those things was the 408-code. In my opinion, discussion about this code seemed circular and incomplete.

The 408-code is often described as solved, but in reality, it is only partially solved, the final 18 characters are still unknown. Furthermore, if we believe the killer to be truthful, his identity should be in part three of this code. Is it in the 18 unsolved characters, which happen to reside in part three? Is it, as others maintain, the GYKE sequence of letters?

There is a lot of debate about this online. Frankly, I was tired of reading the back and forth and decided to do my own analysis of the code. For clarity, and because details are important, let's do a quick review of the facts.

As we know, the Zodiac's 408 Cipher was divided into three parts, and sent to three different Bay Area newspapers, Gibson Publishing, the owner of the *Vallejo Times-Herald*; the *San Francisco Examiner*; and the *San Francisco Chronicle,* on July 31, 1969. This was nearly four weeks after the July 4th murders, and about eight weeks before

Lake Berryessa. Each mailing also included a letter demanding that the enclosed code appear on the front page of the paper the following Friday, or else he'll go on a killing spree.

Part one of the code was sent to the *Vallejo Times-Herald*, which sort of makes sense. After all, so far all the murders had occurred in that area, why not start there? The second letter was sent to the *San Francisco Examiner* with identical text, along with Part two of the code. Part three of the code was sent to the *San Francisco Chronicle*, with a letter identical to the other two, EXCEPT the added line, "in this cipher is my identity."

On the fourth line of the third part of the 408-code is the four-letter sequence GYKE. Richard called himself Gaik, authored articles as Dick Gaik and D. Gaik. I have read some accounts that he also spelled it Gike, but I have never been able to independently verify that.

In no known byline or other writing did he spell it Gyke. This is a very important point to those who discount Richard Gaikowski as a Zodiac suspect. To those who think Richard is not Zodiac, GYKE is just a coincidence.

Yet again we have circumstances that are either relevant, or just coincidence. And possibly One F of a Coincidence, because it's not just that GYKE appears in the code, but that those four letters cipher to AUSE. Hey, maybe it's all a coincidence.

Now consider the possibility that he wrote under the name Geikie. When you have an EI or an IE in some languages like English or German, the second letter determines how it is pronounced. Geikie rhymes with spikey. Geik rhymes with bike, Mike, and…Gaik.

On the other hand, Geikie is a Scottish name, and they pronounce it with a hard E: geeky. It's worth noting that the Scottish pronounces both the EI and the IE in Geikie as a hard E. And while I could find no direct reference for Polish, the ethnic background of Richard, his name contains AI that is pronounced as hard I. So, it is a reasonable conjecture that he would pronounce the EI in Geikie the way he pronounced the AI in Gaikowski. Regardless, punsters and word-jokers use both spelling and pronunciation to make their jokes.

Those who discount GYKE in the code, saying he never spelled it that way, seem to miss the point that it is phonetic. The foundation of puns play is with phonetics—two words that sound the same or similar, creating a joke. GYKE is a phonetic match to "Gaik," as is AUSE to "ows."

My final point to those who discount GYKE in the 408 cipher: Can you imagine if Richard was Zodiac, and he indeed wrote GAIK in the cipher, and had it solve to OWSK? I mean, why bother with a code at all? Why not just confess? If you made it that easy, it would be the equivalent to a confession. Of course you would not do that. One also would not use the name Gaikie, as it would be too obvious, to close to Gaik.

In this cipher is my identity

The 408-code was mostly solved in just a few days. All of part one. All of part two. And almost all of part three. Of the eight lines of part three, only the first seven lines, minus the last letter of line seven, have been solved, leaving the 18 unsolved characters.

When the code was broken, by Don and Betty Harden, they wrote "signature" over the last line. Of course, they thought this must be where Zodiac encoded his name. He had written that this cipher contained his identity no less, so it was obvious. Right? It was a very logical assumption that those final 18 letters were indeed where the identity was, and the killer had changed the code for them to make it harder to crack. My god, anyone could see that.

This final line of the 408-code remains unsolved to this day. Using the same cipher as the rest of the code, it reveals gibberish. So, it is either encoded differently than the rest of the message, is some kind of anagram or component word, or is indeed gibberish.

In the MysteryQuest TV show about Richard, Blaine plays audio that he claims is Richard. As I have said previously, it sure sounds like Richard to me. In the audio clip, Richard talks about the military sending gibberish codes to throw the enemy off.

So I ask, if you were going to hide your name in a cipher, and you really didn't want it to be cracked, might a line of gibberish at the end be the perfect thing to throw people off the trail?

I know this contradicts the thinking that the Zodiac was indeed truthful, but I've only conjectured that he was mostly truthful. More-over, it doesn't have to be all one or the other. By his own writing, Zodiac is aware of the concept of leaving "fake clews" as he spelled it.

Part three of the 408-code is high stakes, he's putting his name in there. He needs to make sure it is not too easy. Outside the box thinking would be called for. Adding in the bogus letters would create some added insurance to throw people off the trail.

And it is a <u>certainty</u> that Zodiac wanted part three of this code to be harder to solve. How can I say it is a certainty? The breakdown of the 408-code in the next section will show that very simply.

408-Code Deep Dive

I decided to break down the code myself, and diagram how it was constructed. From that, I would be able to comment on it free from the noise of 50 years of debate. This process greatly increased my understanding of Zodiac's coding methods, and allows me to state the following opinions on this with cautious confidence.

It is indeed a certainty that Zodiac wanted part three of the code to be harder to solve. We know this by how the code is constructed. This code is not a simple letter-substitution code. For most of the letters, Zodiac used more than one symbol, substituting them in a sequence. For example, the letter E is encoded with seven different symbols: Z, P, W, +, O, N, and E, in a repeating sequence. Starting in cipher part one, the sequence repeats five times perfectly, but on the sixth time, one line above GYKE, it goes awry: Z, P, W, +, W, Z, E, O, Z, +, W.

This pattern of sequences repeating perfectly for a while, before being modified at their end is consistently replicated for other letters: S, I, A, H, R, L , T, N, and O. The letter E has the longest sequence, using seven letters, many others have four letter sequences, some have three or two, and a few letters use just one letter.

The effect of this is that, with a couple of exceptions (that might be mistakes), part one of the code is entirely consistent; part two is almost entirely consistent, with a few exceptions starting at the bottom of this part of the code; but part three is VERY inconsistent. It is clear that Zodiac wanted part three of the code to be harder to crack, and/or he was making exceptions so as to force another message into the puzzle.

Here's the thing, if you did want to do something like encode your name in both the puzzle and the solution of your code, it wouldn't be the easiest thing to do. As I found when making my Berkeley Bear code, it was hard to not have unintended consequences. You could not just change a letter, without checking to see how it affected all the code. One would almost certainly have to make exceptions or do some kind of rigging to make the code work out.

In plain English that means you would likely have to make exceptions in your coding rules to make the joke happen. If the Zodiac's name were indeed in the third part of the code, there would likely be evidence of exceptions or inconsistencies in it.

But this would be a tricky operation. If your exceptions were too clunky, you might very well give yourself away. The perpetrator might actually tip their hand by showing WHERE the exceptions occurred. So I conjectured that the substitutions would be numerous—helping to camouflage the key ones, in part three of the code. I began my diagramming of the code in earnest.

I decided to color-code the solution: very light grey when the code followed its rules, meaning when a letter was encoded in its established sequence. When a letter did NOT follow the established sequence, it is colored black. When there was something I did not understand, or a possible mistake, I marked the symbol in a dark grey. The 18 unsolved characters at the end I put in white with black outline.

When you apply the shading, the point about exceptions becomes obvious.

You can clearly see that the top section has no code exceptions, save for the possible mistakes. The second section begins that way as well, but starting with its final lines there is a large increase in the exceptions. The exceptions continue into the third section of code, which becomes mostly exceptions. Most of the letters in part three that are light grey are those where only one symbol was used to encode the letter, so of course they stayed consistent.

The last 18 characters remain uncracked, seemingly unrelated to the rest of the code. At minimum it uses a different cipher, or has an additional filter, or is an anagram. Or perhaps it is just gibberish to throw people off.

This exercise shows that effort was being made in part three of the code. Why would one bother to switch all of those letter sequences for no good reason? Perhaps just wanted to F with people, maybe just to throw people off the trail. The fact remains that GYKE didn't have to appear, both the G and the E were exceptions to their letter sequences. Without such exceptions, GYKE should have been SYKZ.

The tricky part of this, or perhaps the prank part, is that I'm sure everyone initially thought that the name would be revealed when the cipher was cracked. That was their first take—solve the cipher and the name would be revealed. When it wasn't there, people didn't accept it, and got the idea that Zodiac was lying.

When combined with the fact that the 340 code, which for decades people believed a fake code and used as evidence of the Zodiac lying, was actually a real code, I began to come to the opinion that Zodiac was mostly truthful.

Either way, because of the numerous code substitutions in part three, and the 18 unsolved characters, it is my opinion that the identity of the Zodiac is indeed in there, whether it's GYKE, or someone else.

By Knife By Gun By Rope By Fire

In Zodiac's Halloween card to Paul Avery, he says, "By Knife By Gun By Rope By Fire." This is apparently another comic book reference, this time to a 1952 Tim Holt comic book which contained a Death Wheel citing these options as ways to die.

Under the truthful murderer theory, it would seem a clear indication of the ways Zodiac was killing or intended to kill.

Lake Herman, Blue Rock Springs, and Paul Stine were all by gun. Lake Berryessa was by knife, although he showed the victims his gun, and he tied them up with rope. Still, when he wrote on the car at Lake Berryessa, Zodiac listed that murder as By Knife.

So where were the deaths By Rope and By Fire?

In the July 12, 1971, *Stanford Daily*, Dick Geikie's article Campus Hosts Sixty Summer Workshops shared the front page with some other interesting articles.[173] There was one about Venceremos splitting into smaller groups, and another about Stanford administrator Robert Nelson's house being bombed in the Stanford "faculty ghetto," which is not a ghetto at all. It's a sarcastic term to describe a nice area of campus where many professors and administrators live. Nelson was the administrator who fired the five employees of Stanford Hospital because of the April 6, 1971 sit-in. Luckily, the pipe-bomb caused no injuries, but it did create $1,000 in damage. This got me to thinking…

By Fire

Bombs, pipe-bombs, Molotov cocktails, and arson would all be ways to kill that could be classified as "By Fire." If we take Zodiac at his word and accept that he killed in all four ways he claimed, by gun, by knife, by rope, by fire, and if we accept that at least some of his claimed murders post-October 1969 are true, then we are looking for some murders or attempted murders using fire and bombs.

It is not much speculation at all to talk about bombs, Zodiac sure did, a lot. Beginning with the Nov. 9, 1969 letter where he states he is going to disguise his murders. The letter goes on for several pages talking about bombs, including diagrams and a recipe for a "Death Machine," an elaborate bomb with a timer. This talk of bombs continued in several other of his communications.

I endeavored to find all press accounts of bombs and arson for the years in question, to see if any observation or trend was discernible. Where were the bombs and arson attacks in the Bay Area in the late sixties and early seventies? When did they occur at Stanford or the Mid-Peninsula?

There were a lot of incidents to document, and this process was time consuming. But there were certain trends.

In 1968 and the first two months of 1969, there were many bombings around Palo Alto. These were traced to a Nazi-sympathetic group targeting left-wing groups, namely the Midpeninsula Free University.[174] The arrest and charging of nine individuals on February 14, 1969, appears to coincide with a lessening of such attacks. There were bombings in March and April 1969, but these differ in style and method and police believe these to be pranks by juveniles, including cherry bombs placed in a teacher's mailbox.

Post-arrests, there are only two more events that come close to fitting the profile of these previous bombings.

And while there are indeed bombs, Molotov cocktails and fire associated with the protests of the 1960s, it is interesting to note that the term pipe-bomb does not appear in the *San Francisco Chronicle* during the years 1967, 1968, and most of 1969. It does appear very often from then on.

Stanford's First Bomb Incident

On October 30, 1969, a fake bomb was placed on the Stanford campus, under the Willow Road Bridge over San Francisquito Creek, and a call was made to the Stanford Fire Department at 4:20 pm. The bomb was complete with a mechanism, showing that whoever left it knew how to make a bomb, but in this case the cylinders were filled with dirt and not explosives.

This was an area of very high traffic, particularly during the afternoon rush hour. An actual bomb explosion at this location would have likely killed or injured many people. Placing a working bomb mechanism, albeit with dirt in the cylinders instead of explosives, at this high-traffic location at Stanford, was certainly meant to scare, and signal that the perpetrator had the technical skill to make a bomb, and the ability to place it secretly where it could kill many people.

This is the first bomb event, real or fake, on the Stanford campus during the entire protest era of the late sixties and early seventies. There had been bombs in Palo Alto, Menlo Park and the surrounding area, but this is the first one on the actual Stanford campus.

When I saw the date of the bomb hoax, I wondered if it had made the *Daily*, and if so, would it be in the October 31 issue that had the Zodiac Letter to the Editor? Sure enough, it was on the front page with the headline Bomb Hoax Alarms Stanford Firemen[175]. The story also appeared in the *Peninsula Times-Tribune* October 31 issue[176] and included a photo of the elaborate device, but that seems to be the extent of newspaper coverage of the hoax.

There were other bombs in the area on that same day, one of the final attacks against the Midpeninsula Free University. Later that night, cars were firebombed at 1001 Forest Avenue in Palo Alto, the home of a Free University administrator.[177]

I think it would be easy to conflate these events on the same day, but one must keep in mind that the Willow Road bridge was a complete bomb mechanism, just with dirt instead of explosives, and the car bombs that night were Molotov cocktails, a bottle gasoline plugged with a cloth that is set on fire and thrown.

The Stanford bomb hoax was followed by three bomb threats in the mid to south peninsula in November 1969, at Mountain View High School, Woodside Priory School, and the Pacific Telephone and Telegraph Building in San Jose. The PT&T call resulted in an almost immediate arrest, as the call had been made to the telephone company and was easily traceable.

The next bomb event of significance in this geography is on Feb-

THE ONLY TIME RICHARD GOT ANGRY AT ME

ruary 25, 1970, when a pipe-bomb was left on the campus of San Jose State, near the student newspaper. The blast was in the middle of the night, so luckily no one was injured. The bomb was a construction of gunpowder stuffed in an iron pipe with a fuse mechanism.

1970 Arson at Stanford

On April 23, 1970, three firebombs were thrown into the house used by the Free Campus Movement while a meeting of 20 members was going on.[178] Thankfully there were no injuries. Later that night, a bomb threat was called into KZSU, Stanford's student radio station, but it was a hoax.

On April 24, 1970, there was a particularly bad arson attack on the Behavioral Sciences Building. While there were, thankfully, again no injuries, the blaze caused widespread damage and the tragic loss of many years of irreplaceable research of several professors[179].

Then on May 15, 1970, there was an arson attack on Polya Hall, the building that housed SAIL, the Stanford Artificial Intelligence Lab. Sometime after 2 am the fire was discovered by Professor John McCarthy and was quickly put out, causing minimal damage.[180] The story about this fire shared the front page of the May 18, 1970 *Stanford Daily* with the previously mentioned story about the first Open Campus day at Stanford, the article that contained the quote from the "San Francisco newsman."

Summer Daily 1970?

It was during the search for bombings and arson at Stanford, that I first noticed that the *Daily* archives had no issues from the summer of 1970. As I have said and repeat now, the *Daily* archives are very good, easy to use and very thorough. I was surprised to see no issues in the summer of 1970, and figured that perhaps they had a down year. Certainly, student publications go through lean times, the *Chaparral*, the *Sequoia* and *Quad* had such times, particularly in the chaos of this era. No *Daily* in the summer of 1970 seemed plausible to me. Either way, I didn't labor on this too much, as I had Dick Geikie at Stanford in 1971, from March through August. I wondered, would there be an uptick of bombs and arson during this time?

The Summer of 1971

The conventional wisdom about the violence of these years was that it was in response to the suspension of Professor Bruce Franklin at Stanford. And of course that was a primary cause, as was the Vietnam War and the draft. I am not here to dispute that. What I would like to point out, is that an individual who liked violence, bombs and fires, would be right at home in all this.

This subject, the protests at Stanford and other universities, deserves many books devoted to it, with detailed examination of the causes, the motives, the personalities, the groups, the schisms, the splinter groups, the protests, the takeovers. Taoists. Maoists. High-Browists. I'm not going into the incredible epic tale of Bruce Franklin. This is not the book for that. But you can't discuss this topic without knowing the basic gist of what happened. In that light, here is a very brief summary.

Dinkelspiel Protest

The good times of summer of 1971 have their roots in the very first week of January. The *Stanford Daily* reported in its January 4 issue that the Revolutionary Union (RU) was splitting into two groups, the "Avakian group" that would retain the RU name, and a new group, Venceremos.[181]

Then on January 11, a speech by Henry Cabot Lodge Jr. was disrupted at Stanford's Dinkelspiel Auditorium. Whether people were under the orders of Franklin at the Lodge speech is unclear, but that was the university's position. They brought disciplinary actions against him. At the hearing, Franklin said he wished he had disrupted it more.

Then on January 25, Bruce Franklin was arrested at a rally and charged with felony assault of a police officer[182]. Multiple witnesses said it was an unprovoked attack by the police on Franklin. Actually, they said, "by the pigs."

On January 26, Franklin faced criminal court[183]. On January 28, he faced Stanford Judicial Council (SJC). President Lyman was requesting suspension of Franklin.[184] The meeting had so many attendees it was forced to recess.

On January 31, four students involved with the Lodge disruption were suspended for contempt[185].

On February 9, the Defense Collective representing all the Lodge disrupters walked out of the SJC and its "farcical trial."[186] The next day, February 10, Vietnam activists declared a general strike for noon to protest intervention in Laos. The campus was a powder keg.

The Riot

And that powder keg went off. A long day and night of confrontation, violence, vandalism, arrests and shootings. Protesters occupied the Computation Center and other buildings. In separate incidents, two students were shot by unknown assailants, although an all-points bulletin went out for a 5' 10" white male driving a Volkswagen. Coincidentally, both students were shot in the thigh. Luckily, the wounds were not fatal in either case[187].

President Lyman could not wait any more. On February 12, he suspended Franklin, and the university filed a restraining order against him.[188] Stanford also filed an injunction against 16 individuals deemed to be the ringleaders of campus protests.

On February 16, Franklin ignored his suspension and taught his class to an overflowing crowd.[189]

On February 26, President Lyman laid out the charges against Franklin and the case for dismissal.[190]

On March 3, in San Francisco, thirteen Stanford students were charged with felony counts of violating the Selective Service act.[191] Meanwhile in the Mid-Peninsula, final arguments began in the Injunction Hearing for the 16 defendants. The trial continued through March 5.

On March 5, 1971, the *Chaparral* printed an issue with the headline Justice at Stanford? On the cover are two pictures, one of a policeman in riot gear, the other of President Dick Lyman shown looking wistfully at a headline tacked on a bulletin board that says "Report: Nixon to Head Stanford University."[192] This photo of Lyman coincidentally also ran in the January 15, 1971, *Stanford Daily*, and the 1971 Stanford *Quad*, the only known photo in history to run in all three publications, albeit with drastically different croppings.

Realize that Lyman had only been president for a few months, so the idea he would be thinking of an exit shows just how dire the situation was on campus. For the record, it was just a joke that he was looking for such a quick exit. The origin of the publication containing that headline, and how it came to be posted on a *Daily* bulletin board, is unknown, but it is immortalized on that March 5 *Chaparral* cover.

On March 9, the preliminary injunction was issued against 17 individuals and one organization.[193]

On March 23, Lyman filed formal charges with Stanford's Advisory Board[194].

On June 16, an FBI informer who had been undercover at Stanford testified to a US Senate committee. In the June 22 *Stanford Daily*, Bruce Franklin is quoted as saying, "We were telling people two years ago he was probably a pig."[195]

Franklin's hearing would not be until September, so the tumultuous 1970-71 school year came to an end and summer session began. Dick Geikie has his first *Stanford Daily* byline on June 25.[196]

Between April 5, and July 28, 1971, there were nine bombs in Palo Alto, Stanford, and the immediate vicinity, and fourteen, if San Jose and Santa Cruz are included. Palo Alto, Menlo Park, Stanford, Woodside, Los Altos, San Jose, Ben Lomond, and Santa Cruz would all be hit by bombs, and Stanford's Junipero dorm lounge and the offices of the Stanford Free Campus Movement would be set ablaze by an arson. There had been arson at Stanford before, but the bombs were something new, beginning in the spring of 1971.

Conventional wisdom says this is related to the suspension of Franklin. He had been the central professor involved in the protests for some time. But he was out, almost certainly going to be out forever, and moreover, 17 individuals and one organization had restraining orders placed on them. The thinking of the day was surely the bombs are from the activists of the Mid-peninsula or South Bay. That's a very easy, and very likely explanation. I agree with that explanation. But as I said, can you imagine such a time and place for a serial killer interested in bombs?

If someone was killing and disguising his activity, why not disguise it as political activism? That would be just as good a cover as any.

The Sunshine Express, or Maybe Brigade

The April 5, 1971, bombing of the Bank of America in Ben Lomond, a small town near Santa Cruz, might not be classified with the

THE ONLY TIME RICHARD GOT ANGRY AT ME

bombs around Palo Alto and Stanford, if it were not for an individual who claimed responsibility for it. A male caller, identifying himself as Earl Grant, called the KQED TV station in San Francisco and said he was part of the Sunshine Brigade or Sunshine Express, a group, according to them, sympathetic to the Weathermen[197].

The same person called KQED again on April 15, 1971, claiming responsibility for the bombing of Fairchild Camera on Deer Creek Road in Palo Alto that day[198]. The April 16 issue of the *Palo Alto Times* is the lone reference to the group Sunshine Brigade or Sunshine Express, and it is not explained why there are two names. In between these Sunshine Brigade bombings chronologically was a bombing on April 11, 1971, at the Merrill, Lynch, Pierce, Fenner and Smith office on University Ave. in Palo Alto.[199]

President's Office Bomb

At approximately 3:50 am on Friday, April 23, 1971, a bomb exploded in the attic of the Stanford *Quad* above the President's office[200]. The bomb blew a small hole in the ceiling of the office. The bomb used C-4 plastic explosives. It was discovered that only one of two devices had exploded. A subsequent search of the attic system in the Stanford Quadrangle found a duffle bag full of Molotov cocktails.

Earlier in the evening, a sniper fired into the transformers at the PG&E substation on campus, causing an oil leak. The leak was discovered and mitigated, preventing what officials believed would have been an explosion that would have knocked out electric power to the entire campus. Investigators believed the two events were related[201].

Junipero Lounge Fire

Then two days later, on April 26, 1971 at approximately 3:24 am, a fire was set in the Junipero dorm lounge[202]. According to the April 27 *Stanford Daily*, the arson attack gutted the entire room. Luckily, the lounge area is separated from the student rooms, and the fire was contained to the lounge. Those studying nearby said there was a sudden "whoosh" and blast of hot air. It was speculated that this was a right-wing attack on the dorm that housed many black students and members of various left-wing organizations.

Two other arson attacks within minutes of the Junipero fire were reported, and another fire in Roble dorm that was not believed to be arson[203].

More Bombs

On May 1, a Bank of America branch was bombed in Santa Cruz[204]. A caller to a radio station claimed the bomb for the People's Revolutionary Army. Bank of America was a frequent target of bombs.

On May 6, 1971, a pipe-bomb caused damage to a Pacific Gas and Electric Company substation in Monta Vista[205].

On May 30 and 31, 1971, two pipe-bombs were found in Woodside. One had a cigarette fuse, not yet detonated. The other bomb also did not detonate[206].

On June 2, two pipe live pipe bombs were found in Monta Vista, near where the previous bomb had gone off just a month earlier.[207]

Then on June 7, 1971, a pipe-bomb exploded at the Wells Fargo Bank in Menlo Park causing minor damage[208].

Disaster was averted on June 16, 1971, when an unexploded pipe-bomb was found at the Santa Cruz County Administrative Center. Demolition specialists from Fort Ord disposed of the bomb[209].

Willy and the Poor Boys

On June 29, 1971, a pipe-bomb exploded in front of the Transamerica Title Insurance Corp. office in Palo Alto. A letter written in felt-tip pen was mailed to the Palo Alto Times the next day from Willy and the Poor Boys that claimed solidarity with the workers at Stanford, and used the term "pig" twice. The note was reprinted on the front page of the July 1 Palo Alto Times[210].

Willy and the Poor Boys, is, of course, the title of Creedence Clearwater Revival's epic album, recorded at Wally Heider Studios in San Francisco and released October 29, 1969. The hit album was CCR's third album of that year. It was certified gold in December 1970. The song Down on the Corner, from the album, is about fictional band Willy and the Poor Boys.

Do you know the way?

On July 4, 1971, a pipe-bomb at the IRS office in San Jose caused $500,000 of damage[211].

Hospital-Related Bomb?

On July 12, 1969, a pipe-bomb exploded at the home of Stanford personnel director Robert Nelson-on the Stanford campus. He had fired the five employees involved in the Stanford Hospital, April 6, 1971, sit-in. The bomb caused $1,000 in damage[212].I already noted that in the July 13 *Daily*, Dick Geikie's article on Summer Workshops shared the front page with news of this bomb.

What I haven't mentioned is that *Good Times* covered the Stanford Hospital protest[213]. Their April 16, 1971, issue has a lengthy article on it written by "revoman," a fake name that was used only once. That same issue also carried a syndicated article from the Earth News about the offices of the *Stanford Daily* being raided[214]. This raid, initiated to confiscate the *Daily's* photos of the protest, resulted in the Supreme Court case Zurcher v. *Stanford Daily*, settled in 1978 in favor of the police. *Good Times* didn't cover many things at Stanford at all, but they did cover the hospital protest and its aftermath.

As for Dick Geikie, two of his six articles for the *Stanford Daily* are medical-related: an article on June 25, 1971, about a work/study program for Stanford Hospital workers, and a July 30 article about a San Jose medical clinic set up by Stanford medical students to serve a disadvantaged community. In the San Jose article, Dick Geikie also has the photo credit.

In September 1971, Robert Nelson resigned from his position.

The Second Time Around

On July 24, 1971, there was a pipe-bomb at an armory in Santa Cruz[215]. Also on July 24, there was an arson attack on the offices of the Free Campus Movement[216]. This was the second attack on that office, as an arson had been attempted on April 23, 1970. A member of the Radical Libertarian Alliance was sleeping in the office. There were no injuries.

On July 28, 1971, there was a firebomb at the Bank of America in Ben Lomond,[217] the second bomb at that location that summer. This time there was no call to a TV station and no claim by the Sunshine Brigade, nor anyone else.

Thankfully, amazingly, that was the last mid-peninsula and south bay bomb for the next four months. The area became free of bombings, coincidentally corresponding with the end of summer term.

SLAC Bomb

On December 7, two bombs exploded at the Stanford Linear Accelerator Center (SLAC), the last of the 1971 bombings around Stanford. The bombs cause about $100,000 in damage, but it is noted they were poorly made and poorly placed. Alternate locations would have caused much more damage[218].

In 1987, not knowing what it was, I used a photo of the SLAC damage in a *Chaparral* issue, placed in my Now That editorial that the Chappie editor writes for each issue.[219] There were all kinds of old photos laying around the office, and in the cabinets of the darkroom. We'd go in there, looking for images to swipe for our own issues. My use of the SLAC image is only a coincidence, nothing other than the comedy and wonder of it all. But it does also show another truth: You just don't know what you're going to find laying around the *Chaparral* office.

1972

Protesting, bombs, fires and strife continue into 1972. The events of this year could also fill many books, but here are the briefest of summaries.

Stanford Rehabilitation Movement

By 1972, those demanding a reinstatement of Bruce Franklin as a professor had united under the name "The Stanford Rehabilitation Movement," with rehabilitation being meant for the university[220]. The groups sought a general overhaul of not just the university's policies, but the structure and administration itself. Many of the actions and protests of this year were done in the name of this movement.

On January 13, 1972, a bomb threat was called in for Encina Hall, and there was an attempted arson at Hansen Laboratory that night[221].

There were two events on January 17, 1972, a fire at the Manzanita Trailers office on the Stanford campus[222], and what was described as a giant pipe-bomb that thankfully failed to explode at the Palo Alto electric substation[223].

On January 24, a second Encina bomb threat was called in[224]. Old

Union on the Stanford campus was occupied, and that night, 200 marchers clashed with police.[225]

On January 25, the second day of the sit-in at Old Union was broken up by police.[226]

On February 3, students disrupted the class of controversial professor William Shockley. The students wore white sheets to protest the Shockley's views on racial genetics. Eight students were criminally charged for the disruption and became known as the "Shockley Eight."[227]

On April 17, 350 protesters gathered against the bombings in Vietnam[228].

On April 20, students again disrupted the class of William Shockley.[229] Later that night a torch-bearing crowd of 700 gathered in Palo Alto, and marched on Palm Drive towards Stanford, but were pushed back and dispersed by police.[230]

Violence and unease continued through the night, into the morning of April 21, as El Camino Real was blocked by people participating in a nationwide anti-Vietnam protest. Mass arrests ensued, with over 200 people charged. The *Stanford Daily* reported on April 22 that the police charged the crowd without warning.[231]

On May 8, the *Stanford Daily* reported that to date, 184 protesters had been arraigned.[232]

On the night of May 9, protesters battled police across many campus locations in a long and tense night of violence that resulted in nine arrests[233].

Two nights later, on May 11, 1972, there was another big night of protests, and many fires were set[234].

On May 18, MEChA (Chicano Student Movement of Aztlán) House was completely destroyed in a fire[235]. The *Stanford Daily* reported this fire was an accident, that resulted from a vinyl couch moved too close to a heater. Thankfully, the building was empty at the time of the fire, and there were no injuries. I would ask why an empty house in May, in Palo Alto needed the heat on, and the specific order of events where the couch was pushed against the heater and then the house was deserted, but that's just me.

The next night, May 19, arsonists hit nearby Lathrop House around

11:30 pm, causing damage to its basement. Thankfully, again there were no injuries[236].

The following night, May 19, disaster was averted at the Women's Center, when students discovered 17 gas burners left on in an apparent attempt to blow it up.[237]

Encina Fire

On June 7, 1972, Encina Hall, an original building of Stanford, originally a men's dormitory, that now housed most of the university's administrative offices, burned in what was described as one largest fires in Santa Clara County history.[238] First seen by a resident of the Manzanita Trailers around 9 pm, more than 100 firefighters struggled to bring it under control. When they finally succeeded two and half hours later, the building was extremely damaged. The fire started in the attic of the center section of the building. A fire wall on the west side of the building held, mostly saving this section from damage. A similar fire wall on the east side failed, and much of the east side was gutted along with the center section. Many university records were consumed in this fire.

It has never been proved as arson, but the cause is suspicious in origin, and arson has never been ruled out.

Later that June, 106 of the 231 people arrested on April 21 for blocking El Camino Real pleaded guilty, as did seven of the "Shockley Eight,"[239] Those pleading included a Chappie.

Knife Attacks

On July 8, 1972, a female Stanford graduate student was attacked by a man with a knife in her Palo Alto apartment. The *Stanford Daily* reported that the student was able to fend off the attack, and the attacker fled.[240] There was no description of the attacker, other than it was a man. One other thing of note was that the phone lines in the apartment had been cut. While not conclusive, this implies a premeditation and methodology, rather than a spontaneous attack of rage.

There were no other media reports about this attack that I could find, but in the July 21, 1972 *Stanford Daily*, the victim wrote a letter to the editor, criticizing the Daily article about her attack, saying that it had gotten some key elements wrong, and had failed to print a warning to the community. The letter referenced several other attacks in recent months, but did not provide any details.[241]

Realize that this is just seven months before the Stanford Murders began, two of which were knife attacks. This article makes me conjecture that there might have been many more attacks at Stanford. With so much violence during this era, I wonder about the full extent of such attacks during this time.

More Fire

Bomb incidents continued in 1973. On January 6, a boy found a pipe-bomb in an orchard near Anza Court in Saratoga,[242] and on May 22 a pipe-bomb was dropped in a sewer in Menlo Park[243].

On November 26 the Pacific Gas and Electric Company substation in Los Altos was bombed for the second time.[244] It had been attacked with a pipe bomb in 1971, but this bomb was ten times more powerful than the pipe bomb. A group called Americans for Justice claimed responsibility.

The final area bomb incident of 1973 was on December 19, when a pipe bomb exploded in a Santa Cruz building containing armed forces recruiting and selective service offices. Responsibility was claimed by group who called themselves the Revolutionary Action Squad[245].

Emma Sharon Brown

In the October 24, 1973, *Stanford Daily* I found an article about the death of Emma Sharon Brown, a star undergraduate student about to begin law school.[246] Her life was cut short by a fire at her apartment on October 22, 1973, in East Palo Alto. Authorities ruled the fire an accident[247].

The name seemed familiar. On a hunch I checked back through the articles I had been reading. Sure enough, Emma Brown was quoted in an article about the January 1972 fire in the Manzanita trailers office. She was a resident of the closest residential trailer to the burning office. Her trailer had almost been consumed in the fire but was saved.[248]

The article also revealed that she and her roommates had been living at Junipero the previous April when arson hit there. This gave me pause, and I double checked everything.

I confirmed the horrible coincidence that Emma Brown endured a fire in her dorm in April 1971, a fire next to her trailer in January 1972, and ultimately died in a fire at her apartment in October 1973. She was another star student, earning her undergraduate degree in only three years, and who was beginning Stanford Law School.

The accident, according to authorities, was that Emma Brown fell asleep while smoking in bed. Now it is just my gut reaction, but it doesn't sound right. I mean, I know good students can smoke too, especially in 1973, but smoking in bed is dumb. It just doesn't sound like the actions of a star student.

It sounded out of place, and WTF, fire seemed to follow this woman. I did a wider search for Emma Brown, and I discovered that I was not the first person to conjecture that her death was not an accident.

By Rope - Edward Alan McNeill

Zodiac's bomb letters and references, coupled with the myriad unsolved bombings around the Bay Area could more than account for Zodiac using bombs, the By Fire of the Halloween card. But what about By Rope? On my list of questions, I still had, "Where are the strangulations?"

Leslie Perlov in February 1973, and Janet Taylor in March 1974 were strangulations, but of course their killer has been apprehended and convicted in recent years. John Getreu was found guilty and subse-

THE ONLY TIME RICHARD GOT ANGRY AT ME

quently confessed to both murders.

I specifically searched for cold case strangulation murders at Stanford, or of Stanford students, and lo and behold, I found one.

Between 1 am and 4 am on the morning of July 17, 1976, Edward Alan McNeill, age 27, was found dead in his apartment in Menlo Park[249]. He was a postdoctoral researcher in chemistry at Stanford. There were traces of adhesive around his mouth and the death was ruled a strangulation. There were no signs of struggle.

The similarities of the murder of Edward Alan McNeill to those of David Levine and Eric Abrahamson should be noted. All three occur at times when school is out of session. All three victims were involved in the sciences at their respective universities, Levine in physics, Abrahamson and McNeill in chemistry. Two of the three murders, Levine and McNeill, involved no struggle. All three would have had access to computers.

Star students were emerging as a theme. As a PhD candidate, Paul Stine could be described as a star student, as could Emma Brown. That would be five star college students. It makes one wonder.

I must admit, compiling all of this exhausted me and fazed me. So much violence. So much death. Perhaps you get a similar effect reading it. WTF is going on during these times? I took a break for a few days.

Same Day, Same Serial Killer, Different Paper

After the excitement of finding Dick Geikie, I was at a crossroads, and/or immersed in so much *Chaparral* history and so much Zodiac information. I had looked through as much of the *Chaparral* material I had, I had gone through many, many issues of the *Stanford Daily*. I was exhausted, and it seemed like my sources were exhausted. I decided to expand my searches.

I happened to be searching through the Wisconsin Historical Society archives, which rival JSTOR.org and archive.org, trying various names and terms. I found a bunch of *Berkeley Tribe* PDFs. I had already seen and documented the instances of Blaine and Richard Gaikowski in Tribe issues. At this time, I was really just aimlessly searching. It wasn't my intention to compare the two archives.

But anyway, I decided to search for Blaine in those issues. The search returned the articles I had previously found. But then I noticed two hits for a date I did not have an entry, October 24, 1969.

I scrolled to those results and found Blaine's name on page three of that issue, in the Staff Box[250]. Then I scrolled to page ten, and I couldn't believe my eyes. The main headline of the page read, A Message for the Zodiac Killer, and it was written by Blaine[251].

I couldn't believe what I was reading. And more strangely, the date of October 24, 1969, seemed really familiar. I thought on it a while, and got an idea that should have been ridiculous, but it was not.

I looked up the date of the *Stanford Daily*'s Message to the Zodiac article. Yep. October 24, 1969.

I'm sure you know by now, I heard the weird Close Encounters music, and once again, the hair on the back of my neck stood up. I might have even conjured an image of Devil's Tower on this one.

There were TWO different Message to the Zodiacs on the same day in 1969, one by the guy who was accusing Richard of being Zodiac, and the other from the… *Stanford Daily*?

"What the Fuck is Going On?" I asked aloud.

There, in October 1969, Blaine was writing to, or about, the Zodiac. He didn't arrive in this story in the 1980s, nor the 2000s, here he was contemporaneous with the Zodiac. And writing A Message For The Zodiac Killer on the very same day the *Stanford Daily* writes Message To The Zodiac. That's just weird. And creepy. What does it mean?

The Missing Pages

Then there was this question: How on earth did I not find this already?

I had searched for Blaine. I had entered all his bylines for *Good Times* and *Berkeley Tribe* into the spread sheet. I had been back and forth over this spreadsheet quite a bit. How did I miss this obviously important article?

I went back and reviewed all the files. Yes, I had marked in my notes that I had indeed reviewed the October 24, 1969 *Berkeley Tribe*, and that Blaine's name did NOT appear in it. I went back to JSTOR. org and looked up the issue.

Now this could be purely coincidence, or not, but in the JSTOR online archives that have the October 24, 1969 issue of the *Berkeley Tribe*, the page containing A Message For The Zodiac Killer, and the preceding page, are missing. Upon closer investigation, I found that in total, eight pages of this issue are missing.

This issue of the *Berkeley Tribe* was 28 pages, seven sheets of paper, folded. In the digital archive file, the pages 3, 4, 9, 10, 19, 20, 24, and 25 were missing, meaning the entire sheets of paper in the scanned copy were missing. Pages 3 and 4, combined with pages 24 and 25, compose one missing sheet of paper. Pages 9 and 10, combined with pages 19 and 20 for the other.

It may or may not be obvious to those who have not produced a publication, but magazines and newspapers that are folded in the middle have page amounts that are in multiples of four. This is because each folded sheet, printed on each side of the fold, and each side of the paper, makes four pages. Yes, newspapers occasionally print on half-sheets, which adds two pages and gives the publications page counts like 10 and 14, but for the most part it is always in multiples of four.

So, the copy of this issue on the JSTOR.org server had two pieces of paper missing from this issue, which coincidentally are the two pieces of paper on which Blaine's name was printed, page three, containing his name in the masthead, and page ten, with his byline on the Zodiac article.

The fact that Blaine's article A Message For The Zodiac Killer was not included in the original archive definitely made my research more difficult. Because of this omission, I was unaware of the missing pages for most of a year. It was only with a bit of luck that I discovered them. It is more than a funny coincidence that they are missing, and I would lie if I said I didn't wonder how all this happened.

This discovery greatly changed my impression of Blaine. Not that I disbelieved what he said before, I had confirmed he had written for *Good Times* and would have certainly known Richard, but this put him in the midst of everything happening at the pinnacle of Zodiac hysteria, October 1969.

A Friendlier, Heartfelt Message to the Zodiac

Blaine's letter is more like a personal plea, or letter to a friend, than an article. He sympathized with the Zodiac, and said words to the effect that the police had done worse. Blaine chastised the *San Francisco Examiner*, and said Zodiac would find more help in the pages of Dostoevsky than the *Examiner*. Blaine urged Zodiac to give up his ways, and to also get out of the country, start a new life, grow a beard, to take (smoke) pot and pray, and to not worry about the little minds who wrote foolish things about Zodiac, consulting astrologers and programming IBM computers in hopes of catching him.[252]

Upon reading this, I was stunned. I'm quite honestly amazed that this is not better known. Blaine speaks to the Zodiac as if he is speaking to a friend. Blaine shows a sentiment to the Zodiac. This sentiment is not only what one might have towards a friend, but one that was fitting into an emerging theory that Zodiac was a left-wing activist and had some amount of sympathy with some in that crowd because Zodiac was killing privileged white people. And possibly cops.

Did law enforcement investigate this article? Or was it just passed off as hippies jumping on the Zodiac bandwagon? Did they consider that Blaine was not just writing creative prose, but was actually addressing a person, a smoker of grass, interested in computers?

The final words of Blaine's article particularly caught my eye "... programming IBM computers in hopes of catching him." Had the police talked about using computers, IBM computers, to try to catch Zodiac? Had there been something in the press to that effect? If so, that might explain such a sentence. If not, that seems like a strangely specific thing to mention.

So far, I have not found any reference about the police using IBM computers. It seems like a strange thing to put in such an article, unless you were writing to someone specifically interested in computers, and perhaps was working, or trying to work on, an IBM computer.

Something also worth noting is the timing of A Message For The Zodiac Killer in the *Berkeley Tribe*, which roughly coincides with Blaine ceasing to write for *Good Times*. Six days after the *Berkeley Tribe* article, Blaine's regular Cop Watch article appears in the October 30, *Good Times*, his twentieth consecutive article. Then the streak is broken. There is no Cop Watch in the November 6, 1969, issue. Blaine continues to write the article in November, and that is it. December 4, 1969, is the last record of Blaine working for *Good Times*.

Is it just a coincidence that Blaine stopped working for *Good Times* soon after publishing his Message? Is there a reason that article reads the way it does? Did Blaine become uncomfortable working at *Good Times*? Or is it all just a coincidence?

And speaking of coincidence, we have this very relevant article, regardless of who the Zodiac is, written right in October 1969, almost unknown in the public record about this case. And not just unknown, it just so happens that all relevant pages that lead to it in a key internet archive are missing.

Coincidence?

Now There are Two of Them

That's another bad quote from a Star Wars movie, but it was true: There were two Friday, October 24, 1969, editorials about Zodiac, the *Berkeley Tribe* and the *Stanford Daily*.

While I haven't seen either of these articles discussed very much, if at all, a reasonable explanation is that they are in direct response to, or parodying, the Sunday, October 19, 1969, *San Francisco Examiner* editorial, A Message to the Zodiac Killer. Zodiac hype was at its peak.

Even so, printing on the exact same day is eerily strange. And in both cases, seemingly a very bad idea. Did both writers not see the foolishness and poor taste of engaging a homicidal maniac? Did they both not realize they were placing themselves in danger?

Perhaps a reason why the two editorials might slip under the radar is that October 24, 1969, was a big day in Zodiac press in general. On that day there was widespread newspaper reporting on the meeting between the various investigators and law enforcement divisions working on Zodiac, a sort of Meeting of the Minds.

Zodiac crimes had been committed across multiple law enforcement jurisdictions, including Solano County, the City of Vallejo, Napa County, and of course, San Francisco. There are press accounts of a meeting that included personnel from seven law enforcement agencies around the state.

The articles report that some investigators were exploring the theory that linked the Zodiac to Dick Tracy, but reported that San Francisco officials dismissed it, as the killer had named himself The Zodiac prior to when the Zodiac Gang storyline in Dick Tracy began.

I hope that this was just the police putting out fake information, because if it were not, it was very faulty reasoning. Newspaper comics were done long in advance, and Sunday comics were printed with many weeks lead time. There was just not enough time in one month for investigators to run down every person who might have had access to the Dick Tracy comics before being printed in the paper.

For starters, it could theoretically be any employee of the *Chronicle* or *Examiner*. It could be anyone associated with printing the comics, anyone who handles the actual pages, anyone involved with laying out pages, printing the comics, transporting the comics, storing the comics. And for that matter, it could be a friend of such person. It could be a janitor or maintenance man at any such facility handling this work.

The Dick Tracy similarity to the Lake Berryessa attack, and the intent to have news of the attack in the same edition of the paper is too great to dismiss without hunting down every single person who might have seen the comic beforehand. There was no reasonable way to say there was no link at that time in the investigation.

Nevertheless, dismissing a possible link to Dick Tracy was reported in many articles across multiple papers on October 24, 1969. And in that dismissal, it seems investigators had overlooked what seems painfully obvious: Zodiac HAD to have seen the Dick Tracy comics early. Zodiac worked with the *Sunday Examiner-Chronicle* comics in some way.

Unless it was intentionally false information hoping to trick the killer, it is my assertion the investigators dismissed a Dick Tracy link prematurely.

Blaine's Post

Some weeks later, when I finally found a social media page for Blaine, he wrote on that page something that stunned me: He says that Richard Gaikowski asked him to write his article. Yes, I said that. Blaine says that Richard asked him to write the *Berkeley Tribe*'s October 24, 1969, A Message For The Zodiac Killer.

Certainly by now you have all realized the vista point we are at: If Richard did indeed ask Blaine to write his Zodiac message, what if he had asked staffers at the *Stanford Daily* to write one as well?

Now remember, even if Dick Geikie is indeed Richard, I only have bylines for him at Stanford in the summer of 1971, two years later.

Was he there as early as October 1969?

The DR-70 Astrology Computer

In the July 24, 1969, *Good Times*, the front page headline reads, Nixon Gets His Rocks Off.[253] Coincidentally, or not, "rocks off" is a phrase Zodiac uses in the solution to the 408-code:

"...TO KILL SOMETHING GIVES ME THE MOST THRILL-ING EXPERENCE IT IS EVEN BETTER THAN GETTING YOUR ROCKS OFF WITH A GIRL..."

In this same issue, Richard gets his second *Good Times* byline, although it is the first time it is printed as "d. gaik." Gaik's article is about an astrology group in Berkeley and includes the information that some people are using computers to do astrology[254].

Blaine also has a byline in this issue[255], as does Verne, a confessed fake name for the individual also known as Goatkirk.

I wondered about using computers to do astrology in 1969, and of course, there are many sections of this book that explore the possibility of getting on a mainframe at a Bay Area college.

But I also learned about the early days of standalone computers, what have become to be known as personal computers. In the early 1970s, the personal computer industry was fledgling, guys in their garages or their parent's garage. The entire idea of personal computers was scoffed at by many, who argued that a mainframe, or think "cloud" today, could always provide more computing power than an individual computer.

I learned that in 1977, the Digicomp DR-70 Astrology Minicomput-er debuted, the first commercially available computer designed specifi-cally to do astrology[256].

Digicomp Research was based in Ithaca, New York, started by some Cornell grad students. My interest sharpened on this. David Levine was from Ithaca, the son of a Cornell professor. In 1977, David Levine would have been of grad school age, a similar age to the people at Digicomp. David Levine was building his own computer at Stanford in 1973. It is a certainty that prototyping of the DR-70 had to occur in the years prior to 1977.

This would be a pretty wild conjecture, but was there a chance of overlap between David Levine and the creators of the DR-70? I decided to dig deeper.

When I googled the Digicomp DR-70 Astrology Minicomputer, I found picture of one. I did a double take and had a moment of recognition. The blue device with a black keyboard looked strangely familiar. You see, it didn't look like a computer to me and my 1980s and 90s comprehension. I didn't know what this random piece of old tech was, this keyboard sort of adding machine sort of blue metal… thing. But it jogged my memory. I think there was one of these in Richard's apartment.

To me is just looked like a big, old, clunky adding machine, or some other old technology that I remember seeing, but Richard had things like that in his apartment. I mean, there are old pieces of tech in my house right now. Techies have such things, artists have stuff laying around. All I can say is the picture of the DR-70 looks strikingly similar to equipment I remember seeing at Richard's place.

I ended up speaking with the owners of Digicomp, and found no connection to David Levine nor his father. It was just a coincidence that it was people from Cornell. They did mention to me that a DR-70 was used by Joan Quigley to calculate charts for her clients, including Nancy and Ronald Reagan.

Fake Names in the Ithaca High School Yearbook

While searching for Cornell-oriented material and the DR-70, I was finally able to come across the Ithaca High School Yearbook of 1971, David Levine's high school senior yearbook. Early in the book, there are the seniors, the class government, the Most Likely To's. I recognized David Levine picture right away under Most Scholarly before I even read the name under the picture. David Le Vine.

"Hmmm, that's interesting," I thought. "I wonder if I've been spelling it wrong all this time?"

A few pages later is his senior photo, with his name, "David S. Levine". Ok, so he, or someone on the yearbook staff, is playing a joke with the fake name, or at least, fake spelling.

David's senior photo includes his activities, Astronomy Club President, ECMNC Under-Secretary General, Dramatics Club, Flicks, National Honor Society, Orchestra, PAX.

I went through the whole book. There was no Astronomy Club. He was not listed in the Dramatics Club section, nor did he seem to be in their photo. Same for National Honor Society, Flicks, Orchestra and ECMUNC. Perhaps he was away looking at colleges on the day of the yearbook photos, I thought. I know I missed more school days than normal when I was a senior because we were on trips looking for colleges.

I decided to look through the groups again in case I had missed the Astronomy Club. I never found that group, but upon closer inspection of the photo of the Science Club, I noticed David Levine, or at least someone who looked a lot like him. And the photo caption confirmed it was David Levine. I prepared to include it in my saved files of this project.

Then I did a double take, as I noticed that actually, it DID NOT say David Levine, it said David Leutne. I looked at the photo. It sure looked like David Levine. VERY much like David Levine. Funny about Leutne I thought, because u is so much like v, and t and i are also paired and confused on a joke level. Leutne is like a visual pun or joke of Levine.

I looked next to David Leutne. The next words were Missing: and then four more names. But there were five people in the photo.

"That's weird," I thought. There was no one missing, and in fact, there was one more person than there are names. Someone isn't missing, someone is extra.

I decided this was quirky, but nothing of interest to the case and moved on to the more important task of identifying any Ithaca High graduates who might have gone on to Cornell, and then on to Digicomp.

Kate pointed out that looking at the kids in the Science Club, or who listed Astronomy Club first would be of higher priority, because the chances of them being friends with David Levine would rise.

So, I went back to the Science Club photo. It was comically frustrating again, because the guy sitting right next to David would very likely be a friend of his, and that's where the caption said "Missing:" I decided look through the senior photos to see if I could recognize this guy.

Not only was he easy to find, but there was his name, Seth Messing, and it listed that he was a member of the Astronomy Club as well. It seems Seth, and his friend David, were indeed "messing" with everyone. There was no one missing, SETH was "Missing:" and he was next to his friend using the visual pun "David Leutne".

I realized these guys were sophisticated prankers, and they made puns and jokes out of their own names. "David Le Vine" was indeed on purpose, as was "David Leutne".

In order to get a prank in the yearbook, you need an inside person. Neither David Levine nor Seth Messing was listed as yearbook staff. I looked through the other clubs listed as David Levine's activities to see if I could find a likely person who could have accomplished the jokes. It wasn't too hard to find another individual in the Science Club, who was also on the Flicks Club, National Honor Society, and Orchestra like David Levine, and he was also the Layout Editor of the Yearbook. Layout Editor would be the ultimate insider to help get a joke in the yearbook.

Here came that weird feeling again.

It appeared David Levine was a jokester, a person who liked to play around with his name, with spelling, puns and jokes on a sophisticated level. The probability he would have enjoyed hanging around the *Chaparral* increased, as did the probability he would have hit it off with other punsters and wordsmiths who like to play with the spelling of their name, like Richard.

So Close, Yet So Far – April 2023

So as of April 2023, I had bylines in the *Stanford Chaparral* and *Daily* for an individual named Dick Geikie, who Stanford had confirmed was not a student, and who I could not find in any other internet search. There were also no bylines or mentions of a Dick Geikie in other newspapers. Given the similarity of the name Dick Geikie to Dick Gaik, and given that Dick Gaik is itself a modification of Richard Gaikowski's real name, the idea that Dick Geikie was another such modification was a very real possibility.

And if that were true, it would mean that I had discovered Richard working for the *Chaparral* and Daily in the spring and summer of 1971. And if that were true, for how long was Richard visiting Stanford? Any extension of Richard on campus later than that, up and through September 1973 would increase the likelihood of Richard knowing David Levine.

Dick Geikie's *Daily* articles were about the Computer Music Department, the demise of the Midpeninsula Free University, a medical clinic in San Jose, a work-study program for Stanford Hospital workers, science fiction, and Stanford campus workshops that were open to the public. All of those could provide clues as to Richard's activities while he was on campus.

The staff boxes in the *Stanford Daily* issues from the summer of 1971 could also provide clues, noting Dick Geikie was part of the Night Lackeys, and that sometimes the staff box listed "those who wished to remain anonymous."

I had David Levine, entering Stanford as a freshman in September 1971. In 1972, he ran for Student Senate and won. He was building a computer from scratch for the Physics Department. And while he was not a grad student, the type of student my case theory thinks Richard would try to associate with, he was described as doing the work of a grad student[257]. I knew that David Levine liked to spend hours debating politics and he was a member of his high school film club, both hobbies that would have clicked with Richard. Also, based on his high school yearbook, there was a possibility he liked wordplay, puns, and modifying his own name for comic purposes.

David Levine's roommate, or at least the individual who was to be his roommate, worked for the *Chaparral*, eventually becoming co-editor in 1974. It is unknown when that roommate began participating on the Chappie, but to eventually become editor means he had to have established himself there sometime before. If David accompanied his roommate to any *Chaparral* meetings or parties, it could have increased his chances of meeting Richard.

People Living in the Chappie Office

As the joke goes, 'That would never happen," which means, it happens all the time. I know that various people lived in the Chappie office from the seventies through the nineties. As I described at length, I was one of two people who lived there the summer of 1986. For the other years, I wasn't sure who or when, but I had heard stories.

I had hard evidence that off-campus people, people associated with publications, were in the *Chaparral* office through the summer of 1974. According to the July 16, 1974, edition of the *Stanford Daily*, the university kicked out a group described as off-campus people and had to change the locks on the *Chaparral* office doors. The article reported that these non-students were not only creating their own non-Stanford publication, they were also living there.[258]

The discovery of this situation in the summer of 1974 means the activity was going on PREVIOUS to the summer of '74. If previous means for as long as a year, then we would have that situation going on at the time of David Levine's murder. If previous means two years, and if Richard was one of the non-students working on the non-Stanford publication, we had more than enough chance for David Levine to meet Richard via this connection.

If I was asked to predict how long, previous to summer 1974, people lived the Chappie office, I would estimate that it most likely went back to at least 1969. In fact, one person I interviewed, MB, said that in the early 1970s, people were living in the Stanford *Quad* offices, directly below the *Chaparral* offices. The Storke Building where the *Chaparral*, *Quad*, *Daily* and *Sequoia* magazines had their offices was a hip scene, and relatively unmonitored by the university.

I was tantalizingly close to showing that Richard Gaikowski and David Levine might have known each other, perhaps even LIKELY they knew each other, both with connections to the *Chaparral*. Even if there was just a chance encounter at the *Chaparral* office, or at a political rally on campus, or at a computer terminal center, their mutual interests of politics, computers and pun-making could have led to them talking.

In an article about David, his friends noted that he loved to spend time down in the dorm lounge, debating politics. The combination of politics and an interest in cutting edge computer stuff is exactly why I spent hours talking with Richard during the 1990s. Certainly, the personality types of David and Richard could have easily led to a friendship.

My research to this point had been entirely internet-based, but it was becoming increasingly clear a trip to Stanford, and a review of the *Chaparral* and Hammer & Coffin collections at Green Library was necessary. And the good thing? I didn't have to tell anyone about researching Zodiac murders. As it would be, The Jester, the eternal cosmic joker had provided the situation that this review could be done entirely while researching the history of the *Stanford Chaparral*.

There was now a unity of purpose, a coincidental synergy that was comical to think about. While I haven't mentioned the *Chaparral* anniversary project for some time, I was still compiling its history and scanning old issues concurrently with all of this Zodiac research.

High Chaparral Films

Of the 42 issues of the *Chaparral* from fall 1969 to spring 1974, I had been able to get 10 of them via alums sending them to me. In one I found something that interested me. In the February 15, 1973 *Chaparral*, with a front page about Daniel Ellsberg and Stuart Ramsey coming to Stanford for a conference, there was an ad on page seven for High Chaparral Films, a film series run by the magazine.

I was already aware that the *Chaparral* had a film series in 1980s, before I came to Stanford and VCRs took over, but I was not aware they had a film series as early as 1973. By some point in 1973, Richard was running a speakeasy movie theater on 14th Street in San Francisco, and he would eventually form a film distribution company later in the 1970s. David Levine was in his high school's Flicks Club, so he had at least enough interest in films to join that club.

The slightest potential of overlap I could find in the few issues I had access to was through films. There were 32 other *Chaparral* issues from this era that I only had the front page of, I needed to see the interior pages.

Trip to San Francisco May 2023

There was nothing left to do by internet, or by calling people. I had questions I could not answer for both the *Chaparral* history project, and my Zodiac research, without going to the source. I contacted Stanford's Green Library and requested to see the Hammer & Coffin materials in Special Collections, along with various volumes of the *Chaparral*. I had a few things I was very interested across the years, issues around the Hammer & Coffin founding, the Larrey Bowman issue of 1909, issues of Lansing Warren in 1918, stuff concerning the suspensions of Chappies in 1951 and 1961, and I also requested to see every single issue from 1969 to 1974.

The visit to the library would be over two days, the first focusing on Hammer & Coffin materials, and the second looking at the *Chaparral* issues.

I had specific hopes of what we might find:

1. Just how many Dick Geikie bylines would there be in the *Chaparral*?

2. Would there be any articles or subjects that were also in *Good Times* or connected to Richard?

3. Would the 1971 *Chaparral* staff photo have names with it? Most importantly, would any of those names be Dick Geikie?

4. Would there be a *Chaparral* with David Levine's name in it?

5. Would there be something in a *Chaparral* that directly tied David Levine to Dick Geikie?

It was May of 2023. With much anticipation we prepared to visit the Bay Area and Stanford for the first time in 17 years. Kate and I got on a plane. We hadn't even flown in five years. My how air travel is even worse than it was before.

We landed at SFO, got a rental car, and went to Jack In The Box. Man, just like air travel, the meal it was not as good as I had remembered. Through alumni I was able to get a key code that would let me into the *Chaparral* office, which had been moved to Stanford's Old Union in 2009 when the Storke Building was demolished.

In the Chappie Office

Something I learned from my old days traveling to California from the East Coast, was that you could use jet lag to your advantage. It was easy to wake up early traveling east to west, and Stanford's campus would be largely deserted early in the morning, especially on days like Tuesday, Thursday, Saturday or Sunday, when there were either fewer or no classes. As previously pointed out, times when school was out of session would be even better. We were arriving at the next best time— Dead Week, a period before final exams when no classes were held, and students were presumably studying for them.

And while outsiders coming on campus at say, 2 am might elicit notice from campus security, at 7 am it was entirely legitimate. It wasn't entirely deserted, but the only others who were there were students almost certainly mentally immersed in their own world, their upcoming exams, their research. There certainly wasn't going to be anyone dropping by the Chappie office.

We parked our car in one of the few public parking spaces, walked right through the heart of campus and into Old Union without anyone taking any notice of us. We found the door to the *Chaparral* office, my code worked, and we were in.

I was prepared to hate the current Chappie office, but I couldn't. The spirit of the *Chaparral* was alive and well in the three-room, split-level office, that included an interior staircase, the huge upright coffin, and lots of junk on the walls and floors. There was shit just strewn about, just like the old Storke offices. A comic squalor stream of consciousness over a hundred years long, which even included some of the junk we had left lying around in the 80s in our old location.

I knew the layout of the office from previous video calls and knew the small back room that served as the archives of the *Chaparral* would be a good place to look. It was completely full of stuff, so packed it was hard to fit two people in there. We moved some stuff around, so we had space to work.

After some time looking in the *Chaparral*'s storage room I saw a really thin, oversized volume. I reached for the book in great anticipation. Indeed! This was a bound volume of political era *Chaparral* issues. The issues started with the fall of 1969, the Michael Sweeney era. I had seen the covers of this era before, but never the interiors. I was ecstatic.

"Wow, they really did go for the underground press look of the day," said Kate.

It was indeed an underground press style, albeit a sort-of staid Stanford version of that look. Of course it was. Anti-establishment. Power to the people. Astrology columns. Listings for events all over the Bay Area, with many events in San Francisco.

We were scheduled to see these issues the next day in Stanford's Green Library, so we didn't spend too much time examining them, but there was one thing I REALLY wanted to see. I paged ahead, past these 1969-70 issues including the infamous ROTC issue, hoping that this bound volume contained the Dick Geikie issue from March 1971. We paged through the 1969-1970 school year, and yes, the 1970-71 issues were also in this bound volume!

I turned the pages until I reached issue number two, March 5, 1971, and then on to section two of that issue. And there it was, the *Chap-*

arral with Dick Geikie's byline, with the Missing Link photo. We had seen the scan of this front page, but never the real-life paper. It was quite a moment, and the Close Encounters music was certainly playing in my head.

"Well here we are," I said

The anticipation was incredible as I turned the page, wondering what might be in the interior of this issue.

I turned the page and Kate gasped.

The next two pages of the issue were blank. Completely blank.

"WTF?"

I turned the page again, and found page four of the issue, a seemingly normal page. The next page in the bound volume was page one of the next issue.

I turned the page back to the blank pages. Then back to the front page, then back to the blank pages.

"What on earth does this mean?" I asked.

"It was the seventies," replied Kate. "They were so stoned they left out two complete pages and then printed it."

"That's pretty stoned," I said.

"It was the seventies."

I wasn't quite sure how to process this. The number one reason out of all the reasons we had flown across the country was to see the interior of this issue. Yes, we wanted to see others, but THIS one was the Missing Link. THIS one was the most important. And then we find out it is just a four-page issue with pages two and three completely blank. Who's writing this BS? WTF?

"It was the seventies" repeated Kate.

As stated before, we would be seeing unbound copies of all issues 1969-1974 the next morning in the library, so we didn't spend more time on this at that moment. Maybe this was just some fluke, some mistake. Tomorrow we would see this issue in the library and could confirm what was going on with the blank pages. We put the bound volume aside and proceeded on other goals we had for this visit. We were also there to get as many *Chaparral* issues as we could to add to the digital directory and work towards the 125th Anniversary Book. We snagged perhaps fifty issues from the office for the scanning project.

All Chaparral issues seen

The next day we were back in Green Library, this time to look at *Chaparral* issues. I had originally thought that this would be a great climax, seeing the interior pages of all *Chaparral* issues for the first time, but that had already happened the night before in the Chappie office, even though we had just glanced at them. Now the great question was would the library's copy of the Missing Link also have the blank pages.

We saw every page of the Chaparral from fall 1969 to spring 1974 and took a photo—not as good as scanning, but still effective to document what was on these pages. I looked over each page, but we had to go fast or we would have no hope of doing all we needed to do. A few things stood out: astrology columns, tarot articles, a real underground press look, at least in the 1969-70 school year, a bit more measured in the subsequent years. I saw some things that looked familiar, a photo of a bird covered in oil from the Standard Oil tanker accident in San Francisco Bay, other photos that I recognized from Chappies of my era—we would use old photos we found in the Chappie darkroom.

As we went through the issues, just a quick look over of each page did not yield positive answers to any of my questions.

We got to the 1970-71 school year, and again found issue number 2, and then section 2, the Missing Link issue. I opened it and pages two and three of this issue were indeed blank, just as we had found in the bound volumes in the office. Not that I thought it would be different, but finding the blank pages was so strange, I was interested in seeing another copy of this issue just for my own sanity.

I needed some sanity, because across the entirety of fall 1969 to spring 1974, there were no additional articles by Dick Geikie. There were no mentions of him on any *Chaparral* masthead. Only this one time on this one strange issue.

Seeing the entirety of these issues answered many questions, almost all of them negating my speculations. None of my hopes for the *Chaparral* issues came to fruition. We found the caption to the 1971 staff photo, listing the names everyone in the picture. No Dick Geikie. No other name that might be a fake name. No byline or mention of David Levine

All we had was the issue with Dick Geikie's byline, and it was absolutely an oddball. I reflected on this.

The Mystery of the Blank Pages

So you mean to tell me, that when I reveal to the world that there is a *Stanford Chaparral* issue with a byline for Dick Geikie in 1971, that pages two and three of that four-page section are missing? And when I say missing, I don't mean that the paper is missing, I'm saying there are two blank pages in this four-page section.

I don't know whether to laugh or cry. I can tell you my first inclination was definitely to cry. No additional article by Dick Geikie. No masthead. No other articles with bylines. And no mention of David Levine or anything related to him. Absolutely nothing.

But I also had to laugh.

I want to state plainly that the blank pages' value to this story is likely just comic background. But I also recognize that as the world learns of the Dick Geikie bylines in Stanford student publications, the Missing Link issue with the missing pages is certain to gain a lore BEYOND. As my boss's boss on Madison Avenue would have said over his martini, "That's got a lotta spin..."

2023 Trip Aftermath

So, after all of that, and the emotional rollercoaster of thinking we had a photo of Dick Geikie ended. We did NOT find an issue where both Dick Geikie and David Levine appeared together. We found nothing in relation to David Levine in the *Chaparral* issues, not even a senate recommendation for him which I had hoped to find. There were no student senate recommendations at all in the 1972-73 *Chaparral*s, as there had been in previous years. We had found almost nothing that we had been looking for.

But we had found that the Missing Link issue was completely blank on the inside. And we had photographed every page of every *Chaparral* issue from 1969 to 1974. Who knows what might be found upon their inspection?

And we were left still with: Who the hell was Dick Geikie?

In the midst of all of the theories falling by the wayside, I have to admit I felt some amount of disappointment. It just goes to show that one should always remain measured in their theories and conjectures. But it's good to stay even-handed on the downside as well, our trip had also NOT positively identified Dick Geikie. Dick Geikie remained an unknown individual, and the chance that he indeed was Dick Gaik was still very real. While we had failed to identify him, we also had found NOTHING to disprove he was Richard Gaikowski. The longer it went, the longer he went unidentified, the higher the probability that he was indeed Dick Gaik

As stated earlier, no Dick Geikie or Richard Geikie was ever a student at Stanford. We've also learned that it was not unusual for non-students to be on campus during that era. Underground press newsman Dick Gaik could easily be the tabloid student publications volunteer Dick Geikie. Dick Geikie was somebody, but who?

The Oil Bird

As stated rather recently, who knew what closer inspection of the *Chaparral* issues would yield? We were home a few days when I had a flash in my mind where I had seen the photo of the bird covered in oil from the front of a 1971 Chaparral. My excitement rose as I found it, in an ad for a poster, the photo of the "oil bird" as I came to call it, with the headline Ecology is for the Birds, in the pages of, and available for sale at… *Good Times*.

Ok, so *Good Times* sold the poster, that could mean any number of things. Perhaps they were just running the ad. But it did seem like an in-house ad, I mean, it said send the money to *Good Times*. I needed to find more, and I did. The ad ran in *Good Times* several times, in every issue I looked in, working backwards through 1971. I needed to find when the actual oil spill occurred, and found it started on January 18, 1971, when two Standard Oil tankers collided in San Francisco Bay.

I skipped many issues and when straight to the January 22, 1971, *Good Times*, the first issue after the accident, and there it was.

The cover of the issue was a large photo of the poor bird, and a lot more.[259] The ads for the poster showed a tight cropping of the bird. This cover not only had the bird large, but also showed a lot more of the background, the Golden Gate Bridge, shoreline and mountains.

This was indeed the origin of the poster—the photo was indeed owned by *Good Times*.

We did an image search on this photo and learned that the San Francisco Oil Disaster spawned a generation of ecological movements and bird rescue action groups. The November 11, 1971 Stanford *Chaparral* featured this rescue work on their front page, and used the *Good Times* poster as their feature photo[260].

Up to this point I had avoided asking Stanford or some individuals directly if they knew Dick Geikie, in hopes of discovering more in the *Chaparral* issues. But now there was no reason to not ask. Finding out the truth of this story could justify me asking all kinds of questions about Dick Geikie.

In addition to Dick Geikie, the Missing Link issue had three articles with bylines on the front, and one on the back. I was able to find contact info for all four of these individuals, so I emailed some and called and left messages for others, describing the freak *Chaparral* issue and our 125th anniversary project. I emailed others and asked questions about the oil bird issue. I also emailed other people who worked on the *Stanford Daily* in the summer of 1971. In each case, I asked about a list of names that included Dick Geikie. No one remembered the name or person, Dick Geikie, save for one individual who said the name rang a bell, but did not remember anything else.

Call with D

Then, an individual who also has a byline in the Missing Link issue returned my call.

On their voicemail, I had said that I bet they were not expecting to hear from the *Stanford Chaparral* after all these years. D said they weren't so amazed to hear from the *Chaparral*, because they had forgotten completely about it. In fact, they thought that they had only worked for the *Stanford Daily*, back during the summer session of 1971.

"Well, I have a byline for you in the *Chaparral* from March 1971," I said to them on the phone.

"Oh, that's not possible," they replied. "I was a high school senior in the Midwest in March of 1971. I didn't come to Stanford until the summer."

"That's weird," I said. "Look at the jpg that I just sent you, see, it says March 5, 1971."

They agreed that this was weird, but reiterated they were not at Stanford in March of 1971. They had indeed worked for the *Daily* in the summer and noted that their highlight was interviewing the famous activist, academic, and Marxist, Angela Davis.

People's memories can be more than foggy, but usually not on things like the year they graduated from high school. D was indeed in the Midwest in March of 1971. They did not write articles for the *Daily* until summer of 1971. The March 5, 1971, date on the *Chaparral* had to be wrong.

I should have realized something was amiss with the Missing Link issue, but you just don't think about what you don't think about, and original takes on things, if they are wrong, can really lead you astray.

And it finally all dawned on me.

The Missing Link issue was fake, made with articles taken FROM the *Daily*. Dick Geikie's computer music article was not reprinted in the July 7 *Daily*, it was lifted FROM the July 7 *Daily*.

I went through the *Stanford Daily* issues from summer of 1971 again. And there it all was. The photo of the bike tire was from the front page of the July 9, 1971, issue.[261] And the article by D was on page eleven in the same issue.[262]

The story AAUP Elections Invalidated from the front page of the Missing Link was from page two of the July 7, 1971, *Daily*.[263] Another Missing Link article, Student Meets Premier, was from the front page of the July 23, 1971, issue.[264]

I went looking for the article on page four of the Missing Link. Sure enough, I found it on page four of the July 9 *Daily*.[265] What's more, the layout of the page looked very familiar. It wasn't just an article from a page, it was the entire page reproduced in the Chappie issue!

Now here's the thing, this page, page four, contains an article that says it is a continuation from page three. As we know, page three of the fake *Chaparral* is blank. I wondered...

I rushed to see page three of that *Daily* issue. Sure enough, there was the beginning of that article. For what it's worth, the article is titled Ripped-Off Opinion.[266]

But there was more.

Next to that article, in the upper right of page three, is the staff box. In that box, the Night Staff is listed, but the first listing is a long blank space, complete with an ending comma. For those who want to see this for themselves, go to the *Stanford Daily* Archives and bring up July 9, 1971, page three, and you can verify for yourself what I am describing.

So you tell me: Is the blank space for the first name in the Daily Night Staff section a joke reference to the blank pages in the *Chaparral*? It's a tantalizing idea. Or maybe they just needed to white out someone's name for some reason. But if so, why did they leave the comma? And what on earth would be the reason to white out someone's name?

After reflecting on this for some time, I came to the realization that the blank is might be intentional and related to the two blank pages of the *Chaparral* issue printed a couple weeks later. If this is so, it means this is a particularly sophisticated prank, planned and executed over many days. The maker of the issue wants it known that the blank pages are intentional.

Is the maker of the Missing Link *Chaparral* issue represented by the blank name in this masthead? Possibly. Is the name of the person who made the fake *Chaparral* on the issue itself, or a name on this masthead, or both? Also possible. Is Dick Geikie one of the names in the *Daily* staff box? Yes. Is Dick Geikie one of the names on both the *Chaparral* fake issue and the *Daily* staff box? Yes.

The masthead of the March 5, 1971 Special Edition, indeed has the wrong date. It's real creation date had to be sometime after July 23, 1971. I had assumed, as apparently did the Stanford Library and the Hammer & Coffin Society, that this was Section Two of the March 5, 1971 issue, but actually this was some sort of forgery, made to APPEAR to be Section Two of that issue in March, but actually produced sometime in July or later.

This issue is fishy even if it has nothing to do with Dick Gaik and Zodiac. It is unlike any *Chaparral* that I have found before or since in the magazine's history. This issue, the keystone to this entire story, quite literally labelled The Missing Link, has a blank center spread, has the wrong date, and was pieced together from re-used *Stanford Daily* articles. This very strange *Chaparral* issue was put together, quite literally, by knife.

Blank Pages, Wrong Date, Fake Issue, WTF?

"So, you mean to tell me, that when I reveal to the world that there is a *Stanford Chaparral* issue with a byline for Dick Geikie in 1971, that this is actually a bogus issue? A four-page farce with pages two and three left blank, that is made up entirely of clipped out *Stanford Daily* articles? Not printed in March, but late July or August? Oh joy," I thought.

I'm sure that's paraphrased, but it does basically capture how I was feeling at the time.

Now it was not a question of me laughing or crying. I had to come to grips that I, one time editor of the *Chaparral* and multiple-time maker of fake *Chaparral* issues, had finally found tangible proof that my outrageous conjectures might be right, and it was in the form of a *Chaparral* issue. And not just any *Chaparral* issue. THE *Chaparral* issue with the Dick Geikie byline, the Keystone, the Missing Link… was a FAKE.

My dilemma had just grown more complicated. Much more.

And now I had yet another problem, how and when should I announce this weird discovery?

Talk about a strange and dark thing to put on a school reunion and party. A bombshell like this might even impede the creation of the *Chaparral* anniversary book. There were a lot of nervous nellies in the *Chaparral*. Someone getting antsy was a near-certainty. And what about Stanford itself? How would they take this news? A discovery that the Zodiac had might have actually hung out around campus and no one had ever noticed until now was not exactly good publicity. And the university had been having a streak of bad publicity in recent years. And murder. What is up with Stanford University and murder? It was all quite something to reflect on.

There was only one way it could happen

As we got to June 2023, we had come to the river, or at least I had.

There was more coincidental evidence than ever, beyond where I could doubt it. At minimum, the information was bizarre. A weird *Chaparral* with blank pages, composed from *Daily* clippings, containing the byline Dick Geikie? What on earth was the story here?

It looked like it would be one of two distinct outcomes. The first was that this was truly just One F of a Coincidence, like a *Who Shot R.R.?*-level coincidence, perhaps even greater. That the closeness of Geikie to Gaik was just a comical coincidence, that this strange issue was just some fluke that happened to accidentally use an article with the Geikie byline, and I had just bumbled across these funny items and was making a big deal out of them.

The second was that Dick Geikie was indeed Dick Gaik, and it would be a bombshell, at least to the people following the Zodiac case, and to Stanford University, its alums and community. The thing is, it was going to be news either way, and a coincidence either way. It's just that one would be a "ha ha, that's funny" coincidence, and the other would be an "oh shit! JFC" coincidence.

And that presented somewhat of a problem in my mind.

The *Chaparral* deserved a tribute to its long history, and the 125th anniversary would be the ideal time. People had been talking about making a coffee-table book since I was a student over 30 years ago, maybe even longer. And we had already done A TON of work towards the research and the creation of the online archives, and planning for the anniversary. What about all that work? Two and a half years of effort had been put into the project, now was not the time for navel gazing, it was time for action.

But quite apart from that, although tied at the hip, I also realized at some point I would have to announce what I had discovered about Dick Geikie.

It was clearer than ever that my potential Zodiac discovery could overshadow and inhibit the *Chaparral* 125 project, possibly interfering with the production of the anniversary book, and could cloud any reunion party. And who was I kidding? It's not that it *could* overshadow it, it WOULD without a doubt.

I reflected on this for many days to weeks. Eventually came the answer: "You must write two books."

Perhaps the funniest part of this is I had done all I could to encourage people to write for the *Chaparral* 125th anniversary book, with little success. I tried the carrot approach, also known as the sugar approach. Many cheerleading emails. I made funny graphics, I made funny videos, all to encourage alums to get enthused and take up the cause of the book. I also tried the pity approach. The shame approach. The sarcasm approach. All to no avail. Of course, fellow alum PC was also doing a ton of work, and a smattering of others had done a bit here and there, but that was mostly it.

I had always seen the Chappie book as a group effort and was very frustrated that it wasn't. But now I saw that lack of participation was actually an opportunity.

A plan began to form in my mind.

A Chaparral Anniversary Book MUST come out BEFORE any public Zodiac stuff is mentioned, or even breathed.

The Chaparral anniversary must be insulated from my Zodiac research. Even the stories of the 1930s Chappie-related suspicious death would be downplayed, even taboo, in the 125 book so the subject didn't come up. Any talk of the Zodiac or the Stanford murders would be met with unenthusiasm and attempt to change the subject.

I would proceed under the plan of writing two books, the second of which you are reading now.

A complete Mea Culpa about my own Chaparral fake issues would have to be included in the Chappie book, although sans anything about Zodiac.

The Missing Link issue WOULD be included in the 125th book, because it was a strange and unique issue, but without any mention of Zodiac.

The book would be made REALLY BIG, and hopefully the Missing Link pages would get lost in a book of several hundred pages.

The legitimate researching for the Chaparral book would continue, with the additional benefit of providing cover for pressing the questions that would further the Zodiac research and his possible time at Stanford.

I would work on an accelerated schedule to get many copies of the Chappie 125 book printed and distributed long before October 2024. With self-publishing I could produce an "artist's proof" of the book regardless, and advocate strongly for Chappie alums to buy that book as a guard against the possibility of the book not being printed on an offset press.

When the Chappie book was sent off to the printers, I would then shift into writing the second one, the Zodiac book. It would include a recounting of the Mea Culpa from the Chappie book, followed by a more comprehensive Mea Culpa that included coming clean about my fake Zodiac issue, fake Zodiac code, any joking I had done, and this entire story.

This second book would be kept private for as long as possible, hopefully until after the evening of October 26, 2024, when the Chaparral Anniversary celebration will be concluded. On or after that day, I planned to make my discoveries public. If all went as planned, the Chappies would have a cloud-free reunion, and then my Zodiac book would come out sometime later. I viewed (and still view) that this is a time-sensitive subject. This plan allowed for the quickest possible public reveal of my discoveries while still making the Chaparral reunion the best it could be.

Ironically, or not, I realized that while I was in an almost unbelievable and unique situation, the answer to my challenge was not unlike that of *Chaparral* editors of yore, with a solution that certainly was the right one in every case—PUBLISH! And not later, NOW!

In 1974, when Mike Dornheim saved the *Chaparral*, his key action was not to wait, not get approval, just PRINT the issue Fiscal Responsibility. His decisive action won the day, and saved the day for the *Chaparral*. The time had come for me to utilize the wisdom of Dornheim.

And it was sort of a funny coincidence on a practical level. I mean, it was not like the H & C was going get it together. Jeez, I had brought this entire project to them on a silver platter, and they didn't really respond at all. So what I had long envisioned as a group effort, just something I would contribute to, changed to a book that I was going to have control over. I would be not only the editor of the book, but also the layout manager, the ultimate insider on any publication.

I realized I should stop bitching about the lack of participation and embrace the incredible opportunity that group and managerial apathy had handed to me.

As for putting the Missing Link on its own spread, there were a few reasons.

First off, it is a really unique piece of printing. It's in the Chaparral archives, included as both loose issues and in bound volumes. Stanford Libraries also record it as a real issue. Until these organizations change their mind, the Missing Link must be considered a real issue, I mean, at least according to these authorities. Who am I to dispute them? The Missing Link is perhaps the strangest thing I found in the entirety of the Chappie archives. Why would I not include this unique item in the book?

Secondly, there were just a few copies of the Missing Link issue, perhaps less than ten. They are bound to be pieces of pop culture history regardless of whether they are of evidentiary value. Sounds like quite a souvenir. And others might try to find them. They are a piece of history, and who knows, maybe there's still someone around doesn't want anyone to learn about this serial killer tale? Maybe some people aren't involved at all but just don't want any publicity?

Then there was the very real possibility that crime investigators would want to take all the Missing Link issues, and maybe more, to examine them. This would likely include the copy in Green Library as well as those in the *Chaparral* office. They likely would want the issues I have scanned. Would they be swept up and now be a police file somewhere for a very long time? Perhaps forever?

The bottom line is that this issue, with only a few known copies, it is the veritable Keystone to the case, literally the Missing Link. It would now be reproduced hundreds or thousands of times in the Chappie 125 book. Not just preserved for history, but also each book that was put out into the universe might get into the hands of someone who knew Dick Geikie. As many people as possible need to see it.

Putting a Zodiac clue in the *Chaparral* 125th anniversary book was NOT the reason for the Chappie book. Not at all. But I realized it would indeed help in the selling of the book. Not only would we get sales from people who wanted a great book about a century-plus old humor magazine, but it would also be of interest Zodiacifiles, true crime buffs, and those who just wanted a piece of strange Americana. And, given that I would be the one making the book, laying it out, now less a group endeavor and more a personal crusade, I not only had the opportunity to do it, it almost seemed like I was supposed to do it. Layout artists are the ultimate insiders, only outranked by those operating the press. Pranks are like real estate indeed. And I had just happened upon the deal of the century. Just as they were when the Super Bowl was held next to my freshman dorm, just as it was when the bear's case was left unlocked, Boardwalk and Park Place were again available, for the steal of the century....

Work on the Chappie 125th anniversary book went into high gear.

"With a passion that's intense
You worship and adore,
But the laws of common sense
You oughtn't to ignore."

-- Ko-Ko, The Mikado

ACT IV === YOU WANT MIKADO? YOU FIND IT ======

Stabford

You know, the "b" and the "n" are next to one another on the keyboard, and I don't type that well. That said, I never made the typo "Stabford" for the first couple years writing on this project, and then I made it three times in just a couple days. Too funny. But it sure as hell seemed to me that I better have a section in this book named "Stabford." I even considered renaming the entire book "Stabford."

But really, there are four kinds of murders, if not more, not just "By Knife." But By Knife is the method used in the primary cold case we hope to solve, the stabbing of David Levine outside Meyer Library. I have tantalizingly brought a possible Zodiac suspect on to the Stanford campus, but have NOT tied them definitively to David Levine.

But it gets ever closer.

The Greatest Cover Story of All Time

It seemed the Cosmic Jester was helping, I could work on both books at the same time. As the astrological aficionados would say, "all the stars had aligned" to make this quirky, coincidental situation that not only allowed for unity of purpose, but researching for the *Chaparral* while also researching for Zodiac was perhaps the Greatest Cover Story of All Time. Really.

Consider where I might have been:

"Hi I'm James, class of 1988, and I'm researching the Zodiac killer, and I think I've found he may be at Stanford. I was wondering..."<-CLICK>.

Instead, I got to do this:

"Hi I'm James, class of 1988, and I'm working on a history of the *Stanford Chaparral* to commemorate our 125th anniversary coming up in October 2024. We're actually trying to find every person we can find with a byline, and I have some names that I just can't place..."

"Why yes, we have such records. What are the names?"

An exchange such as this could be used almost universally, especially regarding the unique and unknown (to me) Chappie circa 1969 to 1974. All questions could be posed as Chappie research questions, because they were indeed Chappie research questions, and I was just viewed as someone who was just enthusiastic and nostalgic for my college days. Really nostalgic.

Someone even remarked, "Wow, you're really into the history of the *Chaparral*." Others implied I was obsessed. As I saw it, as long as I was truly researching the *Chaparral* history, which I was, I was telling the truth. This aspect of this caper was particularly interesting and enjoyable to me.

Then there was the other part of this, the additional problem I had made myself—My Dilemma. When all this was revealed, the fact that I had made fake *Chaparral* issues, including a Zodiac-themed fake issue would be an easy way to discount everything I had said. Can you imagine?

"Oh yeah, I made a few fake *Chaparral* issues and put them in the directory, but this one, this fake issue from 1971 is real. A real fake. No really..."

I asked Kate, "How will anyone believe that I, the maker of fake Chaparral issues, have truly discovered a fake Chaparral issue, one that may be evidence in the Zodiac case?"

"You are an expert on fake Chaparral issues," she replied. "Who better than you to discover it?"

Of course, I had also made a parody Zodiac code. But even that had helped me learn a bit about the process of doing so, and had shown me the usefulness of a computer in making one. The only other person

I confided in about his noted that this story was sort of like a Spy vs. Spy from Mad Magazine, with two prankster/jesters, an evil one fifty years ago, and a good one, who is exposing the evil one.

All of that had to be backburnered, as it was time to actually create the Chaparral Magnum Opus.

Layouts for the *Chaparral* 125 anniversary book began in earnest in early June 2023. While preparing for the monthly zoom call, I realized I should really make some pages. I quickly made a protype logo, intending it to be one of several, but I never made another one, dead on the first time. Then a voice said, "just start making something funny."

I became uniquely inspired. In the half hour before the call, I quickly laid out the first interior pages that highlighted two *Chaparral* issues, the classic Purple Ape issue from 1951, and the notorious LSD issue from 1967. Photos and text were strewn about in a designy way, using bright colors, pithy headlines and support graphics. The cognitive temperature for the material: Fisher Price.

Previous *Chaparral* anniversary books had all focused on the interiors of the magazines, so of course they were all in black and white. I wanted to focus on the true stars of the issues, the colorful covers. I also did not want to get bogged down in long, boring pieces of text which likely would become excessive navel-gazings. Stanford students are really bad when it comes to introspection, as in, they do way too much of it. Self-justification claptrap. So much internal dialogue, that even the smallest, simplest idea can be over analyzed, beaten to death--discussions so long that by the time they are over, everyone is too tired to take action.

So I decided to just do, not think; in the layouts I enlarged the covers to occupy about two-thirds of the page with a large, hopefully funny headline next to it, and then just short paragraphs of text and stand-in secondary graphics at the bottom. If I didn't know what the page should say, I just greeked in text and moved on.

The three others at the June meeting were impressed. At the end of the meeting I made some more pages, Layboy Revisited; Salvador Dali; Let's Eat.

I endeavored to make a layout or two every night. The project took on more and more hours. I decided to cease doing other hobbies until the book was done, as I could do perhaps 10-15 pages on a Saturday afternoon, but not if I was doing something else. I also had to curtail creating political memes to do the book. The Chappie 125 project became an all-encompassing endeavor. I even had to give up looking into Zodiac stuff.

Sometime around this time a Hammer & Coffin board member, at least I suspected he was on the board, did contact me and said that we could make a coffee table book, but it could only be 250 pages and we would hire a graphic designer to do it. I was incredulous, I was graphic designer. And for that matter, our alumni group had plenty of other graphic designers. Their plan was to HIRE someone? Well I figured they were so slow moving I didn't need to worry and moreover, that train had already left the station. I just kept making pages.

That incident became my driving force. If anyone wants to know what it takes to make a 400+ page coffee table book about a 125-year-old magazine, the answer is motivation. Or foolishness. But mostly motivation, and this incident certainly provided it. There was easily enough *Chaparral* material for many hundreds of pages. One could just print one cover a page and there would be over 900. Luckily, I was smart enough not to listen to nay-sayers, or bad-idears. At all.

I set a goal of somewhere north of 250 pages and hoped it would be more like 350. Other than that, I didn't really communicate with anyone about the layouts. With hundreds of pages to make, I didn't have time to waste. And frankly, most of the cheerleading I had done to get people to volunteer for the book had proved to be a waste of time. I had no time to waste now.

I just made pages. If I had an idea, I didn't labor over it, I just made it. I laid out hundreds of pages. Some pages contained things that were related, some didn't. There were a lot of partial pages. If I got stuck, I did not sit around brooding over it, I started a different layout.

Keeping the book organized was getting out of hand, so I made Excel spreadsheets. Subjects, decades, people, art, and more. I made layouts in Adobe Illustrator, with often 50 or more artboards, although I had to cut that down to smaller files when data size got out of hand. June, July, August, September--this was my 2023. I even made layouts while traveling in Colorado, the Jersey Shore, and New York City.

By the Chappie Zoom meeting in July, there were many pages, and by the August many more. Then, I decided to send out a group email— not to the entire alumni group, but just to the people who had ever done anything, attended a zoom, scanned an issue. There were about 15 people. I showed them the pages I had made.

The Cavalry Arrives

This finally got some action. The online layouts inspired a good crew to start contributing. Even some of our heavyweight writers contributed. Individuals from various decades, Dead Bowlers, professors, Mickey Mousers. The momentum built, as did the madness of laying it out, through August and September. It looked like the book might even be 450 pages. The more the better I thought, and I had found a print-on-demand vendor that could do up to 680 pages.

Some key help showed up through the summer. Famous writers, prolific writers, funny people started to contribute stories. The 1980 Old Boy who was the wise senior to the foolish sophomores who pulled the Dead Bowler prank rousted them from their graves to produce an epic account of their escapade. Chappies who were part of the Dornheim "Resurrection" contributed several articles. The "Journalism Era," as the Chappies of 1969-74 wanted to be known instead of "Political Era," wrote a fantastic account of their years. The professor showed up, writing long, scholarly sequences about a wide range of subjects, his expertise and knowledge only exceeded by his hilarious and unflinching take downs, criticisms, and call outs of hypocrisy of the *Stanford Daily*. In the rivalry that exists in some minds between the Chappie and the *Daily*, he is an honored titan for the *Chaparral*. The nineties also contributed stories and issues, and there were even 21st century Chappies who submitted pieces, including The Children, as I call the current students, *Chaparral* active staff. And the core of the effort, the enthusiastic, can-do, "non-representative" Chappies of the 1980s.

As the articles came in, I learned some astonishing, mind-blowing things.

The Year of Living Deathily

For example, I got this great essay from JM, explaining his prescient joking about death. I really couldn't believe it. There were many coincidences that fit almost too perfectly into this story.

I had been developing this personal joke about "coincidenses," misspell intentional, which were coincidences for really dense people, or just dumb coincidences in general. At some point, I realized that this joke switched the c and the s just like Zodiac did when he spelled "paradice." Zodiac used this incorrect spelling multiple times, and it is unknown if he just didn't know how to spell it, or if it was his own personal joke. I hereby explain that "coincidense" which you will find throughout the Chappie 125 Book, is not just a dumb coincidence, it is also my inside Zodiac joke. I took a lot of shit for it, from people whose opinion I value, who said I should take it out of the book. Now we can debate whether it is funny, but I could never defend why I was putting it in the book so much, until now.

But I digress. What was really amazing about JM's essay, The Year of Living Deathily, was that not only did he write "Who Shot R.R?," not only was he editor when the "Dead Bowlers" prank was pulled, not only did he instigate the drawing of chalk outlines around campus to promote a *Chaparral* issue which got two staffers arrested by campus police who were waiting for the Memorial Church murderer to return on the 5-year anniversary of the crime; but he also co-wrote, with his girlfriend M (a future professor of mine), a bad review for the album "Double Fantasy" that published on the day John Lennon was shot. Bad timing. Again, a printed article coinciding with a shooting. What are the odds?

As I said in the Prelude, I thought that the Lennon-Ono album should have been titled Love is Deaf.

But talk about latent psychic abilities manifesting themselves in prankish, pop culture comedy ending up in a humor publication, a sort of antenna, or diving rod, for the odd and macabre.

Also, think of me, trying to downplay murder and such subjects in the Chappie 125 book, at least publicly, then this shows up. When this essay that talks about joke coincidences with death was submitted, I was like, "I don't f-ing believe this." The Fs of Coincidence, or Coincidense, just kept on coming. And it wasn't over.

Laughing to Death

I received a story from JB, a *Chaparral* Old Boy from the late 70s. He was a freshman when Mike Dornheim returned the *Chaparral* to its humor format. He submitted an essay telling how he got his first piece in the Chappie.

The story started while he was at the printers in San Francisco with Dornheim, to print Fiscal Responsibility, an extremely important issue in the history of the Chaparral. With the presses about to run, they heard on the radio that there had been a murder in Memorial Church at Stanford the night before. The issue they were printing contained a piece about people laughing to death in Memorial Church. Luckily, they were able to substitute out the article on laughing to death, and ran instead a piece by JB. It was how his first story appeared in the Chappie.

Honestly, upon reading this, I was beginning to wonder how we could have so many coincidences surrounding death, surrounding murder. The *Chaparral* indeed seems to have some sort of psychic energy around it. I decided to turn this all into its own section of the book.

I made a logo for Strange Psychic Events and used it like a stamp on various pages throughout the Chappie 125 layouts. As the Chappie has many strange coincidences throughout its history, there are quite a few in the book.

Doodles Weaver

Doodles Weaver is perhaps the most famous Chappie, at least internally to our organization. He is known as possibly the wildest Chappie, the weirdest. Doodles would not only get one, but two spreads in the Chappie 125 book, one for his comedy and one for his pranks. Back in school, JW told me about Doodles, and how his niece was Sigourney, and she went to Stanford too.

And then, just through the course of research, I stumbled upon the 1971 film, The Zodiac Killer. I hadn't heard of this film before, perhaps it got lost when the 2007 movie came out. However it was, I was only learning of it now. As I read through the IMDB page on the film, there, in the cast, was *Chaparral*'s own Doodles Weaver.

I don't even think it was the Close Encounters music at this point, rather more of the cheesy drum riff after a bad joke. Thank you! I mean, now the coincidences are just getting stupid.

Doodles Weaver in a Zodiac movie? Now I've heard everything. If you believe in something like a Divine Shakespeare, here might be where you say, "Who doth be writing this shit?" Or you might say, "Yet another F of a coincidence."

At this point, I was ready for anything

Of quizzical interest, Doodles is actually credited in the movie as

Doddles Weaver.

"Hmmmmmm" I thought.

Then another mini-coincidence gave the Doodles-Zodiac joke some legs. BH submitted his article for the 1980 *Chaparral* issue, Americana, with a cover that has the Statue of Liberty with its dress blowing up like Marilyn Monroe in the famous scene from the movie The Seven Year Itch. For that layout, his Fun Fact, a little blurb we would add in addition to the main text, was that Marilyn Monroe and Doodles Weaver never appeared on screen together. I had my hook. And it was perfect.

BH was the guy who had caught my fake *Chaparral* Halloween 1916 issue, where I used the Zodiac Halloween card for the graphic. This point was both tantalizing and dangerous, because he might be able to recognize a Zodiac Easter egg in the book if I wasn't careful.

So, when I laid out this factoid, I got a standard Marilyn Monroe photo and Doodles' official press photo. This is how I sent him the layouts for his feedback.

Then, after he had seen and affirmed the layout, I switched the pictures. I got a still of Marilyn from the movie Niagara, where she plays a murderer, and for Doodles, well of course I got a still from his movie The Zodiac Killer.

I never told BH about all of this, but I did put this Marilyn-Doodles Easter egg in the Chappie book for him on page 270 of *The Chappie – 125 Years of Issues*.[267]

Between the coincidences of the submitted articles and the planning and placing of Easter eggs in the book I was creating, my mind wandered on the possibilities of humor and prank within such publications. I reflected more on the Missing Link, and the possible jokes embedded, and moreover, tried to answer the motivation for its creation.

Further examination of The Missing Link

I decided it was time to examine the Missing Link Issue in more depth.

I needed to get the highest resolution scans of both the *Chaparral*, and the original *Stanford Daily* issues that the articles had been lifted from. It was easy to scan the *Chaparral*, I had found an issue when we went to Stanford in May 2023. I scanned it at 600dpi with no compression, creating a very good digital scan of the document, including the dot screen of the Missing Link photo. I was able to confirm the dot screen from the original in the *Daily*, and the reproduction in the *Chaparral* were the same.

The Double Exposures

I used Photoshop to greatly enlarge the 600-dpi front page scan. That is when I noticed that some of the articles were double exposures.

The Dick Geikie article, and the article next to it, had both been double exposed. You could see the two exposures because the text of both articles was out of alignment. The Dick Geikie article was worse than the other, with one exposure about 1/32nd of an inch lower than the other. This is not bad enough to be seen at normal scale, the only effect is that the type appears different than the other type on the page, a bit bolder. The alignment issue showing the double exposure is only seen when magnifying the image to a very large scale.

The other articles on the front and back pages of the *Chaparral* appear to be single exposures.

But for whatever reason, the Dick Geikie article and another were double-exposed. Perhaps their first exposures were too light. If so, it must have been important for these articles to appear correctly, lessening the chance that the issue was just a mock-up. These double exposures also show that the issue was composed photographically, at least in part.

Threes and Fives Again

On May 28, 2023, I realized that the format of the *Chaparral* had changed during this period. While it always was a newsprint tabloid, the number of columns per page had changed over time. Starting in 1969, the *Chaparral* was a three-column format. It stayed that way for two years, through the end of the 1970-71 school year.

Then the *Chaparral* Missing Link issue of the summer of 1971, the Dick Geikie issue, has a five-column format. Of course we know this issue to be fake. But fake or not, it is the first issue with five columns, and the *Chaparral* remains in this five-column format for the entire year and into the next, when it switches to a four-column format.

Yes, you read that right, the issue in question is the first of a format change for the *Chaparral* lasting a full year. This observation led me to the conjecture that this issue might be a mockup, to see what a five-column format would look like.

But if that were the case, that left me with several questions:

Missing Link Questions

Why would they spend money to print such an issue?

If it were a test mock-up, why make multiple copies of a test?

If it were a test, why bother changing the masthead to read "Special Issue"?

Why print it on a two-sheet? If it were a mock-up, you could still print it on a one-sheet and save money.

Why would an organization notorious for having no money print up a bunch of mock-up issues?

Even if they had money, why would they waste it unnecessarily?

Who composed this issue and why? Once composed, who printed this issue and why?

Why are the Dick Geikie and the adjoining article double exposed?

Who archived it with multiple issues like the other issues of that year?

Who folded it into the other, real, March 5 *Chaparral* issues so it appeared to be a section two?

Why did the library get the issue and archive it as Number 2, Section 2?

Why do H&C bound volumes also have it as Number 2, Section 2?

Who created the bound archival volumes that included this issue? Usually this is done by the Hammer & Coffin. Did they do so for this volume? Whoever bound the volumes, were they duped, or were they in on the joke?

Why did the *Chaparral* change its format to five-column, starting with this issue? Coincidence? Or for some reason?

If the issue is an intentional fake, why leave pages two and three blank?

Are the blank pages a mistake? Were they really stoned?

Are the blank pages intentional? If so, why? Is it a joke? A prank?

Is the blank staff box in the July 9, 1971 *Stanford Daily* with a blank space in it related to the blank pages?

Is the joke something to do with "rip off," a term that appears in the photo caption and the same page as the July 9 staff box?

And finally, is this issue an intentional fake to make it appear Dick Geikie was at Stanford in early March 1971, and not somewhere else?

March 1971

When I first discovered the Dick Geikie byline, I noted the March 5, 1971 date. I knew there was speculation on the internet that Richard Gaikowski was involuntarily committed to the Napa County Mental Hospital sometime in early1971. The exact dates this happened are unclear, if it actually happened at all. You can also read online the conjecture Richard might have gone to a commune in Northern California, a few hundred miles north of San Francisco.

At the time I discovered the Missing Link issue, and when I thought it was from March 1971, I wrote in my notes, "If Dick Geikie is Richard, the believed timeline of his whereabouts in early 1971 will have to be changed--NOT in northern California."

But now I was realizing this issue had to have been made sometime after July 23, 1971, in which case the timeline would NOT have to change. Dick Geikie could have been in northern California in March of 1971, and at Stanford in the summer of 1971.

Kate and I had discussed the Missing Link issue extensively. A mistake. A mockup. A joke. Each options seemed as implausible as the other.

Even Further Examination of the Missing Link

I continued to compare the Missing Link issue with the articles in the *Daily* used to construct it, bringing them into Photoshop. I lined up all the articles, pasted on top of the *Chaparral* issue. After completing the front page, I went and got the last page, page four from the July 9, 1971 *Daily* and laid it on top of page 4, of the *Chaparral*. It fit exactly.

"That's strange," I thought. I had assumed the page would have to be scaled down from *Daily* size to *Chaparral* size. But the page was already at the right size. I realized that the *Daily* was printing tabloid size in the summer of 1971. Every *Daily* issue of summer 1971 was a five-column tabloid, not the regular full newspaper size I had assumed because that is what remembered from my time at Stanford. These *Daily* issues were half-size tabloids.

OMG. The theory that this *Chaparral* issue was a mock-up just became much less of a possibility.

And that's because there was no reason to print a mock-up, the five-column tabloid was already being used by the *Stanford Daily*, you could already see what it would look like. The mock-up theory falls away. The Missing Link issue is not a mock-up.

We were down to just a couple possibilities, and they pointed to this being is some sort of a joke, or prank issue.

What the joke is about is unclear.

There was an emerging idea that seemed too crazy to consider, that this was an intentional fake issue, that attempted to make it appear Dick Geikie was at Stanford in early March 1971. The idea wasn't really that crazy, given that this was exactly what I thought for many months. If I had not bothered to investigate deeper, I would have just accepted that he was indeed at Stanford in March.

If this idea truly was the case, it would mean that there might be a crime in early March 1971 that Zodiac was making an alibi for. Of course, the only Zodiac confirmed murders were in 1968 and 69. Zodiac claimed more, but none have been confirmed.

"If the fake issue was truly to make it seem like he was at Stanford in March, then there will be a reason, a murder somewhere during early March NOT near Stanford," posited Kate.

We figured the most likely place to look for a murder would be in northern California.

I returned to Google and other search engines, in search of a Zodiac-like crime in northern California in early March 1971. With the date on the issue being March 5, I figured I would type in March 6 as a likely day to start. And there it was.

Lynda Kanes

Cue the Close Encounters music, the papers of the north bay on March 6, 1971 were lit up like a Christmas Tree, headlined by the murder of Lynda Kanes, a college student whose body had been found the day before, March 5, in the hills above Lake Berryessa.

Amazingly, Kanes was one of two murders in northern California that actually were both on February 26. The specifics of both crimes sound much like Zodiac. Sharon Wilson was a junior at Humbolt College, knifed to death out in nature near Eureka. Her body was found near the mouth of the Mad River. But it is just a coincidence, because this crime was confessed to by a local man working as a cowhand[268].

Lynda Kanes murder also sounded like a Zodiac crime, even more so. But apparently again a coincidence. An individual was arrested, tried and convicted for this crime. Even so, who really killed Lynda Kanes is still a matter of speculation to this day.

Lynda Kanes was a student at Pacific Union College from Porterville, California. As we know, Lake Berryessa victim Brian Hartnell was a PUC student, and Cecelia Shepard had been a year prior before transferring to UC Riverside. Disappearing on February 26, a Napa County Sheriff's posse began a manhunt for Kanes the next morning[269]. Eventually the search was joined by the general public, including hundreds of students from Pacific Union College. After several days of searching, Kanes body was discovered on March 5, on a mountain road on the west side of Lake Berryessa[270], the same side as the Sheperd and Hartnell attack.

As reported in the March 6, 1971, *Napa Valley Register*, a ranking member of the sheriff's department described it as a "bizarre" murder, but did not elaborate on that description[271].

Kanes was found with a wire around her neck, but they were not positive that strangulation was the cause of death. The body had been well camouflaged under a pile of rocks, found in an area that had already been searched. It was subsequently reported that the cause of death was blunt force trauma to her head. In addition to the wire around her neck, her fully clothed body was bound by rope and then wrapped in an American flag and doused with a mixture of gasoline and fuel oil. Other items found near the body were a gas can and an old military-style duffel bag. A chilling detail was learned about the flag--A piece of it was ripped off by the killer.[272]

From the moment she went missing, through the discovery of her body, it was widely speculated this was the work of the Zodiac. It was reported that the students of PUC were especially jittery, which would have been quite understandable.

It turns out the flag, the rope, the duffel bag, and the gas can were all the property of Walter Williams, a local man who lived up in those mountains, known as Willie the Woodcutter.

When Willie the Woodcutter was arraigned, people were in disbelief; local citizens, people who knew Willie could not believe that he could be a murderer. Willie was well liked in the community.[273]

People following the Zodiac murders were also in disbelief. The murder was so very much like Zodiac. It was another student from Pacific Union College, just like Celia Shepherd and Brian Hartnell. It was very near the location of their attack, just up into the hills from Lake Berryessa. The murderer ripped off a piece of the American flag that the body was wrapped in, similar to Zodiac ripping off a piece of Paul Stine's shirt. It was said that they were all waiting for the piece of the flag to show up in the mail--but it never did.

The March 17, 1971, *Martinez Morning News* reported the arrest of Willie on the front page, the article sharing the front page with news about Zodiac's recent letter to the *Los Angeles Times* where he boasts about his "Riverside Activity."[274] This is noted only as a coincidence.

As the days led up to the trial in June, more items were by investigators tied to the accused. Then on July 9, a surprise witness for the prosecution sealed his fate. Walter Williams, aka Willie the Woodcutter was convicted of the crime on July 23, 1971.[275] Williams died in prison in 1978.[276] There are still people who to this day disbelieve he was guilty, conjecturing instead that Lynda Kanes was killed by the Zodiac.

To even consider I might have a piece of evidence about this, in the form of a fake *Chaparral*, sounded like a ridiculous way-too-many-coincidence movie plot, rather than a real story.

"No one is REALLY going to believe this," I thought.

I realized, I needed to learn even more about the *Chaparral* in the early 1970s, both for the *Chaparral* book, AND Zodiac research. So I commenced an even deeper dive.

THE ONLY TIME RICHARD GOT ANGRY AT ME

What Really Happened to the Chaparral in '69

So, what really happened to the *Chaparral* in 1969? I couldn't tell you, but it was, and still is, a key question in the history of the *Chaparral*. And apparently, it's a key part of the history of Stanford and more as well. What led to the protests in February 1970 that caused the suspension of the Chappie's editor? What other fascinating secrets did these years hold? What happened in 1969 that led to the situation in 1971, when the Missing Link prank issue was created?

I decided to read, or at least skim over, every *Stanford Daily* issue, day by day, starting in fall of 1968. It was a sacrifice I had to make. I mean, I didn't have anyone I knew to call, and the few emails I had sent had gone unanswered. So I started reading *Stanford Daily* issues, beginning with the 68-69 school year that set the table for 69-70.

The *Chaparral* produced an issue in the fall of 1968, an attempt to be a "general interest" publication, which cemented the unpopularity of the magazine, and enlarged its debt. It was the only *Chaparral* printed that school year, and by the spring of 1969 it appeared the Chappie had finally given up the ghost.

A3Mania

In the spring of 1969, the A3Movement came to prominence at Stanford, starting with a meeting on April 3rd, 1969, thus naming the movement.[277] As listed on www.a3mreunion.org, the sponsoring organizations were SDS, Resistance, Peninsula Observer, Stanford UCM Staff, Peninsula Red Guard, Junior Faculty Forum, United Student Movement, New University Conference, Committee for New Politics, Palo Alto Concerned Citizens, *Midpeninsula Free* University, North Santa Clara Peace and Freedom Movement, and American Federation of Teachers Local No. 1816.[278] At that meeting, the A3M issued demands to Stanford President Pitzer and the Stanford Trustees.

At 1 am on May 1, 1969, the April 3rd Movement occupied Encina Hall. By 4:30 am, there were about 200 students, as reported by the *Stanford Daily* in their issue *of the same day.*[279]

The Daily story continued that the seizure of Encina Hall was the most serious student demonstration in Stanford's history, as protesters occupied the Universities Business and Payroll Offices, News and Publication office, Personnel office and several others. Encina had been chosen during a long meeting the previous evening where more than

900 people voted to occupy Encina, beating out Hoover Tower, the Space Engineering Building and Stanford Business School.

As I read the May 1 *Stanford Daily* coverage, I was fascinated to see the article was written by *Daily* reporter and future Chappie Old Boy Michael Sweeney.[280]

As reported by in the May 2, 1969, *Stanford Daily*, by daylight on May 1 the cops arrived, a lot of cops in full riot gear, and Stanford issued injunctions and restraining orders. The cops moved in around 7:15 am[281].

Unbeknownst to the cops, the students had voted to get out of there, but they still delayed ten minutes to "gather their belongings." Sometime after 7:30, the last students left.

Whether the university knew that records had been stolen is unclear. Reports of damage to Encina were listed at about $1,000, mostly due to broken windows. It was noted that files cabinets had been opened, and they were being inspected. Files had indeed been stolen, and they would play a big role the following fall.

At the very end of the school year, a meeting was called regarding the dormant *Chaparral*.[282]

Dawn of a New Era

Over the summer of 1969, the *Chaparral* was revived! A group of "50 odd people," led by Michael Sweeney, got the Hammer & Coffin Society to agree to the new management plan--they would pay off the *Chaparral*'s debt of approximately $16,000, and float the magazine over $3,500 more for operations. Remember, these are in 1969 dollars when a brand-new VW Bug cost $1,799.

It was described that the *Chaparral* would be a "literary magazine." I suppose one could argue that since it had printed "words" on "paper" it was indeed "literary magazine," but that is about the extent of it. The 1969 Chappie staff was off to the races, but they produced a radical publication in an underground press style, on newsprint in a tabloid format, like the *Berkeley Barb*, *Berkeley Tribe*, and yes, like the *San Francisco Good Times*.

It was not just a publication. The *Chaparral* became a focal point of campus and mid-peninsula protests, and certainly the center of the OFF-ROTC protests of spring 1970. The *Chaparral* office became a sort of a headquarters of the protest movement.

The old Hammer & Coffin guys were NOT amused. In fact, they were livid.

From the very beginning of the school year in September 1969, the *Chaparral* was in the news with much more frequency than it had been earlier, with mentions in the *Stanford Daily*, references to individuals associated with the *Chaparral*, and regular listings for Chappie meetings. It is clear that the Chappie of fall 1969 was a very active student group.

In the October 16, 1969, *Daily*, there were two letters to the editor that mentioned the *Chaparral*.[283] One lamented the *Chaparral*'s new radical format and said it wasn't funny anymore. The other letter mentioned Reagan, the SDS, George Meany and the Chappie, signed by the obviously fake name Noknox. The *Chaparral* was mentioned in the October 17 , 21 and 22 *Daily* issues as well.

Of course, October 24, 1969, is the date of the Message To The Zodiac Killer editorial in the *Daily*. For what it's worth, the Chappie was NOT mentioned in that issue

The Secret Salaries

Do you remember the Encina protest on May 1, 1969? Well not the actual protest, but my writing about it a few pages earlier? It turns out the protesters DID take some files while they were in Encina. Personally, I'd wager they were taken during the ten minutes they needed to gather their things. Regardless, they appear, sort of out of the blue, but also happening right in the middle of this story!

On the morning of October 27, 1969, mimeographed copies of salary data, Stanford payroll data that was stolen during the protest, showed up at locations around campus.[284] Copies of the 31-page document containing potentially explosive revelations about internal university workings were left randomly around Stanford. The document was signed "Underground Press."[285]

On October 28, the *Daily* ran a front-page story about it, but didn't print individual salaries, except for the President's.[286] Instead, they present averaged data for various departments at Stanford, including the budget for police salaries.

Also on October 28, copies of the salary documents showed up in the mail at the offices of the *San Francisco Chronicle*, the *San Jose Mercury*, the *Stanford Daily*, and… the *Stanford Chaparral*.[287]

Now I am honored that the *Chaparral* was included with these three other bastions of print. But all jokes aside, as the children's game goes, one of these things is not like the other.

The *Chaparral* sticks out as strangely suspicious. I mean, one could argue that the *Chaparral* was a student publication, just like the *Daily*, and that would be somewhat true. But then, as now, the *Chaparral* was not as well-known as the *Daily*, would not be considered a news source like the *Daily*, and moreover, an average student would not think to include the *Chaparral* on a list with the *Chronicle*, *Mercury*, and *Stanford Daily*. And it is almost a certainty that no *Daily* staffer would send the scoop to the *Chaparral*. But, a Chappie WOULD send it to the *Daily*, because that is what everyone reads, and it provides plausible deniability and cover for your prank.

As an old *Chaparral* prankster, I conjecture: This looks a lot like a Chappie prank. At minimum, it got the *San Francisco Examiner* to report that the *Daily* and the *Chaparral* were Stanford's humor magazines![288]

The Empire Strikes Back

Stanford wasted no time publicly threatening legal action against any publication of the secret salaries.[289]

As I wrote in The Chappie – 125 Years of Issues, page 237:

It was a big shitstorm…. Some of the New Left movement even saw this episode as a distraction to their main goals of cessation of the war in Vietnam, ending of the draft, and the removal of ROTC and other Stanford ties to the military-industrial complex.

Stanford made the move to put out "official" salary data, but it is aggregated and averaged by department, not by individual professor. The *Daily* printed that data in their November 5 issue, sharing the front page with the small article at the bottom stating Zodiac had called.[290]

On some of the copies of this issue, a pronounced spot appears on this article, mostly on the chart of salary data.

The *Chaparral* did not waste time exploiting their "fortuitous receiving" of the salary data via the mail. The cover of the November

6 *Chaparral* was titled Should We Print the Secret Salaries? with a cartoon of three Jesters doing speak no evil, see no evil, hear no evil on the cover.[291] Inside, the issue there is an article that discussed the salaries, and asked why it was such a big secret. It promised an in-depth analysis in a future *Chaparral* issue.

On November 13, the Daily, with much fanfare, printed secret salaries, but they were making a joke. They printed not the professors' salaries, but the salaries of the *Daily* staff. The list includes many names, including some likely involved with this story. Of pop-culture note is that Sigourney Weaver is on the list, she earned $10 from working at the *Stanford Daily*.[292]

Then in the November 20 *Chaparral*, letters from individual professors were printed that fully disclosed their salaries and other income arrangements.[293] On some of these issues, a pronounced circular spot appears on the title page of the multi-page section where the salary letters appeared. The spot looks similar to the one in the Daily on November 5, but it is in a completely different location on the page.

I've Got a Little Listing

The October 9, 1969, issue of the *Stanford Chaparral* was the second issue of the school year, the second issue of the Chappie's political era, printed in the style and manner of the underground press. The issue's cover and main theme is the upcoming Moratorium to End the War in Vietnam, set to occur on October 15.[294]

Listings of events occurring around the Bay Area were printed in the back of the issue.[295] Included in the listings under the heading Drama are shows in San Francisco. Hair at the Geary Theater, Jacques Brel is Alive and Well and Living in Paris, at the Marine Memorial Theater, Geese at the Encore Theater, Fantasticks at Ghirardelli Square, You're a Good Man Charlie Brown at the Ghirardelli Theater, Oh! Calcutta! at the On Broadway Theater, and Duchess of Maifi at The Theatre in Berkeley.

There are also numerous films listed under Recommended Cinema and The Committee, the Pitschel Players and the Thieves Market are all listed under a heading Good Time Places.

"That's interesting," I thought.

Then there are listings by date for October 9 through October 22.

These listings include the date and time for performances all over the Bay Area including Grand Kabuki at the Curran Theater, the Buster Keaton Film Festival at the Surf Theater, Cabaret at the Berkeley Community Theater, Charlie Mingus, Country Joe and the Fish, Liberace, Dizzy Gillespie, Nina Simone, Pete Seeger, Victor Borge, and performances of Puccini's La Boheme at the SF Opera House.

All these listings contain the date, time and location for these events.

The first listing for Saturday, October 18 says, "You want Mikado? You find it. It's around." It does not list a venue, nor an address or time.

"That's even more interesting," I thought. "Why not put the time and place?" I assumed it was for the Lamplighters production in San Francisco which debuted that night, but why no information?

This made me curious, so I went back and found the *Daily's* Mikado review from the October 31 issue. The layout was really bad; with cut off letters on the left of the article, and there were white spots on it. As I breezed through pages, I noted that there were other white spots on issues of that time. I wondered if the *Daily* was such a bad client or so broke that they got their issues printed on the cheap machines.

At this point we were deep in production of the Chaparral book, and now it was Zodiac yet again sidetracking my Chappie work. It was easy to fall into the black hole of time that reading about Zodiac had become. Anyway, I was already immersed in such a hole creating the Chappie 125 book.

I put this Mikado business aside.

Tensions on campus build through the end of 1969 and into 1970. The Chaparral produces issues six issues through January. Then comes their most ambitious project yet. The seventh *Chaparral* issue, the anti-ROTC issue, the "Off ROTC" issue, as the movement and protests were named, was the final issue of the tumultuous editorship of Michael Sweeney.[296] The Hammer & Coffin alums had reached their limit, and after protests, broken windows, buildings burned, the University wasn't amused either. This was the end of Michael Sweeney's editorship of the *Chaparral*.

The following school year, the Chaparral produced just three issues, or four if you count the Missing Link to be a separate issue. There are indeed staff boxes on two of the "real" issues, with names listed alphabetically. There is no Dick Geikie listed. Instances of the Chaparral being mentioned in the *Stanford Daily* drop precipitously that school year, save for the calendar listings for various meetings.

Then in the October 1, 1971, *Daily*, the article appears, Chaparral Publishes Again.[297]

The Journalism Years

Up to summer of 2023, I had only made limited progress on talking to political era Chappies, but a group email about a play got a response... from the editor of the 1971-72 *Chaparral*! I had previously tried to contact them without success. But their reply to that email led to contact with them and another Chappie staffer from the early 70s. This was the key event in reconnecting with the Chappies of what had always known as "the political era," but now refer to as the "Journalism Years."

Starting that fall of 1971, the magazine righted the ship. They produced a by-weekly news tabloid that still had cartoons and a glib and often sarcastic editorial, and they stuck to their production schedule. As mentioned, the *Chaparral* produced 17 issues in both the 1971-72 and 72-73 school years, a record. It was still a magazine interested in politics and social justice, but it was not the center of the cyclone, so to speak, in these years.

And so the history of the *Chaparral* was pieced together, from the demise of the humor format in the late 1960s to its underground press and journalism transformation, to its return as a humor magazine in 1974. It was a group effort. PC had researched the very end of the humor era in 1967 and 68, and a fabulous article was contributed regarding the journalism of the era. I had taken photographs of every page when I was at Stanford, so between those photos, cross-referencing them with *Stanford Daily* and other newspaper articles, we created a section in the Chappie 125 book that told the story of these years, and how they survived when so many college magazines bit the dust.

Defense of the Journalism Years

These years of the *Chaparral* had been described to us in the late 1980s as a dark time, when the magazine had been taken over by radicals, and most disparagingly, wasn't funny. This was the entirety of my knowledge of the *Chaparral* circa 1969-74 until present day.

But I want to make clear now, in the 2020s, that the description of that time was unfair, and in a word, wrong. The *Chaparral* has always been a reflection of the times it existed in, interspersing eras as a cutting edge antenna/lightning rod, with other eras when it is on life support. In these aspects, the *Chaparral* during the years 1969 to 1974 fits right in. And it never was free from humor, not by a long shot. Glib, sarcastic, and biting could be used to describe much of the content. One of the greatest parodies of all *Chaparral* history was published during this time, 1973's Campus Report. The issues of this era always had cartoons and sarcastic commentary. They ran a comic about the genders of plain and peanut M&Ms while mocking William Shockley's racist and sexist views—amazingly prescient of the M&M gender "controversy" here in the 2020s. Don't tell me the *Chaparral* isn't strangely psychic.

This era shared another aspect with many other humor eras of the *Chaparral*, it ended with the Chappie in dire financial straits.

The 1973-74 school was the fifth, and last year of the Journalism Years. That year the *Chaparral* produced four issues, but ended the year in substantial debt. The future of the Chaparral was yet again in doubt at the end of the 1974 school year. Then that summer, the Chaparral's position became even more precarious.

Remember the front-page article in the July 16, 1974, *Stanford Daily* I described early on in this book? Consider it now. The *Chaparral* had been shut down by the ASSU Publications board because the magazine's debt was over $2,000 dollars, the locks to the office were changed, and the non-students-living in the *Chaparral* office, who produced a non-Stanford publication while there, were kicked out.[298]

"Now that's more interesting than ever," I thought.

Where Do You Hide a Tree?

It seemed my investigation into all this was as warranted as ever. People living in the *Chaparral*? That wasn't the biggest deal to me. That would never happen. <wink wink>

But non-students, printing their own publication? Who were these people and what were they printing? What was really going on? Inquiring minds want to know.

Except for running my mouth in *Chaparral* Zoom calls a year earlier, I had otherwise been able to mask my Zodiac research. If the subject happened to come up, I would downplay it. Even when the subject of David Lamson came up, the 1920s *Chaparral* editor accused of killing his wife, I played it down.

Everything was going along fine, until... In one of the late 2023 Zoom calls, X brought up my previous Zodiac conjecturing and suggested it should go in the book. I strongly objected. Strongly. It was sort of funny, though. Thirty-five years ago X had created some difficulty for the bear prank, too. It was like history repeating. Anyway, I played down the idea.

That zoom call even had me doing some damage control. I contacted people individually telling them that I thought discussion of Jane Stanford being murdered, the 1930s Chappie murder allegations, the four Stanford Murders in the seventies, or psychopathic serial killers in general was not good material for the *Chaparral* anniversary preparations. It was a reasonable idea, and everyone agreed.

Meanwhile, my fascination with these years of the *Chaparral* grew, as did my reasoning for including a full reprint of the Missing Link in the Chappie 125 book. Even with the additional research, even with corresponding with some of the Chappies from this era, this issue still evaded explanation. And no one remembered Dick Geikie.

I created the spread on the Missing Link issue, and slipped it into what would become *The Chappie – 125 Years of Issues*, a tree, placed deep in the forest of the Chappie 125 book.

Page 394

Around October 2023, I realized it was time start putting all these pages I had generated in order to see just how many pages there were. I had long abandoned the idea of assembling them end to end in one file. With each page very graphics-heavy, and because there were so many pages, I had created the book in more than 50 separate documents. Now, because they needed to be put in some sort of order, it wasn't feasible to arrange the actual layouts at all, so I opened up Excel again. I entered in every layout I had and started arranging them in sections. One long list of pages for the first time ever. I added in many placeholder pages for things like a table of contents, an index, acknowledgments and the like, and also padded sections with extra spreads, additional pages, booze jokes, more religion pages, and Dornheim extras.

I put the Missing Link in among Psychic Events, Occulture, and a spread on Warren G. Wonka, a mythical, fake Stanford character who appeared over the years in the *Chaparral, Daily, Quad* yearbook and more. I made sure this section appeared about three quarters into the book. Normally I would put something like this about two-thirds into a document--the best place to try to hide something in a block of text. But in this book, there were so many pages, hundreds of pages. You could put the Missing Link tree even deeper into the forest and still have plenty of pages for those who look at the book back to front. With so many pages, I thought many would just get tired out before getting three-quarters in.

Plus, I had a secret hope—that the Missing Link spread would land on a funny or auspicious number. I thought it would be funny if it turned out to be page 420, but also thought 333 would be good (half of 666), or 444, for similar reasons; or 411, something like that.

You have to understand—there had been, have been, so many coincidences in this story, you start to make jokes about it and wonder if another is going to happen. So, when I decided to run the column of page numbers, I eagerly awaited to see what page the Missing Link would get. I ran it and…the Missing Link landed on page 394. Hmmm. I was sort of disappointed, that was not any kind of special number that I knew, but whatever. I saved the spreadsheet and returned to the layouts.

Later that evening, I kept thinking I remembered something about a page 394. A sound byte, or something from a movie? Wait. What about Harry Potter? Isn't there a scene where Snape tells them to go to a certain page?

I opened up a search bar. As you are typing and you get to "Snape pa…" the search engine completes it for you: Snape Page 394! I went to YouTube and entered "Snape Page 394" and was taken to clips of the movie Harry Potter and the Prisoner of Azkaban.

Before hitting the Play button, I paused and said to myself, "OK, 394, I bet this clip will have something to consider on this case, some joke or coincidence. Let's see."

I hit Play and watched the scene. Professor Snape enters a class-room at Hogwarts, closing the windows with flicks of his wand and says, "Turn to page three hundred ninety-four." He says again, "Turn to page three hundred ninety-four."

I sat there in bemusement watching the scene.

Now there is no point here other than noting the comical nature of having the voice of the great Alan Rickman saying to go to page 394, because that is what I recommend you do in the book The Chappie – 125 Years of Issues.

Page 394 is where the Missing Link issue is reproduced in its entirety, reduced in size somewhat, but each page is shown, with circles and arrows and a paragraph near each one explaining what each one might be, and the staff box from the key *Stanford Daily* that much of the issue was constructed from.

Let me tell you, there were MANY page rearrangements in the next month, but after cracking up about Professor Snape's instructions, one way or another, I made sure that the Missing Link stayed on page 394.

Delay in the Chappie 125 Book

In October 2023 I sent out for a 60-page test print of the Chappie 125 book. It arrived two weeks later, and it was fabulous. I took photos of the book and sent them to the group. It caused quite a stir.

I had given everyone the deadline of Halloween to get their stuff to me, and after that I was going to be very harsh to latecomers. Keep in mind, my first call for submissions had been in May 2021, with an initial deadline of June 2022. As we approached Halloween 2023, I was contacted by an individual saying the Hammer & Coffin board wanted me to delay the deadlines on my book. I was pretty incredulous.

First off, I really didn't even know exactly who was on the board of the H&C, but I was fairly sure none contributed any article to the book effort, which was OK, people are busy. But why did they say I needed to delay?

I asked a few friends who are H&C members for their opinion about what to do. None of the Hammer & Coffin members I knew were aware of who the board members were, or what they did.

"Who are they and how do they have any authority?" was the general question. Actually, it was pretty much the only question.

Ironically, the Chappie Book needed to be finished by the beginning of 2024 to be of best use for the organization, not just for my timeline. "Finishing" a book is just the beginning, then there is distribution, promotion, and selling. It would be necessary for the book to come out in early 2024 to have time to get people interested in the October celebration. People do indeed plan out their travel plans a year and more out. Hype does indeed take time to get to all interested parties, and to previously uninterested parties.

For example, I planned to hawk and promote the book in April, when we would travel to San Francisco for the annual Hammer & Coffin banquet. Delaying production of the book would put that plan in great jeopardy.

So the request to delay the book was really a bad one, and would have impeded the work to make a great 125th anniversary event. And since the request to delay was being made by those who had not worked on the project, and made quasi-anonymously via an intermediary member, there was no way view it other than kind of strange.

20 Days in November

Ok, some of the days were in October, but doesn't that sound like a movie or play?

I told the intermediary that I wasn't inclined to delay deadlines for the book, BUT, I also believe it's always a good idea to work with people. I have said from the beginning that there were some naysayers and yes-butters in the organization. Such people would be cautious and slow moving regarding any topic or project. Then there was general malaise--this project began because *Chaparral* archives were in such a shambles. I imagined all this was just moving too fast for some people. So, I made a concession to address the board's feelings and concerns.

It was October 26, 2023. I announced to the group that I would delay 20 days, 10 days for anyone to tell me they are writing an article, and how many pages they think they will need, and 10 more days to get the article in. All in all, one day shy of three weeks delay for some people who hadn't been in the process at all for the preceding 30 MONTHS. I sent a group email to the Everyone list with these terms.

The good news was a few people not previously involved with the book saw the email and wrote up articles. One entirely new page about the great 1973 Tresidder Union Theater prank and issue was submitted within the first 24 hours! That's when the *Chaparral* printed, as a prank, that the University was considering adding a movie theater to Tresidder Union. The hoax received rousing support from the public, who did not know it was a hoax. And while a theater was never built at the Union, the University did expand options to see films on campus, a big deal in 1973.

Three days later I had three new articles. A couple more people notified me of their intent to write articles, and I entered their pages into the spreadsheet, and yes, shuffling things around to keep the Missing Link at page 394.

All in all, the delay made the Chappie 125 book better. As far as more articles from the Hammer & Coffin board, they never came, except perhaps for one. A person from Dornheim's era did write a spread, and it is a really great addition to the book. None of the others responded at all, not even an "Okay, got your email." A transparent and clinical discussion was never initiated about the delay.

In early November I had the files about 99 percent ready to go, when a family emergency caused all work to stop. Following that I was summoned to New York by my Japanese friend and patron, who I had first met back in 1994 at the ATA show where Richard signed my book. While having dinner with them, I passed my phone around with a link to the layouts of the Chappie book.

"Do you have a publisher?" I was asked by one in the entourage. "We would be happy to publish this if you need one."

"Oh, I am so sorry," I said, "our alumni group at Stanford will publish it," wondering as the words were coming out of my mouth if I was making a mistake. Would the Hammer & Coffin publish the *Stanford Chaparral* 125th anniversary book? The question seemed absurd, but I honestly was beginning to wonder.

Nevertheless, the Chappie book was almost done: It was at last time for me to put into writing the first part of the solution to My Dilemma, the Mea Culpa where I would confess to the fake *Chaparral* issues I had made. At least most of them.

Mea Culpa to the Mea Culpa

In December 2023, I included a four page section near the end of the *Chaparral* 125th Anniversary Book titled Mea Culpa.[299] It explains my creation of fake *Chaparral* issues during the years 2021-2023.

The gist of the Mea Culpa is found in this book, Act III, That's Not My Issue. It does not include the section Busted, nor How to Make a Zodiac Code, because while the Mea Culpa in the Chappie 125 book is truthful, it does not include anything related to Zodiac.

Hence the need for this section.

Most importantly, I want to emphasize that until I discovered the Missing Link *Chaparral* issue with the Dick Geikie byline, I did not really think I would find any evidence relevant to the Zodiac case, and if I did, I certainly never imagined it would be through a *Chaparral* issue, and absolutely, certainly, and never in a million years, a *Chaparral* FAKE issue. I mean really.

My idea that Richard Gaikowski could have visited Stanford was really just speculation, and given I had already done a fair amount of research on this point and was not finding anything definitive, by late 2022 I thought the chances were near zero, so I was indeed cracking Zodiac-Stanford jokes. I have always liked dark humor, and this subject was rich territory. The *Chaparral* often has joked about death. When I needed to think fast and come up with a creative way of revealing the 1986 UC Bear theft, I thought making a Zodiac code would be a funny way to do it. It seemed funny at the time.

My Dilemma

When I made the discovery of the Dick Geikie byline, any comedy about this was wiped from my mind, and when I fully realized the byline was in a bogus Chappie issue, I wondered how I would ever explain that I too had made fake issues, but I didn't make this one. Who's writing this shit?

But it's not just that I made fake issues. I made a Zodiac one. And a joke code.

I want to reiterate that I was only making jokes like this when I truly believed that it was too far-fetched to think that there could really be a Zodiac-Stanford connection. It just seemed like a gag, gallows humor, dark humor, but ultimately just a joke. Like all the fake issues, pieces of history or pop culture were used to make a plausible but outlandish prank, made better yet because it was being played on my fellow classmates and alums.

Of course, now the fact that I made these pranks, these forgeries, could work to totally undermine the true aspects of this story. It's quite a dilemma, one of my own making, and will always be a difficulty moving forward on this subject.

There is no way to hide my *Chaparral* fake issues. There is no way to undo what I did. And there was really no way to imagine that after all that, I would see the name Dick Geikie in a fake *Chaparral* issue made by someone else in 1971. Who would believe that?

The only path forward was these Mea Culpas. Or is it Mea Culpi? I had cracked Zodiac jokes. As it turned out, the joke was on me.

Where do you hide a tree? Part 2

So, as *The Chappie – 125 Years of Issues* neared completion, I kept mum about the Missing Link spread that was deep in the forest book. Would people get tired, would they suffer from information overload before getting to that page? That was my hope.

It's kind of funny, but the existence of the Mea Culpa sort of works to be additional interference. Also, in the online files I only included the first two pages for the four-page Mea Culpa article.

"You'll have to buy the book to read the last two pages," I told the group.

Just as R had suggested 35 years ago to make a fake bear, the Mea Culpa in the Chappie 125 book was the stand-in for the greater reveal in this book. I could even refer to a "crime being revealed in the book" and presumably and truthfully be talking about the theft of Berkeley's Oskie Bear. All in all, the Mea Culpa would draw attention as the "mysterious part" of the book, further putting the Missing Link as just some random spread in a sea of random spreads.

Where do you hide a tree, indeed.

Sending Off the Chappie 125 Book

In fall of 2023, the enormous effort was coming to its completion. Pages were added, pages were subtracted. We got to what we thought were the final layouts, and PC discovered the story of Chappie Ike Russell, who broke the story of the Titanic while working alongside Guglielmo Marconi. It HAD to go in, and since pages come in multiples of four, three extra pages were also snuck in. I did the final page numbering, securing page 394, and locking in the book at 476 pages, a number harkening the Fall of Rome in 476 AD. I then spent 48 hours manically plowing through each page to make the index. The index was squeezed on to the four pages allotted to it with room to spare, so Paul and I each got a small photo, added some final filler, and… it was finished!

The *Chaparral* 125th anniversary book was completed in early December 2023. It turned out better than I ever imagined, and is quite good if I say so myself; a comprehensive exploration of the *Chaparral*'s long and offbeat lifetime. Colorful, funny, historical.

And for those who were lucky or wise enough to buy one, they would also be getting a reprint of the fake *Chaparral* issue that might lead to the cracking of the greatest cold case of the 20th Century, the Missing Link, literally, that solved the Zodiac.

Now that's quite a proposition.

Truly, the confluence of events and circumstances from across years and years that brought me to this point, this ridiculously funny vista point has made me seriously reconsider questions like, "Was there indeed a 'Divine Shakespeare?'" or "Is this what John Lilly was experiencing when he talked about Earth Coincidence Control Office?" Or, is there indeed a "lattice of coincidence" that lays over top of things?

I wasn't exactly sure what the Hammer & Coffin board thought of my book. I certainly wasn't under any impression that swift action was on the horizon. I sometimes jokingly compared my situation to something similar to Patrick McGoohan's character in the 1960s show The Prisoner.

But as it were, it was the 2020s, not the 1960s, and I was able to print copies of the 125 book free of murmurs and feet shuffling. Self-publishing solved my issue. I sent away for two test print artist's proofs of *The Chappie -125 Years of Issues* for myself. Things always look different on the page, and a couple test prints was a necessity before having the group buy them. What if they sucked?

The night I sent off the files, and they were reported from the vendor as good to go, I sat relieved, in the sort of strange freefall that occurs after a big project is done. The files would be at the printers for at least two weeks. For the first time in seven months, I was not making layouts for the book, not calling up alums to pick their brains or ask where their articles were, not dealing with anything, nothing Chappie at all, just sitting there at the computer with nothing to do....

I looked at my screen, and double-clicked on a folder I hadn't opened in some time, ZODIAC----.

The Halloween Stanford Daily - October 31, 1969

I knew the first thing I wanted to look at, something I had put off for weeks during the crunch time of the book. The Chappie itself had pointed me back to it. "You want Mikado? You find it, it's around." said the October 9, 1969, *Chaparral*. I did want Mikado, so I would find it. It was around. It was in the Halloween 1969 *Stanford Daily*.

In the October 31, 1969, issue, there is a short letter to the editor on page two that takes issue with the Message to the Zodiac editorial the Daily ran the previous week. The letter calls out the perceived poor taste and ill-advised attempt at humor. I tried to find other reactions to that editorial, but looking through *Daily* issues, local press, and other contemporaneous material, this Letter to the Editor was the only reference to the *Daily's* Zodiac message I could find.

As noted, this letter exemplified the conventional take--that it was just bad college humor. The idea that it might have some actual relevance was dismissed, apparently.

Coincidentally, in that very same October 31, 1969, *Stanford Daily*, on page four, is a review of the Lamplighter's production of The Mikado at the Presentation Theater in San Francisco. I say it is a coincidence because of Zodiac's interest in the Mikado. Of course it is easily explainable, the *Daily* ran reviews of lots of shows, including shows in San Francisco. It was just comical to me that the Mikado review was in the same issue with the Zodiac letter to the editor.

So comical, in fact, that the sarcastic side of me thought that maybe there WAS something to it. At minimum, I should at least scrutinize this issue a bit more closely. Even if nothing came from it, it should be included as background and context for the book.

As I continued through a closer look of the October 31, 1969 *Stanford Daily*, I noted that on page three, there was an editorial from the Radical Libertarian Alliance. Yet another funny coincidence, that was the group that had caused me to look more closely at the *Chaparral*.[300]

Then I flipped on to page four again, the Mikado review was due for a deep dive.

The Sparkling Mikado Review

The headline reads, Gilbert & Sullivan "Sparkling Show." The review of the Mikado is without a byline, but it is clear the author loves it and is quite familiar with Gilbert and Sullivan operettas and The Mikado in particular. They refer to "typical G and S complications," and "the inevitable happy ending," both of which imply a familiarity with the material. The reviewer later refers to "the famous song 'Let the Punishment Fit the Crime,'" and notes the performer gave the song a "truly diabolical laugh." The review notes that they can hear all of the lyrics to the songs, something even the D'Oyly Carte company doesn't always accomplish.

So, this is someone who has seen Gilbert and Sullivan before. Someone who has seen the Mikado before, enough to know the story and highlights, enough to reference D'Oyly Cart company shows. The D'Oyly Carte Opera Company is a professional British light opera company that, from the 1870s until 1982, staged Gilbert and Sullivan's Savoy operas nearly year-round in the UK and sometimes toured in Europe, North America and elsewhere.[301]

Now in olden times, The Mikado was performed more than it is now, as were other Gilbert and Sullivan operettas, so there would be some number of people who were familiar with the themes. But seriously, the popularity of 1800s comic opera would not be that large. And of that set of people, there would be an even smaller set who knew The Mikado well, well enough to know which songs were famous and that the Mikado himself performs a "diabolical laugh." Such people would skew older; there would be very few such people of college age.

I don't know about 1969, but in the 1980s, not a lot of people I knew were talking about opera, Gilbert and Sullivan and/or The Mikado, especially around colleges. You might even say, no one was. We were talking about Prince, Beastie Boys, and the like. As for 1969? They could talk about The Beatles, Jimi Hendrix, Janis Joplin. But hey, an 1800s comic opera! Sounds groovy. Not.

The longer you think about it, the more you realize it would seem this reviewer was somewhat of a unique individual. In some ways, a remarkably unique individual.

The fact is, there is only a small subset of the population who would know these things about the Mikado, and a VERY small subset who would have seen it multiple times and be able to remark on the production values, and both this reviewer and Zodiac are in that subset. How many college students in 1969 are in that subset is an interesting question. I posit not many.

A final minor but possibly relevant point is the Mikado review in question has no byline, it was written anonymously. Now, this is not singularly unique. A perusal of the reviews in the *Daily* of this period show perhaps a quarter of them have no byline. But even so, one wonders who this unknown individual so familiar with The Mikado was. If they had just bothered to include a byline, they would have saved us a lot of trouble! As it is, its authorship is unknown.

The Layout of the Mikado Review

The layout of the Mikado review is somewhat peculiar. It seems to be placed on the page hurriedly; it has graphic mistakes, layout mistakes. I noticed that some of the letters in the left-hand column of the article are cut off. Starting at the bottom of the second paragraph and continuing through most of the third, the left-most letters are cut off.

Upon closer examination, what appears to be happening is not so much that the letters are cut off, but rather that the paragraph to the left, a part of a column about bridge, was actually pasted too far to the right, and some of the white paper of that article was went over the letters of the Mikado review, cutting them.

This is sloppy paste-up. Paste-up is the term used to describe the method to design and produce printed pages before desktop publishing took hold. It was a very hands-on process and required a steady hand and precise artistic skills. This is very poor layout work, uncharacteristic of layout artists, who tend to be precise and proud of their work.

A second sloppy thing about the layout of the Mikado review is that the space between the two columns of the review is very wide, wider than the space outside the columns. This is breaking some of the most basic rules of layout, and again looks hurried, slapdash. What's more, this wide space would have presented an easy fix to the previous problem mentioned. There is plenty of room to make the space between the two Mikado article columns thinner, and thus the Bridge column would not have overlapped. But this very simple fix was not done.

The layout of the Mikado review is quite poor, and as such it is quite unique. I haven't found a layout this sloppy looking across many, many *Daily* issues and literally thousands of articles. Isn't it a funny coincidence that a Mikado review, already so Zodiac-esque, would be one of, if not the-poorest laid out article found, ever?

And there is yet another bit of poor quality regarding this article--the printing of the review contains two white spots, or blemishes, obscuring some of the text on each column. The larger of the two spots obscures quite a bit of text. The combination of the spots, the cut off letters, and the poor layout artist work, makes the *Daily's* Mikado review peculiarly bad. Whether that is a coincidence, I do not know.

That said, the layout of the Mikado review is so sloppy, it makes one wonder if it was made under duress, or trying to work too quickly, or by someone in an excited emotional state.

I spent a long time looking at the Mikado review and doing internet searches on the Zodiac's Mikado letters to see if there was anything thing that tied it more closely to them, but I didn't find anything. It really just seemed that it was a coincidence that it appeared in the same issue as the Letter to the Editor talking about the *Daily's* Zodiac joke editorial.

After many days, I finally looked at the rest of the page that contained the review.

The Electric Zodiac

You would think one would just scour every inch of paper when doing something like this, but that opinion has the benefit of hindsight. I focused for weeks on the Mikado review before I ever really looked at the rest of the page, the TOP of page four in the October 31, 1969, *Stanford Daily*.

When I did look, I saw it was a bunch of music reviews, with the first album review being Douglas Leedy's *The Electric Zodiac*. Now that's a funny coincidence, I thought.

But there's more.

At the top of the page, there was a photo of the album cover of The Electric Zodiac. It was a headshot of the artist, Douglas Leedy. In the top left of the album, in small sixties type were the words, "The Zodiac."[302]

I blinked a few times.

Now the review clearly states the album's name was *The Electric Zodiac*. I took to the internet and found another picture of the album online, and it does indeed say "*The Electric Zodiac.*" But in the photo in the *Stanford Daily*, the word "Electric" is missing.

I was stunned. I heard that weird music again. The hair on the back of my neck went up. Again. I don't know about you, but I call that a coincidence. An amazing coincidence. A relatively larger F of a Coincidence than your normal F. (I know I'm in the wrong Act of this book, but it is, truly, an amazing coincidence.)

"This is getting ridiculous." I said.

I can understand that the idea of the perpetrator laying out their own Mikado review in the Stanford Daily might be hard to accept, but now I had this other Zodiac coincidence on the same page.

I wondered about someone whiting out the word Electric. But I realized there is another possibility. In the color photos of the album, I saw the word Electric was cyan (light blue). Light cyan was a color used in print production layouts in those days with lines that helped the artists keep the layouts aligned, but did not show up in the final printing. Anything light blue would go white. It's possible the cyan text disappeared by this process.

Layout artists are well aware of this. In fact, a newspaper that knew it would be running a photo in black and white that contained a lot of cyan color would certainly have it photographed in black and white, known in the industry as "greyscale," ahead of time. Then that greyscale photo would be "screened," meaning turned into a series of discreet black dots that can be printed. This is how all black-ink photos are printed in newspapers and magazines, then and now. But if the color photo was screened directly to black and white, it is possible the cyan color might disappear.

The thing is, even though this could account for the word Electric disappearing, it is still entirely possible, even likely, that the person laying out this page or processing the photo knew very well that Electric would not print, leaving just "The   Zodiac." However it happened, by plan or by coincidence, this appears on the same page as the Mikado review in the Halloween 1969 *Stanford Daily.* If it was on purpose, somebody thought it was funny as hell.

All of the Articles Aligned

I realized that it was now in the interest of this investigation to look at every *Daily* issue of this-period MUCH more closely.

I also reconsidered the white spots on the Mikado review. Could there be any significance or coincidence regarding them? There were two on the Mikado review, one on each column of the article. I conjectured perhaps the copy had not been waxed down on the layout board adequately and had bubbled up, causing the defect, or something like that.

After some time, I discovered that page three of this issue also had spots, two on the bottom center of the page, and another very pronounced spot somewhat above them. Three spots.

Then I noticed that the bottom two spots were in a very similar position to the spots on page four, the Mikado review page. I looked at page four again and it was true, the spots looked similar. But there seemed to be no third spot. But I looked closer and the upper spot was indeed there. It had been hidden because it was in a mostly white area on the page, in the midst of a syndicated article about Bridge . All three spots were on both sides of the paper! This spurred conjecture.

I took a screenshot of all of these pages and stitched them together. I got both pages into Photoshop, and aligned them, flipping page three horizontally, as it would be on the back side of the paper of page four.

Indeed, the spots aligned exactly!

It appeared to me that someone poured something on the page that caused the ink to dissolve, and it bled through to the page on the back of the paper. I mean, how could there be this defect on both sides of the same paper if it were not for a solvent on the printed page, dissolving the ink and bleeding through to the page printed on the back side?

If true, this would mean that someone modified the actual copy of the paper that had been scanned for the archive. And if that were true, it would be another instance of someone modifying the archival records of a publication, somewhat similar to the *Chaparral*'s modified archives with the Missing Link issue.

I heard the strange music in my head. If someone had intentionally poured a solvent on the Mikado article, that would be a strange coincidence. What on earth could be the reasons someone would do that?

And of course, it could just be random damage that just happens to be on the Mikado review.

I continued to closely examine the October 31, 1969 issue. The spots seemed definitely bigger on page 4, so I figured the solvent was poured there, and had bled down to page 3. I wondered if it bled past page three and onto page two, the page that contained the letter to the editor about the *Daily's* Message to the Zodiac. To my disappointment, page two did not have the spots.

I wondered if perhaps the spots only bled a small amount onto page two—perhaps too small to see. Photoshop contains many tools for contrasting and imaging that allow you to examine pages and find things not obvious to the naked eye. Perhaps I should do that with page two? I went ahead and imported it into the same Photoshop document and aligned it to pages three and four.

Well, there was no faint spot on page two, but my disappointment turned out to be wonderment. Cue the spooky music as that eerie feeling came back yet again. When I brought page two into the document and aligned it to pages four and three, I found that page two's Zodiac letter not only fell perfectly underneath the Mikado review, but exactly under the largest spot. Exactly.

Let me restate it for clarity because this is very important: The letter to the editor about Zodiac on page two falls EXACTLY under the largest spot on the Mikado review on page four when the pages are aligned. So when reading the paper, if you have it open to page two on the left, and page three on the right, when you turn page three over, page four opens and the large spot on the page on a Mikado review lands exactly over the Zodiac letter.

"That's one F of a coincidence." I said aloud.

And if this is not just a coincidence, then this is actually more important than the Missing Link *Chaparral* issue. That issue has the name Dick Geikie, but that is all. Taken with the six *Daily* articles in 1971, it only shows that someone named Dick Geikie was on campus and writing for the *Daily*. Neither of those are a crime. No, this is different. Very different.

Here we have a Mikado review sharing the page with the review for *The Electric Zodiac*, yet it's photo only shows "The   Zodiac." The Mikado review is aligned with the Zodiac letter on the page below, with spots on the article making an additional "joke," to make sure you see the alignment, a "Hey! Look right here you idiots!"

I wondered how it could exist if it were not coincidence. What were the possible ways this Zodiac-Mikado quirk could come to be in the pages of the *Stanford Daily*?

The most likely to me was that it was a college prank. The people who thought the editorial was funny could still be making some kind of joke now. They could have read about Zodiac quoting the Mikado, and seen an opportunity for this "hidden joke" in the issue. I realized I need to find the exact date Zodiac referred to the Mikado.

I reviewed the Zodiac timeline. The first Zodiac letter quoting lines from the Mikado was in July 1970, and that information was not released to the public until October 1970, in a Paul Avery article.[303] This possible "prank" I had discovered in the *Stanford Daily* was in October 1969.

OMG!

I have found a possible Zodiac-Mikado connection nine months earlier than Zodiac referenced the Mikado, and twelve months before that information was made public, right there in the *Stanford Daily*.

This would be relevant even if Dick Geikie turned out to be irrelevant, because this specifically connected Zodiac and Mikado regardless of who it was. If this were to check out, this is smoking gun evidence of the Zodiac at Stanford in October 1969.

OMG!

And whether it did or not, it was another One F of a Coincidence. I reflected on what this meant, and what to do next.

White Spots on the Daily

It seemed to me that if the spots had any significance, they would be unique. Now I thought I had seen other spots a few times, but I could not remember. There was only one way to find out. So I commenced the arduous task of closely examining all 1969 *Stanford Daily* issues, again, this time looking for spots.

I started at the October 31 issue and worked forward. The next issue, Monday November 3, had no spots. Tuesday November 4 was also clean.

Wednesday November 5 had a very large spot on the front page. Much to my disappointment, it had only taken three issues to find another spot.

But my disappointment was tempered when I noticed on the bottom of that same front page a small article titled Zodiac Calls, about the call to the Palo Alto police saying they were coming onto the Stanford campus. I had seen this article before, but now in the context of the spots it was even more interesting. The spot was not on the actual Zodiac article, but it was a very prominent, a very circular spot on the top part of the page. For it to be on the same page as a Zodiac article was a bit interesting.

I also found spots in this issue on pages three and four that looked similar to the spots from October 31. I wasn't sure what I was looking at.

Moving on to the November 6 issue, the first thing I noticed was a big feature article at the top of the page, even above the *Stanford Daily* masthead. I wondered if there would be a spot on this article, and indeed there was, a very small one, easily missed, but it was there. That issue also had more small spots on page two, on the staff box.

The November 7 issue had spots on pages one, and the similar spots again on pages three and four. It was becoming apparent that spots on the Daily were not unique at all, in fact, they were a fairly regular occurrence. I began to question my conjecture that a solvent had been used. Perhaps it wasn't that at all, and instead a printing or scanning defect when the archive was made?

There were no spots for the next five issues. But starting on November 17, I found spots on pages three and four; November 19, pages three and four; November 24, pages three and four; November 26, pages three and four; December 3, pages three and four; and December 5, the last issue of the quarter, on pages five and six.

I looked at the first weeks of issues in January, and there were no spots, so I went back to the October 31 issue, and then worked backwards.

There was a possible spot on the October 30 issue, but it was not at all like the other spots I had found, it looked like a paste up error on an ad. I marked it as a "maybe." Then I looked at the October 29, 28, and 27 issues and didn't see any spots on them. With no Saturday or

Sunday issues, the next issue to examine was Friday, October 24, the issue with the Message to the Zodiac article in it.

"If these spots have any meaning, then there will certainly be some in this issue," I thought.

But much to my disappointment, there were no spots in that issue. Nor were there any spots in any issue resembling the previous ones going back to September 26, the first issue of the fall 1969 school quarter. There were a couple issues with print degradation, scratches, or letters trailing off with light printing, but there were no spots anywhere near as pronounced as what I had previously found.

I put all this into a new spreadsheet. It was clear that the vast majority of spots occurred on pages three and four, and that almost every time there was a spot, it was always on a Monday, Wednesday, or Friday. There were also unique spots that occurred during this time period, from October 31 to December 5. An examination of the *Dailys* from the years directly before and after these spots occurred did not uncover any more spots.

All of this aside, I finally realized what many of you likely already have: These spots in the *Daily* first show up on October 31. The first incidence of these spots is on the Mikado review.

One might note again that this is yet another F of a coincidence.

But there's more.

The Recurring 3-Spot Pattern

I noted that many of the spots looked similar. But I wondered, just how similar? I imported all the pages into the Photoshop document that held the October 31 pages. When the pages were aligned, there it was, clearly the three-spot pattern was identical, it only varied by what was printed on the page, and by the density of ink. It could also be hidden if it were in the white space of the page, but it was in the exact same location on multiple pages, on both sides of the paper each and every time.

I confirmed that this exact three-spot pattern occurred eight times, from October 31 to December 5. The pattern appeared on pages three and four, seven out of eight times, with the exception being December 5, the final issue of the quarter, where it appeared on page five and six.

This was not someone pouring a solvent on the paper after it was printed. I tried to imagine what would produce what I was seeing. I conjectured it could be a scanning artifact, but why then would it happen on opposite sides of the same sheet of paper, and why only on a few pages? I honestly couldn't explain what I was seeing by a scanning defect.

A more sound conjecture was that this was a recurring print defect that had to occur at the printer. I called some people who worked on newspaper presses, including G who ran the local newspaper back in Indiana. I knew they had still printed the paper there in the newspaper offices until the early 20th century. G was a family friend, so I gave him a ring.

Upon my description of the spots, G thought that they were likely caused by a crushed blanket—a blanket being a key element in the printing process. Ink was transferred to the blanket, and from the blanket to the paper. And because both sides of the paper would get printed at the same time, a defect on one side showed up on both. G said these were not really "spots" but "blemishes."

He explained that crushed blankets usually happened when something jammed in the press, like some misfed paper.

"Could someone intentionally damage the blanket?" I asked.

"Yes, you could just touch it with your hand, wearing gloves or using a rag. More likely you would ding it with a hammer, I suppose. It would be quite easy," G replied.

"Could you intentionally place the damage over a specific article?" I asked.

"Yes, that would be easily accomplished," answered G.

"And how would one know where to hit the blanket?" I asked.

"Well, you just look. You can see the entire page on the blanket. It's mirrored, but pressmen all know how to read backwards and even if you don't, you can see the articles. You would just ding it right on it," said G.

"Why would the three-spot pattern only occur every once in a while? Why are some issues printed without the spots?" I asked.

G posited a theory: He explained that printers almost certainly had more than one press, and it was vital to keep those presses running as close to 24/7 as possible. Scheduling your time on press is a big deal in printing, especially in the time-sensitive, deadline-oriented printing of newspapers.

He surmised that the press with the crushed blanket was only used when the others, those without the defect, were busy. If there was a print job that was of higher priority, that would get to be run on the good presses, bumping the student newspaper to the press with the defect. The fact that it was always on Monday, Wednesday, or Friday likely meant that there were other jobs of higher priority on those days.

As for not replacing the damaged blanket, it was a time-consuming task, and you might not replace it, if it wasn't too bad, until you had a significant break in your schedule.

"Like during a slowdown around Christmas?" I asked.

"Exactly," replied G.

As for the one issue where the 3-spot pattern occurs on pages five and six, G said that was also easily explained—either there was a different pressman on that day who lined up the pages a different way, or the issue might have been special in some way or had more pages than normal, making it arranged on the cylinder differently. I subsequently discovered that this issue indeed had 14 pages, the largest issue of the year.

So, what I have discovered is that the three-spot defect in the *Stanford Daily* is first seen on October 31, 1969, and it continued on many, but not all, issues until December 5, 1969. It begins on a review of the SF Lamplighter's production of Mikado with a spot on each of two columns, with the largest spot also exactly aligned over a letter to the editor about Zodiac on page two. The occurrences of the blemishes are explained by a crushed blanket on the printing presses, appearing only on days when scheduling at the printing vendor forced the damaged press to be utilized, and not being fixed until sometime after the school term was out, during the Holiday Season.

G's explanations were a real eye-opener. I decided to see if his ideas held up against other professional opinions. I posted scans of the blemishes on a printers' forum, not showing anything relevant to the case or even what newspaper they were from, just closeups of the spots. I explained how they were recurring and asked if anyone knew what would have caused them. The only answer proffered in the thread was the same as G's: a crushed print blanket on the presses.

If this is not all a coincidence, it means the Mikado review was intentionally placed in the layout in position over the Zodiac letter, and the blanket on the printing press used was intentionally damaged to place a spot on it. And since this occurred one year prior to Zodiac making Mikado references, these actions had to be taken by Zodiac himself. The damaged print blanket was used through December 5 and was fixed by the following January. The identical marks prove they were created by the printing press, not a scanning defect.

If the marks are intentional, they were made by the perpetrator. And, it means Zodiac was an individual who worked in newspapers.

The main spot on the Mikado article

When I describe the Mikado review and the spots on it being exactly over the letter to the editor about Zodiac, I thought a graphic example would be helpful.

The main spot on the Mikado article is basically an oval, with sort of a horizontal extension out from the top-right of it. In some ways it appears that the upper right extension was an addition, maybe a second tap with the hammer. The marks applied to page four, one on each column of the Mikado review, lay on top of the Zodiac letter on page two like this:

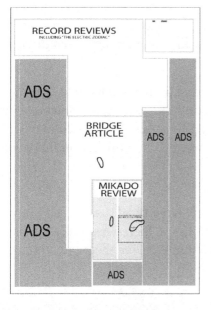

I have also included some of the text from the letter to the editor that appears inside the spot. Again, is it just a coincidence that the words 'The Zodiac" and "Stanford" are in the affected area? Or is it on purpose?

The Unique Spots of the November 17, 1969 Daily

The November 17 issue had unique spots. And the way that they were unique is in itself somewhat unique.

The spots are on page three and four, but not the three-spot pattern. This time there are two spots, each appearing on both pages three and four. What is interesting about these spots is that they coincidentally happen to mark two different articles on hypnosis on the two different pages.

Is it normal for there to be two separate articles on hypnosis in the same issue of the *Stanford Daily*? Well, I wondered myself, so I checked. There was an article on October 3, 1969, "Transcendentalist Where Were You?" that mentioned hypnotism.[304] Then on October 28, 1969, there was another, "Meditation Expands Minds at Esalen Workshop."[305] Then there were the two articles on November 17, 1969, Hypnosis Research Uncovers Problems, on page three, and Hypnosis Tool in Many Fields, on page four.[306] The next article on hypnosis was on March 4, 1970, Hypnotic Happening, about a big show on hypnotism by Stanford's famous psychology professor Phillip Zimbardo.[307]

So no, two articles on hypnosis on the same day of the *Daily* was not a normal occurrence. In fact, it was a pretty unique. Even so, it could just be coincidence, just as it could be coincidence that there are the spots on these articles.

But if it isn't, if the spots are intentional, then we have to consider the possibility that the individual making these spots was interested in hypnosis, perhaps even experimenting. It's almost too much to even consider the ramifications, so I will not speculate further on this point.

Slick Tracy

By going back to the Mikado review page I had discovered *The Electric Zodiac*. At this point, I had to figure there was likely much more I had overlooked. It crossed my mind to give the page with the letter to the editors another look.

Sometimes it takes me forever to see the obvious, but right there on page two of the October 31, 1969, *Daily*, directly below the Letter to the Editor about Zodiac is a comic-strip parody of Dick Tracy: Slick Tracy. For what it's worth, this is the only day Slick Tracy ran in the *Stanford Daily*. Ever. If it is shown there is a Dick Tracy tie-in to Zodiac, this will either be one more clue, or it will be yet another F of a coincidence.

Who's There?

With this discovery, it seemed prudent to give a closer look to the October 24, 1969, *Stanford Daily*, the Message to the Zodiac page as well.

So I did. I didn't see anything too weird, except there was a Letter to the Editor from an obvious fake name, Nok Nok. Fake names in the *Stanford Daily* Letters to the Editor were not that uncommon in the late 60s and early 70s. And we've already covered the fake names of the underground press—ooh those hippies and their love of fake names.

I typed Nok Nok into the Daily search engine to see if this person ever wrote again. It returned zero results, which was strange, because I knew there should be at least one. I tried Nok Nok in the author search box, still no results.

"Hmmmmmmmmmm," I thought.

I reviewed the paper again and noted that Nok Nok was actually NokNok, so I typed that into the search field. STILL no results. I tried the author field, STILL nothing.

I looked closer and thought it actually looked like N okNok.

"That's some strange typesetting," I said.

I typed "N okNok" into the search field, and there it was! It found the Letter to the Editor. The bad news was that it was the only search result, so no way to see anything else "N okNok" wrote about. For what it's worth, the letter itself was a macabre metaphor about "killing" the government.

I wondered about the alternative spelling and so I did a Newspapers.com search: 1968-1969, in California, using the term "knock knock." The search returned hundreds of hits. I did the same search for "noc noc," "noc-noc" and "nocnoc" as well as "nok nok," "nok-nok" and "noknok." There were ZERO instances of these spellings in California newspapers in 1968 and 1969.

So, Nok Nok was not a spelling at all in October 1969. This is hippie pun-speak. Hippies seem to love to use fake names, especially if they were double entendre, or some kind of joke or pun. Misspelling jokes, homonym jokes, puns, rhymes, saying one thing but meaning another. They were and are experts in this and loved fooling "squares," who were/are so literal that you could practically put anything, or almost anything, over on them.

When Zodiac was being investigated in 1970, and he included the Mikado's Little List lyrics in a letter, police found and questioned everyone who had played the role of Ko Ko, the Grand Execution across a wide area, all turning up nothing.

Let's break it down another way. The *Stanford Daily*'s Message to the Zodiac Killer and NokNok letter appear on a page that contains four editorials, all with bylines of real names, including the Zodiac editorial. There is one political cartoon, which is signed, and there is the Daily Staff Box with real names. The page is completed by the Letters to the Editor section, which has six letters, four signed by real names, and one that says "this letter was signed by 16 people," but does not include those names. The remaining letter is signed by N okNok. Out of over two dozen bylines and credits, this is the lone item on the page that uses an obvious fake name.

I thought this was of mild significance, at minimum showing that using a fake name was not as widespread as I thought.

But then I saw it. N okNok, in addition to its obvious begging the question of Who's there? also anagrams to koko ZZ when one rotates the Ns 90 degrees.

Now that is yet another F of a coincidence indeed.

For anyone who thinks it is ridiculous to note this, I reply that it is ridiculous to NOT note this, note it as another funny coincidence. At minimum, it's just one more strange thing, one more Zodiac-Mikado coincidence long before anyone should or could know about the Zodiac-Mikado link. Anyone except the perpetrator. And it seriously begs re-examination of the Daily's Message to the Zodiac editorial on October 24, and the Zodiac calls to Palo Alto October 20 and November 4.

If these things were not coincidence but intentional, this is a discovery of a greater magnitude than the fake *Chaparral* of 1971. If that is the Missing Link, this is perhaps the Rosetta Stone, the Holy Grail, the proverbial Smoking Gun.

2024 - CHAPPIE'S 125TH YEAR

My test prints of the big Chappie book were delivered on December 29, 2023. I showed photos of the book to other Chappies, and then during the January 2024 Zoom call. Enthusiasm exploded. There was much rejoicing.

The printed book was even better than the files on the computer. Bright colors, funny pictures and text. Glossy paper.

As I said before, there are also many "Easter eggs" in the book. Page 270 has the Marilyn Monroe-Doodles Weaver Zodiac conjunction. Again, that's with a still of Marilyn the 1953 film, Niagara, and a still of Doodles from the 1971 film, The Zodiac Killer.

Page 214 has a photo of Mike Dornheim in Memorial Church, with the words of the original caption "ritual murder" whited out in homage to the blank space in the July 9, 1971, *Daily* staff box from the Missing Link blank pages joke.[308] Just to be perfectly clear on this point: in the Chappie 125 book I blanked out the words "ritual murder" in 2024, modifying a caption that originally ran in a 1975 *Chaparral* issue. It's a Missing Link joke, paying homage to where they have a blanked-out name in the Daily staff box.

There's even a one in my Acknowledgments on page 475, where thanking Cornell allows a mention of the DR-70 astrology computer.[309]

I also threw various oblique references to David Lamson into the Chappie book; like a cover from one of his issues on page 185 that depicts a woman hitting a man for unwanted advances,[310] framed by an inverted coffin and with jokes about divorce; and page 261, which features a joint issue he edited with the unfortunately named Cornell Widow.[311] Strange huh? Lamson's picture holding the hammer on page 264 is quite something as well,[312] capped off on page 68 with the amazing 25th Anniversary issue that he edited. One Hundred years ago, our psychic-echo effort from 1924 features on its cover the only depiction in all 125 years of the Jester holding a knife,[313] the one time that holding a blunt object might have made more sense. The knife is for birthday cake, but it is more of a long-bladed stiletto than any bakery knife I've ever seen.

And then on page 355, on the Doodles Weaver spread no less, I included the 1969 clipping from the *Daily* where they jokingly listed the salaries of the *Daily* staff.[314] I already told you this list includes Sigourney Weaver. What I haven't said is that the list also includes the name of the person who wrote the "Message To The Zodiac Killer" editorial for the *Daily*.

And another funny Easter egg that sort of just happened upon me is on page 369. An article was submitted for a 1995 prank titled The Stanford Bike Experiment, a parody of Professor Phillip Zimbardo's notorious Stanford Prison Experiment, which coincidentally was going on during the summer of 1971! It seemed I had, no, I was compelled to put the photo from the Missing Link issue showing the ripped off bike as the graphic for the article.

The last thing I did, I think, was I made sure Dick Geikie made it into the index, on both pages his name appears, page 394 and 395.[315] These are all of the things I can remember I put in the Chappie 125 book.

In early 2024, *Chaparral* alums ordered just over 100 artist's proofs. One Hundred printed books of our multi-year effort to document the Chappie, with the added bonus of having the Missing Link in it! From that point, regardless of what happened, regardless of whether the book was mass-printed or not, regardless if something happened and I never revealed the secret, never wrote the second book, the Missing Link issue had been reproduced, and placed into the hands of about 100 Chappie alums.

We also had a few printed to be promotional copies.

The artist's proofs were sent out, and I waited. Would anyone ask about the Missing Link spread? A month went by and no one said anything. Then another. Would anyone notice? Would anyone care? That was still unknown. The responses from the Chappie alums were pretty much universal praise from the rank and file. There were email threads about various parts of the book, but no one ever brought up the Missing Link.

After a period of back and forth discussions, a decision was made to print 500 copies of the books at an offset press in China. The book would be 93 percent smaller, because for some reason the price to be under $13,000. Printing costs would not come from the big fund started in 2006, it would have to be paid from an old Hammer & Coffin fund that left the funding of the book at the mercy of approval by the University. We waited for a couple weeks with all fingers crossed that Stanford would approve. Finally, approval came. And there was much rejoicing.

The Dawn of the Second Renaissance

As I outlined earlier, it would be much better to insulate the Chappie book and anniversary celebration from anything to do with the Zodiac. Complete isolation.

Of course, I would have to go public eventually. Doing so AFTER the celebration was a lock, but just when and how was still to be determined. I also reflected for quite some time what it might mean for the *Stanford Chaparral* and the Hammer & Coffin Society; what it might mean for Stanford University. Of course, it's a dark tale. But a few things assuaged my concerns.

First, this is about solving a crime. The victims and their families have a right to them being solved. I truly believe this is relevant information, so I indeed have ethical responsibilities to come forward.

Second, I'd like to state something quite bluntly, for the record; something I've observed across this entire, years-long saga: In my opinion Zodiac was an absolutely pompous individual, perhaps one of the most of all time. Pompous. Arrogant. An asshole.

The public learning that an alumni organization at Stanford has a hand in solving the Zodiac mystery, and it just happens to be named the Hammer & Coffin Society? There's my boss' boss on Madison Avenue again, exclaiming over his martini and adding "now" to make a glib *Chaparral* reference, "Now that's got a lot of spin..."

But here's the deal: The name of Hammer & Coffin has its origins from a noble purpose: To mock the pompous and the stuffed shirts, knocking them with a hammer and locking them in a coffin. It's a metaphor for mockery, not a death cult.

Zodiac's letters and taunting of the media are indeed pompous. Taking others' lives for your own kicks is beyond arrogant. So, in many ways, this organization with Coffin in its name and mocking the pompous as its mission is perhaps the perfect one for this type of work.

Third, there would many of people who just thought this was cool and would react overwhelmingly positive. If it did solve the Zodiac case, it would be a cause for celebration, and many victims' families could close the book, at least to some degree. It would be a Chappie who cracked the case. As an organization, we cracked the case.; the old jesters of the *Chaparral* and H & C caught the evil jester. However it happened, it certainly was going to be a way that many, many more people would hear of the *Stanford Chaparral* for the first time.

In any case, A new investigation will hopefully ensue, almost certainly spurring more revelations. Perhaps the David Levine case would be solved, and maybe others. And who knows? It might affect the perceptions of the other Stanford crimes: the bombings, arsons and murders, or even the Memorial Church murder of Arlis Perry. Perhaps the fire that killed Emma Brown would be reconsidered given the new information.

As the hippie anthem proclaims: Let the sunshine in!

After these discoveries are revealed to the public, awareness of the *Chaparral* and the Hammer & Coffin Society will certainly skyrocket. When people are asked to name a college humor magazine, we might get named along with the *Harvard Lampoon*, or even before them. And with such public awareness, any recruiting problems the Chappie might have had in years past will be solved for decades to come. Copies of the Chappie 125 book, the tome with the clue that cracked the case, would make their way into pop culture history.

The Stanford Daily Archives

With the book printed, and the anniversary preparations ramping up, I devoted more and more time to writing this book, which included verifying facts and hunting down loose ends.

One thing that had still bothered me about the spots on the Mikado review is that I had only examined scans of the Daily issues, never the actual paper copies. Even though I had newspaper and printing professionals all in agreement that the marks came from a crushed blanket on the press, what if by some fluke it WAS a scanning error? A huge part of this book rests on the spots. Learning how and when the scans were made became my focus.

I took to finding out more about the *Stanford Daily* Archives, both the online files, and what might physically exist. There had been a lengthy article about the online archive's creation in 2015 by *Stanford Magazine*.[316] Through that, I was able to get connected to the creators of the archives. As I have said, these archives are fabulous. Easy to use and thorough. I was more than thrilled to make contact with the people who made it happen.

It was confirmed that the *Daily* archives were compiled by scanning bound volumes, NOT by microfilm or some other archive method. The bound volumes are, of course, actual paper copies of the *Daily* gathered into one bound book. Thus, the scans are from actual paper.

There were usually two bound volumes made, one for the *Daily's* archives, and one for the editor of the volume. Of course, the Daily is older than the *Chaparral*, and they have two volumes a year, so there are a lot of volumes, and some volumes have unique stories to them. There was a certain amount of detective work that was required to find all of them when the archives were created.

I was confident that the blemishes were from the printing process but wanted to absolutely confirm they were not an artifact from the scanning process. Regardless, I really wanted to examine the actual paper copies in the volumes housed in the *Daily* offices, or perhaps there were other copies in Stanford's Green Library. The *Daily* was very helpful and said I could visit their offices the next time I was on campus. I set up a tentative date for April 2024, when we would be returning to the Bay Area for the H&C banquet.

It was also confirmed that the *Daily* was printed off campus, at a printer in Menlo Park. The *Daily* was described as being a horrible client, the pages to be printed were dropped off in the middle of the night with a request that the finished papers be ready in just a few hours, sometimes their finances weren't great... I could relate—the *Chaparral* was a bad client for our printers too.

I was interested to learn where the *Daily* was printed. I wondered where *Good Times* was printed? Then I realized, if there were spots in *Good Times*, spots like the three-spot pattern in the Daily, then *Good Times* would be printed on the same press as the *Stanford Daily*! I took to the computer with great anticipation...

But there were no spots. I looked at every *Good Times* from October to December 1969 and there were none. It's worth noting that the print quality of the *Good Times* issues was quite good, very few spots or blemishes. I subsequently found that *Good Times* was printed by Waller Press in San Francisco, NOT where the *Stanford Daily* was printed.

Return to Stanford - April 2024

The dual nature of this story and a unity of purpose manifested itself again in the form of our second trip to the Bay Area for both *Chaparral* and Zodiac matters.

The *Chaparral* 125th anniversary events were planned for October, during Stanford's Reunion Weekend. But each year since 1906, the Hammer & Coffin Society has held a banquet in April, the month of the organization's founding. The 2024 banquet was set for April 13. A trip to the Bay Area was in order, to promote the 125 book and the October reunion, to attend the Hammer & Coffin banquet in San Francisco, and to gather more information about Zodiac in the archives of the *Stanford Daily* and *Chaparral*.

First, I wanted to see as many versions of the October 1969 *Stanford Dailys* as I could find. I wanted to confirm once and for all that the marks on the October 31, 1969, issue were indeed on the paper, and on multiple copies, NOT a scanning effect. My intent was to visit the office of the *Daily* to see their bound volumes, review the microfilm copies in the Stanford Library, and attempt to view any paper copies they or the Archives division possessed.

I also planned to return to the *Chaparral* office with video cameras to document the Missing Link issue in the bound volumes and in an envelope of loose issues. For those who might propose this was all an elaborate prank, I needed all the documentation I could get. A video of the issues in their "natural state" in the back room of the *Chaparral* would be invaluable. The back room was in need of some cleaning and organization too--old issues just thrown into boxes, often stacked to the ceiling. Cleaning up and organizing some of the back room would be very good unity of purposes.

And in the midst of all this, I was actually going to attend my first Hammer & Coffin Banquet in 18 years while possibly solving the Zodiac. That's funny.

That's Heavy, Man

This time, I was better prepared for how shitty air travel has become, and we arrived in California in better shape. We landed, got a rental car, ate a great Thai meal in San Mateo. Jack in the Box was relegated to a midnight run for tacos later that night.

We had arranged to have a few extra Artist's Proofs printed, and they were waiting for me at J's house, divided into pristine and slightly damaged groups. Let me tell you, 12 of these books are really heavy. Almost comical. Each one weighed almost eight pounds. The book is the size and shape of a paver.

We just kept them in the trunk the whole weekend and only took out one or two at a time.

I really wanted the Chappie book to stand on its own, to be popular on its own, before any information about its special place in history was known. Once the general public found out there was a potential Zodiac clue in its pages, it would become a publication unique in all history.

The Chaparral Office

As previously noted, when you land in California from the East Coast, you have the advantage of being able to wake up early, even though you are fried. As we had done the year before, we got up and were on campus by 7 am. Now you're not going to see too many people at 7 am at Stanford, but you are guaranteed to see absolutely no one at the Chappie office, even more certainly in the 21st century when they disallow people sleeping there.

We videotaped this visit. We documented the bound volume containing the Missing Link, and the envelope of loose issues, which only had three more left in it.

I confirmed that the Missing Link is indeed intended to appear as Section two of the March 5, 1971 issue, as it is folded into that issue each time. And one can see from the faded paper and folds that this issue had been incorporated into that March 5 issue on purpose. All conjecture this was a mock-up issue, or just some random art experiment that got mistaken as a real issue was obliterated.

Upon reviewing the issues in the *Chaparral* office the second time, I can state unequivocally:

The Missing Link *Chaparral* issue is an INTENTIONAL FAKE, made to look like it was printed on March 5, 1971, but actually produced after July 23, 1971.

We videoed the bound volume that covered two school years: 1969-70, and 1970-71. The Missing Link is indeed incorporated as Section two of the March 5, 1971 issue. Otherwise, this book appears to be a normal bound volume. There was no information about who made the bound volume.

We also found a three-ring binder in a filing cabinet in the *Chaparral* back room, that also held the 1970-71 school-year's issues. The Missing Link issue was included in this binder as well, in sequence, the bogus sequence. Someone had just grabbed the issues of that year, put a three-hole punch in them, and put them in the binder. This was the only such binder we found, no other year's issues had such a binder. I almost think that it was another attempt to slip this issue in as a legitimate issue and have it accepted that it was from March, not July.

The Stanford Daily Offices

After our successful video documentation of the Missing Link in the *Chaparral* Office, we got ready for our appointment at the *Stanford Daily* later that morning. I had asked to see all issues from fall of 1969 until Spring of 1972, but I was mostly excited to finally see a paper copy of the October 31, 1969, issue. *Daily* staffer greeted us and let us in to their conference room where they had the bound volumes pulled out for us.

I eagerly opened fall of 1969, flipped the pages to October 31, turned to page four, the page with the Mikado review and "The Zodiac" at the top. The key page I wanted to see to confirm the spots were on the printed issues... And the spots were not there.

The spots were not there.

I couldn't believe my eyes, but there it was, a perfectly printed page four, no spots, no blemishes; the Mikado review with none of the text missing. I flipped to page three, no spots there either. I went to November 5, page one with the Zodiac article at the bottom of the page. There was no spot at the top. I went to pages three and four, where there should be spots, but there were none.

The Zodiac-Mikado coincidences in the October 31, 1969 *Daily* are very interesting on their own, and the cut off letters on the left column are still there. But since the discovery of the spots, I had come to think of them as being made by the hand of the perpetrator himself, his special exclamation mark on the prank.

But what was going on? The spots logically HAD to be from a printing defect. Yet here I was looking at perfect, immaculately printed pages, actual pages of the *Daily*, with no blemishes. We didn't find any spots in the bound volume of fall 1969, nor any other volume.

The simple explanation that the spots are caused by a scanner defect doesn't hold water either. How could a scanner defect present itself on the front and back of a single piece of paper, perfectly mirrored, but then not be on all the other pages? How and why does a scanner defect show up in eight issues across a six-week period, and then just go away?

The only other item of note from our visit to the *Daily* offices was that they had no volume for summer of 1970. It was becoming clearer there was no *Daily* then.

I pondered the significance of what we had found during lunch, ranging from bewildered to despondent about the spots, or rather, lack of them. We still had a trip to Green Library scheduled, to see the microfilm files and inquire if they had paper copies of the Daily. Would they have the spots or not? I was really not happy as the idea that the defects had been made at the printer had been dealt a serious blow.

The Stanford Daily MICROFILM

Upon inquiring about paper copies of the *Stanford Daily* in the archives at Stanford's Green Library, we were invariably directed to either the *Daily* online archive, or Green's microfilm. Yes, they said they also had paper copies but said that those were fragile and generally not allowed to be handled by the public. I didn't push the issue because I gauged that too much inquiry about the paper issues might raise suspicion about what I was researching. I really didn't want that in April 2024. I could wait until October or later, when many such questions could be asked more freely.

So we found our way to the Media Center in the basement of Green Library to look at the microfilm. Just as at the *Daily* offices, I requested the issues from fall 1969 to spring 1972. And just as before, there were no issues from the summer of 1970.

The staff there helped us thread up the first reel, fall of 1969 to spring of 1970. We scrolled ahead to October 31, and lo and behold, there were the spots!

There were the spots!

As far as I could tell, all the spots across the six weeks were there. October 31, pages three and four. November 5, pages one, three and four, and the rest. I was glad to see them, I was relieved to see them, but I was also more perplexed than ever.

Additionally, the appearance of the issues on microfilm also show that they are not the origin of the scans at the StanfordDaily.com, nor those at NewspaperArchive.com. The printing of the microfilmed issues is poorer, much poorer. The quality is such that it is hard to know if the *Daily* issue used for the microfilm is the same copy of the issue that was the original for the digital scans, but the digital scans certainly were not made from the microfilm.

What can be said with certainty is that the spots are indeed on the microfilm, joining StanfordDaily.com, and NewspaperArchive.com as having them. It can also be said with certainty that the microfilm was made many years ago, likely in the 1970s. While there was no date on the box that said when the microfilm had been made, the age of the box and typography showed it was made not long after the issues had been printed, up to 50 years ago.

It was frustrating; I still had not seen a paper copy of a *Daily* issue with the spots. On the other hand, I had spots on the microfilm in the library from the 1970s and the digital scans online made in 2014, but no spots on the paper copies at the offices of the *Stanford Daily*. What on earth is the answer to this mystery?

We rounded out our visit to Stanford with three meetings about the Chappie's 125th anniversary book, with *Stanford Magazine*, the Alumni Association, and the University Archives. We delivered a complimentary book to each of these offices, as well as a copy for the incoming President of Stanford.

Then we took off in the car to mountains and then the ocean, to Cloud City, San Francisco. There really is no other place like San Francisco. It is truly one of the most beautiful cities on earth, the fog, the hills, the towers, the bay, and it is always great jacket weather.

The annual Hammer & Coffin banquet was a fun event, North Beach soiree in an Italian joint—an oft-chosen cuisine for this party. Several of us "non-representative" alums were staying in the fabulous Majestic Hotel and its beautiful Butterfly Bar, where you can imagine you are in 1901 San Francisco. The evening and weekend were memorable, and there was much rejoicing.

Our Bay Area trip concluded with a night at the East Bay home of DL, sorta close to Vallejo. We gave him the option of where to eat, and he picked Jack In The Box. Yet again, it ain't what it used to be, I say to my sorrow.

Stanford Daily Summer 1970 Volume

Back at home in May 2024, I reviewed the video and photos I had taken at Stanford the month before. One of them was of the boxes the Green Library microfilm was contained in. In that photo I noticed something I hadn't seen before.

On the box containing the microfilm for fall of 1969 and spring of 1970, it says that this is a Mark Larwood Company Silver Film Duplicate, and lists offices in Redwood City, Sacramento, San Francisco, and Detroit. I typed this into a search engine.

On January 31, 1988, TRW Micrographics ran a classified ad in the *San Francisco Examiner* that said the company was formerly known as the Mark Larwood Company. So, the obvious conclusion is that microfilm of the 1969 *Stanford Daily* editions had to have been made before 1988. It is a minor and perhaps obvious point, but I wanted to confirm it. The box typography looks like it is from the early 1970s, and it almost certainly is. Of course it is.

Then I noticed something very interesting on the microfilm box.

Someone had written on the box in ink pen: "June – Aug 70 in Archives."

"That's interesting," I said.

I had pretty much decided there was no *Daily* in the summer of 1970. The question had gone on and off my list of top questions for a large part of this story. When the *Stanford Daily* bound volumes in the *Daily* offices did not include a summer 1970 volume I figured that was the end of it. They had the bound volumes from 1969 through 1971 that we requested to see, but no summer of 1970. The online scans at StanfordDaily.com and newspaperArchive.com also do not have a summer 1970 volume. The microfilm collection at Stanford's Green Library also does not include a summer 1970 volume.

But now, after seeing this photo of the microfilm box, the question was back front and center.

The most likely person to have written on the box was a librarian, and they probably were NOT mistaken. Which means there IS a summer of 1970 *Stanford Daily* volume. And it is in the Stanford Archives. But for whatever reason, it has NOT been documented like the others, not documented in the microfilm of Green Library, not scanned in the online archives of the *Stanford Daily,* not in the bound volumes in the Daily office.

Then I got an idea: If there was something in the summer 1970 *Daily* that was worth making harder to find, then perhaps it was something newsworthy. Perhaps other newspapers had stories about the *Stanford Daily* in the summer of 1970? I turned to the online newspaper archives.

It didn't take me long to find a newsworthy event and confirm that there was indeed a summer 1970 *Stanford Daily*. On Saturday, July 11, 1970, the *Peninsula Times Tribune* reported that out of 6,000 total issues printed, 2,000 issues of the Friday, July 10, 1970, *Stanford Daily* had been stolen. Soon after their drop off around campus, someone went around and snagged them.

I also found other references in the press to the summer 1970 *Stanford Daily*.

The question changed from Was there a summer 1970 *Stanford Daily*? to Why is the summer 1970 *Stanford Daily* not archived like the rest?

Watch Me Make These Spots… Disappear

Back to the spots.

I subsequently confirmed that the *Stanford Daily* was indeed printed in Menlo Park in 1969, and many years before and after that year as well. The *Chaparral* was also printed by the same vendor. The presses ran as close to 24/7 as possible, printing over 70 newspapers across the Bay Area.

The spots, or more correctly, the blemishes on the copies of the *Daily* have been identified by various trade professionals as resulting from a crushed print blanket on the press. This is the only way that the marks could be consistent over time, and on both sides of the paper.

THE ONLY TIME RICHARD GOT ANGRY AT ME

The question remained then, how are there copies of the issues without the blemishes?

For the October 31, 1969, issue, the first where blemishes appear, it is possible the blanket was not damaged until some issues had already been cleanly printed. And it makes sense in one large aspect: if the perpetrator is actually working on the press, and they don't want to get caught, they would certainly like the *Daily* staff to get undamaged copies of the newspaper.

But this conjecture could not at all explain the seven other subsequent issues with the three-spot pattern, on the scanned versions, but not in the *Daily's* bound volume. I was perplexed for many weeks. But then a newspaper press worker who I had consulted with contacted me with the answer: print blanket fixer that could temporarily fix a crushed print blanket.

I don't know the brand name in 1969, but in the 21st Century you can use Blue Swell, which pretty much does what the name says - make the print blanket, which is blue, swell up so it can print pages without the blemish. It only works for a while, but during that time you can get clean copies before it reverts to the blemished state. THAT is how a damaged blanket could still print a few good copies of the paper, and do so over a period of weeks.

Either way, if you could ensure that good copies were the ones that got back to the *Daily,* It would be a way to get away with the prank.

So regarding the *Daily* issues in fall of 1969, each issue could have had some good copies, and then some with the blemishes. From a prank standpoint, it would indeed help you to make sure the good copies made their way to the *Stanford Daily* offices, and those good prints were the ones gathered to make their bound volumes, while other copies, copies with blemishes, made their way to other points around Stanford, including the copies the library and archives gathered. Some of those copies were the ones photographed for microfilm sometime in the 1970s, and some of those were copies scanned in 2014, when the *Daily's* online archives were created.

Blanket fixer could finally explain the occurrence of the blemishes, yet not on every copy. And from a prank point of view, the blanket fixer provides an interesting opportunity--to help NOT get caught. There would be no one asking "What happened to the printing? Why are there these blemishes on the page "

Consider this scenario: the newly-printed *Daily* issue comes back to the office, and the *Daily* staffers see the final product for the first time, they see the blemishes on the paper. Certainly, the editor and any reporter or photographer whose work had a blemish on it would wonder what had happened and ask questions. People take pride in their work. I still have clippings of when I was in the paper, both as news and as the writer. The spots would be a shock to those staffers.

Now consider that the issue comes back to the *Daily* office and everyone sees a correctly printed issue. No questions. Even if a staffer were to see a blemished issue later, it would likely be comprehended as a random defect, there would still be the clean versions delivered to the *Daily* office.

As for the general public getting blemished papers, they could rationalize it as just slip-shod work. It would likely not be bad enough to call in and complain. From this angle, the blanket fixer element makes this prank easier to pull off, and much more plausible.

Even though I still had found no paper issue with the spots, I was sure they must exist. I now had a plausible theory to explain what was observed, and perhaps how the prank wasn't caught as it happened.

With a reasonable explanation of how the Zodiac-Mikado coincidences and the spots on the *Daily* could be accomplished, I was left with a sort of gut-question: Did I really believe someone intentionally did it?

Spots on Paper

I was certain of the print blanket explanation. Nevertheless, as I got to summer of 2024, I still had not examined an actual paper copy containing the blemishes. I had only worked with scans and microfilm of the issues. I was writing this book as such without confirming a blemish on paper.

Then a miracle happened, with the help of my old friend—the *Chaparral*.

I hadn't noticed that during our first visit to Stanford I had photographed a *Chaparral* issue in Green Library with a white spot on one of the interior pages. Late in 2024 I looked again at these 2023 photos, and I saw the November 20, 1969, *Chaparral*, with a spot on the bottom of page three. I wasn't taking note of spots in 2023, but by this time, I was VERY much was.

I knew I had an actual copy of that issue. I excitedly checked it, and it did NOT have the spot. The spot was on the issue held by Green Library but not on mine. Sound familiar? Regardless, the photo confirmed a spot on a paper issue!

The blemish was not like the three-spot pattern, just a single spot that was almost a perfect circle. I remembered that the November 5, 1969 *Stanford Daily* had a very round spot on the front page.

I only had the photo of the page with the spot in perspective, laying on a table, not squared up scans. I brought it into Photoshop, and used the perspective tool to square it up as best I could. I then got the front page of the November 5, 1969, Daily and pasted it on top and was disappointed to see the spots definitely did not line up.

But my disappointment faded as I realized that the *Chaparral* was printed on a smaller sheet of paper than the *Daily*, in fact, exactly half the size. In terms of printing, that likely meant the *Chaparral* was printed at 90 degrees to the *Daily*, and the full two-page spread of the *Chaparral* should be aligned with a single page of the *Daily*. I rotated the *Chaparral* page and scaled it to be exactly half of the size of the *Daily* page.

And there it was.

The spots aligned perfectly! It was the exact size and shape of spot, the exact distance from the edge of the paper. A spot. On Paper. The exact same spot that was on the digital scan of the *Daily*. It was NOT a scanning defect; it was a printing defect. 100 percent certainty. I can't tell you how satisfying it was to discover this spot, on paper. The other spots will indeed be found on paper too, just not on every issue. This part of the mystery was solved. There was much rejoicing.

As I noted earlier, both spots, the November 5 *Daily* and the November 20 *Chaparral*, are on articles about the Secret Salaries.

Occam's Coincidences

The thing about the Zodiac-Mikado coincidences and the spots in the *Stanford Daily*, is that unless you can explain, by my count, 15 incredible coincidences, they appear as if they had to be done BY the Zodiac.

To deny that this was done or influenced by the Zodiac, one must

Hold as "just a coincidence" that a Mikado review and a letter to the editor about Zodiac were in the same issue, October 31, 1969.

Hold as "just a coincidence" that the Mikado review on page four was exactly aligned over the letter to the editor about Zodiac on page two.

Hold as "just a coincidence" that on the same page as The Mikado review there is a review for the album *THE ELECTRIC ZODIAC*.

Hold as "just a coincidence" that in that review, the photo of the album has the word "ELECTRIC" missing, leaving just "THE   ZODIAC".

Hold as "just a coincidence" that the three-spot pattern occurred for the first time in the October 31, 1969, *Stanford Daily* with two spots on the Mikado review, one on each column.

Hold as "just a coincidence" that the largest spot of the three-spot pattern on page four of this issue, occurring on the Mikado review, fits even more perfectly over the Letter to the Editor about the Zodiac on page two.

Hold as "just a coincidence" that this main spot seems to be oblong and has an extension to the upper right, so it appears over the words The Zodiac as well as the word Stanford.

Hold as "just a coincidence" that the layout of the Mikado review looks hurried, slapdash, with strange mistakes that could have been easily fixed.

Hold as "just a coincidence" that the next appearance of the three-spot pattern is in the November 5 *Stanford Daily*, which also includes on its front page a unique and prominent spot on an article about the secret salaries, as well as an article headlined Zodiac Calls.

Hold as "just a coincidence" that the night before, November 4, 1969, the Palo Alto Police received a call from someone who identified themselves as The Zodiac and said they were coming onto the Stanford campus, thus putting the Zodiac article on the front page of that November 5 *Daily*.

Hold as "just a coincidence" that this unique blemish on November 5, 1969, *Stanford Daily*, is found only one other time, on the Novem-

THE ONLY TIME RICHARD GOT ANGRY AT ME

ber 20, 1969, *Stanford Chaparral* and both are on articles about the Stanford professor's secret salaries.

Hold as "just as a coincidence" and view as a prank the October 20, 1969, call to the Palo Alto Times from someone identifying as Zodiac who said they were coming to the area because it was getting too hot in San Francisco.

Hold as "just as a coincidence" that the *Stanford Daily* and *Berkeley Tribe* both ran editorials addressed to the Zodiac on the same day, October 24, 1969.

Hold as "just as a coincidence" that on the same page as the *Daily's* Message To The Zodiac Killer, there is a Letter to the Editor that uses a death metaphor as its topic is signed by N okNok, which can anagram to koko ZZ.

Hold as "just as a coincidence" and view as a prank the fake bomb under the Willow Avenue bridge on the Stanford campus, and subsequent call to the Stanford Fire Department October 30, 1969, which gained a front-page story on the October 31, 1969 *Daily*, the same issue with the Mikado review. This incident is the first bomb event, real or fake, on the Stanford campus, and was only "fake" because the tubes were just filled with dirt, not explosives, the rest of the device, timer, wiring and mechanism were all real working bomb parts. The perpetrator was indeed threatening that they had the capability and know-how to make a real bomb. Zodiac starts writing about bombs in his letters just one week later.

If you poo-poo this section, disavow the spots on the *Stanford Daily* as too fantastical, too far-fetched to be real, if you can't get your head around an individual who may have both volunteered at the *Daily* and worked nights at the printing presses, know that you must adopt all of these points.

At some point Ocaam's Razor cuts in. The solution is indeed fantastical, but I ask you, which explanation is the simplest now?

If you do not believe all these points were just random coincidences, then The Zodiac, whoever he was, was responsible for these things.

It's Around

"You Want Mikado? You Find It It's Around."

I kept thinking about this listing in the October 9, 1969 *Chaparral*, and always came back to the same thing: They had to pay for this to be typeset. Someone had to write it up, submit it to the ASSU typesetting shop, and it was added on the bill. Why no time and place? Why the attitude? What is the joke?

The Chaparral said, "You want Mikado? You find it. It's around." So I went looking.

Of course, in October 1969, no one knew to look for Mikado-Zodiac coincidences. It would be a year before the public knew Zodiac liked The Mikado. The issues of the *Stanford Daily* passed into history unnoticed.

Here is the kicker—a point I did not understand until much closer examination of all of this: Zodiac REALLY liked the Mikado. He didn't copy down lyrics to the Mikado, he quoted them from memory, and we know so because he gets several of the lyrics wrong.

Just as some in the 1980s incorrectly thought Huey Lewis' sang "the Heart of Rock 'n Roll was in Cleveland," Zodiac thought that "All children who are up in dates, and floor you with 'em flat" was "All children who are up in dates, and implore you with implatt." He also thought "And all third persons who on spoiling tête-à-têtes insist" was "And all third persons who with unspoiling take those who insist."

There are several of these mistakes. He makes similar mistakes in both the 1970 and 1974 letters. He got some of the lyrics wrong, which means he was quoting from memory. This means he was a real fan, a real Mikado aficionado. The review in the *Stanford Daily* was written by a Mikado aficionado too. Do I dare say the C-word, or do I just raise an eyebrow and let all of you say it aloud?

And there's more.

I compared the Little List letter against the libretto of the Mikado. There are some interesting things to observe.

For example, Zodiac leaves out the chorus of the song—he only sings the part of Ko-Ko. So even though he is doing it from memory, even though the song is undoubtedly playing back in his mind, a playback that certainly includes the chorus, he only sings Ko-Ko.

As for the lyrics he mis-quotes, they are often just an incidental word, "and" instead of "the" and the like. There are other lyrics he seemingly mis-heard, as previously shown. But then there is the second half of the second verse, where his memory seems to break down for a line.

"And the lady from the provinces, who dresses like a guy, and who 'doesn't think she dances, but would rather like to try," is written by Zodiac as, "And the lady from the provences, who dress like a guy who doesn't cry"

That is the first only true breakdown of the lyrics as written by Zodiac. Then in the following line, Zodiac does something totally unique, he writes his own lyrics. Yes, Zodiac briefly parodies the song—at the final, climactic ending of the second verse.

The line "And the singular abnormality – the female novelist" is changed by Zodiac to read, "*And that singular abnomily, the girl who never kissed*"

I don't know about you, but the red light is flashing in my head. As a three-time Dr. Demento songwriter/performer I can tell you: One clear parody line in the otherwise correct song lyrics is significant, on purpose. One clear parody line about the girl who never kissed. Never kissed who? The Zodiac? Did she kiss other boys but not him? Oh my god, Zodiac is writing about Darlene.

Of course this is speculation about Darlene. But it seems pretty clear that somewhere, sometime, some girl refused to kiss, and it was still bothering him. So much so as to inspire him to make the only parody section in his production angst about some girl, tied to the Grand Executioner persona.

For what it's worth, this verse is followed by "I don't think she'd be missed I'm **sure** she wouldn't be missed." The emphasis on "sure" is in the Gilbert and Sullivan score. As a Mikado aficionado, I'm sure he knows about the emphasis on sure.

The Mikado was more important to the Zodiac than I first comprehended.

Going back to that October 9, 1969, *Chaparral* issue, I think someone must have asked about including a Mikado listing, but for whatever reason, the staff, or just the person doing the listings, did not want to do it. It's not a question of location, there are plenty of San Francisco listings. It's not a question of genre, they have the listing for the opera La Boheme, as well as the Grand Kabuki listings. Why on earth did they not just list the details for The Mikado?

Then there is the wording of the listing. It's sarcastic. It's dismissive.

I am VERY familiar with *Chaparral* editorial processes, and the culture of Chappies. It sure looks like someone was annoyed with someone else, and it made it into print. The "you" in the listing is not the collective you, it is a specific person.

And whoever this person was who was interested in The Mikado, they were persistent. I mean, a single request, a single mention would not result in the sarcastic listing that got printed. I think someone brought up Mikado multiple times, and for whatever reason, the staff was like, FU. I mean, why even bother printing this without the time and address if it was not some kind of joke pushback?

The *Chaparral* does indeed run joke listings, so this Mikado line is not completely out of nowhere. For example, in that same issue, the final listing for October 11 is Belly Dancing: Ken Pitzer & his Trained Seals, top of Hoover Tower, 1 am. The key question is this: What pushed the staff to have the FU response? You don't go to FU over trivial matters, it had to be FU-worthy. What on earth could be FU-worthy about the Mikado? Perpetual requests about it would be one way.

I think maybe the listing was even a fallback request, after a proposal for a feature article was shot down--someone still wanted at least a listing. Maybe everyone was sick of hearing about the Mikado by then.

Here's the deal: Each new issue of a magazine like the *Chaparral* begins with a germ session, staff members meet to suggest ideas and exchange information. They modify the ideas and decide what will go in the issue. The theme and cover story are also determined in a germ session with the editor having final say.

I remember them well, some of the most fun experiences of my life. Wild. Raucous. Drunken. Hilarious. Free flow of ideas, people spouting wit and sarcasm and puns in real time. Others struggling to get it all written on the chalkboard or notebook. This is exactly the process that the *Who Shot R.R.?* article and issue were born.

Of course we were doing comedy issues, but the political tabloid issues would have similar meetings where the plan of the issue came together. Article ideas, who to lambast, who to protest, what sarcastic cartoon to draw, whose cause to champion, where to get drugs, what was hip?

For the issue in question, everyone was psyched for the upcoming October 15 Vietnam Moratorium. It was a very exciting and important moment for the protest movement—it was going nationwide! There were lots of angles, and lots of stories worth writing about.

It was also early in the quarter, and they were still flush with dough, so there would be lots of people who wanted their article or artwork put in. The issue would be 24 pages, and there was a fair number of ads. All these factors make it very likely there was more content than there were pages to put it on.

I conjecture that someone in one of these germ sessions suggested that they do a feature, or at least a review, on the Mikado production going on up in San Francisco. I further conjecture that this idea was viewed as "Squaresville" to at least some significant proportion of the staff. I mean, there were important things at hand. The Moratorium would be six days after this issue—making it of extreme importance for getting the word out. This was a huge nationwide protest, predictions proved true that it was the day Vietnam protests went mass. The Mikado? A British opera from the 1800s about Japan? Sounds establishment, colonial. Were they really going to use their precious pages on that?

If this conjecture is correct, it's quite possible the guy already had the feature written, or at least the Lamplighter's press release, with photos or graphics. Do you think it focused on The Grand Executioner, or the Little List song? It's possible.

When it was not accepted for publication, of course that was disappointing. Perhaps he even said something about it, or offered to shorten it, but it still wasn't going in. Perhaps he just kept asking and the answer was still no. Perhaps he then tried to get a listing of the performance in the events in the back of the *Chaparral*.

Apparently, however it went down, it became a thing or a joke for some portion of the *Chaparral* staff. Anyone who is a Chappie, or worked on a publication, especially a glib, sarcastic one, knows about inside jokes, knows about paste-up hi-jinks. This is my conjecture explaining the October 9, 1969 *Chaparral*, listing: You want Mikado? You find it, it's around.

Realize that someone actually had to order those words to be type-set. Someone had to type it up on a typewriter, send it to the typesetting office, and pay for it. The need for sarcasm was so great, that they went to the trouble of printing it in the issue, while NOT printing a time and place. It's a retort. It's mocking someone. It's making fun of someone who REALLY wanted something about Mikado in that October 1969 *Stanford Chaparral*, because the show was one of his favorites, and could provide a prank perhaps greater and more sophisticated than even the Dick Tracy gag. An appearance of Mikado's Grand Executioner would bring the house down.

If he couldn't get a Mikado article in the *Chaparral,* no matter. Maybe he could get something in the *Daily?*

I hope the enclosed "key" will prove to be beneficial to you in connection with the cipher letter writer.

-Concerned Citizen, August 10, 1969

ACT V === THE BURRITO at the END of the UNIVERSE======

In January 2002, Kate and I journeyed to Hawaii one last time to attend John Lilly's funeral, stopping for a night in San Francisco on the way.

It was almost dark when we landed at SFO, and it was cold and rainy. I got a car and proceeded straight to Richards.

"It's so weird we are not going to Jack in the Box," I said.

We did not stop at our normal place, because we were going to have dinner with Richard. I had called from New York, and he had said he only had time in the early evening. We went to his place on Guerrero and hung out a while. At some point B came over and the four of us went to get burritos. Mission burritos. If you've never eaten in the Mission, I recommend it.

After eating, we headed to our hotel, The Red Vic, leaving Richard and B at the front of the restaurant. That was the last time we saw Richard.

I think a burrito metaphor may be apt, trying to wrap up these various ingredients into a coherent meal. I hope nothing falls out the bottom. I liken this section to the Burrito at the End of the Universe. At least this part of the universe.

What would you do?

I find this situation a most unlikely story, involving my school and its student publications in a twist no one saw coming. As I said from the first words of this book, I wouldn't blame anyone if they did not believe all this. More murder stories about Stanford? That would never happen.

But I stand by my discoveries and point to the reality that victims and their families to have a right to have their cases solved. I believe this must be investigated. And while I am delaying the release of this information so as to not shadow the Chaparral's anniversary, once that is completed there will be no ethical way for me to not come forward with this information, and to lay out my interpretation of it.

It sure seems to me that there is a there, there.

Coincidence? Or CoincidenSe?

Now as we have seen, coincidences DO exist. It IS possible that you could write a parody of Dallas but change it to Who Shot R. R.? and put it in a *Chaparral* issue some months later, only to have that issue debut on the very day that Reagan is shot, but there is truly NO connection, it's just a coincidence. It truly was a coincidence.

It is indeed possible that one could write an article about people laughing themselves to death in Memorial Church and it could be just about to print in the *Chaparral* when the radio reports that someone was actually murdered in Memorial Church the night before. You might indeed be able to switch out the article literally minutes before it was going to run, and all of this would truly just be a coincidence.

It can also be a complete coincidence that you are pranking the Stanford campus by drawing chalk outlines of bodies on the sidewalk--like in murder investigations--and it is purely a coincidence that it turned out to be the fifth anniversary of that Memorial Church murder. That the cops arrest you because they were waiting undercover to see if the perpetrator would return on that anniversary is just a sort of darkly comical punctuation on that coincidence.

And it can also be a total coincidence that you were researching your college humor magazine, and just happen to recognize your friend's fake name in a fake issue and realize this was of extreme significance to the greatest cold case murders of the 20th Century.

It's not just possible that these things happened, these all actually happened.

So what do you think?

Was the Zodiac making Mikado mischief in the Stanford student publications in fall of 1969? If so, how long might this individual have been on campus? Is Dick Geikie really Richard Gaikowski, with by-lines and a bogus *Chaparral* issue in 1971? Did the "scene" in 1969 to 1971 actually extend up through 1974? Could this have anything to do with the murder of David Levine and the other Stanford murders?

I've reflected on these questions for a long time now. One thing I can tell you is that this needs to see the light of day. I say it again, this needs to be investigated, and other events in the timelines of the Zodiac and of Stanford University need to be re-examined.

The October 20 call to Palo Alto police; the two Zodiac Messages in the *Daily* and *Berkeley Tribe* on October 24; the October 30 Willow Bridge bomb hoax; the October 31 Zodiac Mikado coincidences; the November 4 call from the Zodiac and accompanying November 5 *Daily;* these all need to be reconsidered in the context of the information in this book.

Any non-natural deaths around the Mid-Peninsula during this time period also need to be re-examined. If it is confirmed that Zodiac was on the Stanford campus during these years, all such incidents and non-natural deaths bear re-examination and re-evaluation, all suicides, apartment fires, routine robberies, killings of anger, and a few fake accidents, etc. should be looked at again.

Observations and Conjectures

Of course, at this point I have spent considerable time over many years considering the Zodiac case, and I have made several observations and conjectures. My decades of watching Columbo are now going to be put to use: I throw my burrito into the ring.

Conjecture: Zodiac worked in newspapers or printing.

This isn't my conjecture; I'm just stating I agree with the various investigators who posited this from early in this story. Zodiac seems quite familiar with newspaper lingo; and overwhelmingly chooses newspapers to place his communications rather than TV or radio stations. I believe he saw the Dick Tracy comics before the general public, indicating he worked in the newspaper or printing industry.

Beyond these points, the things I have discovered involve the creation and manipulation of publications.

Conjecture: The Dick Tracy Zodiac comic was a coincidental opportunity.

I conjecture that the killer was signing his letters with a gun-sight, a circle and cross image he was also familiar with because it is a registration mark used in printing. Then, quite coincidentally, one of his favorite comic strips began an astrology-themed storyline. He was ecstatic, and the name "The Zodiac" was born. When the gang is shown in a later strip wearing black hoods with white astrology symbols, also known as zodiac symbols, he took it as a sign and commenced to make the hood.

Conjecture: Zodiac was NOT a resident of Vallejo

In the police reports about the Blue Rock Springs attack it states that at 12:10 am Vallejo police dispatcher Nancy Slover takes a call from a female that says that two juveniles were being shot at "at Blue Rock Springs parking lot." Then at 12:40 the killer calls and states "... if you go one mile east on Columbus Parkway to the public park...." The killer is describing the location of the bodies but is not familiar with the name of the park. The killer is giving directions to the scene, directions for someone driving via Interstate 80.

I wanted to test this idea as best I could, so I used the directions tool on Google Maps. Of course, the roads are somewhat different in 2024 than they were in 1969, but I verified that most major freeways and streets were indeed in existence then.

If you ask for directions to the Blue Rock crime scene from downtown Vallejo, it routes you out Springs Road to Columbus Parkway, and then north to the park. I tried it from various spots around Vallejo, the downtown, the police station, the location of Darlene's house, and it always gave me this result. In no case did it route me on to I- 80.

But once you start from locations outside of Vallejo, like San Francisco, and Oakland from the south, Fairfield and Sacramento from the north, it routes you on Interstate 80 and has you exit at Columbus Parkway and head east 1.7 miles. I did the same test for several other locations including Martinez and even out to Stockton—it always routes you on to I-80 to the Columbus Parkway exit.

Given that the Zodiac did not use the name of Blue Rock Springs Park, and that he uses the directions coming from I-80, I think it is most likely he did not live in Vallejo.

Conjecture: Zodiac was a resident of San Francisco.

I conjecture that Zodiac was a resident of San Francisco, at least by some point in 1969, because he measured himself against the San Francisco Police Department. In his letters he often ended with a scorecard: SFPD – 0 Zodiac – 13, and the like. In the "Exorcist" letter of January 27, 1974, the letter concludes: Me – 37 SFPD – 0. He was really fixated on the San Francisco Police Department. Not the Solano or Napa County Sheriff departments, not the Vallejo Police Department, not the FBI nor California State Police. Zodiac kept score against the San Francisco Police Department. I conjecture that is so because that is where he lived.

Conjecture: The Zodiac mostly told the truth in his letters.

From what we can verify, Zodiac's letters are often truthful. He is indeed the perpetrator in the five confirmed killings. He gives correct details of the crimes. He actually killed people; he didn't make it up. He also said he was going to stop "announcing" his murders on November 9, 1969. For what it's worth, he indeed stopped announcing.

The 340 code, long regarded as "gibberish" by many, and thus added to the "lying Zodiac" line of thought, was finally cracked. It was not gibberish, just too sophisticated to be cracked for 51 years. It was real. I think when Zodiac says something, we should mostly believe it.

Conjecture: There are indeed more Zodiac murders.

If Zodiac mostly tells the truth in his letters, there are indeed more victims. These will be cold cases, obviously, but also murders incorrectly labelled as accidents, murders where someone was incorrectly convicted, and even some solved murders where another individual confessed to them might be Zodiac, or Zodiac-assisted.

As for victim count, the question is one of probabilities. Taking 37 as the highest victim claim, that means there are up to 32 additional victims beyond the five official ones.

If you believe Zodiac lied 90 percent of the time after October 1969, that will still leave 10 percent of the time he told the truth, calculating to 3.2 additional murders, rounded to three, and giving Zodiac a total of eight victims. If you believe Zodiac lied 50 percent of the time after October 1969, that still leaves 50 percent of the time he told the truth, calculating to 16 additional murders, giving Zodiac a total of 21 victims.

In all of this, the LEAST likely, to me, is that he told the truth 100 percent of the time up through October 1969, and told lies 100 percent of the time beginning in November 1969. That is a nearly impossible proposition. So, you see, it is quite likely there MUST be additional victims, the tricky questions are who, and how many?

Conjecture: Zodiac killed by gun, by knife, by fire, and by rope

These are the ways to die listed on the Halloween card sent to Paul Avery. The four methods are apparently lifted from a 1952 Tim Holt comic. Under the theory that Zodiac told the truth, there should be murders of all four types. This is not to say blunt force trauma should be ruled out of hand. Cold cases and unnatural deaths of all types should be examined as potential Zodiac murders.

Conjecture: Zodiac Indeed Used Fake Clews

Now that I have made the case for a truthful Zodiac, let me point out what I believe to be an obvious time he was not truthful and attempted throw people off the trail.

In the Bomb Letter of November 9, 1969, Zodiac says he left fake clews (his misspelling of "clues") for the cops when he spent so much time wiping down Paul Stine's cab, unaware he was being witnessed.

> *"If you wonder why I was wipeing the cab down I was leaving fake clews for the police to run all over town with, as one might say, I gave the cops som bussy work to do to keep them happy. I enjoy needling the blue pigs."*

I think there are two things one can take from this passage.

First, obviously the idea of leaving "fake clews" has crossed the mind of Zodiac. Whether he actually left fake clues is unknown, but he was aware of the tactic. It is almost certain he did so at some point.

Second, it is clear that Zodiac is lying, and here's why: Zodiac would certainly be aware of what uncaught criminals and pranksters know instinctively--that once the crime has been committed you need to GET THE F OUTTA THERE—get away from the crime scene ASAP. As the instantaneous prank, or instantaneous crime would be uncatchable, the ones that take a long time to commit are eminently CATCH-able.

Prior to the crime, right up to the moment that the first anti-social act is committed, you can mosey around, case the situation, change plans if you need to, make sure no one is watching. Sure, you don't want to be seen, but if you are, you can still abort the mission, you haven't done anything wrong yet.

All this changes once the crime is committed. Then the clock is running. Seconds count. Moreover, you are in great danger and that danger is rising. Fast. Every second you hang around the crime scene your risk rises. Stay there one minute, two minutes, anything over a few seconds, and the risk of being seen skyrockets. As people, cars, police may be approaching from any direction (or as children who did see Zodiac and told their parents, who then called the police), the risks rise exponentially, not linearly.

There would have to be a very good reason to spend any time at the scene, let alone a minute or two. A VERY good reason that would justify the risk. This would not be the time to dally around leaving fake clues. You can leave fake clues later, when it's vastly safer. That's what he's doing in the letter—leaving fake clues--trying to devalue and obscure that he screwed up and was seen thoroughly wiping down the cab. Zodiac's claim that he used airplane glue on his fingertips is also attempting to throw off investigators.

No, the only thing that would be worthwhile to stay at the crime scene that long would be to obscure REAL CLUES or the even scarier POTENTIAL REAL CLUES. You do more because you think the possibility exists something could lead back to you.

Wiping down the car and emptying Stine's pockets had to have been important to the killer. He thought his, or someone else's, fingerprints could be on that driver side door. Or a hair follicle or something on the dashboard, the steering wheel. And he thought something in Paul Stine's pockets might also lead back to him. A business card, an address, a show program, it could be anything. While he was doing all of this, he was unaware he was being watched.

Then, after reading the articles in the press and noting the children had watched his time-consuming behavior at the murder scene, he realized it was a path to catching him. It became in his interest to cast doubt upon wiping the cab and emptying the pocket as being significant. Add in the time it took to rip the shirt and he's really risking getting caught.

I conjecture that later, upon realizing he had been witnessed, he came up with the idea of "fake clews."

Conjecture: The 408 Code is indeed solved by the Concerned Citizen letter

All through the past couple years the debate, and joking about when and when not to use quotes, double-quotes, single quotes, quotes for titles, quotes for jokes, quotes for quotes, and the various meta meanings for quotes, including in legal documents and consequences, has been central to our lives, including the Chappie book and zoom calls, the writing and editing of this book and any and all parts of daily conversation.

In that context, I would just like to ask why the Concerned Citizen put quotes around the word "key" in his August 10, 1969 letter that contained a correct solution to the 408 code? I conjecture that it is because "key" is special. "Key" isn't really the key to the cipher, it is the "key".

In my opinion as a prankster and wordsmith, I agree with those who posit that GYKE solves to AUSE when you have the "key." This opinion has been around online for years, I only note that if Richard Gaikowski is indeed confirmed to be the perpetrator, this is certainly what is meant by "In this cipher is my identity," in the letter to the Chronicle accompanying part 3 of the code.

Conjecture: Zodiac Planned or Committed a Mikado-themed Murder

I propose that Zodiac was planning a Mikado-themed murder for October 1969. But something happened, circumstances changed. This might be in direct relation to the Paul Stine murder, or not. Zodiac hadn't been able to get a Mikado feature article in the *Chaparral* or in another publication. Did the small review in the October 31 Daily suit his purposes?

Did Zodiac perform a Mikado-style murder sometime between October 1969 and July 1970 and we just don't know about it? I think it's quite possible. But unlike Lake Berryessa, there was no one to report the "prank," no one to see the Ko-Ko outfit, or the sword, or whatever. So, I conjecture he wrote about it in the letter(s) of July 1970.

Conjecture: The 340 Code was Computer Assisted

I had wondered about Zodiac being a "coder" from the beginning, and the cracking of the 340 Code seemingly points to it as well. When finally solved in 2020, the encoded message was quite generic, almost nothing new. One wonders if the Zodiac was getting bored.

But what was not generic was how the message had been scrambled, letter by letter in a knight move pattern across the cipher. That is where Zodiac placed his energy. Scrambled so well, it took 51 years, and much more powerful computers than I believe he was using to solve it.

I conjecture that a piece of software was written, from a terminal on a computer mainframe, most likely at a Bay Area college at night. The code was not split into three separate code blocks as homage to the 408, it was done because of memory limitation or a quirk in the coding.

He ran the code on the first section. It was so easy! Then he loaded the second section. The computer now scrambled letters in seconds! I conjecture that before running the remaining two lines of text, he tweaked a parameter of the code, resulting in the braided effect of the last two lines. Unlike the "messy" scrambling of the 408 Code, here shifting is done with machine-precision

Conjecture: Zodiac's interest in computers brought him to colleges

In the late 1960s and early 1970s, finding computer time would be difficult, especially for "secret" purposes. This drew him to college campuses. He would especially be interested in meeting science students and graduate students, who would be more likely to have access to computers with loose or no supervision. This is not just common sense, but it fits how computer time was valued in that era. Terminals were occupied all hours of the day and night, at all times of the year. Students took what they could get, often a 3 am or similar spot. A non-student would absolutely have to accept off-peak times and dates to get on a computer, regardless of what they were working on. For someone who wanted secrecy about what they were doing, late nights and when school was out of term would certainly be the most likely times.

In 1969, several colleges could have provided had the opportunity for a non-student to get on a computer, but arguably the best place in the Bay Area, and perhaps the entire USA, was Stanford.

There were many opportunities to start hanging around Stanford, perhaps through the Midpeninsula Free University, perhaps through summer workshops, perhaps by political protests. Either way, friends and contacts were made on campus. With newspaper expertise, one gravitated to student publications located in the Storke Publications Building. There were a few hip scenes going on there.

As a non-student he never wanted a byline, doing things here and there, assisting with paste up; even writing the occasional article, filler or things like a review of a San Francisco theatrical show, always anonymously.

He fit in around Stanford for many reasons: computers, politics, art, printing magazines, counterculture; all were subjects that he was interested in and had skills in. This new life around the Mid-Peninsula was even farther away from Vallejo than San Francisco.

Conjecture: The call to Palo Alto Times was authentic.

In the October 20, 1969, call to the Palo Alto Times, someone claiming to be Zodiac says, "I am leaving the city because it is getting too hot" in SF. I conjecture this call was authentic and that Zodiac was indeed visiting the Mid Peninsula.

Conjecture: The Daily's Zodiac Message could have been suggested

Even though a bad idea can come from anywhere, I suggest examining whether the October 24, 1969, Message to the Zodiac Killer editorial was suggested to the staff as a joke idea. Who was involved in the decision to run the article, and who might they have known? The circumstances surrounding the printing of this article are key to answering questions regarding this case.

Happy Halloween Eve!

As the sun went down on Thursday, October 30, 1969, the threat to Stanford grew, like shadows grow from day to the night as darkness falls on the campus. The Willow Bridge Fake Bomb was the first bomb-related incident at Stanford, real, threat, or hoax. It wasn't a prank phone call, it was a real working bomb apparatus, just with dirt instead of explosives.

That same evening, into the night past midnight, a *Stanford Daily* was laid out with extremely interesting coincidences. Extremely. Thursday nights were already big party nights on campus, and it would be Halloween at midnight!

Regarding the plausibility that a non-student could have affected the layouts and printing of the October 31, *Stanford Daily*, let me just say, I have experience in these matters. When you are the editor of a student publication, you do many things to get workers, and in particular, paste-up workers when you have to go to press.

How work Gets Done at a Student Publication

There is a *Chaparral* cartoon from 1943, that shows a desperate editor Jester, downing aspirin among piles of articles and drawings, trying to put together an issue while three extremely happy jesters, not paying any attention to the editor toast with frothy beers. I lived this situation, literally. Every *Chaparral* Editor has lived it, and I'm sure every *Daily* Editor has too.

As *Chaparral* Editor, you HAVE TO produce while the rest of the volunteer staff is there to have fun—what other point is there? And yeah, it's still a school. There are midterms, papers, and actual class to go to. Then there is socializing.

The thing about partying on campus is there are certain facts that determine certain outcomes. College students, especially those in a joint like Stanford, take weekend trips, to the mountains, to the beach, to LA, to father's chateau. They especially take them in the first part of a quarter, pre midterms. Thus the biggest ragers (wild parties) on campus are NOT on the weekend, NOT on Friday night. They are on THURSDAY night, when you can easily convince nearly everyone to "start their weekend early, and besides, Jackie, and Greg, and the crew are going to Tahoe this weekend, so we're having the party tonight. Come on, you can cut a Friday class…"

Of course, we only printed four issues of the *Chaparral* a year, so you could move your layout times around, to avoid big party nights. But whenever it happened, the Editor had to dish out a lot of tough love (and pizza or some other method) to get people to actually work. No *Chaparral* would ever have paste-up on such a night--everyone would have been like "FU." The *Daily*, on the other hand, was on a much more rigid schedule and HAD to paste-up that night.

So when I say that the Thursday before Halloween 1969 would be a hard night to get paste-up workers, I speak from experience. It would have been a perfect storm of no one wanting to work or people being gone. I could add a snarky comment about it being 1969 and note that some potential workers might have decided to do LSD on such an evening, but it is not needed. Pity the poor soul responsible for rounding up layout artists on this night.

If there was someone who wanted to help, a reliable, experienced person who was volunteering, on this night that would be difficult to get volunteers, it would be a godsend. Such a person could easily get a larger than normal share of the layout duties. They might even layout whole pages of the issue. Better yet, it was the guy from the night crew at the printers who had a car and could even run the layouts over to them later tonight...

Now when I talk about pranks being the result of opportunities, this is what I mean. There would have been fewer people than normal at the *Daily* on this night, and some other people were relatively drunker, relatively higher, or just relatively checked out more on this evening, and thus the opportunity was presented, and seized.

Here was the chance to put the beloved Mikado in print, with the connection to Zodiac, and in the Halloween issue no less. As they say, "the stars all aligned."

Conjecture: Later that Day at the Printers

"We had a jam last night...crushed the blanket in three places. I got it cleared, but it needs to be replaced."

"Son of a bitch. We can't swap that out now, we make so little money on that job. We'll have to muddle by on that press until we can replace it in a few weeks..."

THE ONLY TIME RICHARD GOT ANGRY AT ME

Conjecture: Zodiac Calls November 4, 1969

I conjecture that the night of Tuesday, November 4, 1969, the *Stanford Daily* had some of the same crew it had on the night of Thursday, October 30. On that evening, the issue was taking shape. The big news was that the university had responded to the secret salary scandal with some public relations material. I would imagine that it was not well received by the students as it just provided averaged data in a chart, with a press release written to make the university look good, and the people who stole the salaries look bad.

I conjecture this spurred someone to pull a prank around this article. It was perhaps a happy coincidence that they were going to be on press that night anyway.

I further conjecture they went to a pay phone and called the Palo Alto police, said they were Zodiac and that they were coming on the Stanford campus and that was truthful. Unbelievably truthful. as I conjecture the call was likely made FROM the campus or the immediate vicinity.

The call had been at 9:05 pm. News of the call and resulting police scramble certainly made its way to the *Daily* offices later that night, requiring them to revise the front page to squeeze in the Zodiac story.

Then sometime in the wee hours of the morning, an increasingly practiced hand at the press popped that university propaganda chart with a clean, head-on hit with a hammer, done with such precision and touch that it made a nice circular impression on the front page, while barely affecting the page two print on the underside.

November 5, 1969 is the only time such a front-page and pronounced spot appeared on any issue of the *Stanford Daily*, coincidentally with the only Zodiac article to ever appear on the front page.

As previously noted, the circular spot was found again, on the November 20, 1969 *Chaparral*, confirmed to be on the paper. This blemish has only been identified two times, both on articles about the stolen professor salaries. Is this a coincidence?

It had been a while since I had heard the Close Encounters music, but I began to wonder. I had conjectured that the *Chaparral* was involved with the theft of the professor salaries in May of 1969, or at least the publicity of them in October 1969. And now the discovery of two spots, two unique spots, both on salary articles? It seemed strange.

For those keeping score, we now have two instances of blemishes on Stanford student publications where we have the legitimate question of whether the damage is intentional or not. With two instances, the probability that they are indeed intentional does indeed rise, although by how much is unclear.

The Seven Symbols - Chaparral Dec. 4, 1969

The December 4, 1969, *Chaparral* has a very strange page titled "Life is Good,"[317] a recurring article in this era of *Chaparral*s, with a hippie cartoon logo for its typography. The layout for this particular article is quite unique and includes a bunch of registrations marks across the middle of the page. Registration marks are often used in print production, and as stated before, are also the circle and cross symbol Zodiac used to sign his letters.

The page also feels special because it ends with a quote of sentiment similar to Richard's opinion on the value of astrology:

Life is also bad. Astrologers have always known that day, hours, and stars determine men's lives. Monday night proved that they are right.

"Life is bad," refers to the title of the article. "Monday night" refers to the draft numbers that had just been picked in Washington, determining the birthdays of those to be sent to Vietnam.

I had seen this page before, but I really didn't think it was anything worth noting. There were rolls of registration mark tape all around a paste up room. Someone thought it was cool to paste them into the layout. And it was about the draft, and who would die, so the gun-sight imagery worked. I did not mark this page down as a Zodiac coincidence.

But late in the process of this book, I returned to this page to answer a question that had developed in my mind: How many registration marks were on this article, and how many victims was Zodiac claiming at this point in time?

I found the page and I saw what I feared. By then I had become so familiar with the Zodiac timeline that I didn't even have to verify that in early December of 1969 Zodiac was claiming seven victims, so of course I wasn't that surprised when I saw seven registration marks, or Zodiac symbols if you rather, across the center of the layout.

Now it was widely reported in the press that he was claiming seven, so anyone could have put seven there, intentionally or unintentionally. Yet again, another funny coincidence. But it does make one wonder...

Stanford Murders - What If Zodiac was really at Stanford?

Sure, three of the four identified Stanford Murders have been solved. But wouldn't it be another F of a Coincidence if a serial killer were indeed on campus at the same time? That would be really weird, and consider the ramifications.

If it is confirmed that Zodiac was on the Stanford campus during these years, all such incidents and non-natural deaths bear re-examination and re-evaluation. Perhaps take a second look at the death of Mark Rosvold, whose body was found WHILE they were looking in the Page Mill quarry for Leslie Perlov, and who is believed to have died on the SAME day.[318] Regardless of the search engine or terms I used, Perlov and Rosvold were the only bodies ever found at the quarry.

Yes, yes, I know the police investigated and ruled these two events are not related. But if so, we have another One F of a Coincidence, one as big as any in this book. There are no other days in all of history that bodies were found in there, at least not recorded by the internet. Just these two, dying on the same day, and they are NOT related? The odds are astronomical. This is quite worthy of further review.

And a big thing to note if connections were indeed found: it could imply that Zodiac didn't always work alone. Or perhaps more likely, he wasn't without friends and associates. If it were shown Zodiac was indeed at Stanford, exploring whether he could have known John Getreu would be a worthwhile investigation. All of this, of course, also has bearing on how we look at the murder of Janet Taylor.

I don't imply direct involvement, but I do wonder about the associates and friends of Zodiac. Whoever he was, he must have had them. When contemplating a decades-long saga, years and years of not being caught, one wonders about the life of Zodiac, who he knew, who he fooled, and perhaps who he commiserated with? Did he ever find a kindred spirit? Could he have known Karl Francis Werner? Could he have known Steven Crawford?

The Bloody Handprint

Believe it or not, I didn't really pay much attention to the Memorial Church murder of Arlis Perry until rather late in my research. I knew that the murder was particularly awful, and I knew that law enforcement had recently identified the guy through DNA, Steven Crawford, the security guard who had been under suspicion from the beginning, and who killed himself when they went to arrest him.

I didn't think there was any particular reason to study this case, because it was solved. It wasn't until late in this process and I was coming to grips that Zodiac may well have been hanging around campus, even in 1974, that I read the details of this horrible murder. It either was, or made to look like, a ritual murder. The victim had been sexually violated with a candlestick.

Before DNA testing confirmed perpetrator Steven Crawford was at the scene of the crime, he had been ruled out because he had passed a lie-detector test. He had also been ruled out, along with several other suspects, because his hands did not match the print taken from the candlestick at the scene[319]. The bloody handprint. Investigators took many handprints from all over the church and compared them with handprints from around 50 of possible suspects, including those of Steven Crawford, but never got a match to anyone.[320]

"Wait, what?" I said to myself. I reread the passage. Crawford's hand does not match.

"So you mean to tell me that there are hand prints that were good enough to rule out this person as a suspect all these years, but now that we have DNA we are going to ignore that they don't match?" I said those words aloud as it was so striking to me.

For 44 years the handprint was used to exculpate Crawford. That's interesting. Now I'm not saying he is not guilty--the DNA proves he was there. I'm saying the handprint on the candle does not match Crawford. Unless there was some incredibly faulty aspect of the handprint, this points to a second person being involved in this crime.

Yes, I said that.

There has to be another person. Whose handprint is it? Is there an explanation why the handprint does NOT match Steven Crawford, because for 44 years the handprint not matching was good enough reason to not arrest him. Either there was some mistake involved or the handprint was more inconclusive than exculpatory, but in absence of such, the handprint belongs to someone else.

A Lot of Strange and Bizarre People

Three years after the event, the Memorial Church murder was still a relatively recent cold case. As reported in the October 14, 1977, *Peninsula Times Tribune*:

Investigators pursued leads which included the questioning of more than 50 people, the comparison of fingerprints at the murder scene with those of about 50 people who were known to be in and around the church.

"We came across a lot of strange and bizarre people who either lived in the (Stanford) area or who were drifting through."[321]

Investigators did report that all of the more than 50 people did indeed check out. But there was one lone individual out of seven late night visitors to the church that they never found, never to be identified, described as a white male with sandy hair approximately 5' 10".

Perhaps the handprint was his?

David Levine

David Levine, the lone cold case of the Stanford murders. Solving this crime remains a duty we have, to him and to all the victims. If Zodiac was at Stanford, does this change our perception of this crime? Keep in mind that even if my discoveries are validated, they are in 1969 and 1971; David Levine was killed in 1973.

The prevailing view in the 2020s is that the murder was a random killing by a stranger, the hypothesis put forward on the very day it happened, September 11, 1973. Investigators posited this theory in the first news articles about the murder.

Investigators also said they had no idea why David Levine would have been out walking at 1 to 3 am on campus, which shows they had no idea about the life of the student and campus activity. There is no chance that a thorough investigation could have been done on the same day the murder happened, so, there is no way that this first take could have any solid basis. No. Way. That is obvious.

If they indeed conducted a thorough investigation and then came to the same conclusion as their first take, well that's possible, but it has yellow lights flashing as to poor logic and confirmation bias. Nevertheless, the random stranger hypothesis has taken hold.

Conjecture: The Zebras did not kill David Levine nor Eric Abramson

The second theory on the death of David Levine is that his murder and the murder of Eric Abramson in Berkeley were part of the Zebra Killings. This idea is still often posited by people today as the answer to the Levine murder, but I find this idea quite unlikely. Here's why:

In May of 1974, eight months after Levine and five months after Abramson, both cold cases were included in a long list of murders claimed by San Francisco Mayor Alioto to be part of the Zebra Killings, murders perpetuated by a "black terrorist group," against whites. According to Alioto, they were responsible for over fifty unsolved murders around California[322].

Of the 56 listed murders, forty used a gun, sixteen were by a knife. Of those sixteen knife attacks, nine were by machete or meat cleaver. Four murders list knife or stabbing or cut but provide no details about the type of knife used. This leaves three attacks committed with a similar, 8 to 10-inch knife.

One of the three, was a bizarre and gruesome case, John Doe #169, also in fall of 1973, where the victim was cut up and wrapped in plastic and dumped on Ocean Beach in San Francisco. The other two were David Levine and Eric Abramson.

Now the Zebras were known for shooting people and quickly getting away by car. It was unclear why any knife victims were included. And while some of the murders included descriptions of the attackers, thus leading to their inclusion on the list, no such information was provided about how Levine and Abramson were tied to the Zebra killings. Also starkly missing from the list of victims, was why and how did the San Francisco Police Department have all this information on murders across the entirety of California? Wouldn't the FBI or California State Police be the agencies to release such information? I described all this to Kate.

"Sounds like Mayor Alioto was up for reelection," said Kate.

As it turns out, not reelection, but a bigger election. Mayor Alioto was running in the California Democratic Gubernatorial Primary in June 1974 and was polling a distant second place to Jerry Brown. The announcement of the killings was statewide news. Eight of the "Death Angels" were arrested, with a lot of national press and fanfare. Alioto not only got press across California, but it was also carried in papers from coast to coast.

Four of the eight were released on May 4, 1974.[323] The four remaining suspects were tried, and eventually convicted of 22 murders, 21 by gunshot, and one stabbing, John Doe #169.[324] No information was listed in the papers relating how investigators linked John Doe #169 to the Zebra Killings, other than it was contemporary to the crimes. It is completely unlike their other murders, and quite frankly, much more like a serial killer than a terrorist group.

When the four of the eight initially arrested were released, there was some ado that one of the four was going to be charged with the murder of Eric Abramson. The DA announced on a Friday that the following Monday there would be an indictment.[325] But over that weekend the statement was retracted, with the DA saying there was insufficient evidence to file a criminal complaint.[326]

And that was the last time the murder of Eric Abramson, or David Levine for that matter, was mentioned in the press, that I could find, other than articles noting the anniversaries of their deaths or charitable awards set up in their name—and noting that they were still cold cases.

I can tell you it appears to me that the Zebras did not kill Levine and Abrahamson. It was already being reported that Abramson was not considered a Zebra victim when the four suspects were released.[327] Zebras shot people, with a quick escape. The Levine and Abramson murders are strikingly alike, and strikingly NOT like the other Zebra killings, both with an 8 to 10-inch knife, just like Lake Berryessa.

Here in the 2020s, the idea that terrorists killed David Levine persists. But it is apparent this idea is less of a legitimate criminal theory, and more of a political stunt by a campaign in need of a gamechanger.

Conjecture: Who killed David Levine?

It's possible that David Levine was murdered by someone who knew him. Perhaps they had become acquaintances because of their shared avocations of computers, debating politics, films, and comic wordplay. The individual knew David Levine's schedule, could see when his time on the mainframe would be ending, and knew when he would be traveling from the lab to his apartment. The murderer was able to get close enough to strike a fatal blow with no struggle not because it was a total surprise out of the darkness, but because David Levine knew the individual.

David Levine was a roommate, or was scheduled to be the roommate, of a future *Chaparral* editor - the chances he visited the *Chaparral* office, or met people from there, are high. This story runs through the offices of the *Chaparral*, the *Daily*, and the scene in and around the Storke Publications Building.

This point deserves much closer examination.

I wonder about computer logs of the era. Do they exist? If so they should be scoured for the name, or potential fake name, of the killer. The same should be done for participant lists of any workshops from the summer of 1973, or other programs that could have been attended by non-students.

I was surprised to see that the ASSU Senate, of which Levine was a senator, advertised a meeting for August 2, 1973,[328] but found no reporting of that meeting. If the minutes or record of attendees to that meeting exist today, they should also be examined.

Moreover, I propose this entire case needs to be re-examined from the angle that a non-student interested in politics, computers, publications, and film is potentially the perpetrator.

Conjecture: Who Killed Eric Abramson

I propose that the same individual killed Eric Abramson on December 20, 1973, under similar circumstances. Computer logs and class lists for UC Berkeley should also be examined for the killer's name, and/or fake name. Any connections between the two student newspapers, the *Stanford Daily* and the *Daily Californian*, should be explored, both via possible staff overlap, via the printing vendor, or other possible connections between Berkeley and Stanford.

By Knife

In addition to the Levin and Perry murders, there were more knife attacks during this time period. As noted earlier, the July 14, 1972 *Stanford Daily* reported that a female graduate student had thwarted an attack by a man with a knife in her Palo Alto apartment the previous Saturday night, July 8.[329] On July 21, 1972, the victim wrote a letter to the *Daily* and referenced several other attacks in recent months that had not made the press.[330]

What was the knife-attack survivor referencing in her letter? How many more knife attacks, and other attacks, have slipped under the radar?

I reiterate that if it is confirmed that Zodiac was on the Stanford campus during these years, all such incidents and non-natural deaths bear re-examination and re-evaluation, all suicides, apartment fires, routine robberies, killings of anger, and a few fake accidents, etc. should be looked at again.

By Fire

If Zodiac were telling the truth in his letters, then Zodiac's discussion of bombs almost certainly means he was responsible for some of the MANY bombings between 1969-1974 around the Bay Area. I conjecture that "by fire" in the Halloween card of 1970 refers to arson AND bombs. I conjecture that it's possible that political protest could have provided the means of meeting people with knowledge of bomb-making.

I propose investigation should be focused on the Zodiac's bomb diagrams and recipes to look for similarities to other bombs in the area, and comparison specifically to the Willow Bridge fake bomb at Stanford on October 30, 1969.

I propose that the May 15, 1970, arson at Stanford's Polya Hall, the home of the SAIL program, is a candidate for re-examination, as are the Ben Lomond pipe-bomb of April 5, 1971, and the Palo Alto Fairchild Camera bomb on April 15, 1971.

Of course, the April 24, 1971 bomb in the attic above the Stanford President's office should be reexamined too. This action was bold and intended to generate big headlines. How close was the construction of this bomb, or any bomb, to the descriptions in Zodiac's bomb letters?

The arson attack on the Junipero lounge two days later, on April 26, 1971, should be looked at, as should the January 17, 1972, arson attack on the Manzanita Trailers office.

The June 29, 1971, bomb at the Transamerica Title Insurance Corp office in Palo Alto is another possible candidate to be a Zodiac-related bomb. More on this one later.

The July 12, 1971, pipe-bomb at the home of Stanford personnel director Robert Nelson's home is something to be re-examined, as is any connection to the Stanford Hospital sit-in. *Good Times* didn't cover Stanford that much, but they did this event,[331] along with the resulting police raid on the *Stanford Daily* offices[332]. Two of Dick Geikie's articles for the *Stanford Daily* in summer of 1971 are medical-related, including one about a work-study program offered to the Stanford Hospital workers. Richard Gaikowski had been an Army medic.

The arson on July 24, 1971, at the offices of Free Campus Movement is another that bears re-examination, as are the many arson attacks around Stanford in May and June of 1972.

And for the last By Fire event, I propose that the death of Emma Brown on October 22, 1973, should be re-investigated in lieu of the information provided in this book. Were the three fires that occurred near Emma Brown, the Junipero Dorm arson, the Manzanita Trailer arson, and the East Palo Alto fire that resulted in her death just coincidence, or were they related and intentional?

By Rope

The murder of Edward Alan McNeill on July 17, 1976, should also be re-investigated. McNeill was a grad student in chemistry and could also have had self-supervised access to Stanford's computer system. He was strangled without struggle in his own apartment[333]. It would seem one would have to know their attacker for such a circumstance. This murder is much less famous but appears to be another 1970s Stanford cold case murder.

By Gun

I repeat again this passage from the November 9, 1969 Zodiac letter:

> *"So I shall change the way the collecting of slaves. I shall no longer announce to anyone. When I commit my murders, they shall look like routine robberies, killings of anger, a few fake accidents, etc."*

Recognize that "etc." means Zodiac made an open-ended statement that there may be other methods, and that he is in the process of thinking of other methods. It is a cold fact that making a murder look like a suicide would be one method to disguise a murder. In fact, if investigators think the victim took their own life, then they will not even be looking for a murderer. It follows that making murders look like suicides would be likely method of a serial killer trying to not get caught.

Three days after the death of Edward Alan McNeill, biochemistry grad student David R. Charney committed suicide by self-inflicted gunshot[334].

Good Times – Stanford Coincidences

Again, what do you think? Can we really find a connection here? Was there any more hard data, not conjecture, I could find that may point to Richard Gaikowski hanging around Stanford? The following instances are not presented as proof of anything, just the ways I could find a *Good Times* and Stanford overlap.

Chaparral Good Time Places

Starting in 1969 with the first Michael Sweeney issues, the *Stanford Chaparral* contained listings for events in San Francisco and around the Bay Area, with one recurring heading, Good Time Places.[335] There are usually three listings under this heading: The Committee and the Pitschel Players, both in San Francisco, and the Thieves Market in Alameda. Good Time Places run throughout the fall of 1969.

The Magus

In the September 18, 1969, issue of *Good Times*, Goatkirk wrote an article about The Magus, what is perhaps more commonly known as the Magician tarot card.[336] The Magus is card number One, and sits between The Fool card, number Zero, and The High Priestess, number Two.

The October 23, 1969, *Stanford Chaparral* also contains an article about The Magus tarot card.[337] For what it's worth, the articles are not very much alike. That said, there aren't articles about the other tarot cards in either publication. The High Priestess never gets her own article (figures), but also none for The Tower, Wheel of Fortune, The Hierophant, Temperance, Death, nor Satan. Not in the *Chaparral*. Not in *Good Times*.

Were people particularly interested in The Magus in September and October 1969? Is this just a normal covering of a pop culture subject? Or was it just a couple people, or one person, who wanted to write Tarot articles? Again, it's a minor point that I only bring up because I know Richard was interested in Tarot. I'm sure many people were interested in Tarot.

William Hinton

There is an ad in the Feb. 19, 1969 *Stanford Daily* for a talk by William Hinton, author of *Sanshen*, regarding the Chinese Cultural Revolution, who would be speaking on February 21 at Dover Hall in San Francisco, and on February 22 at UC Berkeley,[338] and on Feb 27, he spoke in the Physics Tank at Stanford, sponsored by the Political Union and the SDS[339]. In the August 21, 1970 *Good Times*, Dick Gaik writes about reading Hinton's book, "Iron Oxen."[340]. In the December 3, 1970 *Stanford Daily* there was an ad for William Hinton who would be speaking that night at UC Berkeley[341]. In the December 18, 1970 *Good Times*, Dick Gaik interviews William Hinton[342]. The article mentions he had recently given talks at Berkeley, Merrit Collage, Stanford and others.

Lanh Dao Caoboy

In the Nov 26, 1970, issue of *Good Times*, former *Chaparral* editor Michael Sweeney wrote a feature article on South Vietnamese leader Nguyễn Cao Kỳ.[343]

Kelsie

Kelsie cartoons ran in the *Stanford Chaparral* starting in 1961,[344] and continued through the mid-1970s, a long and involved collaboration with the *Chaparral*. Some issues had several Kelsie cartoons and even Kelsie sections. On May 17, 1971, the cover of *Good Times* was a Kelsie cartoon.[345]

Oil Bird

The November 11, 1971 cover of the *Chaparral* has a picture of a bird covered in oil caused by the Standard Oil tanker spill in San Francisco Bay.[346] That photo was a *Good Times* original photo from the cover of their Jan 22, 1971 issue.[347] *Good Times* also made and sold a poster from the picture titled Ecology is for the Birds.[348]

Since it was sold as a poster, it is possible that the *Chaparral* just used it. But it's also possible they got permission. Now when you reprint a screened photo, the chances of moiré pattern are great. You try to get to the original photo if you can. I think it is possible that someone had access to the original photo, and let the *Chaparral* use it. Or gave the ok to reproduce it. If so, this would be a confirmed interaction between *Good Times* and the *Chaparral*.

A Warship Can Be Stopped

In the October 15, 1971 *Good Times*, the featured page two article is about the USS Coral Sea, written by Dick Gaik.[349] This article was picked up and syndicated by the Liberation News Service.

In November 1971, members of the *Chaparral* attended the USS Coral Sea protests, and there was an article in the *Chaparral*.[350] The *Chaparral* staff photo of November 1971 shows many "A Warship Can Be Stopped" posters from this protest[351]. Members of *Good Times* also attended this protest and multiple people wrote articles about it, including Dick Gaik.[352]

Who was Dick Geikie?

And of course, we are still left with the ultimate question: Is Dick Geikie Dick Gaik? It is the biggest *Good Times*-Stanford question and/or coincidence of all.

If this potentially bombshell revelation is confirmed, please repeat this immeasurably key point in your head:

He worked more for the *Daily* than the *Chaparral*.

He worked more for the *Daily* than the *Chaparral*.

Of course, this old Chappie is joking. We do know Dick Geikie overlapped at least some with the *Chaparral* because the July 1971 *Daily* article he wrote about the Free University's demise contains an interview with Chappie Tim Coburn[353].

I have tried hard to find Dick Geikie, and have always come up empty. I finally figured if I couldn't find who Dick Geikie was, I should at least try to find everyone else in the 1970-71 Chaparral. Now this really could be another of Occam's Coincidences, but this is what I found.

Of the five names on the Missing Link issue, I can verify four of them. Three students and one non-student. All four exist. The one that remains elusive is Dick Geikie. I decided to take this further. I counted 29 people who have bylines or are listed in the staff boxes a staff box in the 1970-71 *Chaparral* volume, including the Missing Link issue. Of these, there are two obviously fake names, "Red Star" and "Anne R. Key." There is also someone just listed as "Carter." Of the 26 other names that all appear to be actual names, I believe I have found 25. The only name I have not been able to track down is Dick Geikie.

As for the *Daily*, we know Dick Geikie indeed authored six articles in the summer of 1971. Actual, real articles. Dick Geikie also appears in the staff box multiple times. For what it's worth, other times the staff box refers to "people who want to remain anonymous."

Dick Geikie wrote two medical-oriented articles, one about Stanford med students opening a clinic in San Jose, and another about a work-study program for Stanford Hospital workers. He wrote one about a computer music class that mentions most people taking it are not Stanford students. He wrote one about summer workshops being offered on campus to non-students. He also wrote about science fiction films and about the Free University's demise. All six articles could arguably be called interests of Richard Gaikowski.

So, if Dick Geikie is not Dick Gaik, it sure is a coincidence he writes about similar subjects.

Remember that Stanford confirmed that no one by that name of Dick Geikie nor Richard Geikie ever attended the university. The lone possible Dick Geikie in the entire US of the proper age resided in New England, was not known to ever visit California, and likely in Europe during the time in question.

So, if Dick Geikie is not Dick Gaik, where the hell did he go? Why is there no record of him? Who wrote those articles? Was it the "San Francisco newsman" quoted in the May 18, 1970, *Stanford Daily* article about Open Campus Day?

Now Open Campus would have been just one way for non-students to come on campus, another likely way was the Midpeninsula Free-University.

Remember the Chappie interviewed for the article about the Free-U, Tim Coburn? In the September 25, 1973 *Stanford Chaparral*, Tim

Coburn wrote:

"The Free U was a center of many activities: classes for bread baking, encounter groups, dance, and yoga mingled more or less happily with straight engineers and a few genuine psychotics." [354]

The Missing Link Issue of the Chaparral

The Missing Link is self-named and might be exactly what it advertises. It is not a fluke. It is a VERY intentional prank. The blank pages are intentional, planned, as is the blank name in the staff box of the Daily from which many articles were lifted. They reference being ripped off. The name on the Daily masthead on the July 9 issue of the Daily was intentionally missing, also "ripped off."

One can see that it was a months-long plan to create this forgery. This is no mistake by stoners, although some might have been smoking grass. This is also not a mock-up layout to see the *Chaparral* in five-column format. This appears to be a completely intentional prank issue.

Whether it was intended as an alibi, or just a joke, is unknown. But in effect, it worked to throw me off the trail. For many months I incorrectly believed Dick Geikie was at Stanford by March 5, 1971. I had to go to Stanford and look at the issues in Green Library and in the Hammer & Coffin archives to discover that the issue was fake, not from March, but from the summer.

In addition, if we weren't in the internet era, it would have been very unlikely that I could discover the Missing Link issue was constructed from lifted articles from the *Stanford Daily*. How would anyone pre-internet discover the issue was not from March? It would be even more a longshot.

As for the bogus issue's production, there was reportedly a printing press in the basement of one of the computer centers on campus. It is said that at some point, the "radicals" took over the press. I think it is possible the Missing Link was printed this way.

It is indeed a strange issue. The reasons for its production are at the center of this book's questions. The stark possibility remains it has something to do the murder of Lynda Kanes.

Lynda Kanes

The motivation for the Missing Link issue remains unclear, but it coincidentally gives someone writing under the name of Dick Geikie an alibi that he was not in northern California in the days of early March 1971, but hanging around Stanford. A March 5 byline implies one was in the vicinity for at least a few days prior to the printing date. Seven days prior to March 5 is February 26, 1971, the date of Lynda Kanes' murder. March 5 is the date her body was discovered.

The issue was constructed in the summer of 1971, coincidentally during the trial of Walter Williams, aka "Willie the Woodcutter," the individual arrested, tried and convicted for the murder of Lynda Kanes.

I conjecture that the bomb and note of June 29, 1971 with the note from "Willy and the Poor Boys" is a joke reference to Willie the Woodcutter. It could just be that the name Willie was coming up in the news and they felt sorry for Willie. Or they liked CCR. When a name was needed to sign the note, someone suggested Willy. Or someone could have REALLY been interested in Willy the Woodcutter, and his murder trial.

I conjecture that at some point in early summer someone noticed the *Chaparral* printed earlier that year with the date March 5. They recognized it as the date Lynda Kanes was found and realized the prank opportunity.

It's possible that the articles chosen for the Missing Link issue could have been selected purposely because of their dates. There are some coincidences worth noting.

One article selected was from July 23, the date that Walter Williams, aka Willie the Woodcutter, was found guilty of the murder of Lynda Kanes. The July 7 article was chosen because that was the date of the "surprise" witness that pretty much assured Willie's conviction.

The rest of the Missing Link issue is constructed with articles lifted from July 9, including Dick Geikie's computer music article, the entirety of page four, and the *Daily* staff box. I conjecture this date does not have a Willie tie-in and instead is a prank of opportunity based on when certain people who may or may not have wished to remain anonymous were going to be on the night crew.

As I outlined in the beginning of the book, pranks are like real estate, you have to work with what reality gives you. The keystone of this prank was there would have to be an instance of Dick Geikie being on the night crew of the *Daily*, on an evening when he had the ability to affect the layout. A night with similar circumstances to the evening of October 30, 1969, when it was likely hard to get paste-up workers. It's possible every night was similar to that night in the midst of summer term, but that week was also a holiday week. Independence Day was on a Sunday, so Monday July 5, was an observed holiday. The normal summer *Daily* Tuesday issue was pushed to Wednesday July 7. Were people still on vacation on July 8, and thus more outside help than normal was needed? It seems a reasonable proposition.

The *Daily* staff box was known for some comedy, and that evening of July 8, 1971, they thought it would be funny to blank out the first name, leaving the comma for it of course. Had it been "ripped off" perhaps? Whatever the joke was, they did it. Someone did it, and Dick Geikie is one of the other names in that staff box.

Later that summer, the Missing Link was constructed, and printed, and folded into several existing, real, March 5, 1971 Chaparral issues, then slipped into the archives of the Hammer & Coffin in the Chaparral office, also getting included in the bound volume archive, and also presented to Stanford's Green Library with the bogus issue included, duly recorded and categorized.

I think that Dick Geikie, or whoever it was, may not have been able to act without someone knowing--someone might have helped blanking out the name in the *Daily* staff box, or the creation of the fake *Chaparral*. Others must have known about it. I propose all this was presented to others as a prank, with the blank name and the blank pages are the joke. Maybe it was the bylines that had been "Ripped Off," or that they were the "Missing Link." I think the others at the Stanford Daily and Stanford Chaparral were duped--thinking they were doing one prank, while Dick Geikie secretly knew they were doing another.

It's funny how things work out. Making a Chaparral issue under the auspices of one project goal, while secretly altering that very issue for the ends of another, is a theme of this story. A wild fractal iteration of art imitating life, or something like that.

Etc.

I repeat again the November 9 letter:

"So I shall change the way the collecting of slaves. I shall no

longer announce to anyone. When I commit my murders, they shall look like routine robberies, killings of anger, a few fake accidents, etc."

Earlier I addressed this in regard to making murders look like suicide. It took me months to realize that this is also an open admission Zodiac intends to frame people in some cases. He is going to kill people, and then make it look like something else happened, create a rational explanation that someone else did it and NOT Zodiac.

So let me say it in more plain terms because this is important: Zodiac implies sometimes he will frame someone else for his murders.

If one was going to identify a murder that could be a frame, the Lynda Kanes murder would be a reasonable choice. I say so because of the nature of the facts used to convict Willie show how it could be done and are also so obvious that it begs belief. I mean, there were several possessions of Willie's just laying near the body. What kind of murderer would just leave all their stuff next to the body? No one is that stupid. Also, the body was wrapped in his flag. Again, who is that stupid? No one. It is so simplistic, the evidence is so bluntly displayed, it really could have been a frame.

Even fifty years later, people are still in disbelief Willie the Woodcutter murdered Lynda Kanes. An article in the May 7, 2021, *Napa Valley Register* still asks if Lynda Kanes was killed by Willie the Woodcutter, or the Zodiac?[355]

The body was near Lake Berryessa, and near Pacific Union College where Kanes was a student like Brian Hartnell and Cecelia Shepherd had been. The body was wrapped in a flag, and the killer ripped off a swatch of it.

For those looking for additional tie-ins, the murder was near Napa State Hospital.

I had gone looking for a murder in early March of 1971 or so, because of the March 5 *Stanford Chaparral* Missing Link fake issue, a killing somewhere away from Stanford, likely in northern California, with aspects that looked like Zodiac. Lynda Kanes was murdered on February 26, but her body wasn't found until March 5, the same date as the *Chaparral* Missing Link.

Is that the joke?

Or is the joke something to do with "rip-off?" I searched all press reports of the Willie the Woodcutter trial, and I never, ever saw an explanation why a piece of the flag was torn off, or if that piece had ever been found. Most importantly, I never read any account or even theory of why was it torn off BY Willie? Because unless that can be explained, there is a hole a mile wide in this case and the conviction of Willie the Woodcutter.

National Treasure

By Summer 2024, over a year had passed since the discovery of the blank pages. The Chappie 125th Anniversary book was long completed and preparations for the October anniversary in full swing. The second book, this book, was deep into production. Finally, eventually, an idea formed in my head. It was mostly a joke at first, a ridiculous idea, but it kept nagging at me.

The theory the Missing Link was a planned joke had held up. The blank pages are part of that planned joke, a VERY well-planned joke. I had thought on this point for most of a year; the blank pages had gone from being perceived as a mistake, a "how stoned were they in the seventies?" to thinking it was the most important part of the issue.

I posed the idea in the form of a question: What would be the joke about blank pages in a magazine, if it was a very well-planned joke? Given all the effort that was being put into this prank, the composition, printing, sliding into the archives and the library effort, what would be the funniest, most sarcastic, most insidious joke you could make with blank pages?

Upon much reflection, weeks and weeks through this long tale, at long last answer came back: "Well, that is where you would put the secret message."

It seemed that this was really getting ridiculous. I was absolutely jumping the shark.

But even so, I hadn't even bothered to scan the blank pages. Who would scan blank pages? See, the jokes were already springing from this comical situation. Who would scan a blank page indeed? And beyond that, who would scan blank pages on a really nice large-format scanner at quite high resolution, and then put the images through all the image processing power a professional computer graphics artist could muster? That person would be me.

I scanned in the blank pages, pages two and three, at 600 dpi. I already had scanned pages one and four months earlier.

I brought the files of the blank pages into Photoshop, and started to apply various contrast and color adjustments to the page. I made many Photoshop layers, trying various methods of image processing. The scans were in RGB (Red Green Blue) format, so I was able to work on each color separately as well as the composite, checking changes in hue as well as brightness, and isolating anything that did not look normal, whatever that means. The pages are over fifty years old and significantly yellowed, and the areas around the folds in the issues are worse. This is made even more obvious when processing and contrasting the images.

Another issue compounding the problem is that you see through the paper, and when contrasting, the printing on the other side gets more prominent, with a large amount of it bleeding through and easily seen. Also, the very fabric of the paper becomes quite visible through the process of contrasting. One is left with a sort of Rorschach image, with splotches and clouds across the page, with the reverse image of the page on the back also coming through the haze.

That said, some of those splotches appeared to be different than the rest - writing perhaps, not part of the structure of the paper nor coming through from the reverse side. I identified three different examples of this. First, there appears to be typeset letters on the page. There is what appears to be a B in Times New Roman font in the upper left of page three, and there may be more letters to the right of it. There is also most of a serifed, sort of ornate S also on the top half of page three.

I investigated the subject of watermarks on newsprint, and did not find anything conclusive, but watermarks were indeed put into paper stock, including newsprint. It seems reasonable that these type-set-looking letters could be watermarks. They appear to have hard edges, very different than the other splotches and marks.

The second type of things I found appear very much to be hand-written letters. The best example is near the center of the bottom half of page two, where the letters appear, perhaps J.P.V. and then perhaps three or four more letters that are, much less visible. The V might be the symbol for Aries in Greek astrology, or perhaps a narrow Y. The J might actually be a D. And while I can't identify the symbols for sure, they are definitely there. Their image is quite pronounced when subjecting the pages to high contrast image processing, although they are completely invisible to the naked eye.

The third type of marks may also be hand-written letters, may actually be the same as the second type, but I put them in a third category because they are much less pronounced than the JPV, with a wider, fuzzier stroke. They are mostly to completely illegible but appear to be spaced roughly like letters. They are spread out across both pages, with a particularly interesting vertical run of them from the top to bottom halves of page three. This crosses the centerline area, which is completely faded out, but some think the first four letters may spell DEAT, with the rest of the letters too faded to see. On some days, I am one of those people who think so.

There may be LEX at the top of page two and an A at the bottom. There may be a ZO or 70 in the top section of page three. These sorts of marks appear across a lot of the pages. And while some interact visually with where there is printing on the reverse side, many of them appear on unprinted sections. Moreover, they cross both printed and unprinted sections (on the reverse side of the paper) and thus seem to be independent of the printing process. While illegible, they appear to be spaced like letters.

Or this is all just nuts and could they just be anomalies in the paper brought out by the process of contrasting them to such a high degree.

A friend suggested that heat brings out messages in invisible ink. "Just use a blow dryer," he said.

And so it was that I set up a video camera on a tripod, set up nice lighting, took the Missing Link, laid it out on a clean board, and videoed myself applying hot air from a blow dryer to the blank pages for several minutes.

No image appeared.

I put that issue on the scanner and again scanned at 600 dpi. When I brought it into the computer and applied the contrasting effects, it seemed to me that the marks I thought might be type were all somewhat less pronounced than before.

"Shit! What if I caused the ink to evaporate?" I wondered.

As it would be, the movie National Treasure was on TV. We had never seen the movie, but I was generally aware of the premise that there was a secret treasure map on the back of the Declaration of Independence.

'This should be a hoot," I said, "and it's a funny coincidence with the Missing Link blank pages." What a great excuse to finally watch what looked to be a pretty corny movie. We watched with skeptical anticipation. Well, as people who have seen the movie know, there is indeed a message on the back of the Declaration of Independence, which they bring out using heat - combined with lemon juice.

I hadn't used lemon juice. Who knew? A couple days later I readied a lemon and the blow-dryer for a second attempt, but before I did, I noticed that National Treasure was on TV again. I delayed my experiment and watched up through the lemon juice scene. When they apply the juice and heat to the Declaration of Independence, they also say that an "expert should be the one to do it." It was almost like a message being sent to me, from the wise people in Hollywood.

I came to the correct reasoning, that I am definitely NOT an expert, and I could easily screw up these issues. Issues that could possibly be material evidence in this case.

Can you imagine coming this far and boning it? I could.

I decided to wait for experts to see if there was an invisible message on the blank pages of the Missing Link issues. And I say issues because any message would have been written by hand, with potentially something different on each one.

I stopped all tinkering and wasting energy along these lines, I put away the blow-dryer and used the lemon in a drink, and put full focus on writing the book, this book you are reading now.

Sometime after the *Chaparral* 125th reunion, I would put The Missing Link issues into the hands of a crime lab. Will there be a invisible message revealed on the blank pages, the splotchy tan and brown paper that so many ways resembles a toasted flour tortilla wrapping a delicious Mission burrito?

Now That would be beyond amazing.

ACT VI ==THE END (FOR NOW)==

The Tower

After the assassination attempt on President Ronald Reagan, Nancy Reagan contacted Joan Quigley in San Francisco, and arranged for her to assist and/or make all scheduling decisions concerning President Reagan and the White House. It is unknown whether the Reagans ever learned of the *Chaparral*'s *Who Shot R.R.?* piece, or if that affected their decision to contact Quigley. Either way, there, in 1981, Stanford's humor magazine stumbled into a story of Reagan, astrology, and violence. Now over 40 years later, we again stumble into a story of Reagan, astrology, and violence.

Is there a Divine Shakespeare writing this, for lack of a better metaphor, comic opera? I mean, come on! Or is it come on?

But there's more.

Comically, or not; coincidentally, or not; the Stanford conservative stalwart Hoover Institute, resident of the iconic tower and architectural headliner of the hallowed campus, acquired all of Joan Quigley's papers in 2017.[356] This is not just a pop-culture sidebar, it's a proper resting place for such materials that in many ways makes so much sense.

Of course, it's a reasonable idea that they want the Quigley papers because of their relevance to Ronald Reagan. It's also reasonable that historians would want to inquire just how closely Reagan indeed used astrology in his decision-making. Quigley was THE astrologer for the Reagan's during the period of his Presidency, and she lived in San Francisco. She owned one of the first DR-70 astrology computers. It is totally believable and reasonable that the Hoover Institute might want to curate the information she had regarding Reagan.

So sure, it's all very reasonable. But it's also funny as hell.

It seems this funny story has brought me back full circle to what started this strange journey: Ronald Reagan and astrology. Well, that and Richard getting angry about it. Nancy called Joan because of Ron getting shot.

Did Joan Quigley and Richard Gaikowski both own a DR-70? Could they have known each other? Could Richard have gotten angry because he was defending an individual he knew? It's a very interesting question.

The joke reason I named this section "The Tower." Is because The Tower is one of the Major Arcana tarot cards, just like The Fool, The Magus, and 19 others.

It's always pretty heavy to draw The Tower in a Tarot reading. One wonders what secrets The Tower may hold regarding this story.

Coinc'o'dences

Cosmic, or rather, comic coincidences kept happening through this journey. Like this one.

In my quest to learn about The Mikado, my myriad searches for Gilbert and Sullivan led the internet to show me another musician, Gilbert O' Sullivan. While I do remember the tune to one of his songs, his name had escaped my notice these several decades I have lived on earth. That all changed in a big way, and the haunting smoothness of Clair was the earworm of the late summer 2024.

The day I discovered Gilbert O' Sullivan coincided with the day I realized I needed to try to get the rights to use the opening quote for this book, Miller's rap on coincidence from the 1984 movie "Repo Man." This movie is one of my favorites, and like many people my age, there are multiple lines of Repo Man dialogue that are just embedded in our lexicon. "The more you drive, the less intelligent you are." "Blanks get the job done too" "You find one in every car, you'll see."

Perhaps the movie's best known catch phrase is "plate of shrimp," from the same scene as the quote I was requesting. At any point in my life, a friend might say "plate of shrimp" as a joke. And not just my friends. The use is widespread among those who know. I think there was even a band in the 1990s called Plate of Shrimp.

And of course the opening quote of this book, spoken by Miller the ethereal mechanic guy of the repo lot.

"A lot of people don't realize what's really going on. They view life as a bunch of unconnected incidents and things. They don't realize that there's this, like, lattice of coincidence that lays on top of everything."

I found writer-director Alex Cox's website, and sent out an email asking him for permission. I really thought it was a longshot, but who knows? And it worked! I was ecstatic to receive a reply later the same day, approving my use of the quote. There was much rejoicing.

But he informed me that I had the quote wrong. I had found it on-line and just copy and pasted it into the email. That source was written more colloquially, incorrectly using "o'" for "of" and "n'" for "and." Just change the 'n back to and, and the 'o back to of and it would be good and approved for the book.

I was so happy, I put Repo Man on. Even though I have seen it dozens of times, I wondered if there would be a coincidence in it I hadn't seen before. As I watched the movie, I slowly pecked out a reply to Alex. I told him just the slightest bit more of what I was doing, that the story dealt with murder, and that I was writing the book under the pen name "James Bigtwin." I typed and retyped this email a few times throughout the movie's running.

I knew the movie so well, that I knew the scene with the sign for a Plate of Shrimp would be coming soon. I watched more closely thinking I might see a new coincidence in this scene—but there was no need to watch closely. As this scene opens, the word "LEVINE" is large on screen, on a sign in the upper right corner for several seconds.

"Look at that, look at that,' I said to Kate. "Levine."' sort of shaking my head in disbelief.

The scene continues to when we get to the shot where the sign for the plate of shrimp is in the window. I see it reads "Plate 'O' Shrimp."

"OMG!" I said to Kate. "I've been referring to "plate OF shrimp" all these 40 years. It's plate 'O' shrimp!" I finally sent my email. And then it dawned on me. Gilbert 'O Sullivan and Plate 'O Shrimp, on the same day, decades later. Only noted here for the comedy of it all.

I watched Repo Man to the end, including the credits. As the last chord of music faded out at the end of the credits, my computer dinged again. It was Alex's reply, asking if I wanted my tombstone to say J. Suhre or J. Bigtwin?

Cover Story

From the very beginning of the 125 Project planning, it was suggested we try to get an article in *Stanford Magazine*. Some early connections were made, and in 2024 it came to fruition: they would indeed do an article on the Chaparral 125th anniversary. I was interviewed along with several other alums.

In early September, the article became available online. I was very pleased with it as it cast the Chaparral in a very positive light, AND it also included stuff about our pranks. The photo of the Dead Bowlers was reprinted! Reprinted in *Stanford Magazine*! Now that is amazing.

Then in early October I got the issue in the mail. We made the cover!. We. Made. The. Cover! Never in my wildest dreams would we be on the cover of *Stanford Magazine*.

"The first of two times you will be on the cover," said the voice in my head.

So, the Chaparral was already getting great press and public awareness, before the reunion. It would help out book sales. That October 2024 *Stanford Magazine* issue really added to the excitement of preparations for the Chappie Reunion. I slid my copy directly into my backpack of stuff I was taking on our trip.

THE END - As of October 9, 2024

Tomorrow we leave on our cross-country drive to the Chaparral 125th Anniversary at Stanford and back.

It's a bit mind-blowing, the path that has led to this vista point. Interweaving storylines that have their threads throughout my entire life, now coming together in what has the potential to be quite a climax - however the cards fall. Have I solved the Zodiac crimes? Or is it just One F of a Coincidence? Does the *Stanford Chaparral* have some strange psychic energy surrounding it? Or just random chance? It's an amazing story either way, and I'm as eager as anyone as to find out the truth.

The only time Richard got angry at me was not enough to be significant on its own, but it did lead me to learn about the Zodiac killings. Ironically, coincidentally, or just comically, it was only because I had become familiar with the Zodiac story that I was able to recognize what I was seeing years later while researching the history of the *Stanford Chaparral*.

I think of other weird quirks—like I was only the Editor of the *Chaparral* because the Chappie star in the class one year older than me left school early to be in a rock band. If not for this quirk of history, I would never have become Editor. If I had never been Editor, would I have bothered with the 125th Anniversary Project? I'm not sure. It certainly would have been less likely.

The same with Covid. If it were not for "the Plague" of 2020-21, would the Chappie 125 Project have happened? It certainly wouldn't have been as extensive and might not have happened at all.

All these things had to occur for this story to happen. Or as that old saying goes in perhaps its most blithely sarcastic use ever, "All the stars had to align."

Now that all these trails have converged, and the evidence points to a conclusion so fantastical, so improbable, so coincidental that it strains credulity, I tell you I would doubt it as well. Especially from someone with prank credentials like mine. But aye there is the rub. This story is indeed true. And if it is just a coincidence, it is at least a *Who-Shot-R.R.?*-level coincidence, if not higher.

It's almost enough to make one believe in a sort of Divine Shakespeare. Almost.

At the *Chaparral*, we have joke sayings and folklore. Back in the office we used talk about the Immortal Jester, or The Eternal One, a joke about a metaphysical clown responsible for humor in the universe. One of a Jester's joke superpowers is temporary limited invisibility. Now you might question the value of temporary invisibility but let me tell you it is indeed powerful. It might mean you don't get caught on a prank; that the police or your parents don't see you for that brief moment.

But in regard to this story, temporary invisibility meant that I could research the history of the *Chaparral* and ask a lot of questions under the legitimate purpose of writing a *Chaparral* history book – with the added benefit of simultaneously researching the Zodiac, the Zodiac at Stanford, or at least some strange coincidences that could make one THINK the Zodiac was at Stanford. What a fortuitous and unplanned, but moreover perfect cloak of temporary invisibility to have for this task. I couldn't dream up such a scenario, it just happened.

LOL.

Now as the 125 Reunion weekend approaches, that temporary invisibility will be coming to an end. It is also a certainty that the relative obscurity the Chappie has lived in will also come to an end. At minimum, thousands of people who never heard of the Stanford Chaparral before were now going to, because of the Chappie 125 book, the events, and the renewed momentum of the entire group. Then after that, even more people will learn of us.

I reiterate that I will do everything possible to have the *Chaparral* 125th anniversary book, events, and party all happen BEFORE any news breaks about these Zodiac discoveries. The *Chaparral* has been a good thing for so many people, with countless people working on it. The Chappies deserve a fun party that talks about the *Chaparral*, the jokes, the art, the issues, and the good times and camaraderie, not this bizarre and macabre sidebar. Our party will be about the *Stanford Chaparral*, for the *Stanford Chaparral*. If all goes as planned, not only will we have perhaps the biggest alumni gathering in Chaparral history, but also increase our visibility both on campus and the public in general. October 2024's momentum will bring a close of an era, forever marked in history by the big book, initiating the dawn of a new era, a Second Renaissance.

But I digress. The bottom line is I'm not going to do anything to overshadow the *Chaparral*'s Reunion in October 2024. But once the party is over, I will have to reveal.

Of course, these timelines are not without other influences. With each passing day my energy decreases. As time goes on, people who might provide key information to this story are passing away. It is not like I can just wait indefinitely to go public. People with possible evidence of a crime are ethically compelled to come forward. The victims and families have a right to have their cases solved. So, I will work to announce as soon as it is feasible in late 2024.

And then there is still My Dilemma. Yes, some Chappies know that I had made fake *Chaparral* issues to prank fellow Chappie alums and slipped them into the 125 book. Anyone reading the Mea Culpa will know that too.[357] Ha ha ha.

But now…

Now I am going to claim Zodiac was possibly at Stanford over a few years and might have worked for the *Daily* and *Chaparral*? Sure. Happens all the time. That big dude pranking us? Fake issues? That would never happen. It will be most interesting to see how all that plays out.

We decided we are driving to California - a cross-country trip, allowing us to also go to Ohio, to Colorado, to Reno, perhaps New Mexico, and other places around the Bay Area as needed. It will make our time in California more flexible. We love the road trip.

I have also determined this book's story ends now, here in early October 2024—WITHOUT key questions answered. I apologize to the reader who has come this far with me, but there is no other way.

The last weekend of October will be the largest gathering of *Stanford Chaparral* alumni for many decades, one of the largest reunions in all history. Perhaps even some *Stanford Daily* alums will be in attendance too.

For those who are keeping score, October 31, 2024, will be the 55th anniversary of the Zodiac-Mikado coincidences in the *Stanford Daily*. Sometime after that I will reveal.

I will send a condensed version of this book to selected outlets, Bay Area press and law enforcement. And I will submit my research to Stanford, along with a list of requests for information, class lists and computer logs. I will announce that I have included the Missing Link issue in the Chappie's 125th anniversary book, as well as a few other Easter eggs inserted into the pages. And I will make the book you are reading now available to the public.

We set out on this western road trip to still looking to answer the remaining ultimate questions:

31 Questions

1. Who was Dick Geikie? Was Dick Geikie Dick Gaik? And if so:

2. What was the full extent of Dick Geikie's activities at Stanford?

3. Did Dick Geikie suggest to the Daily staff to write the Message to the Zodiac editorial on October 24, 1969?

4. Who made The Missing Link fake *Chaparral* issue? Was this issue made by Dick Geikie?

5. Who knew Dick Geikie? Does someone remember Dick Geikie?

6. Who submitted the *Chaparral* issues of 1971, including the fake Missing Link issue to Green Library, and when did that occur?

7. What is the significance of the blank pages in The Missing Link issue?

8. Is there a secret message written on these pages?

9. Do they reference the blank space in the July 9, 1969, *Stanford Daily* staff box?

10. What was the reason for the sarcastic Mikado listing in the October 9, 1969 *Stanford Chaparral*?

11. What accounts for the Mikado-Zodiac coincidences in the October and November 1969 *Stanford Daily*?

12. Who wrote the Mikado review? Who laid out that page?

13. Was it intentionally placed to be directly over the Zodiac Letter to the Editor on the page below?

14. Was it intentionally placed on the same page as a review for an album *The Electric Zodiac*, with a picture of the album with the word Electric missing, leaving just "The Zodiac"?

15. What caused the spots or blemishes in the *Stanford Daily* on issues between October 31 and December 5, 1969?

16. Are the blemishes on the October 31, 1969 Stanford Daily intentional to mark the Zodiac Mikado article alignment?

17. Are the blemishes on the November 5, 1969 *Stanford Daily* and the November 20, 1969 *Stanford Chaparral* both intentionally on articles about the "secret salaries," or is it just a coincidence?

18. Are the blemishes on the two hypnosis articles in the November 17, 1969 *Daily* intentional and significant?

19. How close did the fake bomb under the Willow Road bridge at Stanford on Oct. 30, 1969, match the description of the Death Machine in Zodiac's Bus Bomb letter of November 9, 1969?

20. Are there records at Stanford for classes and other information from the early 1970s?

21. Who is on the student list for Leland Smith's Computer Music course in summer of 1971?

22. Who participated in the "60 Summer Workshops" spoken of in Dick Geikie's July 13, 1971, article?

23. Who were the Stanford Hospital's Work-Study participants in summer 1971?

24. Do the computer logs of 1969-1974 exist? Is Dick Geikie's name on them?

25. Who was David Levine's roommate in 1972-73?

26. Could Dick Geikie and David Levine have known each other?

27. Who were the "non-students" living at the *Chaparral* and making an "off campus" publication, who were ultimately removed from the offices in July of 1974?

28. What is in the summer 1970 *Stanford Daily* volume?

29. Where was the color comics section two of the *SF Chronicle-Examiner* printed in 1969?

30. Who is every single person who could have seen Dick Tracy comics, especially Sunday comics, before the general public?

31. And a question that has bugged me ever since reading about the "solved" October 1974 Memorial Church murder: Why did the bloody handprint on the candle not match and rule out the security guard for 44 years, but now DNA has now shown him to be the sole perpetrator?

The questions I have been cautious to ask, the theory I have been hesitant to let be known, will finally be brought into the light. As we pack for the cross-country trip to the Stanford Chaparral 125th Anniversary Reunion, this strange, movie-like saga builds towards its presumed climax.

Will "The Only Time Richard got Angry at Me" just be "One F of a Coincidence?" or is it the clue that finally solves the greatest cold-case murders of the 20th Century, The Zodiac?

I apologize for leaving you hanging. But this story is as far as it can go. For now.

Imagine what coincidences lie ahead.

--- THE END ---

I think it's possible, even probable, that coincidences are explained by fractal mathematics. If fractals govern not just materials and systems, but human interaction, history, and even consciousness itself, coincidences would abound, as they seem to do.

– James Bigtwin

===EXTRA STUFF======

Acknowledgments

Well first off, there would be no book without my wife Kate, but I will elaborate on that at the end.

Regarding this book's strange cousin, *The Chappie – 125 Years of Issues*, a full recounting of the individuals and institutions that made that book happen is found on page 475 of that 'heavy' book.[358] But here I will just acknowledge their incredible work and my regret that I was unable to tell them about all of this until now, especially those who worked the most on the book, and those putting time into the reunion weekend.. The 125th anniversary will cause more people to hear about the *Chaparral* than have for several decades. Then after that, we have this item that will put the name *Stanford Chaparral* on the lips of people coast to coast.

I state for the record that no one in the *Chaparral* or Hammer & Coffin other than myself knew about my discoveries during the creation and printing of the Chaparral 125 book, except DL, my close friend and confidant, who was apprised of the information as it happened as insurance against my untimely demise.

The *Stanford Chaparral* bears acknowledgment yet one more time, for it was my affection for that magazine that spurred me to research it. Without that, this story would not have happened.

It also would not have happened without the excellent archives of the *Stanford Daily*, from whose pages I learned so much of the history of Stanford. As I Chappie, I duck down to see that none of my compatriots hear my praise: Our school has been served well by the *Stanford Daily*, and it continues to do so, chronicling not just the news of the day, but our very lives.

Stanford Special Collections has always been so friendly and helpful. Some of the same individuals helping people looking for John C. Lilly materials helped us access Chaparral and Hammer # Coffin collections at Green Library. Our visits to the library were hilights of our journeys to Stanford. Their resource of online Quad yearbooks and Froshbooks was also of great importance to the research of this book.

Stanford Alumni Association was of immense help while I was researching bylines of the Chaparral and Daily, and has been a big help in planning the Chappie reunion weekend.

I used several online newspaper archives. I spent countless hours on newspapers.com, newspaperarchive.com, genealogybank.com, as well as the archives of jstor.org, archive.org, the Wisconsin Historical Society, and of course utilizing the power of Google and Bing searches. And you need both. Take Crosby for example. If you want to know about it you can Google Crosby or you can Bing Crosby.

The Internet Archive also has the Way Back Machine, a very important and useful resource.

Many, many librarians have helped me look up things, and give advice on how to go about research. In addition to Stanford Libraries, I received assistance from the libraries of Palo Alto, San Francisco, the state of California, San Francisco State University, Cornell University, Washington State University, University of Oregon, and yes, University of California at Berkeley.

I spoke with Glenn Fleishman, author of How Comics Were Made. about comics and their production, and also corresponded with people from the Billy Ireland Cartoon Library and Museum at Ohio State University.

I spoke with G about newspaper printing, as well as other Goss press operators. Consultation on comic matters was sought and received from Chappies, Josh and Gregor. And I want to thank the individual who included that old printing bill when they sent the dusty envelope of Chaparrals. I also want to thank the ECCO agents in Japan and elsewhere on the planet Earth.

Through all this has been the support of friends and family, most certainly the Saturday zoomers, Latchaw, Missy, DDA, Ron, Aldo, Lindsey, Kevin, Fiona, ZB, The Dr., Helen, Gretchen, Rich, Kate...

In addition to providing ice cream, Gretchen provided advice, checks on reality, and assistance editing the text.

Firstly and lastly there is Kate, who read and edited this manuscript multiple times, who pointed out many key things and asked essential questions through this journey. It was she who gasped when we opened the Chaparral bound volume and saw the blank interior pages of the Missing Link for the first time. It was she who said, and I "quote," "If you only make jokes about others, and never about yourself, you don't have a sense of humor, you're just an asshole." Of course, nothing would happen without her, my muse and soulmate.

Bibliography

Tom Voigt, Zodiac Killer: Just the Facts, 2021
Robert Graysmith, Zodiac, St. Martins Press, 1986
Robert Graysmith, Zodiac Unmasked, Berkeley Press, 2002
Thurman Watts et al, The Best of the Scribes of Heru, Volume 1, 2024
Donald Regan, For The Record, Harcourt Brace Jovanovich, 1988
Joan Quigley, What Does Joan Say?, Birch Lane Press, 1990
Glenn Fleishman - How Comics Were Made, 2024
Richard White, Who Killed Jane Stanford, W.W. Norton & Co, 2022
The Chappie - 125 Years of Issues, Hammer & Coffin Corp., 2024

Websites

zodiackiller.com - maintained by Tom Voigt
zodiackillerfacts.com - maintained by Michael Butterfield
zodiackillerciphers.com - maintained by David Oranchak
zodiacciphers.com - maintained by Richard Grinell
wisconsinhistory.org - Wisconsin Historical Society
JSTOR.org - A service of ITHAKA
archive.org - The Internet Archive
cartoons.osu.edu - Ohio State University
newspapers.com
newspaperarchive.com
genealogybank.com
chappieArchives.org - Archive of the Stanford Chaparral
archives.stanforddaily.com - Archive of the Stanford Daily
theonlytime.org - The website for this book

Video and Film

History Channel; MysteryQuest (S1, E3); The Zodiac: San Francisco Slaughter, September 30, 2009
Zodiac, 2007, Directed by David Fincher
This is the Zodiac Speaking, 2007, Directed by David Prior
The Zodiac Killer, 1971, Directed by Tom Hanson
Deaf/Punk, 1979, Richard Gaikowski
Repo Man, 1984, Written and Directed by Alex Cox
Close Encounters of the Third Kind, 1977 Directed by Steven Spielberg

About the Author

James Bigtwin grew up on a grain and livestock farm in Indiana; 6-time champion 4-H livestock showman for sheep and swine; HS class salutatorian and 4-year varsity athlete in basketball and track; earned a degree in economics at Stanford and was the Editor of the *Stanford Chaparral* and also Business Manager; floated a 35 ft. sheep balloon over the 1985 Stanford-Berkeley football game; one of three who freed Oskie from the Berkeley union; was a desktop publishing pioneer; painter of mixed media dog and UFO Dukey paintings; founded the TechnoRomantics group and parties in NYC; co-founder of Disorient parties; has drawn thousands of mandala designs on self-coded software; performed at the Montreux Jazz Festival with Virtual Reality founder Jaron Lanier; made virtual sets for ABC, Discovery Channel, ESPN, winning a 1999 Broadcast Design Gold for SportsCentury; has had three songs on Dr. Demento; created website for Dr. John C. Lilly and presented with him in Tokyo and Paris; coded dolphin recognition software and other programs for underwater touchscreen with Dr. Ken Marten; created Japan's first VRML website for Digital Garage; earned an advanced degree in banking from the Graduate School of Banking at Colorado; branding and branch expansion expert for community banks retail businesses; organized a Guinness World Record for the largest serving of fried chicken; designed many Joe Camel billboards and ads; ran a canoe race and festival drawing people from 31 states and three countries before being removed "for the good of the community"; is the basis for the character Jim Kuback on the cult TV show Mission Hill; appeared in The Onion under the name of Chaparral Field Marshal Mike Dornheim; and authored and designed the *Chaparral* 125th anniversary book where he discovered evidence, or coincidence, of the Zodiac Killer on the Stanford campus.

My Credentials

There is still proof online that I knew Richard Gaikowski. The "Wayback Machine" still shows Richard's old website for New Realities Video. On an internet browser, go to: https://archive.org. Once there, put http://www.slip.net/~richgaik/ into the prompt. Then view a snapshot of the site from April 4, 2000 or earlier. The front page background graphic are colored lights on black—a background I created from my coding in Macromedia Director (now Adobe Director). Then, if you click on the eyeball graphic with the link titled, "Who?" you will get to a page with a picture of Richard leaning on a TV, with the same picture appearing on the TV screen. The background is black. There is the text, "I like screwing with what some people think is reality." The word "reality" is a link. Press on that link, and you get to a page on a maroon background with various links. Under the heading "Fun & Games" there is the link "Eye Candy." This link leads to a "Not Found" page at interport.net, which reads,

"The requested URL /~bigtwin/PULSATORS/pulsvideo32.html was not found on this server."

For years I have gone by the art name "Bigtwin," (adding James on the front in recent years) and it is well known I have worked on my own programming titled "Pulsators" since the mid 1990s. A version of "Pulsators" is what was used to create the initial background artwork on the front page of Richard's site. This programming is no longer available on the internet, as it was created in Macromedia/Adobe Director Shockwave, a format long obsolete for online. If you know how to make a DCR file from Director work on a web browser, you may be able to play around with this software. Perhaps with old computers. Nevertheless, this shows Richard's website linking to mine.

You can also use the Wayback Machine to view my website at the time. At the web.archive.org prompt, enter http://users.rcn.com/bigtwin and view the page at 2003 or earlier, you can find my "BKG" files, one of which is the background on Richard's site, and you can also find my "Links" page http://users.rcn.com/bigtwin/linkpage.html where you will see that I linked to Richard Gaikowski. That link, btw, is the next line above a link to the *Stanford Chaparral*.

Coincidence?

My other piece of hard evidence supporting that I knew Richard is his signature in my Guest Book from my art shows. This is from my opening reception at Artists Television Access in San Francisco on March 16, 1994.

I also have some emails to and from Richard into early 2003. So there you have it.

Endnotes

1........ July 1998 – As a member of Jaron Lanier's band Chromataphoria
2........ 1984, Non Musicians – Bringing Me Back Today; 2019, LeChat & Jethro – Christmas is Over; 2022, James Bigtwin - Insane in the Ukraine
3........ The Lampoon castle, Edmund Wheelwright, architect, 1909.
4........ The Onion, July 17, 2002, p 1
5........ San Francisco Chronicle, May 5, 2004, p B7
6........ New York Magazine, June 1994, p 52. Photo taken in my room at Bernal Heights, San Francisco
7........ MacWorld, March 1991, pages 3 and 146
8........ Saturday Night Live, S4.E12 · Sat. Feb 17, 1979
9........ TIME Magazine, May 17, 1968
10...... The Chappie – 125 Years of Issues, Hammer & Coffin Corp. 2024, page 236
11...... Stanford Daily, July 16, 1974, p 1
12...... Stanford Daily,November 26, 1974, p 6
13...... Donald Regan, For The Record, Harcourt Brace Jovanovich, 1988
14...... Joan Quigley, "What Does Joan Say?", Birch Lane Press, 1990
15...... San Francisco Examiner and Chronicle, Nov. 24, 1985, page C-11
16...... Stanford Daily, May 19, 1986, p 10
17...... Peninsula Times-Tribune, August 6, 1986, p 4
18...... San Francisco Chronicle, August 5, 1986, p 5
19...... Oakland Tribune, August 6, 1986, p 13
20...... San Francisco Chronicle, August 26, 1986, p 18; August 27, 1986, p 14
21...... San Francisco Chronicle, August 5, 1986, p 5
22...... Stanford Daily, August 8, 1986, p 3
23...... Stanford Daily, August 12, 1986, p 6
24...... Stanford Daily, August 12, 1986, p 1
25...... "Who Stole the Bear", Stanford Magazine, Tom Smegal, Nov-Dec 1998
26...... San Francisco Chronicle, May 5, 2004, p B7
27...... Rapid City Journal, Feb. 24, 1954, p 8
28...... Martinez News-Gazette, December 8, 1964, p 1
29...... Sioux Falls Argus-Leader, April 2, 1960, p 10
30...... Aberdeen American-News, June 1, 1960, p 2
31...... Aberdeen American-News, December 8, 1960, p 29
32...... Huron Daily Plainsman, February 1, 1962, p 1
33...... Huron Daily Plainsman, April 2, 1963, p 2
34...... Rapid City Journal, July 31, 1963, p 2
35...... Martinez News-Gazette, December 8, 1964, p 1
36...... San Francisco Examiner, August 27, 1965, p 40
37...... Contra Costa Times, May 28, 1965, p 8
38...... Contra Costa Times, October 13, 1965, p 41
39...... Vallejo Times-Herald, October 13, 1965, p 3
40...... Martinez News-Gazette, December 31, 1965, p 1
41...... Good Times, July 17, 1969, Article name
42...... Good Times, July 24, 1969, Article name
43...... Good Times, May 14, 1969
44...... Good Times, September 17, 1971
45...... SF Free and Easy guide, 1980
46...... https://www.imdb.com/title/tt9866528/?ref_=nm_flmg_job_1_cred_t_8
47...... San Francisco Chronicle, May 5, 2004, p B7
48...... San Francisco Sunday Examiner and Chronicle, September 19, 1976, p 58

49...... San Francisco Chronicle, May 5, 2004, p B7
50...... https://www.imdb.com/title/tt8609082/?ref_=nm_flmg_knf_t_2
51...... https://www.imdb.com/title/tt8652820/?ref_=nm_flmg_job_1_cred_i_6
52...... https://www.imdb.com/title/tt8671594/?ref_=nm_flmg_knf_t_3
53...... San Francisco Sunday Examiner & Chronicle Datebook, Mar 20, 1983, p 18
54...... https://beyondchron.org/1960s-underground-newspapers-sf-public-school-transportation/
55...... Kelleher, Michael D.; Van Nuys, David (2002). "This is the Zodiac speaking", into the mind of a serial killer. Praeger.
56...... Solano-Napa News Chronicle, August 1, 1969, p 1
57...... San Francisco Examiner, August 1, 1969, p 3
58...... San Francisco Chronicle, August 2, p 4
59...... San Francisco Examiner, August 3, 1969, p 9
60...... San Francisco Examiner, August 4, 1969, p 1
61...... Vallejo News Chronicle, August 4, 1969, p 2
62...... San Francisco Examiner, August 4, 1969, p 4
63...... Vallejo Times-Herald, August 9, 1969 p 1
64...... San Francisco Examiner, September 29, 1969, p 10
65...... Napa Valley Register, September 30, 1969, p 1
66...... San Francisco Examiner & Chronicle Sunday Edition, October 28, 1969
67...... San Francisco Chronicle, Oct 15, 1969, p 1
68...... San Francisco Examiner, October 19, 1969, p 1
69...... Oakland Tribune, October 22, 1969, p 1
70...... San Francisco Examiner, October 23, 1969, p 1
71...... San Francisco Chronicle, November 12, 1969, p 1
72...... Napa Valley Register, November 12, 1969, p 1
73...... San Francisco Chronicle, May 1, 1970, p 8
74...... Peninsula Times Tribune, December 20, 1969, p 3
75...... San Francisco Examiner, December 29, 1969, p 5
76...... San Francisco Chronicle, April 22, 1970, p 1
77...... San Francisco Chronicle, May 1, 1970, p 8
78...... Vallejo Times-Herald, October 18, 1970, p 3
79...... San Francisco Chronicle, November 16, 1970, p 4
80...... https://www.imdb.com/title/tt0061973/?ref_=nv_sr_srsg_1_tt_8_nm_0_in-_0_q_the%2520mikado
81...... Paul Avery, Gilbert and Sullivan Clue to Zodiac, San Francisco Chronicle, October 12, 1970, p 5
82...... San Francisco Chronicle, Oct 31, 1970, p 16
83...... Los Angeles Times, March 16, 1971, p 3
84...... San Francisco Chronicle, March 26, 1971, p 16
85...... San Francisco Chronicle, March 26, 1971, p 1
86...... Sacramento Bee, December 28, 2023, p 3A
87...... San Francisco Examiner, July 18, 1971, p 1
88...... San Francisco Sunday Examiner and Chronicle, May 13, 1973, p 10
89...... Palo Alto Times, April 12, 1971, p 1
90...... Napa Valley Register, April 13, 1971, p 7
91...... Vallejo Times-Herald, April 17, 1971, p 2
92...... San Francisco Examiner, April 29, 1971, p 1
93...... Palo Alto Times, September 2, 1971. p 1
94...... San Francisco Chronicle, January 31, 1969, p 22
95...... https://www.history.com/news/the-zodiac-killer-a-timeline, Michael Butterfield, History Channel, A&E Television Networks, 2017

96...... Riverside Daily Enterprise, July 11, 1971, p 2
97...... https://www.history.com/shows/mysteryquest/season-1/episode-3
98...... San Francisco Chronicle, October 15, 2002, p 1
99...... Stanford Daily, October 10, 1986, p 4
100.... Michael Levenson, 51 Years Later, Coded Message Attributed to Zodiac Killer Has Been Solved, F.B.I. Says, New York Times, December 11, 2020
101.... https://www.youtube.com/watch?v=-1oQLPRE21o
102.... Stanford Quad, 1971, p 348
103.... Peninsula Times Tribune, May 30, 1933, p 1
104.... Bernard Butcher, Was it Murder? Stanford Magazine, January/February, 2000
105.... Richard White, Who Killed Jane Stanford, W. W. Norton and Company, 2022
106.... Palo Alto Times, February 16, 1973, p 1
107.... Salinas Californian,, May 17, 2019, p A4
108.... Palo Alto Times, March 26, 1974, p 1
109.... Palo Alto Times, March 28, 1975, p 1
110.... Salinas Californian, May 17, 2019, p A4
111.... San Francisco Chronicle, September 15, 2021
112.... New York Times, January 12, 2023, Man Pleads Guilty to 1973 Murder of Stanford Graduate
113.... Palo Alto Daily Post, September 27, 2023, https://padailypost.com/2023/09/27/serial-killer-john-getreu-dies-in-prison/
114.... Palo Alto Times, October 14, 1977, p 10
115.... San Jose Mercury News, June 29, 2018, p 1
116.... Palo Alto Times, September 11, 1973, p 1
117.... Palo Alto Times, September 11, 1973, p 1
118.... Palo Alto Times, September 12, 1973, p 1
119.... Berkeley Gazette, December 21, 1973, p 1
120.... San Francisco Examiner, May 2, 1974, p 4
121.... Stanford Daily, February 22, 1971, p 4
122.... Stanford Daily, November 11, 1971, p 1
123.... WIN Magazine, March 1, 1971, p 35
124.... Good Times, October 16, 1969, p 17
125.... WIN Magazine, March 1, 1971, p 35
126.... WIN Magazine, March 1, 1971, p 36
127.... East Village Other, September 8, 1970, p 11
128.... Good Times, September 4, 1969, p 9
129.... Good Times, September 4, 1969, p 18
130.... Good Times, September 11, 1969, p
131.... Good Times, September 11, 1969, p
132.... Good Times, September 26, 1969, p
133.... Good Times, October 2, 1969, p
134.... Good Times, October 16, 1969, p
135.... Good Times, October 23, 1969, p
136.... Good Times, October 23, 1969, p
137.... Good Times, October 30, 1969, p 17
138.... Good Times, November 6, 1969, p 19
139.... Good Times, November 6, 1969, p 17
140.... Good Times, November 20, 1969, p 16
141.... Good Times, November 27, 1969, p 12
142.... Good Times, November 27, 1969, p 13
143.... Good Times, December 4, 1969, p 18
144.... Good Times, February 13, 1970, p 22

145.... Good Times, February 27, 1970, p 2
146.... Good Times, April 16, 1971, p 2
147.... Good Times, September 17, 1971, p 24
148.... Good Times, June 2, 1972, p
149.... Good Times, July 24, 1969, p 6
150.... Stanford Daily, June 25, 1969, p 7
151.... Stanford Daily, July 9, 1969, p 8
152.... Stanford Daily, July 9, 1969, p 3
153.... Stanford Daily, July 13, 1971, p 1
154.... Stanford Daily, July 13, 1971, p 6
155.... Stanford Daily July 27, 1971, p 1
156.... Stanford Daily, July 30, 1971, p 6
157.... Stanford Daily, July 30, 1971, p 2
158.... Stanford Daily, August 3, 1971, p 7
159.... Stanford Daily, August 3, 1971, p 7
160.... Stanford Daily, August 6, 1969, p 1
161.... Stanford Daily, August 6, 1969, p 2
162.... Stanford Daily, August 10, 1969, p 1
163.... https://web.archive.org/web/20000817164232/http://www.slip.net/~richgaik/
164.... https://web.archive.org/web/19990129023155/http://www.users.interport.
net/%7Ebigtwin/linkpage.html
165.... Stanford Daily, October 24, 1969, p 2
166.... San Francisco Examiner, October 19, 1969, p 1
167.... Stanford Daily, October 31, 1969, p 2
168.... Stanford Daily, June 14, 1979, August 15, 1980, June 20, 1981, August 13,
1982, January 1, 1984, September 20, 1984, January 1, 1985, September 23, 1985
169.... Stanford Daily, November 5, 1969, p 1
170.... Palo Alto Times, October 21, 1969, p 1
171.... Stanford Daily, May 18, 1970, p 1
172.... Stanford Daily, May 25, 1970, p 1
173.... Stanford Daily, July 12, 1971, p 1
174.... Peninsula Times-Tribune, February 15, 1969, p 1
175.... Stanford Daily, October 31, 1969, p 1
176.... Peninsula Times-Tribune, October 31, 1969, p 4
177.... Redwood City Tribune, November 1, 1969, p 4
178.... Stanford Daily, April 24, 1970, p 1
179.... Stanford Daily, April 27, 1970, p 1
180.... Stanford Daily, May 15, 1970, p 1
181.... Stanford Daily, January 4, 1971, p 4
182.... Stanford Daily, January 26, 1971, p 1
183.... Stanford Daily, January 27, 1971, p 1
184.... Stanford Daily, January 29, 1971, p 1
185.... Stanford Daily, February 1, 1971, p 1
186.... Stanford Daily, February 10, 1971, p 1
187.... Stanford Daily, February 11, 1971, p 1
188.... Stanford Daily, February 13, 1971, p 1
189.... Stanford Daily, February 17, 1971, p 1
190.... Stanford Daily, March 1, 1971, p 1
191.... Stanford Daily, March 4, 1971, p 1
192.... Stanford Chaparral, March 5, 1971, p 1
193.... San Francisco Examiner, March 10, 1971, p 3
194.... Stanford Daily, March 29, 1971, p 1

195.... Stanford Daily, June 22, 1971, p 1
196.... Stanford Daily, June 25, 1971, p 7
197.... Palo Alto Times, April 16, 1971, p 3
198.... Palo Alto Times, April 16, 1971, p 3
199.... Palo Alto Times, April 12, 1971, p 3
200.... Stanford Daily, April 26, 1971, p 1
201.... Stanford Daily, April 26, 1971, p 6
202.... Stanford Daily, April 27, 1971, p 1
203.... Stanford Daily, April 27, 1971, p 4
204.... San Francisco Examiner, May 1, 1971, p 1
205.... Palo Alto Times, May 6, 1971, p 1
206.... Palo Alto Times, May 31, 1971, p 1
207.... Palo Alto Times, June 2, 1971, p 1
208.... Palo Alto Times, June 2, 1971, p 2
209.... Evening Free Lance, June 16, 1971, p 1
210.... Palo Alto Times, July 1, 1971, p 1
211.... Palo Alto Times, June 5, 1971, p 1
212.... Stanford Daily, July 13, 1971, p 1
213.... Good Times, April 16, 1971, p 2
214.... Good Times, April 16, 1971, p 3
215.... Santa Cruz Sentinel, July 25, 197, p 1
216.... Stanford Daily, July 27, 1971, p 1
217.... Santa Cruz Sentinel, July 29, 1971, p 9
218.... Palo Alto Times, December 1, 1971, p 1
219.... Stanford Chaparral, Fall 1987, p 3
220.... Stanford Daily, January 13, 1972, p 1
221.... Stanford Daily, January 14, 1972, p 8
222.... Stanford Daily, January 18, 1972, p 1
223.... Palo Alto Times, January 17, 1972, p 1
224.... Stanford Daily, January 25, p 6
225.... Stanford Daily, January 25, p 1
226.... Stanford Daily, January 26, p 1
227.... Stanford Daily, February 4, 1972, p 1
228.... Stanford Daily, April 18, p 1
229.... Stanford Daily, April 21, p 6
230.... Stanford Daily, April 21, p 1
231.... Stanford Daily, April 22, p 1
232.... Stanford Daily, May 8, p 1
233.... Stanford Daily, May 10, 1972, p 2
234.... Stanford Daily, May 12, 1972, p 1
235.... Stanford Daily, May 19, 1972, p 1
236.... Stanford Daily, May 22, 1972, p 1
237.... Stanford Daily, May 22, p 1
238.... Palo Alto Times, June 8, 1972, p 1
239.... Stanford Daily, June 20, p 1
240.... Stanford Daily, July 14, 1972, p 4
241.... Stanford Daily, July 21, 1972, p 2
242.... Los Gatos Times Observer, January 9, 1973, p 1
243.... The Times, May 22, 1973, p 10
244.... Palo Alto Times, November 27, 1973, p 1
245.... Los Angeles Times, December 19, 1973, p 3
246.... Stanford Daily, October 24, 1973, p 6

247.... Palo Alto Times, October 23, 1973, p 2
248.... Stanford Daily, January 18, 1972, p 1
249.... Stanford Daily, July 23, 1976, p 1
250.... Berkeley Tribe, October 24, 1969, p 3
251.... Berkeley Tribe, October 24, 1969, p 10
252.... Berkeley Tribe, October 24, 1969, p 10
253.... Good Times, July 24, 1969, p 1
254.... Good Times, July 24, 1969, p
255.... Good Times, July 24, 1969, p
256.... Computer History Museum, https://www.computerhistory.org/collections/catalog/102746921
257.... Stanford Daily, September 23, 1973, p 1
258.... Stanford Daily, July 16, 1974, p 1
259.... Good Times, January 22, 1971, p 1
260.... Stanford Chaparral, November 11, 1971, p 1
261.... Stanford Daily, July 9, 1971, p 1
262.... Stanford Daily, July 9, 1971, p 11
263.... Stanford Daily, July 7, 1971, p 2
264.... Stanford Daily, July 23, 1971, p 1
265.... Stanford Daily, July 9, 1971, p 4
266.... Stanford Daily, July 9, 1971, p 3
267.... The Chappie – 125 Years of Issues, Hammer & Coffin Corp. 2024, Page 270
268.... The Times-Standard, May 1, 1971, p 1
269.... Petaluma Argus-Courier, February 27, 1971, p 10
270.... San Francisco Examiner, March 6, 1971, p 1
271.... Napa Valley Register, March 6, 1971, p 1A
272.... Napa Valley Register, March 12, 1971, p 2A
273.... Napa Valley Register, March 17, 1971, p 13A
274.... Martinez Morning News, March 17, 1971, p 1
275.... Napa Valley Register, July 23, 1971, p 1A
276.... Sacramento Bee, Feb 27, 1978, p 7
277.... http://a3mreunion.org/about-1.html
278.... http://a3mreunion.org/archive/1968-1969/68-69_april_3_meeting/68-69_april_3_meeting.html
279.... Stanford Daily, May 1, 1969, p 1
280.... Stanford Daily, May 1, 1969, p 1
281.... Stanford Daily, May 2, 1969, p 1
282.... Stanford Daily, May 23, 1969, p 8
283.... Stanford Daily, October 16, 1969, p 2
284.... Stanford Daily, October 28, 1969, p 1
285.... The Times, October 29, 1969, p 12
286.... Stanford Daily, October 28, 1969, p 1
287.... Stanford Daily, October 29, 1969, p 1
288.... San Francisco Examiner, October 29, 1969, p 19
289.... San Francisco Examiner, October 29, 1969, p 19
290.... Stanford Daily, November 5, 1969, p 1
291.... Stanford Chaparral, November 6, 1969, p 1
292.... Stanford Daily, November 13, 1969, p 1
293.... Stanford Chaparral, November 6, 1969, p 3
294.... Stanford Chaparral, October 9, 1969, p 1
295.... Stanford Chaparral, October 9, 1969, p 27
296.... Stanford Chaparral, February 14, 1970

297.... Stanford Daily, October 1, 1971, p 1
298.... Stanford Daily, July 16, 1974, p 1
299.... The Chappie – 125 Years of Issues, Hammer & Coffin Corp. 2024, p 466
300.... Stanford Daily, October 31, 1969, p 3
301.... D'Oyly Carte Opera Company, https://en.wikipedia.org/w/index.php?title=D%27Oyly_Carte_Opera_Company&oldid=1210294468
302.... Stanford Daily, October 31, 1969, p 4
303.... San Francisco Chronicle, October 12, 1970, p 12
304.... Stanford Daily, October 3, 1969, p 4
305.... Stanford Daily, October 28, 1969, p 3
306.... Stanford Daily, November 17, 1969, p 3 & 4
307.... Stanford Daily, March 4, 1970, p 1
308.... The Chappie – 125 Years of Issues, Hammer & Coffin Corp. 2024, p 214
309.... The Chappie – 125 Years of Issues, Hammer & Coffin Corp. 2024, p 475
310.... The Chappie – 125 Years of Issues, Hammer & Coffin Corp. 2024, p 185
311.... The Chappie – 125 Years of Issues, Hammer & Coffin Corp. 2024, p 261
312.... The Chappie – 125 Years of Issues, Hammer & Coffin Corp. 2024, p 264
313.... The Chappie – 125 Years of Issues, Hammer & Coffin Corp. 2024, p 68
314.... The Chappie – 125 Years of Issues, Hammer & Coffin Corp. 2024, p 355
315.... The Chappie – 125 Years of Issues, Hammer & Coffin Corp. 2024, p 471
316.... Stanford Magazine, That's Old News, Sam Scott, January/February 2015
317.... Stanford Chaparral, December 4, 1969, p 3
318.... Palo Alto Times, February 16, 1973, p 1
319.... Stanford Daily, Murder at Memorial Church remains unsolved 40 years later, Caleb Smith October 10, 2014
320.... Peninsula Times Tribune, October 14, 1977, p 10
321.... Palo Alto Times, October 14, 1977, p 10
322.... San Francisco Examiner, May 2, 1974, p 4
323.... Vallejo Times-Herald, May 4, 1974, 1
324.... Oakland Tribune, March 14, 1976, p 1
325.... Vallejo Times-Herald, May 4, 1974, 2
326.... Berkeley Gazette, May 7, 1974, p 13
327.... Vallejo Times-Herald, May 4, 1974, 2
328.... Stanford Daily, July 31, 1973, p 3
329.... Stanford Daily, July 14, 1972, p 4
330.... Stanford Daily, July 21, 1972, p 2
331.... Good Times, April 16, 1971, p 2
332.... Good Times, April 16, 1971, p 3
333.... Stanford Daily, July 23, 1976, p 1
334.... Peninsula Times Tribune, July 23, 1976, p 2
335.... Stanford Chaparral, September 25, 1969, p 23
336.... Good Times, September 18, 1969, p 16
337.... Stanford Chaparral, October 23, 1969, p 3
338.... Stanford Daily, February 19, 1969, p 8
339.... Stanford Daily, February 27, 1969, p 6
340.... Good Times, August 21, 1970, p 16
341.... Stanford Daily, December 3, 1970, p 2
342.... Good Times, December 18, 1970, p 12
343.... Good Times, Nov 26, 1970, p 2
344.... Stanford Chaparral, April 1961, inside front cover and page 19
345.... Good Times, May 17, 1971, p 1
346.... Stanford Chaparral, November 11, 1971, p 1

347.... Good Times, January 22, 1971, p 1
348.... Good Times, June 11, 1971, p 27
349.... Good Times, October 15, 1971, p 2
350.... Stanford Chaparral, November 11, 1971, p 1
351.... Stanford Chaparral, November 11, 1971, p 2
352.... Good Times, November 12, 1971, p 2
353.... Stanford Daily, July 27, 1971, p 1
354.... Stanford Chaparral, September 25, 1973, p 1
355.... Napa Valley Register, Was 1971 PUC student a victim of Willie the Wood-cuttter or The Zodiac killer, Jennifer Huffman, May 7, 2021,
356.... https://oac.cdlib.org/findaid/ark:/13030/c8kp86wv/entire_text/
357.... The Chappie – 125 Years of Issues, Hammer & Coffin Corp. 2024, p 466
358....The Chappie – 125 Years of Issues, Hammer & Coffin Corp. 2024, p 475

Index

340-code 91, 103, 127, 129, 137, 206, 328, 329
408-code 85, 86, 87, 114, 115, 131, 143, 190, 200, 201, 202, 203, 227
1960s 5, 26, 104, 145, 199, 207, 280, 329
1970s 25, 29, 81, 103, 108, 152, 153, 162, 171, 177, 179, 184, 196, 227, 232, 233, 264, 306, 307, 309, 329, 342, 344, 363
1980s 28, 61, 77, 82, 99, 100, 125, 137, 146, 150, 152, 179, 222, 233, 255, 271, 282, 314
1990s 12, 14, 29, 61, 64, 72, 82, 83, 129, 148, 149, 184, 192, 232, 371
2000s 16, 72, 222
2010s 82
2020s 28, 59, 83, 140, 272, 280, 337, 339

A

ABC Television 9, 90, 120, 121, 136, 370
Abramson, Eric 158, 160, 161, 338, 339, 340
Ackroyd, Dan 18
Adams, Bristow 23
Adobe 57, 254, 370, 371
Adweek Magazine 57
Albany, New York 79, 98, 99, 112
Alien Dreamtime 11, 13, 129
Alioto, Mayor Joseph 161, 338, 339
Allen, Arthur Leigh 100, 115
All the President's Men 44
Al X 147
Anastacio, Valtinho 57
Angwin, California 88
Animal in Car 45, 47
Anne R. Key 346
April Third Movement 265
Archive.org 187, 221, 370, 371
Artists' Television Access 13
ASSU 25, 28, 162, 314
ASSU - Associated Students of Stanford University 23, 30, 40, 179, 272, 340
Astrologer 32, 355
Astrology 32, 67, 68, 70, 74, 117, 121, 123, 125, 126, 130, 132, 153, 175, 176, 177, 180, 181, 194, 198, 227, 324, 334, 352, 355, 356
Avery, Paul 96, 97, 127, 128, 149, 206, 264, 288
    addressed as Paul Averly 96, 97
A Warship Can Be Stopped 199, 345

B

Baby On Board 45
Bayshore Blvd 10, 65, 68, 71, 73
Belli, Melvin 90, 91, 92, 120, 127
Belushi, John 18
Ben Dover 163, 164, 165
Ben Lomand, California 212, 215, 341
Berkeley Barb 123, 124, 266
Berkeley Bear 35, 51, 52, 56, 141, 189, 204
Berkeley Tribe 122, 123, 124, 221, 222, 223, 224, 226, 266, 313
   1969_10_24 issue 225
Bernal Heights, San Francisco 10, 61, 62
Bigtwin, James 57, 61, 72, 136, 365, 371
Bilek, Kathy 98, 103
Blaine 99, 100, 113, 121, 122, 123, 124, 131, 132, 202, 221, 222, 223, 224, 226, 227
Blake, Sam 137
Blood Rock 199
Blue Rock Springs 84, 85, 102, 103, 110, 114, 119, 206, 324, 325
Bowman, Larrey 23
Branner Hall 20, 21, 36, 37, 157, 170, 172
Broadcast Design Awards 370
Brookville Lake Dam 33
Brown, Emma 220, 221, 300, 342
Bruno, Giordano 26
Burning Man 14, 65, 136
Bus Bomb Letter 92
Butterfield, Michael 108
buzz cut 15, 163, 199

C

California 18, 19, 53, 72, 77, 78, 84, 86, 92, 97, 98, 112, 132, 136, 140, 161, 182, 186, 187, 234, 261, 262, 263, 295, 302, 303, 325, 338, 339, 346, 348, 350, 361
Cannabis Club of San Francisco 82
Carter, Jimmy 31
Chaparral 6, 7, 23, 24, 25, 28, 31, 137, 165, 170, 183, 188, 189, 192, 212, 237, 239, 240, 242, 246, 252, 253, 257, 264, 265, 268, 270, 271, 272, 276, 311, 314, 315, 318, 322, 323, 331, 333, 340, 343, 345, 346, 348, 349, 360, 361, 363, 367, 370, 375, 376, 377, 378, 379
Chappie 6, 7, 21, 22, 23, 25, 27, 28, 29, 30, 31, 32, 35, 39, 41, 45, 46, 47, 49, 56, 140, 142, 145, 146, 147, 149, 152, 162, 170, 171, 179, 183,

184, 189, 191, 193, 198, 199, 200, 216, 218, 231, 232, 234, 235, 237, 241, 245, 246, 247, 248, 252, 254, 255, 256, 257, 258, 265, 266, 267, 268, 269, 270, 271, 272, 273, 274, 275, 277, 279, 280, 297, 298, 300, 303, 306, 317, 345, 359, 360, 361, 372

Chappie 125 book 270, 273, 300
Chappie - 125 Years of Issues, The 7, 27, 258, 268, 273, 275, 277, 279, 280
Chess 138
Church of the SubGenius 63
Cincinnati Bengals 36
Circle Jerks 63
Close Encounters of the Third Kind 15, 66, 153, 161, 162, 222, 236, 333
Coburn, Tim 184, 345, 347
coincidense 255, 256
Colorado 18, 52, 254, 361
Columbia University 18, 19
Columbo 49, 323
Columbus Parkway 85, 324
Computer Music 175, 183, 363
Cornell University 18, 155, 227, 228, 229, 297
Country Joe and the Fish 270
Covid 136, 138, 359
Crawford, Stephen 154, 155, 336
Creedence Clearwater Revival 214
Crushed print blanket 291, 292, 300

D

Daily Commercial News 78
Daly City, California 90, 120
Davis. Sammy Jr. 53
Dead Bowlers prank 30
Dead Kennedys 20, 63
Dead Week 234
DEAF/PUNK movie 1979 82, 127, 128
Death Angels 339
Death machine 92
Death Machine Letter 92
Deep Throat 44
Deukmejian, George 53
Dickson, Don 57, 175
Dick Tracy 35, 89, 225, 226, 295, 318, 323, 324, 363
Digicomp 227, 228, 229
Digicomp DR-70 227, 228, 355

Digital Garage 5, 13
Dinkelspiel Auditorium 210
Discovery Channel 9
Disorient 136, 370
Divine Shakespeare 3, 257, 280, 359
DNA 12, 75, 97, 100, 152, 154, 336, 363
Doda, Carol 26
Dolphins 5, 6, 106, 107, 135, 136
Dornheim, Mike 6, 28, 29, 30, 34, 170, 246, 255, 256, 274, 277, 297
Drake, Vicky 26
Dr. Demento 6, 136
Drummer film 1973 81
Duchess of Maifi 269
Duck Number 147
Dukey 13, 62
Dunbar, Jim 90, 120

E

Earth News 215
East Palo Alto, California 342
East Village Other 165
Efron, Brad 26
El Camino Real 217, 218
Electric Zodiac, The 194, 284, 285, 287, 294, 362
Elway, Coach Jack 50, 55
Encina Hall 216, 218, 265, 266, 267
    Fire 1972_06_07 218
Esalen 294
ESPN 9, 136, 370
Exorcist letter 127

F

Faculty ghetto 151, 206
Fake Names 169, 228
Faraday, David 84
Farmer's Union 10, 124, 125, 163
Ferrin, Darlene 84, 110, 111, 112, 315, 324
Festival of Bards movie 1978 82
Fincher, David 96, 108
For The Record 32
Franklin, Bruce 210, 211, 212, 216
Franklin, Professor Bruce 210
Free Campus Movement 209, 212, 215, 342
Fresno, California 47, 51, 52

Furlong, Debra 86, 91, 103

G

Gaik, or D. Gaik 80, 81, 115, 122, 123, 167, 169, 174, 180, 181, 182, 185, 187, 188, 190, 191, 196, 201, 227, 230, 239, 242, 244, 261, 344, 345, 346, 361
Gaikowski, Richard 6, 9, 10, 13, 68, 73, 77, 80, 100, 112, 114, 116, 119, 120, 124, 159, 163, 167, 169, 170, 174, 180, 183, 187, 188, 190, 192, 201, 221, 226, 230, 232, 239, 261, 278, 342, 346, 370, 371
Garr, Teri 161
Geikie, Dick 180, 181, 182, 183, 184, 185, 186, 187, 188, 189, 190, 191, 192, 195, 196, 200, 201, 206, 209, 212, 215, 221, 226, 230, 231, 234, 235, 236, 237, 238, 239, 240, 241, 242, 243, 244, 247, 259, 260, 261, 262, 271, 273, 278, 279, 287, 288, 298, 323, 342, 345, 346, 347, 348, 349, 361, 362, 363
Geikie, Richard 182, 186
Getreu, John 154, 220, 335
Gilbert and Sullivan 94, 282, 315
Gillespie, Dizzy 270
Goatkirk 164, 165, 166, 167, 168, 169, 227, 343
Goldcatcher 100
Golden Gate Bridge 239
Goodyear Blimp 36
Grand Executioner, The 314, 315, 317, 318
Grand Kabuki 270, 315
Graysmith, Robert 100
Greenwich Village, NYC 11, 60
Guerrero Street, SF 11
Guy Du Lac 169
GYKE 114, 131, 143, 144, 200, 201, 202, 203, 205, 206

H

Hagman, Larry 31
Hair 269
Halloween card 96, 127, 128, 149, 206, 220, 258, 341
Hammer & Coffin 24, 25, 233, 270, 349, 367, 372, 377, 378, 379
  vault 50, 51
Hammer & Coffin Society 24, 25, 27, 32, 38, 39, 50, 51, 68, 73, 136, 137, 138, 139, 140, 141, 144, 146, 152, 192, 198, 232, 233, 242, 254, 260, 266, 267, 275, 276, 277, 280, 299, 300, 302, 306, 347
Hansen Laboratory 216
Hargadon, Dean Fred 19
Harrington, Marvin 48
Harry Potter 274

Hartnell, Brian 88, 89, 91, 263, 264, 350
Harvard Lampoon 6, 147, 300
Hawaii 14, 52, 65, 72, 105, 151, 321
Hearst, Patty 99
Hinton, William 115, 344
History Channel 100, 121
Hitchcock effect 54
Hoover Tower 172, 266, 316
Huey Lewis 314
Humbolt College 263
Huron Daily Plainsman 78
Hypnosis 294

I

I Have a Little List 94
Indiana 9, 10, 12, 13, 17, 19, 21, 30, 64, 69, 72, 73, 104, 136, 139, 164, 291
International Cetacean Education Research Centre (ICERC) 105
Ithaca, New York 155, 227, 228, 229

J

Jack In The Box 10, 41, 43, 65, 68, 71, 73, 234, 307, 321
Jarl Van Eycke 137
Jeep Waggoneer 43
Jeep Wagoneer 46
Jensen, Bettilou 84
Jester 69, 145, 147, 170, 181, 232, 251, 297, 359
Joe Camel advertising 58, 59, 60, 136, 139, 370
joke names 123, 190
Jordan, Stanley 57, 175
Journalism Years 271, 272
Jstor.org 221, 222, 223

K

Kanes, Lynda 263, 264, 347, 348, 350
Kansas City, Missouri 133
Kelsie 344
Kennedy, Donald 53
Kesey, Ken 150
Kirkland, Kenny 57
Ko-Ko 94, 250, 314, 329
KQED 213
KZSU 209

L

La Boheme 270, 315
Lake Berryessa 35, 88, 102, 119, 150, 153, 158, 201, 206, 226, 263, 264, 329, 339, 350
Lake Herman Road 84, 85, 102, 103, 110, 206
Lambo prank 37
Lamplighter's 281, 292
Lamplighters 270
Lamson, David 151, 152, 273, 297
Lanier, Jaron 57, 136, 192, 370
Lathrop House 217
Lay, Anita Amanda 170
Lennon, John 6, 256
Let's Eat - Chaparral issue 39, 40, 253
Let's Eat Steak prank 39
Let the Punishment Fit the Crime 282
Levine, David 152, 153, 155, 156, 157, 158, 159, 160, 161, 162, 170, 171, 172, 173, 174, 177, 188, 221, 227, 228, 229, 230, 231, 232, 233, 234, 238, 300, 337, 338, 339, 340, 363
Liberace 270
Liberation News Service 345
Libertarianism 163, 164, 165
Library of Congress 140, 148
Lilly, Dr. John C. 5, 14, 72, 105, 134, 135, 136, 192, 280, 370
Little List letter 94, 314
Lord High Executioner 94
Los Altos, California 49, 212, 214, 219
Los Angeles, California 97
Luiz, Fernando 57
Lyman, Dick 210, 211, 212
Lynch, John 87

M

Macintosh 57, 60, 63, 82
Macromedia 370, 371
Macromind Director 10
Madison Avenue 5, 35, 57, 73, 238, 299
Mageau, Mike 84, 85, 110
ManzanitaTrailers 157, 172, 216, 218, 341
Marijuana 10, 64, 66, 82, 131
Martinez, California 78, 324, 372
Martini 238, 299
McCarthy, Professor John 175, 209

McNeill, Edward 220, 221, 342
MEChA 217
Menlo Park, California 24, 208, 212, 214, 219, 221, 301, 308
Meyer, Charley 24
Meyer Library 152, 153, 155
Mickey Mouse Clocktower prank 20, 30, 35, 53
Midpeninsula Free University 184, 198, 207, 208, 231, 265, 330
Mikado, The 93, 94, 95, 96, 98, 99, 250, 270, 281, 282, 283, 284, 286, 287, 288, 290, 292, 293, 294, 296, 300, 304, 312, 313, 314, 315, 316, 317, 318, 328, 362
Mingus, Charlie 270
Mirrielees Apartments 155
Missing Link Chaparral issue 178, 181, 196, 236, 238, 240, 241, 242, 243, 245, 247, 258, 259, 260, 261, 262, 265, 273, 274, 275, 277, 278, 279, 280, 286, 287, 297, 298, 302, 303, 304, 346, 347, 348, 350, 353, 354, 361, 362
Mission Hill 23, 136, 370
M&Ms 272
Molotov cocktails 206, 207, 208, 213
Monroe, Marilyn 258, 297
Montreux Jazz Festival 6, 136, 370
Mount Diablo 93
Muncie, Chuck 30
My Dilemma 142, 144, 189, 252, 277, 360
MysteryQuest 100, 121, 202

N

Napa County 88, 112, 225, 261, 263, 325
Napa County Mental Hospital 261
Napa State Hospital 187, 350
Napa Valley Register 263, 350
Narlow, Ken 112
National Enquirer 67
National Treasure 351, 353, 354
Nelson, Robert 206, 215, 342
Neumann, Moose 22, 170
New Left 268
NewsBase 82
NewspaperArchive.com 306
Newspapers.com 187
New York 9, 11, 12, 13, 17, 19, 56, 57, 60, 61, 62, 64, 65, 72, 77, 79, 98, 102, 112, 136, 155, 163, 164, 227, 254, 277, 321, 372, 374
New York City 9, 11, 12, 13, 18, 19, 56, 64, 65, 72, 163, 164, 254
New York Knickerbocker News 79, 98

New York Times 17, 374
Niagara, film 1953 258, 297
Nixon, Richard 26, 64, 211, 227
NO2 tank 22
NokNok 295, 296, 313
Non Musician 33
Northern Ireland 79

O

Oh! Calcutta! 269
Ohio 20, 361
Oil Bird 344
Old Boy 22, 23
Old Farts 136, 137, 140
Old Page Mill Road 153
Old Union 217, 235
On Broadway Theater 269
Ono, Yoko 6
Open Campus 196, 197, 198, 209, 346
Oppenheim, Morrie 24
Oranchak, David 137
Oskie 42, 45, 46, 47, 48, 49, 50, 51, 52, 53, 54, 55, 56, 143, 148, 279

P

Pacific Gas and Electric Company (PG&E) 214, 219
Pacific Union College 88, 263, 264, 350
Page 394 273, 274, 275
Palo Alto, California 26, 29, 36, 45, 57, 63, 153, 156, 194, 195, 207,
208, 212, 213, 214, 216, 217, 218, 220, 265, 312, 313, 330, 333, 341,
342, 375
Palo Alto Times 156, 195, 208, 213, 214, 313, 375
PARADiCE 96, 128
Paris, France 14, 27, 105, 269
Peggy 38
Pence, Mike 72
Perlov, Leslie 152, 153, 154, 220, 335
Perry, Arlis 152, 153, 154, 336
Photoshop 58, 259, 261, 286, 287, 290, 311, 352
Pie Throwing prank 40, 48
Pipe-bomb 93, 206, 207, 209, 214, 215, 216, 219, 341, 342
Pipe-bombs 206, 214
Polya Hall 197, 209, 341
Presentation Theater 281
Presidio 89, 117, 168

Press Club 23
Pulsators 10, 192, 371
puns 202, 230, 231, 296, 316

Q

Quigley, Joan 32, 228, 355

R

Radical Libertarian Alliance 162, 163, 165, 180, 184, 215, 281
Rapid City Journal 78
Reagan, Nancy 31, 32
Reagan, Ronald 14, 31, 32, 64, 66, 67, 68, 74, 116, 121, 125, 126,
130, 132, 153, 164, 181, 228, 267, 322, 355, 356
Red Star 346
Regan, Donald 32, 125, 369, 372
Repo Man 63
Revolutionary Action SQuad 219
Revolutionary Union (RU) 210
revoman 164, 168, 215
Roble Gym 41
Rocky Horror Picture Show 43
Rosvold, Mark 335
ROTC 27, 28, 146, 235, 266, 268
Round Table Pizza 53
Roxie Theater 13, 81, 82, 124, 129

S

Salcedo, Joaquin 57
San Francisco 5, 9, 10, 11, 12, 13, 14, 18, 23, 24, 26, 30, 31, 32, 47,
51, 56, 60, 61, 62, 65, 68, 71, 72, 73, 74, 75, 77, 78, 79, 81, 82, 85, 86,
89, 90, 91, 93, 96, 97, 98, 99, 100, 101, 108, 114, 116, 117, 118, 120,
127, 133, 135, 143, 160, 161, 165, 168, 180, 192, 193, 194, 197, 201,
207, 209, 213, 214, 224, 225, 233, 235, 256, 261, 266, 268, 269, 270,
276, 281, 302, 306, 307, 313, 315, 317, 321, 324, 325, 330, 338, 343,
344, 355, 371, 373
San Francisco Chronicle 30, 31, 47, 77, 85, 86, 87, 89, 91, 93, 96, 98,
99, 114, 143, 144, 201, 207, 226, 268, 363
San Francisco Deaf Club 82, 127
San Francisco Earthquake 1906 23, 24
San Francisco Examiner 78, 81, 82, 85, 86, 89, 90, 143, 193, 201,
224, 225, 226, 307, 363, 373
   1969_10_19 issue 90, 225
San Francisco Forty-Niners 36
San Francisco International Airport (SFO) 10, 73, 234, 321

San Francisco Oil Disaster 240
San Jose, California 86, 91, 184, 208, 209, 212, 214, 215, 231, 268, 346
San Jose Mercury 268
San Mateo, California 47, 303
Santa Clara County 218
Santa Cruz, California 212, 214, 215, 219
Saratoga, California 219
Saturday Night Live 18, 372
SDS 265, 267, 344
Secret Salaries 267, 269
Seeger, Pete 270
SF Good Times 27, 79, 80, 81, 82, 115, 117, 118, 119, 120, 122, 123, 124, 131, 163, 164, 165, 166, 167, 168, 169, 173, 174, 180, 181, 190, 191, 199, 215, 222, 223, 224, 225, 227, 234, 266, 301, 342, 343, 344, 345, 379
SFnet 61, 129
Sheep in an Anthrax T-Shirt 61
Shepherd, Cecelia 264, 350
Sherlock Holmes 49
Shockley Eight 217, 218
Shockley, Professor William 217, 272
Simone, Nina 270
Slick Tracy 294, 295
Snape, Professor Sevaris 274, 275
Snoozy, Kathie 86, 91, 103
Solano 84, 225, 325
Son of Sam 108
South Dakota 10, 64, 77, 78, 124, 125
Stamford, Connecticut 186
Standard Oil 237, 239, 344
Stanford Alumni 182, 185
Stanford Artificial Intelligence Lab, SAIL 175, 209
Stanford Axe Committee 50, 55, 56
Stanford Band Shak 56, 191
Stanford Bike Experiment 298
Stanford Business School 266
Stanford Chaparral
    1969_10_09 issue 166, 269, 281, 317, 362
    1973_09_25 issue 346, 379
    Campus Report, 1973 30, 272
    Groin issue 26, 27
    Layboy issue 26, 253
    political era 28, 140, 145, 151, 170, 198, 235, 269, 271
    Purple Ape issue 26, 253

Stanford Computer Music 231
Stanford Daily 5, 6, 21, 26, 28, 29, 30, 39, 45, 46, 47, 48, 137, 144,
145, 162, 183, 184, 185, 186, 191, 192, 194, 197, 200, 206, 209, 210,
211, 213, 215, 217, 218, 221, 222, 226, 231, 240, 241, 242, 243, 255,
258, 261, 262, 265, 267, 268, 271, 275, 281, 284, 285, 288, 289, 292,
294, 295, 296, 300, 301, 302, 304, 305, 306, 307, 308, 309, 311, 312,
313, 314, 331, 333, 340, 342, 344, 345, 346, 347, 349, 361, 362, 363,
367, 372, 374, 375, 376, 377, 378, 379
    1969_05_01 issue 266
    1969_05_02 issue 266
    1969_10_16 issue 267
    1969_10_24 issue 222, 225, 267
    1969_10_28 issue 267
    1969_10_31 issue" 270
    1969_11_05 issue 268
    1969_11_13 issue 269
    1969_11_17 issue 294, 362
    1970_05_18 issue 197
    1970_05_25 issue 197
    1971_06_22 issue 212
    1971_06_25 issue 212
    1971_08_06 issue 80, 169, 185
    1972_05_18 issue 217
    1972_07_12 issue 218, 341
    1973_10_24 issue 220
    1974_07_16 issue 272
    1986_05_19 issue 40
    May 18, 1970 issue 209
StanfordDaily.com 306, 307
Stanford Fire Department 207, 313
Stanford Football Team 55
Stanford Froshbook 200
Stanford Hospital 168, 183, 206, 215, 231, 346
Stanford Hospital workers 342
Stanford, Jane Lathrop 151, 273
Stanford Library 140, 151, 179, 242, 302
Stanford Linear Accelerator Center (SLAC) 216
Stanford Linear Accelerator (SLAC) 216
Stanford Memorial Church 23, 24, 152, 154, 171, 256, 257, 297, 300,
322, 336, 363
Stanford Murders 153, 155, 171, 173, 218, 273, 335
Stanford Quad yearbook 21, 145, 150, 151, 162, 184, 191, 200, 209,
211, 213, 232, 274
Stanford Rehabilitation Movement 216
Stanford's Green Library 198, 232, 233, 235, 237, 247, 301, 305, 307,
308, 347, 362
Stanford University 6, 18, 20, 40, 186, 189, 211, 243, 244, 299, 323

Stanford Women's Center 218
Star Wars 159
Stine, Paul 89, 92, 96, 102, 103, 107, 116, 117, 119, 120, 168, 206, 221, 264, 326, 327, 328
Storke Publications Building 21, 27, 41, 45, 48, 149, 187, 191, 232, 234, 235, 330
Sunshine Brigade 213, 215
Sunshine Express 212, 213
Super Bowl XIX 21, 36, 37
Sweeney, Michael 27, 28, 235, 266, 343, 344
Symbionese Liberation Army (SLA) 99

T

Tarot 67, 68, 69, 70, 74, 113, 130, 165, 166, 167, 168, 343
Taylor, Janet 152, 153, 154, 220, 335
TechnoAmish 9
Technoromantics 11, 60, 62
TechnoRomantics 136, 370
Terra House 38, 39, 57
The Beatles 282
The Dicks 63
The Exorcist 98, 99
The Fool 69
The Onion 6
the Play 18
The Residents 63
The Simpsons 23
the Sixties 198
The Stanford Axe 37, 42
The Storefront Cinema 81
The WELL 61
The Zodiac, 2007 movie 108
The Zodiac Killer, film 1971 257, 258
The Zodiac movie, 2007 75
This Is My Black Movie 81
Time Magazine 26, 67
Tim Holt comic book 206
'tis better to have lived and laughed, than never to have lived at all 6
Tracy, California 94
Tresidder Union 18, 276
   1973 Theater prank 276
Twain, Mark 61
Type-O-Tonalator 105

U

Unabomber 108
USS Coral Sea 199, 345

V

Vallejo, California 84, 85, 86, 87, 88, 91, 112, 113, 201, 225, 307, 324, 325, 330
Vallejo Times-Herald 85, 201
Venceremos 169, 206, 210
Versailles, France 105
Video Toaster 63, 82
Vietnam 63, 210, 211, 217, 268, 269, 317, 334
virtual reality 5, 57, 136
Virtual Reality 370
Voigt, Tom 100, 112, 113, 117, 122

W

Wally Heider Studios 214
Watts, Jeff Tain 57
Wayback Machine 370, 371
Weathermen, The 213
Weaver, Doodles 146, 257, 258, 297, 298
Weaver, Sigourney 146, 269, 298
Wells Fargo 214
Werner, Karl Francis 86, 98, 103, 335
Where do you hide a tree 279
Where Do You Hide a Tree 272
White House 32, 355
white spots 270, 284, 286
Who Shot R.R.? 14, 31, 188, 244, 316, 355
Williams, Walter 264, 348
Willie the Woodcutter 264, 348, 350
Willow Bridge 341
Willow Road 207, 208, 363
Willy and the Poor Boys 214
Wilson, Sharon 263
Winbigler, Donald 26, 148
WIN magazine 163
Wisconsin Historical Society 221
Wonka, Warren G. 170, 274
Woodside, California 208, 212, 214
WOXY 20

Y

Young and Rubicam 58
YouTube 82, 120, 274

Z

Zebra Killings 161, 172, 338, 339
Zodiac
  Zodiac Mania 90
Zodiac communications
  November 9, 1969, letter 342, 349
Zodiackiller.com 100, 112, 113
Zodiackillerfacts.com 108
Zodiac-Mikado coincidence 96, 288, 296, 304, 310, 311, 361
Zoom calls 136, 137, 138, 139, 141, 152, 153, 179, 189, 254, 272, 273, 297

I didn't make this book end on page 394 on purpose, it just happened.

Made in the USA
Las Vegas, NV
10 May 2025

21956231R00226